ODYSSEUS/ULYSSES

Major Literary Characters

CHELSEA HOUSE PUBLISHERS

Major Literary Characters

DAVID COPPERFIELD
Charles Dickens, *David Copperfield*

ROBINSON CRUSOE
Daniel Defoe, *Robinson Crusoe*

DON JUAN
Molière, *Don Juan*
Lord Byron, *Don Juan*

HUCK FINN
Mark Twain, *The Adventures of Tom Sawyer, Adventures of Huckleberry Finn*

CLARISSA HARLOWE
Samuel Richardson, *Clarissa*

HEATHCLIFF
Emily Brontë, *Wuthering Heights*

ANNA KARENINA
Leo Tolstoy, *Anna Karenina*

MR. PICKWICK
Charles Dickens, *The Pickwick Papers*

HESTER PRYNNE
Nathaniel Hawthorne, *The Scarlet Letter*

BECKY SHARP
William Makepeace Thackeray, *Vanity Fair*

LAMBERT STRETHER
Henry James, *The Ambassadors*

EUSTACIA VYE
Thomas Hardy, *The Return of the Native*

TWENTIETH CENTURY

ÁNTONIA
Willa Cather, *My Ántonia*

BRETT ASHLEY
Ernest Hemingway, *The Sun Also Rises*

HANS CASTORP
Thomas Mann, *The Magic Mountain*

HOLDEN CAULFIELD
J. D. Salinger, *The Catcher in the Rye*

CADDY COMPSON
William Faulkner, *The Sound and the Fury*

JANIE CRAWFORD
Zora Neale Hurston, *Their Eyes Were Watching God*

CLARISSA DALLOWAY
Virginia Woolf, *Mrs. Dalloway*

DILSEY
William Faulkner, *The Sound and the Fury*

GATSBY
F. Scott Fitzgerald, *The Great Gatsby*

HERZOG
Saul Bellow, *Herzog*

JOAN OF ARC
William Shakespeare, *Henry VI*
George Bernard Shaw, *Saint Joan*

LOLITA
Vladimir Nabokov, *Lolita*

WILLY LOMAN
Arthur Miller, *Death of a Salesman*

MARLOW
Joseph Conrad, *Lord Jim, Heart of Darkness, Youth, Chance*

PORTNOY
Philip Roth, *Portnoy's Complaint*

BIGGER THOMAS
Richard Wright, *Native Son*

CHELSEA HOUSE PUBLISHERS

Major Literary Characters

ODYSSEUS/ ULYSSES

Edited and with an introduction by
HAROLD BLOOM

CHELSEA HOUSE PUBLISHERS
New York ◇ Philadelphia

Jacket illustration: Herbert Draper, *Ulysses and the Sirens* (detail) (1909)
(Bridgeman Art Gallery/Art Resource).

Chelsea House Publishers

Editor-in-Chief   Remmel T. Nunn
Managing Editor   Karyn Gullen Browne
Picture Editor   Adrian G. Allen
Art Director   Maria Epes
Manufacturing Manager   Gerald Levine

Major Literary Characters

Senior Editor   S. T. Joshi
Associate Editor   Richard Fumosa
Designer   Maria Epes

Staff for ODYSSEUS/ULYSSES

Picture Researcher   Patricia Burns
Assistant Art Director   Noreen Romano
Production Manager   Joseph Romano
Production Coordinator   Marie Claire Cebrián

© 1991 by Chelsea House Publishers, a division
of Main Line Book Co.

Inatroduction © 1991 by Harold Bloom

Printed and bound in the United States of America

3 5 7 9 8 6 4

Library of Congress Cataloging-in-Publication Data

Odysseus/Ulysses / edited with an introduction by Harold Bloom
p.   cm.—(Major literary characters)
Includes bibliographical references and index.
ISBN 0-7910-0924-6.—ISBN 0-7910-0979-3 (pbk).
1. Odysseus (Greek mythology) in literature. 2. Literature,
Comparative—Themes, motives. I. Bloom, Harold. II. Series.
PN57.O3O39 1991
809'.93351—dc20
90-20355
CIP

CONTENTS

THE ANALYSIS OF CHARACTER

Harold Bloom

"Character," according to our dictionaries, still has as a primary meaning a graphic symbol, such as a letter of the alphabet. This meaning reflects the word's apparent origin in the ancient Greek *charactēr*, a sharp stylus. *Charactēr* also meant the mark of the stylus' incisions. Recent fashions in literary criticism have reduced "character" in literature to a matter of marks upon a page. But our word "character" also has a very different meaning, matching that of the ancient Greek *ēthos*, "habitual way of life." Shall we say then that literary character is an imitation of human character, or is it just a grouping of marks? The issue is between a critic like Dr. Samuel Johnson, for whom words were as much like people as like things, and a critic like the late Roland Barthes, who told us that "the fact can only exist linguistically, as a term of discourse." Who is closer to our experience of reading literature, Johnson or Barthes? What difference does it make, if we side with one critic rather than the other?

Barthes is famous, like Foucault and other recent French theorists, for having added to Nietzsche's proclamation of the death of God a subsidiary demise, that of the literary author. If there are no authors, then there are no fictional personages, presumably because literature does not refer to a world outside language. Words indeed necessarily refer to other words in the first place, but the impact of words ultimately is drawn from a universe of fact. Stories, poems, and plays are recognizable as such because they are human utterances within traditions of utterances, and traditions, by achieving authority, become a kind of fact, or at least the sense of a fact. Our sense that literary characters, within the context of a fictive cosmos, indeed are fictional personages is also a kind of fact. The meaning and value of every character in a successful work of literary representation depend upon our ideas of persons in the factual reality of our lives.

Literary character is always an invention, and inventions generally are indebted to prior inventions. Shakespeare is the inventor of literary character as we know it; he reformed the universal human expectations for the verbal imitation of personality, and the reformation appears now to be permanent and uncannily inevitable. Remarkable as the Bible and Homer are at representing personages, their characters are relatively unchanging. They age within their stories, but their habitual modes of being do not develop. Jacob and Achilles unfold before us, but without metamorphoses. Lear and Macbeth, Hamlet and Othello severely modify themselves not only by their actions, but by their utterances, and most of all through *overhearing themselves,* whether they speak to themselves or to others. Pondering what they themselves have said, they will to change, and actually do change, sometimes extravagantly yet always persuasively. Or else they suffer change, without willing it, but in reaction not so much to their language as to their relation to that language.

I do not think it useful to say that Shakespeare successfully imitated elements in our characters. Rather, it could be argued that he compelled aspects of character to appear that previously were concealed, or not available to representation. This is not to say that Shakespeare is God, but to remind us that language is not God either. The mimesis of character in Shakespeare's dramas now seems to us normative, and indeed became the accepted mode almost immediately, as Ben Jonson shrewdly and somewhat grudgingly implied. And yet, Shakespearean representation has surprisingly little in common with the imitation of reality in Jonson or in Christopher Marlowe. The origins of Shakespeare's originality in the portrayal of men and women are to be found in the *Canterbury Tales* of Geoffrey Chaucer, insofar as they can be located anywhere before Shakespeare himself. Chaucer's savage and superb Pardoner overhears his own tale-telling, as well as his mocking rehearsal of his own spiel, and through this overhearing he is emboldened to forget himself, and enthusiastically urges all his fellow-pilgrims to come forward to be fleeced by him. His self-awareness, and apocalyptically rancid sense of spiritual fall, are preludes to the even grander abysses of the perverted will in Iago and in Edmund. What might be called the character trait of a negative charisma may be Chaucer's invention, but came to its perfection in Shakespearean mimesis.

The analysis of character is as much Shakespeare's invention as the representation of character is, since Iago and Edmund are adepts at analyzing both themselves and their victims. Hamlet, whose overwhelming charisma has many negative components, is certainly the most comprehensive of all literary characters, and so necessarily prophesies the labyrinthine complexities of the will in Iago and Edmund. Charisma, according to Max Weber, its first codifier, is primarily a natural endowment, and implies a primordial and idiosyncratic power over nature, and so finally over death. Hamlet's uncanniness is at its most suggestive in the scene of his long dying, where the audience, through the mediation of Horatio, itself is compelled to meditate upon suicide, if only because outliving the prince of Denmark scarcely seems an option.

Shakespearean representation has usurped not only our sense of literary character, but our sense of ourselves as characters, with Hamlet playing the part of the largest of these usurpations. Insofar as we have an idea of human disinterestedness, we tend to derive it from the Hamlet of Act V, whose quietism has about it a ghostly authority. Oscar Wilde, in his profound and profoundly witty dialogue, "The Decay of Lying," expressed a permanent insight when he insisted that art shaped every era, far more than any age formed art. Life imitates art, we imitate Shakespeare, because without Shakespeare we would perish for lack of images. Wilde's grandest audacity demystifies Shakespearean mimesis with a Shakespearean vivaciousness: "This unfortunate aphorism about art holding the mirror up to Nature is deliberately said by Hamlet in order to convince the bystanders of his absolute insanity in all art-matters." Of *Hamlet*'s influence upon the ages Wilde remarked that: "The world has grown sad because a puppet was once melancholy." "Puppet" is Wilde's own deconstruction, a brilliant reminder that Shakespeare's artistry of illusion has so mastered reality as to have changed reality, evidently forever.

The analysis of character, as a critical pursuit, seems to me as much a Shakespearean invention as literary character was, since much of what we know about how to analyze character necessarily follows Shakespearean procedures. His hero-villains, from Richard III through Iago, Edmund, and Macbeth, are shrewd and endless questers into their own self-motivations. If we could bear to see Hamlet, in his unwearied negations, as another hero-villain, then we would judge him the supreme analyst of the darker recalcitrances in the selfhood. Freud followed the pre-Socratic Empedocles, in arguing that character is fate, a frightening doctrine that maintains the fear that there are no accidents, that overdetermination rules us all of our lives. Hamlet assumes the same, yet adds to this argument the terrible passivity he manifests in Act V. Throughout Shakespeare's tragedies, the most interesting personages seem doom-eager, reminding us again that a Shakespearean reading of Freud would be more illuminating than a Freudian exegesis of Shakespeare. We learn more when we discover Hamlet in the Freudian Death Drive, than when we read *Beyond the Pleasure Principle* into *Hamlet.*

In Shakespearean comedy, character achieves its true literary apotheosis, which is the representation of the inner freedom that can be created by great wit alone. Rosalind and Falstaff, perhaps alone among Shakespeare's personages, match Hamlet in wit, though hardly in the metaphysics of consciousness. Whether in the comic or the modern mode, Shakespeare has set the standard of measurement in the balance between character and passion.

In Shakespeare the self is more dramatized than theatricalized, which is why a Shakespearean reading of Freud works out so well. Character-formation after the passing of the Oedipal stage takes the place of fetishistic fragmentings of the self. Critics who now call literary character into question, and who proclaim also the death of the author, invariably also regard all notions, literary and human, of a stable character as being mere reductions of deeper pre-Oedipal desires. It becomes clear that the fortunes of literary character rise and fall with the prestige of normative conceptions of the ego. Shakespeare's Iago, who wars against being, may be the first deconstructionist of the self, with his proclamation of "I am not what I am." This constitutes the necessary prologue to any view that would regard a fixed ego as a virtual abnormality. But deconstructions of the self are no more modern than Modernism is. Like literary modernism, the decentered ego came out of the Hellenistic culture of ancient Alexandria. The Gnostic heretics believed that the psyche, like the body, was a fallen entity, mechanically fashioned by the Demiurge or false creator. They held however that each of us possessed also a spark or pneuma, which was a fragment of the original Abyss or true, alien God. The soul or psyche within every one of us was thus at war with the self or pneuma, and only that sparklike self could be saved.

Shakespeare, following after Chaucer in this respect, was the first and remains still the greatest master of representing character both as a stable soul and a wavering self. There is a substance that endures in Shakespeare's figures, and there is also a quicksilver rendition of the unsettling sparks. Racine and Tolstoy, Balzac and Dickens, follow in Shakespeare's wake by giving us some sense of pre-Oedipal sparks or drives, and considerably more sense of post-Oedipal character and personality, stabilizations or sublimations of the fetish-seeking drives. Critics like Leo Bersani and René Girard argue eloquently against our taking this mimesis as the only proper work of literature. I would suggest that strong fictions of the self, from the Bible through Samuel Beckett, necessarily participate in both modes, the sublimation of desire, and the persistence of a primordial desire. The mystery of Hamlet or of Lear is intimately invested in the tangled mixture of the two modes of representation.

Psychic mobility is proposed by Bersani as the ideal to which deconstructions of the literary self may yet guide us. The ideal has its pathos, but the realities of literary representation seem to me very different, perhaps destructively so. When a novelist like D. H. Lawrence sought to reduce his characters to Eros and the Death Drive, he still had to persuade us of his authority at mimesis by lavishing upon the figures of *The Rainbow* and *Women in Love* all of the vivid stigmata of normative personality. Birkin and Ursula may represent antithetical and uncanny drives, but they develop and change as characters pondering their own pronouncements and reactions to self and others. The cost of a non-Shakespearean representation is enormous. Pynchon, in *The Crying of Lot 49* and *Gravity's Rainbow,* evades the burden of the normative by resorting to something like Christopher Marlowe's art of caricature in *The Jew of Malta.* Marlowe's Barabas is a marvelous rhetorician, yet he is a cartoon alongside the troublingly equivocal Shylock. Pynchon's personages are deliberate cartoons also, as flat as comic strips. Marlowe's achievement, and Pynchon's, are beyond dispute, yet they are like the prelude and the postlude to Shakespearean reality. They do not wish to engage with our hunger for the empirical world and so they enter the problematic cosmos of literary fantasy.

No writer, not even Shakespeare or Proust, alters the available stock that we agree to call reality, but Shakespeare, more than any other, does show us how much of reality we could encounter if only we retained adequate desire. The strong literary representation of character is already an analysis of character, and is part of the healing work of a literary culture, which implicitly seeks to cure violence through a normative mimesis of ego, *as if it were stable,* whether in actuality it is or is not. I do not believe that this is a social quest taken on by literary culture, but rather that we confront here the aesthetic essence of what makes a culture *literary,* rather than metaphysical or ethical or religious. A culture becomes literary when its conceptual modes have failed it, which means when religion, philosophy, and science have begun to lose their authority. If they cannot heal violence, then literature attempts to do so, which may be only a turning inside out of the critical arguments of Girard and Bersani.

I conclude by offering a particular instance or special case as a paradigm for the healing enterprise that is at once the representation and the analysis of literary character. Let us call it the aesthetics of being outraged, or rather of successfully representing the state of being outraged. W. C. Fields was one modern master of such representation, and Nathanael West was another, as was Faulkner before him. Here also the greatest master remains Shakespeare, whose Macbeth, himself a bloody outrage, yet retains our imaginative sympathy precisely because he grows increasingly outraged as he experiences the equivocation of the fiend that lies like truth. The double-natured promises and the prophecies of the weird sisters finally induce in Macbeth an apocalyptic version of the stage actor's anxiety at missing cues, the horror of a phantasmagoric stage fright of missing one's time, of always reacting too late. Macbeth, a veritable monster of solipsistic inwardness but no intellectual, counters his dilemma by fresh murders, that prolong him in time yet provoke him only to a perpetually freshened sense of being outraged, as all his expectations become still worse confounded. We are moved by Macbeth, however estrangedly, because his terrible inwardness is a paradigm for our own solipsism, but also because none of us can resist a strong and successful representation of the human in a state of being outraged.

The ultimate outrage is the necessity of dying, an outrage concealed in a multitude of masks, including the tyrannical ambitions of Macbeth. I suspect that our outrage at being outraged is the most difficult of all our affects for us to represent to ourselves, which is why we are so inclined to imaginative sympathy for a character who strongly conveys that affect to us. The Shrike of West's *Miss Lonely-hearts* or Faulkner's Joe Christmas of *Light in August* are crucial modern instances, but such figures can be located in many other works, since the ability to represent this extreme emotion is one of the tests that strong writers are driven to set for themselves.

However a reader seeks to reduce literary character to a question of marks on a page, she will come at last to the impasse constituted by the thought of death, her death, and before that to all the stations of being outraged that memorialize her own drive towards death. In reading, she quests for evidences that are strong representations, whether of her desire or her despair. Such questings constitute the necessary basis for the analysis of literary character, an enterprise that always will survive every vagary of critical fashion.

EDITOR'S NOTE

This book gathers together a representative selection of the best criticism, old and new, that has been devoted to Odysseus (Ulysses, in Latin and subsequent literature) as a major literary character. The critical extracts and essays are reprinted here in the chronological order of their original publication. I am indebted to S. T. Joshi for his skills as researcher and editor. Though this volume centers upon Homer, Sophocles, Dante, Shakespeare, Tennyson, Joyce, and Kazantzakis, there are references to other appearances of the figure of Odysseus/Ulysses.

My introduction centers upon the ambiguities and ambivalences in the portrayals of Odysseus/Ulysses by Homer, Dante, Shakespeare, and Tennyson, before what could be termed the apotheosis of Ulysses in Joyce's gentle and compassionate Poldy, best of Blooms.

The critical extracts begin with Aristotle and Horace and then continue with such eminent critics and writers as Samuel Butler, G. Wilson Knight, Maurice Blanchot, and Italo Calvino. Fuller scale critical essays commence with George de F. Lord's placement of the *Odyssey* in Western tradition, and G. E. Dimock, Jr.'s equally classic analysis of the complexities involved in the name of Odysseus.

In Hugh Kenner's view, Shakespearean and Homeric parallels intersect in the character of Joyce's Poldy. George Scouffas sets the Odysseus of Kazantzakis in the context of the tradition, while W. R. Elton shrewdly reads Shakespeare's Ulysses as a study in moral relativism. The issue of morally antithetical qualities in Ulysses returns in R. F. Storch's exegesis of Tennyson's dramatic monologue.

Michael Beausang suggestively relates Joyce's Bloom to myths of the dying vegetation god, after which John Freccero rather severely interprets Dante's Ulysses from what he asserts was Dante's own Augustinian perspective.

In Martha Nussbaum's reading, the Odysseus of Sophocles' *Philoctetes* is seen as a kind of moral Utilitarian, while Richard Ellmann, Joyce's distinguished biographer, sees Poldy, Joyce's Ulysses, as an only partly comic synthesis of the Greek and Hebraic moral traditions.

Jean Pépin traces the intricate movement from Neoplatonic to Christian allegorizations of Ulysses, after which the philosophy of Homer's *Odyssey* is seen by R. B. Rutherford as one in which Odysseus develops progressively into a figure of moral authority. In this book's final essay, Sheila Murnaghan studies the moral superiority of Odysseus, in relation to the suitors, as a dialectic of recognition and blindness.

INTRODUCTION

O dysseus (Ulysses, in Latin) is in its origins a name of the utmost ambiguity, suitable to a figure at once so singular and so pervasive in Western literary tradition. The name appears to mean everything that is contrary to a blessing: anger, hostility, a curse, a vexation. Ambiguity extends to the question of passivity or activity: is the bearer of the name a curse's victim or a curser's agent? Somewhere behind the name a god's displeasure lurks and the ambiguity therefore is a religious matter. The hero of the *Odyssey* is a hero-villain in Dante's *Inferno* and in Tennyson's dramatic monologue, "Ulysses," and very much a hero again (whatever his author's intentions) as the lovable Poldy of Joyce's *Ulysses*. But the *Odyssey*'s indubitable hero has his equivocal aspects: he is a trickster, in some ways remarkably comparable to the Jacob of the J writer or Yahwist, the Bible's inaugural genius. Each is a double man, Odysseus and Jacob; each is both hero and heel, triumphant warrior and reluctant fighter. Jacob wins the name of Israel by holding out through an all-night, crippling wrestling match, fought against a nameless angel, and yet Jacob has been a fearful man of peace, dreading the vengeance of his rough brother, Esau. Odysseus, when he has to do so, fights with power and prowess, but according to the Neoplatonist Proclus, this wiliest of the Achaeans pretended madness in order not to be drafted for the war against Troy. The deepest affinity between Odysseus and Jacob is that each is more a storyteller than a quester, and each tells a story of his own survival. The Ulysses of Dante (and of Tennyson) is a survivor only in an equivocal sense, but Joyce's Poldy, at once Odysseus and Israel, is again the most authentic of survivors.

Since we are all condemned men and women, with a kind of indefinite reprieve (I cite Walter Pater's paraphrase of Victor Hugo), we are immensely interested in survivors, and identify with them in literature, rather more readily than we identify with tragic victims, or even with epic heroes too much contaminated by death, Achilles or the Jonathan of the Book of Samuel. Survivors impress us by their completeness, and Joyce found in Odysseus/Ulysses the paradigm of the complete man. Homer, according to the critic Longinus, was in his sunset years when he wrote the *Odyssey*. Whatever we think of that metaphor, the poet of the *Odyssey* had undergone a considerable change in stance and temperament, if indeed he was the same poet who wrote the *Iliad*. Odysseus is pursued by a divine wrath, but the direct antagonists he encounters are not worthy of him. Achilles had Hector as opponent, and Aeneas was to have Turnus, but Odysseus battles monstrous beings or else humans greatly inferior to him. Yet Odysseus is so metamorphic or adaptable a figure, that no enemy (short of a god) quite suits him. There is no one else remotely like him in the Homeric poems, no one else so mature, worldly, intellectually curious, or as we now might say, so realistic. To that add that there is no one else nearly so cold as Odysseus; he is a master of reality, but the price of the mastery is that he has been hardened. Prudential heroism is not necessarily ingratiating, and no hero ever has been so little doom-eager as Homer's Odysseus. Self-controlled, pragmatic, he is the paradigm of the will-to-live, and teaches us survival through cunning and endurance. No other Western literary character has so illustrious a history.

II

Pindar, greatest of Greek lyric poets, seems to have begun the long tradition of reversing Homer, by transmuting Odysseus from a wily hero into a hypocritical villain, a deceiver of others. As such a villain, Odysseus is perhaps most memorable in the *Philoctetes* of Sophocles, where he renders the scandalously famous motto of a deceitful counselor: "We can be honest men after this," or tell the truth when we can afford to, in the future. Bad enough, one can think, but not much compared to the appearance of Odysseus in the *Hecuba* of Euripides, where the quondam hero of epic is reduced to a melodramatic demagogue justifying the sacrifice of Hecuba's daughter, Polyxena, in order to quiet the ghost of Achilles. For sheer iciness, the Odysseus of the *Hecuba* is unmatched.

When Odysseus became the Roman Ulysses, he started out well, as a stoic hero in Horace, but received a darker portrait in the second book of Virgil's *Aeneid*. Aeneas appropriately (from his perspective) gives us an Ulysses who was the harshest of enemies, and yet Aeneas himself, in many of his best qualities, is clearly modeled by Virgil upon Homer's heroic and hardy wanderer. This Virgilian ambiguity contrasts with Ovid's rather personal identification with Ulysses, and Virgil fathers Dante, whose vision of Ulysses in *Inferno* XXVI has surpassed even Homer's influence upon subsequent poets. Dante's ambivalence towards Ulysses is interpreted by John Freccero in Augustinian terms:

> What separates Ulysses' definitive death by water from Dante's baptism unto death and subsequent resurrection is the Christ event in history, or grace, the Christ event in the individual soul.

But Dante the poet is not St. Augustine, and the death of Ulysses is not so definitive in more poetic terms. Why does Dante remain silent when confronting Ulysses? Virgil the poet addresses the hero of the *Odyssey,* but Dante the pilgrim cannot. Yet the poet writing the *Inferno* has invented an extraordinary metaphor for his own enormous imaginative ambition. Ulysses leaves Circe not for Ithaca and Penelope but for an ultimate quest, in order to know what is beyond the limits of the world. If Dante is silent, it is because he is dangerously moved, lest the questing parallel become an identity. Ulysses has become a speaking flame in Hell, but any poetic reader soundly prefers this anti-Aeneas to Virgil's prig of a hero. Are we to doubt that Dante, most prideful of poets, also does not prefer Ulysses? His eloquent silence testifies that here, as elsewhere in him, the poet and the moral theologian are not necessarily fused together.

III

What are we to make of the Ulysses of Shakespeare's *Troilus and Cressida?* Like the other truly equivocal characters in Shakespeare, Ulysses provokes a remarkable range of contradictory responses in critics. The play is sublimely rancid, and scarcely has heroes or villains, but if there is a villain, it must be Ulysses, who comes close to being one of Shakespeare's grand negations, and has in him more than a touch of Iago, whom partly he prophesies. There are great speeches by Ulysses in the play, particularly if they are read out of context, but within the play we are compelled to interpret them as ironic, the irony being Shakespeare's and not Ulysses'. Consider the heart of Ulysses's oration on order and degree:

> Take but degree away, untune that string,
> And hark what discord follows. Each thing meets
> In mere oppugnancy. The bounded waters
> Should lift their bosoms higher than the shores
> and make a sop of all this solid globe;
> Strength should be lord of imbecility,
> And the rude son should strike his father dead;
> Force should be right, or rather right and wrong—
> Between whose endless jar justice resides—
> Should lose their names, and so should justice too.
> Then everything include itself in power,
> Power into will, will into appetite,
> And appetite, an universal wolf,
> So doubly seconded with will and power,
> Must make perforce an universal prey
> And last eat up himself.

These are somber commonplaces, indubitably true, and phrased by Ulysses with authority and eloquence, yet in context they are merely prelude to a complaint of how the notoriously sulking Achilles and his favorite, Patroclus, pass time in their tent roaring at their own parodies of the Greek generals. When Ulysses speaks more eloquently still, it is even more marvelous out of context and even more trivial in terms of the play's actions and motions. Achilles, scorned by the other leaders at the wily suggestion of Ulysses, asks angrily: "What, are my deeds forgot?" Ulysses' extraordinary reply would be worthy of another Hamlet urging Shakespeare's Hamlet onward, but in context it is only the cunning of a grand manipulator spurring a brutal egomaniac back to the slaughter-field:

> Time hath, my lord, a wallet at his back,
> Wherein he puts alms for oblivion,
> A great-sized monster of ingratitudes.
> These scraps are good deeds past, which are devoured
> As fast as they are made, forgot as soon
> As done. Perseverance, dear my lord,
> Keeps honor bright. To have done, is to hang
> Quite out of fashion, like a rusty mail
> In monumental mock'ry. Take the instant way;
> For honor travels in a strait so narrow
> Where one but goes abreast. Keep, then, the path;
> For emulation hath a thousand sons
> That one by one pursue. If you give way,
> Or hedge aside from the direct forthright,
> Like to an ent'red tide they all rush by
> And leave you hindmost;
> Or, like a gallant horse fall'n in first rank,
> Lie there for pavement to the abject rear,
> O'er run and trampled on.

Since, in the play, Ulysses means only that Achilles had better get out there and butcher Hector (which he proceeds to do, as dishonorably as possible) or else Ajax will become everyone's idol, we have to believe that the irony this time belongs to Ulysses, as well as to Shakespeare. We are a long way off from the Odysseus of Homer, whose cold reserve was accompanied by an extraordinary sense of being open to all life. Shakespeare's Ulysses is a superb sophist, but only a parody of an epic hero.

IV

Eloquence marks every version of Ulysses as a literary character, even Joyce's average sensual man, Poldy the Jew of Dublin. After Homer, Dante, and Shakespeare, one might have thought that not even Tennyson, the English Virgil, could have accomplished an overcoming of the eloquence of his giant forerunners. Yet

Tennyson's is at once the most adroit and the most sublime of all the portraits of Ulysses. A daemonic dramatic monologue, its seventy lines pack in the English poetic tradition of the hero-villain from Shakespeare through Milton's Satan on to the High Romantic voyagers of Byron and Shelley, while assimilating also hints from Homer and the principal design of Dante's Ulysses. It is as though Tennyson, desperately searching for comfort after the death of his beloved friend, Arthur Henry Hallam, just did not know where to stop absorbing the tradition in this beautiful but bewildered poem. Retrospectively, Tennyson asserted that it gave his "feeling about the need of going forward, and braving the struggle life perhaps more simply than anything in *In Memoriam.* And yet the poem is founded on Ulysses the evil counselor in Dante's *Inferno* XXVI rather than on the Ulysses of the prophecy of the blind sage Tiresias in the *Odyssey,* XI, 100–137. Unlike moralizing critics of Dante, Tennyson admired the Ulysses of the *Inferno,* and his own heroic wanderer does go forth indomitably to seek knowledge. But so subtle and equivo- cal is Tennyson's poem, that we are compelled to realize that its speaker loves no one, scorns his wife and son, and ends by echoing Milton's defiant Satan:

> Though much is taken, much abides; and though
> We are not now that strength which in old days
> Moved earth and heaven; that which we are, we are;
> One equal temper of heroic hearts,
> Made weak by time and fate, but strong in will
> To strive, to seek, to find, and not to yield.

Satan, in his first speech in *Paradise Lost,* proclaims: "And courage never to submit or yield / And what is else not to be overcome?" By assimilating Ulysses to the Miltonic Satan, Tennyson adds yet another dark shading to the fortunes of Ulysses.

V

James Joyce set out to make his Ulysses, Leopold Bloom, the representation of the *complete man,* on the model of Homer's Odysseus. Magnificent as Poldy is, his completeness seems to me nowhere so important as is his vitality, his curiosity, above all his kindness. Warm, gentle, endlessly compassionate, Poldy is our cen- tury's closest approximation to a Shakespearean character, an even wiser Bottom. Goodness is notoriously difficult to represent in language, and Joyce was so wary of his own deep, inward identification with Poldy that he overironized his narrative stance in regard to his epic hero. Yet that is what Poldy remains, a Ulysses free of coldness and suspicion, indeed a Ulysses who cleanses that name of all odium and tricksterism. Poldy shares with Odysseus the drive for knowledge, the yearning for home, yet also the restless need to be different, to be elsewhere. And like Odys- seus, Poldy is a great affirmer of the common life, of the good of everyday existence. Whether or not Joyce knew it, or intended it, Poldy's most Jewish quality is his quest for the Blessing, in the Biblical sense that means: more life. Shakespeare's Iago-like Ulysses could not be further away from Joyce's Ulysses, and yet Poldy is Shakespearean, more Shakespearean than the Ulysses of the magnificently sour *Troilus and Cressida*. A power that Joyce shared with Shakespeare and with Dickens emerges triumphantly in Poldy, the power of so representing benignity as to augment benignity, as to extend our own conceptions of what benignity might yet come to be, come to perform.

Poldy is no saint but an amiable sinner, *one of us,* yet a thoroughly good man, better than we tend to be. There is no hatred in Poldy, no violence and no regard for violence. The ambiguity of the figure of Odysseus/Ulysses, his capacity for mischief-making, for provoking ill deeds in others, sometimes directed against Ulysses himself, survives in Poldy only in its passive form. If Poldy is victimized, still he is not to be thought of primarily as a victim, and his nimbleness protects him from ultimate harm. He is certainly the only Ulysses we can love, and the only Ulysses whom it would be absurd to accuse of evil counsel. It is an aspect of Joyce's triumphalism that we can accept even this as part of the possibilities of an Ulysses:

—Are you talking about the new Jerusalem? says the citizen.

—I'm talking about injustice, says Bloom.

—Right, says John Wyse. Stand up to it then with force like men.

That's an almanac picture for you. Mark for a softnosed bullet. Old lardyface standing up to the business end of a gun. Gob, he'd adorn a sweepingbrush, so he would, if he only had a nurse's apron on him. And then he collapses all of a sudden, twisting around all the opposite, as limp as a wet rag.

—But it's no use, says he. Force, hatred, history, all that. That's not life for men and women, insult and hatred. And everybody knows that it's the very opposite of that that is really life.

—What? says Alf.

—Love, says Bloom. I mean the opposite of hatred.

—H. B.

CRITICAL EXTRACTS

ARISTOTLE

Unity of plot does not, as some persons think, consist in the unity of the hero. For infinitely various are the incidents in one man's life which cannot be reduced to unity; and so, there are many actions of one man out of which we cannot make an action. Hence the error, it appears, of all poets who have composed a *Heracleid*, a *Theseid*, or other poems of the kind. They imagine that as Heracles was one man, the story of Heracles must also be a unity. But Homer, as in all else he is of surpassing merit, here too—whether from art or natural genius—seems to have happily discerned the truth. In composing the *Odyssey* he did not include all the adventures of Odysseus—such as his wound on Parnassus, or his feigned madness at the mustering of the host—incidents between which there was no necessary or probable connexion: but he made the *Odyssey*, and likewise the *Iliad*, to centre round an action that in our sense of the word is one.

—ARISTOTLE, *Poetics* [c. 335 B.C.E.] 1451a, tr. S. H. Butcher
(London: Macmillan, 1895; 4th ed. 1907), pp. 33, 35

HORACE

Yet, in display of what courage and wisdom can also accomplish,
Homer has offered a useful example for us in Ulysses,
Tamer of Troy, who with shrewdness of eye made inspection of many
Cities and customs of men, who while voyaging far in his quest for
Homeward return for himself and his crew endured hardships aplenty,
Ever undrowned by the waves of adversity driving against him.
Songs of the Sirens you know of, you know of the potions of Circe:
How, had he greedily drunk them in folly, as did his companions,

7

He would have languished, a slave to a slut, in a brutish existence,
Foul as a dog and rejoicing in filth like a pig in a quagmire.

> —HORACE, *Epistles* [20 B.C.E.], Book 1, Epistle 2, lines 17–26,
> *The Complete Works of Horace*, tr. Charles E. Passage (New York:
> Ungar, 1983), p. 263

R. C. JEBB

It is curious to compare the Odysseus of this play ⟨Sophocles' *Philoctetes*⟩—one of the poet's latest works—with that of the *Ajax*, which was one of the earliest. There, Odysseus appears as one who has deeply taken to heart the lesson of moderation, and of reverence for the gods, taught by Athena's punishment of his rival; and, if there is no great elevation in his character, at least he performs a creditable part in dissuading the Atreidae from refusing burial to the dead. Here, he is found avowing that a falsehood is not shameful, if it brings advantage (v. 109); he can be superlatively honest, he says, when there is a prize for honesty; but his first object is always to gain his end (1049ff.). He is not content with urging Neoptolemus to tell a lie, but adds a sneer at the youth's reluctance (84f.). Yet, as we learn from Dion, he is 'far gentler and simpler' than the Odysseus who figured in the *Philoctetes* of Euripides. The Homeric conception of the resourceful hero had suffered a grievous decline in the later period of the Attic drama; but Sophocles, it would seem, was comparatively lenient to him.

In the *Ajax*, it will be remembered, Odysseus is terrified at the prospect of meeting his insane foe, and Athena reproves his 'cowardice' (74f.). His final exit in the *Philoctetes* is in flight from the bent bow of the hero, who remarks that he is brave only in words (1305ff.). And, at an earlier moment in the play, he is ironically complimented by Neoptolemus on his prudence in declining to fight (1259). All these passages indicate that the conventional stage Odysseus to whom Attic audiences had become accustomed was something of a poltroon. But it is instructive to remark the delicate reserve of Sophocles in hinting a trait which was so dangerously near to the grotesque. For it is no necessary disparagement to the courage of Odysseus that he should shrink from confronting Ajax,—a raging maniac intent on killing him,—or that he should decline to be a passive target for the 'unerring' shafts of Philoctetes,—or that he should refrain from drawing his sword on his young comrade, Neoptolemus.

> —R. C. JEBB, "Introduction" to *The Philoctetes* by Sophocles
> (Cambridge: Cambridge University Press, 1890), pp. xxx–xxxi

SAMUEL BUTLER

At the very outset of the ⟨*Odyssey*⟩ (i. 13) the writer represents Ulysses as longing to get back to his wife. He had stayed a whole year with Circe, and but for the remonstrances of his men would have stayed no one can say how much longer. He had stayed seven years with Calypso, and seems to have remained on excellent terms with her until the exigencies of the poem made it necessary to send him back to Ithaca. Surely a man of his sagacity might have subtracted Calypso's axe and auger, cut down the trees at the far end of the island, and made his raft years ago without her finding out anything about it; for she can hardly have wanted either axe or auger very often.

As for the provisions, if Ulysses was not capable of accumulating a private hoard, his cunning has been much overrated. If he had seriously wanted to get back to Penelope his little cunning that is put in evidence would have been exercised in this direction. I am convinced, therefore, that though the authoress chooses to pretend that Ulysses was dying to get back to Penelope, she knew perfectly well that he was in no great hurry to do so; she was not, however, going to admit anything so derogatory to the sanctity of married life, or at any rate to the power which a wife has over her husband.

—SAMUEL BUTLER, *The Authoress of the* Odyssey
(London: A. C. Fifield, 1897), p. 142

EDWIN A. SCHELL

Great memories have their rise in great moments when fancy leaps to some gorgeous imagery, when induction discovers some new principle or a great hope is stirred. A nightingale in the thicket, a flash of sheet lightning shows a night landscape, a faded leaf in an old book, a hymn dear to the heart, the sun on some far mountain peak, sets the soul into subtle yearning and ecstasy. So once we saw the sun on the Muir Glacier and through all the strange propinquity of sea and shore it rises yet; so once we heard Madame Nilsson's voice, and above all crash of orchestra or bird note of tumultuous soprano it forever sings. *Tales of a Wayside Inn, Marpessa,* "Ode to a Waterfowl"—each haunts you with question music and Eternal Hope. Once having heard, you are

On your way attended,
By a vision splendid.

The Book of Job has that fascinating thrill for every age and race. It is a special duty for the educated, and has made its way by a thousand channels into the knowledge of men and women of ordinary intelligence. So has the *Odyssey*. Whether the work of one brain or many, no matter how badly translated, its surging billowy hexameters, the legends isolated and detached which it contains, its pleasurable variety—these make it the most wonderful single poem and the greatest epic in all literature. Disregarding the fact that it is verse, and not prose, its adventure, character-sketches, and dramatic culmination make it the first, the finest, and most stirring romance yet written. No incident in any modern novel parallels in intensity the blinding of the huge one-eyed giant Cyclops; the great enchantresses of litera-ture, Dido, Cleopatra, Acrasia, are inferior to Circe, who changes sailors into swine. Vergil borrowed his descent into hell from the *Odyssey,* and Dante took it from Vergil; Æolus, with his bag of winds, Scylla and Charybdis are fearsome fables from the mists of time; no women stronger, more beautiful and more stately than Penelope and Nausicaa were ever sketched; Andrew Carnegie, who has imagina-tion as well as business sagacity, read the *Iliad* and pronounced it monotonous; the world would rather have his opinion of the *Odyssey.*

So Ulysses reaches me, sets me to vibrating, and brings an elevating excite-ment of the soul. John Milton wrote: "It is of great concernment in the church and commonwealth how books demean themselves, as well as men, and therefore confine, imprison, and do sharpest justice upon them as malefactors." The converse of the Milton statement must also be obligatory upon us: if we are to suppress books that demean themselves ill, we are under bonds to commend books that furnish initial impulse and give outlook for high thinking. This gladly is undertaken. Besides, who does not love to introduce his friends to other friends, and perhaps boast of the great men he has met? If you climbed upon the rear of a Pennsylvania coach and shook hands with General Grant, your father meanwhile commanding you to take off your hat, of course you may tell it; likewise if you asked President McKinley to appoint your father postmaster, which he did, or in company with a bishop dined with Edison, you will tell of it—how the great wizard talked, looked, and seemed to you. So, though never having had speech with Tennyson, but having read "Ulysses," we have had speech with him and may somewhat parade our friendship and admiration. It has all of Tennyson's keen observation of nature, scientific knowledge in poetical form, and complete triumph over doubt and dis-couragement. Tennyson for a glance seems Aryan and frontiersman. Back of him you can almost see Pelasgian with his huge two-wheeled cart, woman yoked with the bull, or in wooden ship with cormorant or wolf's head carved upon its beak. Anything that can thus stir memory and passion for men and things long since turned to dust is art at its highest and, mayhap, revelation:

> And when the stream
> Which overflowed the soul was passed away
> A consciousness remained that it had left
> Deposited upon the silent shore
> Of memory images and precious thoughts
> That shall not die, and cannot be destroyed.

Homer, too, grows human, comes out of the myth and carries us back to the dim twilight of history. It is *juventus mundi.* There are no iron ships; few wooden ones, for the race has scarcely progressed beyond lashing logs together as rafts. Only a few planks, adze-hewn, keep out the sea. Horse and dog are scarcely domesti-cated. The world is not far removed from reckoning its years by the revolving moons, whereby the antediluvians attained the great ages credited to them in Genesis. The seasons for a year of 365 days fitted about the year B.C. 146; 1,440 years earlier the year again coincided with the seasons, and then back of that another cycle they probably began to count time by the annus. Tubal Cain has hammered out in the first forge the first metal weapon and the song of the sword begins to pierce the sky and make its moan. The sea beach is lined with sirens and harpies; each waterfall has a god; every grove a divinity. Circe and Calypso, not gowned with Worth or Paquin, but near to nature's heart, smite on the senses and heat their madness in the veins. There is a glow and fancy in the world, for it is young, rich with imagination not yet chilled, and pulsing with a freedom not yet fettered by civilization. So, having read this poem, I have seen Ulysses. He stands forth the hero of our migratory and exuding race, a man who has been to the wars, perhaps to the end of the world and looked over the wall, and come home again. The finest pictures are often painted in words and the finest statues chiseled in language. So here the exquisite art of Tennyson has put before us an old king, gray with honors, walking about Ithaca. He has a face that women turn to look at a second time, tall like King Saul, brawny, athletic, and, though an old man, even yet agile. Some of Tennyson's men seem overbred and lack the virility which Browning has caught in Hervé Riel or Saul. Not so with Ulysses. He is drawn here puissant, quick, shifty with his spear, not given to blubbering like Æneas, nor sulking like Achilles, but veritably he of the Wooden Horse, wily as only himself, councilor with Nestor. As you read you can imagine Frederick the Great walking about Sans Souci, sending a sword to Washington, living Rossbach and Leuthen over again; or Washington at Mount Vernon, shield off, lance at rest, overseeing his estate, or riding over to Alexandria, sitting in the Masons' lodge, and with hat on, perhaps, as we are told, even in the Master's chair. There is added to the picture a touch of Abraham migrating to the land of promise, Balboa overlooking the Pacific, Stanley lean and breathless from the vast interior of Africa, Peary hooded and deep-chested from the frozen pole. Each and all of these are figured in this king of Ithaca, and who knows but in some dim century yet to come this which Tennyson has written shall be expanded and grafted into the epic as the twenty-fifth book of the *Odyssey!*

—EDWIN A. SCHELL, "Tennyson's 'Ulysses,'" *Methodist Review* 95, No. 2
(March 1913): 192–95

EZRA POUND

What is James Joyce's *Ulysses?* This novel belongs to that large class of novels in sonata form, that is to say, in the form: theme, counter-theme, recapitulation, development, finale. And in the subdivision: father and son novel. It follows in the great line of the *Odyssey,* and offers many points of more or less exact correspondence with the incidents of Homer's poem. We find there Telemachus, his father, the sirens, the Cyclops, under unexpected disguises, bizarre, argotic, vera-cious and gigantesque.

Novelists like to spend only three months, six months on a novel. Joyce spent fifteen years on his. And *Ulysses* is more condensed (732 pages) than any whole work whatsoever by Flaubert; more architecture is discovered. ⟨. . .⟩

Bloom, advertising agent, the Ulysses of the novel, the sensual average man, the basis—like Bouvard and Pécuchet—of democracy, the man who believes what he reads in the papers, suffers *after his soul's desire.* He is interested in everything, wants to explain everything, to impress everybody. Not only does his celerity and aptness for picking up what is said and thought everywhere, chewed over by everyone a hundred times a week, serve Joyce as a literary device, but the other characters are chosen to support him, in order to pick up the vanities of circles other than his. ⟨. . .⟩

Joyce uses a scaffold taken from Homer, and the remains of a medieval allegorical culture; it matters little, it is a question of cooking, which does not restrict the action, nor inconvenience it, nor harm the realism, nor the contemporaneity of the action. It is a means of regulating the form. The book has more form than those of Flaubert. ⟨. . .⟩

The action takes place in one day (732 pages) in a single place, Dublin. Telemachus wanders *beside the shore of the loud and roaring sea;* he sees the midwives with their professional bags. Ulysses breakfasts, circulates; mass, funeral, bath house, race track talk; the other characters circulate; the soap circulates; he hunts for advertising, the "ad" of the House of Keyes, he visits the national library to verify an anatomical detail of mythology, he comes to the isle of Aeolus (a newspaper office), all the noises burst forth, tramways, trucks, post office wagons, etc.; Nausicaä appears, they dine at the hospital; the meeting of Ulysses and Telema-chus, the brothel, the brawl, the return to Bloom's, and then the author presents Penelope, symbol of the earth, whose night thoughts end the story as counter-weight to the ingenuities of the male.

Cervantes parodied but a single literary folly, the chivalric folly. Only Rabelais and Flaubert attacked a whole century, setting themselves against a whole idiotic encyclopedia—in the form of fiction. The Dictionaries of Voltaire and Bayle are not under discussion. It is no small thing to get into the Rabelais-Flaubert class.

—EZRA POUND, "James Joyce and Pécuchet" [1922], tr. Fred Bornhauser,
Shenandoah 3, No. 3 (Autumn 1952): 14–17

G. WILSON KNIGHT

Ulysses' speech ⟨in Shakespeare's *Troilus and Cressida*⟩ forms a perfect statement of the case for the moral order against the high mystic philosophy of tragedy and passion. Nor is this to twist the natural meaning of a dramatic speech; for we must observe that the speeches in *Troilus and Cressida* are primarily analytic rather than dramatic, and, if we are to understand its peculiar meaning we must be ready, as are the persons of the play, to respond to the lightest tones and shades of its philosophy. This reading of the argument as a discussion of tragedy does not conflict with the dramatic situation. Agamemnon has expressed a profound and sympathetic commentary on the progress of the war. He has spoken like a mystic; but mystics seldom make good generals. Agamemnon is thus closely analogous to the Duke in *Measure for Measure*. Both speak wisdom, especially the profound mystic wisdom of the tragic philosophy. Both are, however, impractical in the ordinary sense. From the view-point of Thersites Agamemnon is an honest man enough, but a fool (v. i. 56–8). Ulysses answers Agamemnon's gentle and noble acceptance of misfortune by suggesting that his actual conduct of the war lacks the co-ordinating and directing quality of regal discipline. This we can well believe from what we see of the Greek army. There are, then, two layers of thought here: the purely dramatic and the profoundly universal and philosophic meanings. They are not properly separate, but rather two aspects of the same thing. We have an illuminating instance of what often happens here: the persons are all obsessed with the desire of analysis, and, in the process of their search for truth, continually raise the particular into the realm of the universal. Here the crucial problem of the play is at issue: since intuition and faith accept the tragic philosophy, reason and intellect reject it. In this instance, the intuition-intellect opposition is obviously one with that of individualism and order. Ulysses, exponent always throughout the play of reason, statecraft, and order, attacks the intuitional and emotional—one might almost say the 'sentimental'—arguments of Agamemnon and Nestor. And it must be observed that both sides use the peculiar Shakespearian symbols of disorder and tempest which are fundamental in tragedies of the *Macbeth* and *King Lear* type. For, besides the tempest-imagery of the passages already quoted, there is, in Ulysses' speech, a reference to unnatural, disorderly phenomena in earth and sky such as I discuss elsewhere in relation to *Julius Caesar* and *Macbeth*:

> ... but when the planets
> In evil mixture to disorder wander,
> What plagues, and what portents! what mutiny!
> What raging of the sea! shaking of earth!
> Commotion in the winds! frights, changes, horrors,
> Divert and crack, rend and deracinate
> The unity and married calm of states
> Quite from their fixure!   (I. iii. 94)

The relevance of this to Shakespearian tragedy is obvious; nor could a better commentary be found on Shakespeare's disorder-symbolism than this carefully constructed order-speech of Ulysses. It should be observed that Ulysses' arguments win the day.

—G. WILSON KNIGHT, "The Philosophy of *Troilus and Cressida*,"
The Wheel of Fire (1930; rev. ed. London: Methuen, 1949), pp. 50–52

FRANK BUDGEN

"I am now writing a book," said Joyce, "based on the wanderings of Ulysses. The *Odyssey*, that is to say, serves me as a ground plan. Only my time is recent time and all my hero's wanderings take no more than eighteen hours."

A train of vague thoughts arose in my mind, but failed to take shape definite enough for any comment. I drew with them in silence the shape of the Uetliberg-Albis line of hills. The *Odyssey* for me was just a long poem that might at any moment be illustrated by some Royal Academician. I could see his water-colour Greek heroes, book-opened, in an Oxford Street bookshop window.

Joyce spoke again more briskly:

"You seem to have read a lot, Mr. Budgen. Do you know of any complete all-round character presented by any writer?"

With quick interest I summoned up a whole population of invented persons. Of the fiction writers Balzac, perhaps, might supply him? No. Flaubert? No. Dostoevski or Tolstoi then? Their people are exciting, wonderful, but not complete. Shakespeare surely. But no, again. The footlights, the proscenium arch, the fatal curtain are all there to present to us not complete, all-round beings, but only three hours of passionate conflict. I came to rest on Goethe.

"What about Faust?" I said. And then, as a second shot, "Or Hamlet?"

"Faust!" said Joyce. "Far from being a complete man, he isn't a man at all. Is he an old man or a young man? Where are his home and family? We don't know. And he can't be complete because he's never alone. Mephistopheles is always hanging round him at his side or heels. We see a lot of him, that's all."

It was easy to see the answer in Joyce's mind to his own question.

"Your complete man in literature is, I suppose, Ulysses?"

"Yes," said Joyce. "No-age Faust isn't a man. But you mentioned Hamlet. Hamlet is a human being, but he is a son only. Ulysses is son to Laertes, but he is father to Telemachus, husband to Penelope, lover of Calypso, companion in arms of the Greek warriors around Troy and King of Ithaca. He was subjected to many trials, but with wisdom and courage came through them all. Don't forget that he was a war dodger who tried to evade military service by simulating madness. He might never have taken up arms and gone to Troy, but the Greek recruiting sergeant was too clever for him and, while he was ploughing the sands, placed young Telemachus in front of his plough. But once at the war the conscientious objector became a jusqu'auboutist. When the others wanted to abandon the siege he insisted on staying till Troy should fall."

I laughed at Ulysses as a leadswinger and Joyce continued:

"Another thing, the history of Ulysses did not come to an end when the Trojan war was over. It began just when the other Greek heroes went back to live the rest of their lives in peace. And then"—Joyce laughed—"he was the first gentleman in Europe. When he advanced, naked, to meet the young princess he hid from her maidenly eyes the parts that mattered of his brine-soaked, barnacle-encrusted body. He was an inventor too. The tank is his creation. Wooden horse or iron box—it doesn't matter. They are both shells containing armed warriors."

History repeats itself. The inventor of the tank also found his Ajax at the War Office in the shape of Lord Kitchener.

It seems to me to be significant that Joyce should talk to me first of the principal character in his book and only later of the manifold devices through which he presented him. If the two elements of character and material can be separated this is the order in which he would put them. On the home stretch back to Bellevue a question grew in my mind.

"What do you mean," I said, "by a complete man? For example, if a sculptor makes a figure of a man then that man is all-round, three-dimensional, but not necessarily complete in the sense of being ideal. All human bodies are imperfect, limited in some way, human beings too. Now your Ulysses . . ."

"He is both," said Joyce. "I see him from all sides, and therefore he is all-round in the sense of your sculptor's figure. But he is a complete man as well—a good man. At any rate, that is what I intend that he shall be."

—FRANK BUDGEN, James Joyce and the Making of Ulysses (New York:
Harrison Smith & Robert Haas, 1934), pp. 15–17

W. K. C. GUTHRIE

The outstanding feature of epic as displayed in the *Odyssey* is simplicity. It is the tale of the hero who has to pass many dangers on sea and land, outwit giants and other monsters, and accomplish in general a number of feats of courage and ingenuity before he reaches the final goal from which his purpose, so far as it is serious, has never swerved, and is welcomed by his dear wife at his own fireside. In all this he has working with and for him a goddess who has chosen him for her especial favourite. As Jason had the help of Hera, and Aeneas of his mother, so Odysseus was able to defeat all perils by joining to his own wits the divine powers of Athena. The assistance she gave him lay in such devices as hiding him in a cloud, or going before him in human form to ensure him a friendly reception, for help of this sort suited the problems he had to face. We are, that is to say, in a genuine fairy-tale world, not one indeed where human personalities are submerged, but where motives are simplified, where our chief joy is to see the hero first mocked, then outwitting or outdoing his mockers, where, to put the point briefly, there is no moral and no one but a fool would spoil a good story by looking for one.

It is otherwise with tragedy, and especially with the tragedy of Sophocles. Human motives and their justification, the moral relations between gods and mortals, provide questions that have demanded, not perhaps to be answered, but at any rate to be probed and brought forcibly before the notice of men. Realizing this, we shall be prepared to find a very different sort of story when we meet Odysseus again as he emerges from the mind of Sophocles, and surely the first question we shall want to ask is, What has become of the old partnership without which the *Odyssey* cannot be imagined? That hand-in-glove work of man and goddess, in reading which Homer asked no more of us than that we should admire its smooth efficiency and enjoy the adventures in which it plays a part—how does it appear when subjected to the searching light of moral criticism? A glance at one scene will let us see that it will have to be altered beyond recognition. Odysseus has been landed on Ithaca asleep. His friend and counsellor meets him in the guise of a young man and tells him that it is truly Ithaca he has come to. 'Ithaca,' says he musingly, 'yes, I've heard of Ithaca', and proceeds to spin a long and detailed story about why he left his home in Crete. And Athena smiles and says, 'He would be a clever man, or god for that matter, who could get the better of you. But I'm pretty cunning myself, and not even you knew it was I who was talking to you.' 'No, you took me in there,' answers Odysseus, 'but for all I know you're fond of me, you're not going to get me to believe that story about this being Ithaca.' 'Just the same as ever', is Athena's reply. 'And, do you know, that's the real reason why I don't give you up, just because you're cautious and tricky like myself.'

No one would expect us to take these cheerful conspirators too seriously. How are they to be transformed into figures fit to appear on the tragic stage? That to my mind is not only the way to approach the character of Odysseus in the *Ajax*, but even, in spite of the overwhelming interest of the central figure, one of the most fascinating questions which the play raises.

The old partnership is again at work, and we are presented at the opening of the play with one of those scenes so familiar to us from Homer, of the man and his patron-goddess plotting and taking counsel together. At those meagre facts all resemblance to Homer stops. The difference in atmosphere, in the relations between the two, is as complete as it could be. In the *Odyssey* one gets the impression that although Athena may have one or two mechanical powers which Odysseus lacks, the ability to metamorphose herself or to cast a cloud over whom she will, Odysseus' superb and never-failing wits make him a worthy and no less active partner. It is a conception rather like that of Jehovah and his great men in the negro versions of Bible stories. The heroes of Israel have to ask permission to use a miracle, for they cannot work it without his aid, but it is sometimes their brains and not his that make it any use employing a miracle at all. ' "But I jes' don't see," say de Lawd, "what making de sun stop still have got to do wid beating dese here five kings." "Dat's all right Lawd", say Joshua. "You jes' go right back and sit on yo' cloud and leave de rest to me." ' So one felt that if only these arbitrary powers had been given to Odysseus, he would have shown himself at least as intelligent and cunning in their use as his divine patron.

This relationship has now undergone a striking change. At the very first we are shown the hero παπταίνων, peering about in a puzzled way. The one-time wily Odysseus is completely at a loss. There is suspicion attaching to Ajax, and he is trying to find out if it is justified. Athena can tell him that. The deed was Ajax's. But this if anything increases his bewilderment. What purpose could the mighty Ajax

have in such an insanely wanton act? Athena, who is throughout mistress of the
proceedings, explains what she has done, and before Odysseus can interrupt is
calling Ajax forth for the unpleasant purpose of displaying his mania to Odysseus in
order that he may publish it abroad with sufficient vividness among the Argives:

ὡς πᾶσιν Ἀργείοισιν εἰσιδὼν θροῇς.

That when thou hast seen it thou mayest proclaim it to all the Greeks.

Through the scene Odysseus is at a total disadvantage. Gone are the days when in
the pages of Homer he and Athena used to plan, with mutual approval and
practically as comrades, for his safe return. He is in the grip of a power which, while
acting in his own interests, carries him off his feet and has no respect for his own
plans and wishes whatsoever. With taunts of cowardice and the most unworthy
remark οὔκουν γέλως ἥδιστος εἰς ἐχθροὺς γελᾶν; ("And to mock at foes—is
that not the sweetest mockery?") she forces him to view a sight for which, very
properly, he has little relish. We have here neither the brave, resourceful hero of
epic nor the cold and remorseless plotter which he becomes in the *Philoctetes*. We
have a very human figure, reluctantly consenting to an ally who is divine only in the
sense of being more powerful, while his heart is heavy to think that both he and
Ajax alike are mere playthings for such powerful beings to deal with as the whim
may take them.

You may say at this point that the view we have taken goes too far, and
involves forgetting that the purpose for which Ajax had set out, and from which he
had only been turned aside by the intervention of Athena, was a horrible one, the
murder in cold blood of the foremost of the Achaeans: you may also point to the
fact that he had consistently treated the gods with scant respect and preferred to
rely on his own right arm rather than on divine assistance, so that the course of
events is just the conventional Greek sequence of ὕβρις and ἄτη, with nothing
more subtle, nothing of more human appeal, beneath it. I should be surprised to
find that it was so in a play of Sophocles, and I do not think it is.

First, it is not the simple action that matters in a Sophoclean tragedy, but the
mind and the motives behind it. Athena has saved Odysseus and his fellow-
chieftains, but has done it not so much for their sake as in order to fasten a horrible
doom on Ajax. Clearly there were more merciful methods of turning him from his
purpose than this of putting him in the midst of a writhing heap of dying cattle,
gibbering his insane triumph as it were over the bodies of his rival and his enemies.
Killing him would have been one of them. There is clearly another purpose in this
than the saving of lives, a purpose which involves that Odysseus, shrinking back in
natural repulsion, shall be forced to look on a ghastly, inhuman sight. He looks, Ajax
passes in again, and the purpose is revealed. Ὁρᾷς, Ὀδυσσεῦ, τὴν θεῶν ἰσχὺν
ὅση; ("Seest thou, Odysseus, how great is the strength of the gods?") 'I see,' replies
Odysseus in effect, 'and the sight gives me no pleasure. I see that he, my enemy, is
bowed low beneath an evil doom, and all it suggests is that I no less, and indeed all

men on earth, are but phantoms and shadows of men.' 'Then see,' replies Athena, 'that you keep to your own station and behave not arrogantly towards us, τοὺς θεούς.'

The *might* of the gods is here as great as it ever was. Sophocles is not denying, he is emphasizing, the old dictum that ὕβρις will be followed by ἄτη, as far as it is simply a question of fact. Whether the essence of *justice* is contained in such a system, when the ὕβρις may consist simply of a personal slight felt by a being who is superhuman in power but in character can have more than a human share of vanity, jealousy, and other weaknesses, but it will be followed surely by a κακὴ ἄτη just because the power lies in the hands of this being, that, I suggest, is a question which is left, to say the least of it, in doubt.

If ever there was an uneasy mortal, it is Odysseus at the end of this scene. What are we to think of the next occasion on which we hear of him? It is from the chorus of Ajax's sailors, bewailing the madness of their lord. Τοιούσδε λόγους ψιθύρους πλάσσων εἰς ὦτα φέρει πᾶσιν ᾿Οδυσσεύς ("Such are the whispered slanders that Odysseus breathes into all ears"), they say. Here, I would suggest, is a fine piece of irony. Consider the attitude of Odysseus throughout the last scene, and especially the words with which, after being thoroughly revolted by the thought of seeing Ajax in his present condition, he closes.

> ἐποικτίρω δέ νιν,
> δύστηνον ἔμπας, καίπερ ὄντα δυσμενῆ,
> ὁθούνεκ᾽ ἄτῃ συγκατέζευκται κακῇ.
> ὁρῶ γὰρ ἡμᾶς οὐδὲν ὄντας ἄλλο πλὴν
> εἴδωλ᾽, ὅσοιπερ ζῶμεν, ἢ κούφην σκιάν.

And I pity him in his misery, for all that he is my foe,
because he is bound fast to a dread doom: I think of mine
own lot no less than his. For I see that we are but
phantoms, all we who live, or fleeting shadows.

'Thus in the *Ajax*,' wrote J. A. Symonds, 'Sophocles contrives to reverse the whole situation, by showing in the end Ajax sublime and Odysseus generous, though at the first the one seemed sunk below humanity and the other hateful in his vulgar scorn of a fallen rival.'

If you extract vulgar scorn of a fallen rival from the little speech just quoted, or indeed from any word of Odysseus in this scene, you do not attach the same meaning to Greek as I do. This is not the man to go straight away and publish abroad with relish the tale of what he has seen. That was Athena's suggestion, not his. He has been thoroughly shaken, and has gone away to think it over, and the result of his meditation, on this view, is the attitude he adopts when he reappears at the end of the play. Surely on this interpretation we are not only giving unity and meaning to the tragedy, in so far as the position of Odysseus is important to it, but are less than on any other view forcing the Greek to bear a certain meaning which on our own standards we think it should have rather than one which, taken as it stands, it would naturally suggest.

A few words more in confirmation of the part we have assigned to heaven on this view of the tragedy. We should not attach too much importance to the language of Ajax, who is being expressly depicted as a god-hater. Yet his words as a whole are calculated to increase our sense of the power of the gods rather than our sense of their justice: εἰ δέ τις θεῶν / βλάπτοι, φύγοι τἂν χὦ κακὸς τὸν κρείσσονα ("But if a god send harm, verily e'en the base man can elude the worthier"). The evidence of Tecmessa is more striking, for she is presented at first as pious and god-fearing. She protests with the cry εὔφημα φώνει ("You speak blasphemies") against her husband's blasphemies, and is altogether at one with the conventional attitude of the chorus. After Ajax's death, when the chorus conclude an antiphonal account of the hard fate which assuredly awaits Tecmessa and her child with the words 'But may heaven prevent it', she cannot stand it, nor bring herself to echo the pious prayer which has now lost all meaning for her. 'But all our troubles are the work of heaven', she cries. 'Such is the evil which Zeus's daughter, the dreadful goddess, Pallas, causes to spring up out of her love for Odysseus.' Athena did it. In doing it she saved Odysseus' life, but he no less than others was driven despite himself where her will, not his, led. When a truly noble action is to be performed, when Odysseus shows his generosity by not only insisting on the due burial of his fallen enemy but effecting a reconciliation with that enemy's brother, then it is human beings who are the protagonists: the powers of heaven are conspicuously absent.

—W. K. C. GUTHRIE, "Odysseus in the *Ajax*," *Greece and Rome* 16, No. 3 (October 1947): 115–19 (translations from the *Ajax* by R. C. Jebb)

W. B. STANFORD

Odysseus does not actually appear on the scene for long in any of Euripides' tragedies. But his single appearance in *Hecuba* is unforgettably detestable and he lurks in the background of *Troades* and *Iphigeneia at Aulis* as a sinister, malign influence. (His part in *The Cyclops* and *Rhesus*, if this play is by Euripides, need not be discussed in detail here: both plays are closely derived from Homeric episodes, and have had little influence on the main Ulysses tradition.) As it happened, *Hecuba* became one of the most popular of Euripides' plays in later times, much to Odysseus' disadvantage. Seneca strengthened its influence by conflating it with Euripides' *Troades* in his own *Troades*. Similarly Odysseus' part in the Iphigeneia play was much imitated by French neo-classical dramatists like Rotrou and Racine, with varying degrees of emphasis on his culpability.

Hecuba (produced about 424 B.C.) presents an Odysseus without a redeeming feature. Troy has fallen. According to custom all the adult Trojan males have been slaughtered. The fate of the women and children has now to be determined. The ghost of Achilles has demanded the sacrifice of Polyxena, daughter of Hecuba. Here Euripides chooses to lay the whole blame for her death on Odysseus. The cyclic *Destruction of Troy,* as far as is known, did not implicate Odysseus at all. Possibly Stesichorus—if one can rely on the testimony of the Tabula Iliaca—had involved Odysseus with Neoptolemus and Calchas in the sacrifice. But Euripides makes him bear the whole odium for it. The other Greeks are represented as merciful and compassionate in comparison.

Before Odysseus enters the chorus of captive women describes him as 'that shifty-minded, popularity-seeking, smooth-spoken prater' (v. 13). It is true that the speakers are Trojans, naturally biased against their conqueror. But Euripides' sympathy is clearly on their side and their view, like that of most tragic choruses, may be taken as expressing a widely-held opinion. It would be hard for anyone to win popular approval after such an introduction, and Euripides gives Odysseus no chance to do so. After a highly emotional scene between Hecuba and her daughter, designed to enlist the audience's sympathy on their side, Odysseus enters. Euripides makes him perform the duties normally assigned to a herald, in order to emphasize his harshness. His announcement of Polyxena's doom is brutally laconic. Hecuba appeals to him for mercy. She has reason, she thinks, to hope for special consideration. She reminds him how, when he came into Troy disguised as a beggar, she detected him and spared him. Odysseus admits that the recollection touches him deeply, and acknowledges his debt of gratitude. Hecuba reminds him of his promises to repay her as soon as he could. Now is his opportunity to show his sincerity. Odysseus cynically dismisses those promises as 'speeches devised to avoid death'. At this Hecuba breaks into a scathing denunciation of demagogues who will promise anything to win political advantages, creatures careless of all debts of gratitude and ruthless towards their friends as occasion demands. Here, in other words, Odysseus meets the full tide of Autolycan odium, the furious hatred of a victim of deceptive promises. But we must be on our guard. It may be Euripides who is the deceiver here.

No doubt many simple, kindly Athenians gnashed their teeth at Odysseus' villainous ingratitude, as Hecuba described it. But some of Euripides' more critical hearers may well have asked two pertinent questions. What is the authority for this touching story of Hecuba's kind-heartedness? And what has Odysseus' conduct here to do with political demagogy? Homer had, indeed, related how Helen had encountered Odysseus on his spying expedition into Troy, and had seen through his disguise and treated him kindly. But there is no suggestion in extant earlier Greek literature—though the possibility of some now lost source cannot be excluded—that Hecuba knew anything about it. Besides, if one thinks for a moment and does not let emotion cloud one's critical faculties, does it not imply an entirely improbable situation—that the queen of a beleaguered city should spare the most dangerous of its enemies when she has caught him spying? In contrast Helen's help was natural. She was a Greek, and apparently tired of Troy and Paris by then. But would all Odysseus' proverbial skill in pleading have persuaded Hecuba to let him return unscathed with his valuable information to the Greek camp? It would have been a flagrant betrayal of all she held dear.

A second consideration is equally damaging to Euripides' carefully contrived villainization of Odysseus. The charge of being a typical demagogue had been already made against him by Pindar. In fact there is no justification for it in his Homeric or cyclic career as we now know it, as the ancient commentators on Homer emphasized. Pindar and Euripides simply chose to distort his character to make him a whipping-boy for contemporary politicians. Euripides' presentation here is good theatre, and well calculated to inflame hostility against Odysseus. But it hardly stands closer examination.

When Hecuba turns again from denunciation to pleading, Odysseus replies coldly. First he formally discharges his debt of gratitude to Hecuba by saying that he will keep her personally from all harm. But Euripides makes it sound more like a politician wriggling out of a commitment than anything else. Then Odysseus argues about public as distinct from private debts of gratitude: every political body must honour its benefactors, especially after their death, if it hopes to promote loyalty and public spirit. The ghost of the greatest Greek champion demands the sacrifice of Polyxena. To refuse it would be both ungrateful and politically inexpedient. 'I myself', Odysseus adds, 'would be content with few possessions in this life, provided that my tomb was duly honoured after my death'. This personal touch closely resembles his remark to Agamemnon in *Ajax*. Uncertainty of dating precludes any deductions about priority. But the difference of context creates a marked difference in tone. In *Ajax* Odysseus refers to his own mortality out of sympathy with a defeated foe. Here in *Hecuba* he refers to his own ambition to have an honoured grave as part of his argument in favour of sacrificing Polyxena, and as a statement of personal agreement with a general principle of political expediency.

His last arguments to Hecuba are frankly chauvinistic. Greek women have lost many relatives in this war: why should not some Trojan women suffer now? Blood is thicker than water. If the Trojans wish, like barbarians, to make no difference between kindred and enemies and neglect the honour of their illustrious dead—so much the better for the more pious Greeks. Euripides, the humanitarian, is, of course, speaking with fierce sarcasm here. He means that if the barbarians are those who refuse to exclude foreigners and strangers from their compassion, then let us turn to those barbarians for hope of a kinder world—as, in fact, he himself did when he left Athens for the court of Archelaus in Macedonia later. Like St. Paul, he turned to the Gentiles.

After Odysseus' callous speech Hecuba makes a last effort. Remembering that he, too, has children, she tells her daughter Polyxena to throw herself at his feet and appeal to his feelings as a father. At this Odysseus draws in his hand and turns away his face, either through a momentary flicker of emotion or else simply to avoid her ritual gestures of supplication, or for both reasons. Later Hecuba offers to die in Polyxena's place. Odysseus insists that this is not what the ghost of Achilles desires. He remains silent while the mother and daughter tearfully part. Then he silently leads the victim away for sacrifice. This is the last that is seen of him in the play.

Apart from the explicit denunciations by the Trojan women who naturally detest Odysseus, Euripides' own dislike of him in this play can hardly be disputed.

Euripides visualizes him as the extreme type of chauvinistic and militaristic power-politician, correct as any Nazi Gauleiter and as impervious to personal or emotional appeals. Odysseus has not even the excuse of anger, envy, or vengefulness here, as he had in the Palamedes incident. It is his sheer inhumanity that repels us, and his ability to believe that political loyalty can justify murder. Most sinister of all in the light of recent events in Europe is his convenient doctrine that to class a people as 'barbarians' is a valid reason for treating them as beasts.

Odysseus does not appear personally in Euripides' *Troades* (415 B.C.) but his malignant influence pervades the play. It was he, according to Euripides' version, who inexorably urged the death of Astyanax, which is the essence of the tragedy. When Hecuba hears that she is to become his slave she describes him (vv. 281ff.) as the 'abominable, treacherous, justice-fighting, law-breaking monster with a two-ply tongue'. Cassandra gains some comfort in predicting (vv. 431ff.) the sufferings of his Odyssean wanderings. The titles of two other plays in this trilogy, *Palamedes* and *Sisyphus,* suggest further antipathy to him.

In Euripides' last play, the *Iphigeneia at Aulis,* Odysseus once more suffers from the principle *les absents ont toujours tort.* He does not come on the scene, but Menelaus and Agamemnon discuss him privately (vv. 522ff.). They suspect that if they refuse to sacrifice Iphigeneia, he will denounce them to the army to gain popular influence, for nature has made 'that seed of Sisyphus' ever quick to change and to side with the mob. 'Yes', Menelaus replies, 'he is possessed by ambition, that potent curse'. Later in the play (vv. 1362ff.) it is alleged that Odysseus was ready to compel Iphigeneia's sacrifice by force of arms if necessary. An impartial observer might have pointed out that the expedition was doomed to failure unless the sacrifice took place, and that Odysseus could have been acting purely for the sake of a Greek victory at Troy. But the Atreidae imply, as does Achilles later (vv. 1362–4), that he is exploiting the situation in his own interests. Odysseus is given no opportunity of defending himself.

The theme of selfish ambition was also dominant, apparently, in Euripides' lost *Philoctetes.* In the opening scene Odysseus soliloquizes on the hardships of a career of self-advancement, wondering whether he can really be so intelligent in being prepared to suffer so many trials and dangers for the sake of reputation. Would it not be wiser to live a quiet life free from troubles and business instead of spending himself like this? Then, Miltonically, he reflects, that fame is the spur to greater deeds. With a touch of cynicism he comments, 'surely nothing that lives is more vainglorious than man', and goes off to deceive Philoctetes with a sardonic effrontery, compared with which his villainy in Sophocles' play seemed 'gentle and candid'. Here he is the veteran *politique* valuing his reputation and advancement above both virtue and ease. But he is too intelligent to deceive himself about his motives or to be entirely self-satisfied. There is something almost Shakespearian, or at least post-machiavellian, in this self-consciousness.

These last two plays provide further examples of how Euripides can distort a heroic quality into a contemptible fault. Ambition in the sense of desire for honour and glory—*philotimia*—is the main motive for heroic action in Homer and in much of later Greek literature. 'Ever to be best' was their ideal, and a hero who ignored it was quite exceptional. The same competition for excellence can be observed in Greek athletics and in the literary festivals. If Euripides himself had been entirely exempt from it he would not have competed for the prize at the Dionysia. Ambition can, of course, be a grave moral fault. But without it the whole heroic world would have collapsed in lethargy and torpor. Further, the Homeric Odysseus, as has been described, was much less under the influence of the desire to win glory than any other hero. With a few lapses, as in the Cyclops incident, he observed the Delphic maxim of 'Nothing in excess' almost as faithfully as Socrates. Lucian in his *Dialogues of the Dead* (29) is more faithful to the Homeric spirit than Euripides in this matter. In Hades, Agamemnon asks Ajax why he had spurned Odysseus' friendly approaches (as described in chapter seven). Ajax reaffirms his implacable hatred. Agamemnon argues that, after all, Odysseus had only aimed at 'that most pleasant thing, renown' in the contest for Achilles' arms. His efforts to gain the prize were, he insists, just what one would have expected from any normal hero. The fact is that Odysseus' conduct in the earlier tradition gives no special grounds for charges of ambition and self-aggrandisement. Euripides is heaping on Odysseus the dislike he felt for the upstart Cleons of his own time.

It is seldom possible to prove that an author's attitude is identical with that of his characters, but most critics have agreed that Euripides is less detached from the opinions expressed by the sympathetic figures in his plays than Sophocles. His consistent tone of antipathy and disparagement towards Odysseus in the plays already mentioned—and a similar impression is made by the fragments of his plays on the Ulysses theme—in contrast with the two-sidedness of Sophocles' approach in *Ajax* and *Philoctetes,* seems to confirm the view that Euripides personally disliked the character of Odysseus as he saw it. What most repelled Euripides, apparently, was Odysseus' inhumanity in his treatment of the weak, no matter how much the doctrine of the greater good of the greater number seemed to justify it. Euripides had a unique sympathy for the individual in the grip of ruthless personal forces, and at times, unlike Sophocles, he seems to have allowed his feelings to overcome his dramatic technique. Euripides, again in contrast with Sophocles, had not been very successful himself in his own career. He had suffered much from the calumnies of witty and unscrupulous contemporaries. That is not to say that he was simply working off his personal spleen on Odysseus. But his own experience enabled him to understand the pathos of the losing side of life. Doubtless considerations of dramatic technique contributed to his villainization of Odysseus, but less, it would seem, than in Sophocles' more objective portraits.

Euripides' influence on the later Ulysses tradition was great, especially when reinforced by Seneca's adaptation of his *Hecuba* and *Troades.* As a result the standard role for Ulysses in European drama was that of the crafty man of policies, sometimes directing affairs with malign omniscience, sometimes merely executing the commands of others with inexorable precision. Obviously Euripides was not

solely responsible for this. Pindar, Aeschylus, Sophocles, and others to be mentioned in the following chapters, combined to bring Odysseus into contempt. But
it was Euripides who most successfully enlisted the deeper feelings of his own
contemporaries and of posterity against the grandson of Autolycus and favourite of
Athene.

If one accepts Euripides' portrait of Odysseus as a cynical but unrepentant
power-politician, a disillusioned but unrelenting careerist, the well-known scene at
the end of Plato's *Republic* forms a fitting epilogue to his earthly life. It comes at the
end of the Vision of Er. The souls of Homeric heroes are assembling to choose
bodies for their next reincarnation. Ajax, still angry at his defeat in the award of
Achilles' arms, chooses to be a lion, symbol of unbounded strength and courage.
Agamemnon takes the body of an eagle, unassailable lord of the sky. Thersites,
ambitious for consummate buffoonery, would like to enter the body of an ape. Last
of all comes the soul of Odysseus. He now knows the futility of all ambition. What
he seeks is the life of some humble citizen unoccupied with public affairs. He
searches for it among the lives that the previous heroes had tossed aside like
unwanted bargains at a sale. It is not easy to find. When he comes to it, he seizes
it gladly. Even if he had been given first choice, he says, he would have chosen this
'unofficial' life above all others.

Plato shows genuine sympathy here. If Odysseus had been all that fifth-century
writers had said, ambitious, unscrupulous, unsuccessfully successful, disliked by the
good, denounced by the honest, well might he have chosen the *fallentis semita vitae*
for his next life. And from another point of view Plato's vision was uncannily
prophetic. When after many vicissitudes in the literatures of Italy, France, Germany,
England, and Spain, Ulysses came to choose his fullest and perhaps greatest metamorphosis since the *Odyssey,* he did take the body of a 'private, unofficial person'—
the bourgeois 'hero' of Joyce's *Ulysses.*

—W. B. STANFORD, "The Stage Villain," The Ulysses Theme: A Study in
the Adaptability of a Traditional Hero (1954; rev. ed. New York:
Barnes & Noble, 1964), pp. 111–17

MAURICE BLANCHOT

The Sirens: evidently they really sang, but in a way that was not satisfying, that only
implied in which direction lay the true sources of the song, the true happiness of the
song. Nevertheless, through their imperfect songs, songs which were only a song
still to come, they guided the sailor towards that space where singing would really
begin. They were therefore not deceiving him; they were really leading him to his
goal. But what happened when he reached that place? What was that place? It was
a place where the only thing left was to disappear, because in this region of source
and origin, music itself had disappeared more completely than in any other place in
the world; it was like a sea into which the living would sink with their ears closed

and where the Sirens, too, even they, as proof of their good will, would one day have to disappear.

What sort of song was the Sirens' song? What was its defect? Why did this defect make it so powerful? The answer some people have always given is that it was an inhuman song—no doubt a natural noise (what other kind is there?), but one that remained in the margins of nature; in any case, it was foreign to man, and very low, awakening in him that extreme delight in falling which he cannot satisfy in the normal conditions of his life. But, others say, there was something even stranger in the enchantment: it caused the Sirens merely to reproduce the ordinary singing of mankind, and because the Sirens, who were only animals—very beautiful animals because they reflected womanly beauty—could sing the way men sing, their song became so extraordinary that it created in anyone who heard it a suspicion that all human singing was really inhuman. Was it despair, then, that killed men moved to passion by their own singing? That despair verged upon rapture. There was something marvellous about the song: it actually existed, it was ordinary and at the same time secret, a simple, everyday song which they were suddenly forced to recognize, sung in an unreal way by strange powers, powers which were, in a word, imaginary; it was a song from the abyss and once heard it opened an abyss in every utterance and powerfully enticed whoever heard it to disappear into that abyss.

Remember that this song was sung to sailors, men prepared to take risks and fearless in their impulses, and it was a form of navigation too: it was a distance, and what it revealed was the possibility of traveling that distance, of making the song into a movement towards the song and of making this movement into the expression of the greatest desire. Strange navigation, and what was its goal? It has always been possible to believe that those who approached it were not able to do more than approach it, that they died from impatience, from having said too soon: "Here it is; here is where I will drop anchor." Others have claimed that, on the contrary, it was too late: the goal had always been overshot; the enchantment held out an enigmatic promise and through this promise exposed men to the danger of being unfaithful to themselves, unfaithful to their human song and even to the essence of song, by awakening in them hope and the desire for a marvellous beyond, and that beyond was only a desert, as though the region where music originated was the only place completely without music, a sterile dry place where silence, like noise, burned all access to the song in anyone who had once had command of it. Does this mean that there was something evil in the invitation which issued from the depths? Were the Sirens nothing more than unreal voices, as custom would have us believe, unreal voices which were not supposed to be heard, a deception intended to seduce, and which could only be resisted by disloyal or cunning people?

Men have always made a rather ignoble effort to discredit the Sirens by accusing them flatly of lying: they were liars when they sang, frauds when they sighed, fictions when they were touched—nonexistent in every way; and the good sense of Ulysses was enough to do away with this puerile nonexistence.

It is true, Ulysses did overcome them, but how did he do it? Ulysses—the stubbornness and caution of Ulysses, the treachery by which he took pleasure in the spectacle of the Sirens without risking anything and without accepting the consequences; this cowardly, mediocre and tranquil pleasure, this moderate pleasure, appropriate to a Greek of the period of decadence who never deserved to be the hero of the *Iliad;* this happy and confident cowardice, rooted in a privilege which set him apart from the common condition, the others having no right to such elite happiness but only to the pleasure of seeing their leader writhe ludicrously, grimacing with ecstasy in empty space, but also a right to the satisfaction of gaining mastery over their master (no doubt this was the lesson they learned, this was for them the true song of the Sirens): Ulysses' attitude, the amazing deafness of a man who is deaf because he can hear, was enough to fill the Sirens with a despair which until then had been felt only by men, and this despair turned them into real and beautiful girls, just this once real and worthy of their promise, and therefore capable of vanishing into the truth and depth of their song.

Even once the Sirens had been overcome by the power of technology, which will always claim to trifle in safety with unreal (inspired) powers, Ulysses was still not free of them. They enticed him to a place which he did not want to fall into and, hidden in the heart of the *Odyssey,* which had become their tomb, they drew him—and many others—into that happy, unhappy voyage which is the voyage of the tale—of a song which is no longer immediate, but is narrated, and because of this made to seem harmless, an ode which has turned into an episode.

This is not an allegory. A very obscure struggle takes place between every tale and the encounter with the Sirens, that enigmatic song which is powerful because of its insufficiency. A struggle in which Ulysses' prudence—whatever degree he has of truth, of mystification, of obstinate ability not to play the game of the gods—has always been exercised and perfected. What we call the novel was born of this struggle. What lies in the foreground of the novel is the previous voyage, the voyage which takes Ulysses to the moment of the encounter. This voyage is a completely human story, it takes place within the framework of human time, it is bound up with men's passions; it actually takes place and is rich enough and varied enough to consume all the narrator's strength and attention. Once the tale has become a novel, far from appearing poorer it takes on all the richness and breadth of an exploration, one which sometimes embraces the immensity of the voyage and sometimes confines itself to a small patch of space on the deck and occasionally descends into the depths of the ship where no one ever knew what the hope of the sea was. The rule the sailors must obey is this: no allusion can be made to a goal or a destination. And with good reason, surely. No one can sail away with the deliberate intention of reaching the Isle of Capri, no one can set his course for it, and if anyone decides to go there he will still proceed only by chance, by some chance to which he is linked by an understanding difficult to penetrate. The rule is therefore silence, discretion, forgetfulness.

We must recognize that a certain preordained modesty, a desire not to have any pretensions and not to lead to anything, would be enough to make many novels irreproachable books and to make the genre of the novel the most attractive of genres, the one which, in its discretion and its cheerful nothingness, takes upon itself the task of forgetting what others degrade by calling it the essential. Diversion is its profound song. To keep changing direction, to move on in an apparently random way, avoiding all goals, with an uneasy motion that is transformed into a happy sort of distraction—this has been its primary and most secure justification. It is no small thing to make a game of human time and out of that game to create a free occupation, one stripped of all immediate interest and usefulness, essentially superficial and yet in its surface movement capable of absorbing all being. But clearly, if the novel fails to play this role today, it is because technics has transformed men's time and their ways of amusing themselves.

The tale begins at a point where the novel does not go, though in its refusals and its rich neglect it is leading towards it. Heroically, pretentiously, the tale is the tale of one single episode, that in which Ulysses encounters the inadequate and enticing song of the Sirens. Except for this great, naive pretension, apparently nothing has changed, and because of its form the tale seems to continue to fulfill its ordinary vocation as a narrative. For example, *Aurélia* is presented as the simple account of a meeting, and so is *Une Saison en Enfer,* and so is *Nadja.* Something has happened, something which someone has experienced who tells about it afterwards, in the same way that Ulysses needed to experience the event and survive it in order to become Homer, who told about it. Of course the tale is usually about an exceptional event, one which eludes the forms of everyday time and the world of the usual sort of truth, perhaps any truth. This is why it so insistently rejects everything which could connect it with the frivolity of a fiction (the novel, on the other hand, contains only what is believable and familiar and yet is very anxious to pass for fiction). In the *Gorgias,* Plato says "Listen to a beautiful tale. Now you will think it is a fable, but I believe it is a tale. I will tell you what I am going to tell you as a true thing." What he told was the story of the Last Judgment.

Yet if we regard the tale as the true telling of an exceptional event which has taken place and which someone is trying to report, then we have not even come close to sensing the true nature of the tale. The tale is not the narration of an event, but that event itself, the approach to that event, the place where that event is made to happen—an event which is yet to come and through whose power of attraction the tale can hope to come into being, too.

This is a very delicate relationship, undoubtedly of a kind of extravagance, but it is the secret law of the tale. The tale is a movement towards a point, a point which is not only unknown, obscure, foreign, but such that apart from this movement it does not seem to have any sort of real prior existence, and yet it is so imperious that the tale derives its power of attraction only from this point, so that it cannot even "begin" before reaching it—and yet only the tale and the unpredictable movement of the tale create the space where the point becomes real, powerful, and alluring.

*   *   *

What would happen if instead of being two distinct people Ulysses and Homer comfortably shared their roles, and were one and the same presence? If the tale Homer told were simply Ulysses' movement within the space opened up for him by the Song of the Sirens? If Homer's capacity to narrate were limited by how far he went as Ulysses—a Ulysses free of all impediments, though tied down—towards the place where the power to speak and to narrate was apparently promised to him as long as he disappeared there?

This is one of the strange things about the tale, or shall we say one of its pretensions. It only "narrates" itself, and in the same moment that this narration comes into being it creates what it is narrating; it cannot exist as a narration unless it creates what is happening in that narration, because then it contains the point or the plane where the reality "described" by the story can keep uniting with its reality as a tale, can secure this reality and be secured by it.

But isn't this a rather naive madness? In one sense, yes. That is why there are no tales, and that is why there is no lack of tales.

To listen to the Song of the Sirens is to cease to be Ulysses and become Homer, but only in Homer's story does the real encounter take place, where Ulysses becomes the one who enters into a relationship with the force of the elements and the voice of the abyss.

This seems obscure, it is like the embarrassment the first man would have felt if, in order to be created, he himself had had to pronounce in a completely human way the divine *Fiat lux* that would actually cause his eyes to open.

Actually, this way of presenting things simplifies them a great deal—which is why it produces these artificial or theoretical complications. Of course it is true that only in Melville's book does Ahab meet Moby Dick; yet it is also true that only this encounter allows Melville to write the book, it is such an imposing encounter, so enormous, so special that it goes beyond all the levels on which it takes place, all the moments in time where we attempt to situate it, and seems to be happening long before the book begins, but it is of such a nature that it also could not happen more than once, in the future of the work and in that sea which is what the work will be, having become an ocean on its own scale.

Ahab and the whale are engaged in a drama, what we can call a metaphysical drama, using the word loosely, and the Sirens and Ulysses are engaged in the same struggle. Each wants to be everything, wants to be the absolute world, which would make it impossible for him to coexist with the other absolute world, and yet the greatest desire of each is for this coexistence and this encounter. To bring Ahab and the whale, the Sirens and Ulysses together in one space—this is the secret wish which turns Ulysses into Homer and Ahab into Melville, and makes the world that results from this union into the greatest, most terrible, and most beautiful of all possible worlds: a book, alas, only a book.

Of Ahab and Ulysses, the one with the greater will to power is not the more liberated. Ulysses has the kind of deliberate stubbornness which leads to universal domination: his trick is to seem to limit his power; in a cold and calculating way he finds out what he can still do, faced with the other power. He will be everything, if he can maintain a limit, if he can preserve that interval between the real and the imaginary which is just what the Song of the Sirens invites him to cross. The result is a sort of victory for him, a dark disaster for Ahab. We cannot deny that Ulysses understood something of what Ahab saw, but he stood fast within that understanding, while Ahab became lost in the image. In other words, one resisted the metamorphosis while the other entered it and disappeared inside it. After the test, Ulysses is just as he had been before, and the world is poorer, perhaps, but firmer and more sure. Ahab is no longer, and for Melville himself the world keeps threatening to sink into that worldless space towards which the fascination of one single image draws him.

The tale is bound up with the metamorphosis alluded to by Ulysses and Ahab. The action that the tale causes to take place in the present is that of metamorphosis on all the levels it can attain. If for the sake of convenience—because this statement cannot be exact—we say that what makes the novel move forward is everyday, collective or personal time, or more precisely, the desire to urge time to speak, then the tale moves forward through that *other* time, it makes that other voyage, which is the passage from the real song to the imaginary song, the movement which causes the real song to become imaginary little by little, though all at once (and this "little by little, though all at once" is the very time of the metamorphosis), to become an enigmatic song always at a distance, designating this distance as a space to be crossed and designating the place to which it leads as the point where singing will cease to be a lure.

The tale wants to cross this space, and what moves it is the transformation demanded by the empty fullness of this space, a transformation which takes place in all directions and no doubt powerfully transforms the writer but transforms the tale itself no less and everything at stake in the tale, where in a sense nothing happens except this very crossing. And yet what was more important for Melville than the encounter with Moby Dick, an encounter which is taking place now and is "at the same time" always imminent, so that he keeps moving towards it in a stubborn and disorderly quest, but since this encounter is just as closely related to the source, it also seems to be sending him back into the depths of the past—Proust lived under the fascination of this experience and in part succeeded in writing under it.

People will object, saying: but the events they are talking about belong primarily to the "lives" of Melville, Nerval, Proust. It is because they have already met Aurélia, because they have tripped over the uneven paving stones, seen the three church towers, that they can begin their own vision. Unfortunately, things are not that simple. All the ambiguity arises from the ambiguity of time which comes into play form, an image, a story, or words—that will let us share a vision close to their own vision. Unfortunately, things are not that simple. All the ambiguity arises from the ambiguity of time which comes into place here and which allows us to say and to feel that the fascinating image of the experience is present at a certain moment, even though this presence does not belong to any present, and even destroys the present which it seems to enter. It is true, Ulysses was really sailing, and one day, on a certain date, he encountered the enigmatic song. And so he can say: now—this is happening now. But what happened now? The presence of a song which was still to be sung. And what did he touch in the presence? Not the occurrence of an encounter which had become present, but the overture of the infinite movement which is the encounter itself, always at a distance from the place where it asserts itself and the moment when it asserts itself, because it is this very distance, this imaginary distance, in which absence is realized, and only at the end of this distance does the event begin to take place, at a point where the proper truth of the encounter comes into being and where, in any case, the words which speak it would originate.

Always still to come, always in the past already, always present—beginning so abruptly that it takes your breath away—and yet unfurling itself like the eternal return and renewal—*"Ah,"* says Goethe, *"in another age you were my sister or my wife"*—this is the nature of the event for which the tale is the approach. This event upsets relations in time, and yet affirms time, the particular way time happens, the tale's own time which enters the narrator's duration in such a way as to transform it, and the time of the metamorphoses where the different temporal ecstasies coincide in an imaginary simultaneity and in the form of the space which art is trying to create.

—MAURICE BLANCHOT, "The Song of the Sirens: Encountering the Imaginary" [1959], *The Gaze of Orpheus and Other Literary Essays,* tr. Lydia Davis (Barrytown, NY: Station Hill Press, 1981), pp. 105–13

ANDONIS DECAVALLES

This modern epic of 33,333 lines, first published in the original Greek in 1938 in Athens, is undoubtedly the greatest long poem of our time, a colossal achievement in art and substance. It is the mature product of Kazantzakis' deep familiarity with the best in world-literature and thought, of intense living, traveling, and thinking. The creator, himself another Odysseus, came to know "the cities and minds of many people", and made them his own in a passionate record of wide experience to which he has given meaning and value. Its hero, Odysseus, is Homeric only so long as he does not conflict with Kazantzakis' own self. It is not without significance that the old Adventurer was re-created once more in his own native land, and in his own tongue. Odysseus has never ceased to be the supreme and lasting em-bodiment of Greece, its spirit of an unfailing faith in life and freedom, of enrichment and rebirth through ever new experience. Yet the range in which Odysseus shapes and fulfills his destiny in this new poem is far wider than when he gave us his old,

Homeric report. Three thousand years of further physical and spiritual exploration
have passed since then.

The great longing of Homer's Odysseus was for *nostos,* "homecoming", a
return to Ithaca and Penelope after perilous adventures. But those adventures
were not sought after, for he had been driven into them by angry Poseidon. The
genius of Homer's hero lies in that he turned these precarious adventures into
soul-enriching experiences. Kazantzakis' Odysseus, in contrast, is not home-bound.
After his Homeric return, he finds Ithaca meaningless. He is unwanted for what he
has become: violent, blood-thirsty, lawless, ungodly (a product of later literary
tradition from the Greek dramatists on.) So he sails off again, with a gang of rogues.
From Sparta he steals the still-blossoming Helen, symbol of perfect classical beauty.
In Crete he achieves the overthrow of the decadent Minoan society of King Ido-
meneus, and leaves Helen behind that she may give birth to a new, healthier race
through her marriage with one of the blond, Northern, Doric barbarians. Then he
reaches Egypt, and sails up the Nile in search of its headwaters. An attempt to
overthrow Pharaoh's decayed social order fails. Later, he builds his Ideal City, a
Utopia which, just before its inauguration, is destroyed by an eruption. This marks
his second major freedom: from society, war, and glory in manhood; his first
freedom had been from woman. From now on he is alone, an ascetic as he
wanders to the southernmost end of Africa, meeting on the way a series of spiritual
and mystical experiences embodied in representative types of Don Quixote, Hamlet, Faust, Buddha, the Hedonist, the Primitive Man, the Poet, the Courtezan and,
finally, Jesus Christ in the form of a young Negro fisher-lad. Thence, in a coffin-
shaped boat, he sails towards the Antarctic to achieve his third and final freedom,
from freedom itself. When naked, stripped of all but Memory and Love, he faces
Death on an iceberg, he recognizes his own mirrored self.

In this progress, which cannot be summed up in any few lines, there is still
the notion of the Homeric homecoming, but Ithaca is now the hero's own soul,
the fulfillment of his own being, a full self-conquest as the supreme gain. What
appears as a progress through rejections is really a progress through conquests
and affirmations. Life is good and Death is good. The motive power of the Quest
is fire, the Sun, God, clarity, man's burning body and heart and mind, wherein all
things become one and priceless, where the antitheses merge into a universal
synthesis:

> O Sun, my quick coquetting eye, my red-haired hound,
> sniff out all quarries that I love, give them swift chase,
> tell me all that you've seen on earth, all that you've heard,
> and I shall pass them through my entrails' secret forge
> till slowly, with profound caresses, play and laughter,
> stones, water, fire and earth shall be transformed to spirit,
> and the mud-winged and heavy soul, freed of its flesh,
> shall like a flame serene ascend and fade in sun.

What a precious message of love to come in our time of disparity, what warm affirmation of life, not unrealistic, for a world of anxiety, bitterness, disaffection, fren-
zied rejection or predilection. For the partial, here is the complete man offered,
powerful and integral, able to create his own fate against Fate, his Manhood above
God.

—ANDONIS DECAVALLES, "The Torrent and the Sun," *Poetry* 95, No. 3
(December 1959): 176–77

G. S. KIRK

⟨. . .⟩ the *Odyssey* as a whole fails to achieve the profound monumental effect of the
Iliad. This is partly because the main theme is less universal and less tragic; but to
a large extent it is caused by the actual character of Odysseus. The man of many
trials and many devices, the canny, suspicious, boastful and ruseful victim of fortune
and his own qualities, is obviously less magnificent than the god-like Achilles, the
swift and insanely proud warrior; he is also less real, strangely enough, and less
credible. Achilles is often petty and unimaginative, in many ways like a destructive
and acquisitive child, but there is something sympathetic in him: he represents some
of the commonest aspirations and failings of human nature, though on a superhuman scale. Odysseus is a more specialized being, a curious mixture of heroic and
intellectual qualities that can never have been frequent in any society. Moreover he
is not drawn in much depth: partly the difficulty lies in reconciling the Iliadic Odysseus, who is clever and persuasive but still a great warrior in the classic mould, with
the ingenious braggart, poisoned arrows and all, that he has become in some parts
of the *Odyssey*. For even within the *Odyssey* itself his character is inconsistent
in—for the unitarian audience—a rather unfathomable way. The faithful husband
who rejects a life of divinity with Circe and Calypso is estimable enough; he makes
a nice symbol of the conservative and social demands of man and the power of his
affections, even at the cost of survival; yet he does not accord with the dangerously
conceited victor over the Cyclops. In fact this Odysseus of the sea-adventures
makes too strong an impression for the good of the whole poem, in the rest of
which the hero's character is more consistently sound and gentle—though always
suspicious. Admittedly the hero of the false tales is not usually an appealing figure,
and one suspects that the real Odysseus quite admired his creations; but otherwise
the generous master of servants, the patient victim of insults, the determined and
ultimately affectionate husband, is admirable enough. The trouble is that he does
not turn out to be very interesting. Largely this is because of the role the main poet
has seen fit to assign to Athene, and to the altered conception, different from that
of the *Iliad*, of the way in which the gods rule the life of mortals. During the
sea-adventures, at least, Athene is absent from Odysseus' side—because she could
not risk offending Poseidon, as she explains later, but also perhaps because some
of the earlier sea-tales did not have this kind of divine participant; and, though the
audience still knows that the hero will survive, his ordeals seem more terrifying as

a consequence. Once he is accompanied at almost every step by the goddess, either heavily disguised or in her plainest anthropomorphic form of a tall, beautiful and accomplished woman, the tension of Odysseus' actions and dangers is surely reduced. This may not seriously affect his moral stature, but it diminishes his interest as a hero developing with his circumstances. The growth of Telemachus' character under the goddess's guidance is heavily emphasized; but his father is too mature and too cunning for this kind of unfolding, and the only quirks and anomalies of his character, as we have seen, are probably the rather worrying product of the conflation of different themes and different kinds of epic material.

—G. S. KIRK, *The Songs of Homer* (Cambridge: Cambridge University Press, 1962), pp. 364–65

CHARLES PAUL SEGAL

The Return of Odysseus can be regarded as a return to humanity, in its broadest sense: a return to the familiar, man-scale realities of Ithaca, but also a renewal of the basic human relations with parents, wife, son, friends and retainers, and country. In the course of reclaiming these relations Odysseus undergoes a varied series of experiences, testing him as he tests those he encounters on Ithaca, and culminating in his visit to the land of the dead and his vision of mortality, the antithesis of the immortal life offered by Calypso. She is the point from which Homer begins the tale of Odysseus' wandering and the point at which the hero himself concludes it on Scheria (see 12.450–53). The long series of trying vicissitudes is thus framed on both sides by the stillness of Calypso's island where the hero has refused immortality but yet is far removed from mortal life. If the Return is seen as a reclaiming of humanity, then Calypso becomes significant as a point of suspension, a point of enforced removal in which the hero's human qualities have been entirely dormant and from which he is seeking to return. Homer's silence about details of Odysseus' years with Calypso perhaps reflects the mystery and impenetrable, irrecoverable quality of this 'suspension.' Her island too is distant even for the gods (see 5.100–102), and embodies somehow the mystery, ambiguity, remoteness of the sea itself: it is the very 'navel of the sea' (1.50), while Calypso is the daughter of 'baleful-minded Atlas who knows the depths of all the sea and himself holds up the high pillars which hold apart earth and sky' (1.52–54). Odysseus' place of 'concealment,' then, is itself of the primal essence of the sea; and he is held by the goddess in whom are reflected the crossing and binding together of the cosmic substances, earth, sky, and sea. The man who is to return to mortality first appears against a vast, threatening (see ὀλοόφρων, 1.52) scale that far overshadows his manhood. Yet Homer presents Odysseus on Ogygia at the moment when he is fully ready for his Return, when all his thoughts are dominated by it. The goddess who 'hides' (Kalypso-*kalyptei*) can hide the hero no longer from the human world to which his deep, inextinguishable mortal nature draws him (see 5.215ff.). The visit to Hades

marks an acceptance of mortality generically and, in Teiresias' prophecy, an acceptance of his own death from which he can no longer turn away.

From Calypso to the Phaeacians: the longest and most perilous of Odysseus'
voyages, twenty days in duration, twice the length of the voyage from the Island of
the Sun to Calypso on Ogygia. The two journeys are similar. In both Odysseus is
shipwrecked by a god and travels alone, with great hardship. The first has a
negative result: the losing all his companions, and seven years of idleness, totally
removed from humanity; the second a positive result: an almost immediate return
to the world of men. Perhaps the doubling of the length of the journeys indicates
the magnitude of difficulty in finding his way back to humanity (or the point of
transition to humanity, Scheria) after full 'suspension' from it, in recreating or
reconstructing after loss or removal. Psychologically, the seven year absence on
Calypso's island could be understood as a state of shock and weakness, an inability
to return to reality until enough strength has been gathered. Odysseus himself is
helpless to return until the gods intervene, stimulated by Athena, the embodiment,
in part, of Odysseus' rationality and patience, his clear and integrated vision of
himself as what he is, and therefore the reality of his bond with Ithaca and human
life. She is the vitality and resiliency of his inner human self that has not ceased to
work in his behalf, though he knows it not.

To reach the Phaeacians requires a tremendous effort, against the usual overwhelming odds. But why, to return to the question broached before, should this
passage be so crucial and why should the Phaeacians be chosen as the point for the
review of Odysseus' adventures? The answer requires a careful examination of the
entire Phaeacian episode in the *Odyssey* as a whole.

Noteworthy first is the juxtaposition of Calypso and the Phaeacians. The
Phaeacians, with their activity, agility, seamanship, are antipodal to the inactivity
enforced on Ogygia and to the lack of means of transportation which Calypso
alleges to Hermes (5.141–2) and which causes Odysseus to shudder when Calypso
announces that she will send him home (5.175–9). Odysseus must create from the
basic materials his own means of transport, whereas the Phaeacians provide them
gladly and easily. Similarly, the loneliness of Ogygia, the lack of human contact,
contrasts with the Phaeacians' fondness for society and collectivity (they are first
described in terms of their 'community and city,' δῆμόν τε πόλιν τε, 6.3, and the
building of the wall, houses, and division of fields by their previous king, 6.9–10).
Return to the Phaeacians is thus a major step in the return to humanity, for different
as their way of life is from Ithaca, it is still recognizably human. Scheria thus forms
an essential stepping-stone from the complete suspension of Ogygia to the complete involvement of Ithaca. Odysseus' activity in building a raft is thus not only a
literal requisite for his physical passage, but also a symbolical reengagement of his
rational faculties and his active temperament that are the psychological prerequi-
sites for his return, a reassertion of his power to act creatively upon his environment and master it for his own ends. Here he begins to reestablish the peculiarly
human power of *technē* which appears later, as will be seen, in his victory over the
Cyclops (note the similes of 9.384–6, 391–3) and his construction of his marriage-

bed (23.192–201). It is this same skill which established his fame in his heroic past: the building of the Trojan horse. Once these faculties have been reactivated, the passage over the 'great void (or abyss) of the sea' (μέγα λαῖτμα θαλάσσης, 5.174), though attended by great suffering, cannot be entirely hindered, as Poseidon knows (5.288–9). The safe arrival among the Phaeacians, therefore, cancels the paralyzing enchantment of Ogygia and marks the accomplishment of the most difficult part of Odysseus' return to humanity. Here too Athena, the image of his rationally acting self, helps him directly for the first time in his overseas adventures (7.14ff., 13.316–23), though there is still no mention of his consciously recognizing her until he is actually on Ithaca (13.322–3), where she again becomes dominant in his actions and his consciousness. From Scheria to Ithaca is the easiest of Odysseus' passages, the only one made entirely without effort on his part, in sharp contrast with the voyage from Ogygia, where Zeus decreed that he must return without aid of gods or men (5.31–2), another indication that this latter passage is the cardinal one, the principal point of crisis and transition.

In the kindliness of his reception by the Phaeacians, the joyful vitality and curiosity he finds among them, their assurance of his return, and their generous giving of gifts, they appear as a neutralization of the dangers he has met in the outlandish world between the Ciconians and Scheria. While they are friendly and benign, they are not going to hold and allure him by 'necessity' or enchantment, like Calypso or Circe, but agree easily to speed him on his way. At the same time they are clearly human, and in the games of Book 8 Odysseus can again assert with overwhelming success (8.186ff.) some of the heroic strength of his past life, as he has not been able to do for nine years. Yet they are also somewhat removed from the common sufferings and toil of ordinary mortals. It is this balance of involvement and removal (to be further discussed below) which makes possible Odysseus' review of the past: he is on his way back to mortality but not yet fully involved in it, and hence can reflect on and review his experiences in the non-human, 'unreal' world before reentering the reality of Ithaca. The Phaeacians provide a restorative framework in which he can integrate the real with the unreal, the imaginary with the familiar. They recall too, both in the lays of Demodocus and the games (see esp. 8.215–22), Odysseus' heroic past at Troy and his warlike prowess, which he shall have to call upon soon in defeating the suitors. Hence they face backward as well as forward, back to the adventures after Troy and to Troy itself, and forward to the future struggle with the suitors. Though at peace themselves, they hark back to the spirit of war and the image of heroic self-assurance which Odysseus is to renew in himself. They stand between Odysseus' great exertions on both sides of reality and provide a calm vantage point in the midst of his grim efforts. His arrival there, thrown up by the waves, his safe sleep and awakening before Nausicaa, is a rebirth, a restoration to life after the quasi-death on Ogygia. He emerges from the water entirely naked, stripped of all that has been outgrown and outlived, but ready to be reclothed for the resumption of his human life on Ithaca. The Trojan war is now far in the past, a subject of song; and even his post-Trojan adventures are seven years removed, a removal emphasized by the fact that they are presented as a tale and

Odysseus, in telling them, likened to a bard (11.368, μῦθον δ'ὡς ὅτ' ἀοιδὸς ἐπισταμένως κατέλεξας). Both aspects of his past now focus on the future, and Odysseus' review of the totality of his experiences in the unreal world occurs in the very shadow of his return to reality: but one eagerly awaited dawn separates the two worlds (see 13.35).

The very act of recounting his adventures is a mark of Odysseus' readiness to return. He has lived through a full complement of experiences carrying him from the heroic to the fantasic, from the intelligible to the non-human, from war to inaction, from his position as a leader of men, surrounded by his companions, to total isolation in the seas off Thrinacia and Scheria. Now, no longer immediately involved, he has reached a point of integration and synthesis for reentrance into his humanity. In his tale to the Phaeacians he is making the synthesis final and strong, fixing the past in readiness for the future.

The tale to the Phaeacians is told by the man who has lived it, with its uniqueness and personal vividness in his own mind. He has not only lived it in the past, but relived it inwardly and absorbed and grasped it synoptically for the future. What Odysseus tells, then, is remembered experience, inwardly formed and transmuted. His tale, consequently, must be in the first person, and the change back to third-person narration again in the thirteenth book is striking. The books of his tale, 9–12, have, by contrast with the others, a subjective coloring and privacy, a separateness in a universe of their own, which make them appear indeed as the account of a voyage of the soul, from life to death and back to life. Whatever the symbolic associations of the adventures themselves, their presentation in the first person as a recollected totality can be taken as what the inner man has acquired—like the gifts of the outer man—in passing through a rich multiplicity of experience, a formed and crystalized whole which cannot be communicated literally or objectively, but only in the strangeness of its own terms. They represent certain basic conditions and experiences of human life transformed into a different plane, a key or tonality beyond and foreign to ordinary reality and hence requiring a different form of expression, the personal language of imagination. Not that the actual diction or style of Books 9–12 differ from the other books, but their first-person form and content and their place in the narrative as a whole mark them off as special, as does their removal from the ordinary modes of action and relation in the known world; and their interruption of the forward-moving time-scheme of the poem, their function as a flashback, contributes further to their 'unreality.' The problem for Odysseus is to bridge the gap between the two worlds, between the past accumulation of private experience (or the private aspect of all experience) and his present and future relations with the public, external, directly communicable realities on Ithaca. If Ogygia represents a withdrawal or suspension of his relations with external reality, then his Phaeacian tale is the re-sifting and re-erecting of his inward world to bring it into contact with the reality and objective human demands of Ithaca.

—CHARLES PAUL SEGAL, "The Phaeacians and the Symbolism of
Odysseus' Return," *Arion* 1, No. 4 (Winter 1962): 20–24

ANTHONY BURGESS

'Ulysses' and 'Ulixes' are, as every schoolboy used to know, Latin forms of the Greek 'Odysseus'. Odysseus was, even quite early in life, Joyce's favourite epic hero, and, knowing something of Joyce's temperament, one can see why. Most primitive poetry is about fighting, and the ancient epic naturally extols fighting qualities, making its heroes out of heavyweights gifted with blind courage, brute strength and a garnishing of conventional virtue. Physical violence was repugnant to Joyce—there is very little of it in his books—but he responded readily enough to more intelligent ways of overcoming an enemy—organisation, coolness, tact, cunning. These qualities are all to be found in Odysseus, and to them we can add various endearing imperfections of character. He longs to get home to his wife, but he is not averse to fornication with nymphs and goddesses. This wife is a second-best to Helen, whose hand he failed to win, and it is good loser's decency on his part to persuade all the suitors to join him in swearing an oath to protect Helen from violence. Yet when Helen is carried off to Troy he tries to evade his obligations by pretending to be mad. Still, once launched on the expedition he proves wise and cunning in counsel and prudently brave in war. He is more likeable than Achilles and Ajax and Æneas; he is more human, more Bloom-like. The *Iliad* gives us a sharp picture of him.

Odysseus' qualities call for celebration in a separate epic poem, and the *Odyssey* is devoted entirely to his adventures after the fall of Troy. It covers the ten years between his demobilisation and his arrival home in Ithaca to wrest the little island kingdom from the suitors of his presumed widow Penelope. Most of the adventures which fill the ten years are related in retrospect, the actual events of the poem taking about six weeks. Before we meet Odysseus we meet his son Telemachus (this opening section of the poem is called the *Telemachia*). Telemachus, like Hamlet, is sick at heart. Various island princes are seeking the hand of his mother, but she has—with a cunning perhaps learned from her husband—been putting them off by promising to come to a decision when she has finished weaving a winding-sheet for Laertes, Odysseus' father. What she weaves during the day she unravels at night, but, at the opening of the poem, this trick has been discovered: she must choose her husband now. It becomes urgent for Telemachus to get news of his father. He faces the prospect of having a stepfather whom he hates (he hates all the suitors, but Antinous, the candidate with the shortest odds, is the worst of them all); moreover, these insolent princelings are wasting the substance of the little kingdom of Ithaca very fast. Telemachus goes off to consult Nestor at Pylos and Menelaus and his wife Helen at Sparta: they may have news of his father. Meanwhile, the suitors prepare an ambush against his return.

We come now to the *Odyssey* proper. Odysseus has been living for seven years on the island of Ogygia, detained there by the goddess Calypso. He wants to go home, but she will not let him. But Zeus, father of the gods, steps in and orders his release, and Odysseus builds himself a raft. He sails on it for seventeen days and comes within sight of Scheria, where the Phaeacians live, but then Poseidon, the

sea-god, blows up a storm and destroys the raft. Odysseus, as we shall hear, put
out the one eye of Poseidon's giant son Polyphemus, and he will not be allowed to
forget it. Odysseus floats for two days on the sea, buoyed up by a scarf which Ino,
sea-goddess, has given him, and at length he is cast ashore on the coast of Scheria.
Nausicaa, daughter of the king Alcinous, finds him and looks after him. In the palace
the bard Demodocus sings to him about his own exploits—including that of the
Trojan Horse—and Odysseus, who has up to that moment concealed his name,
now tells the Phaeacians who he is and recounts his perilous story.

He tells of the raid on the Cicones at Ismarus, then of the land of the
Lotus-Eaters, where so many of his men succumbed to the will-destroying, home-
forgetting fruit. After that we hear about the one-eyed giant cannibals called Cyclopes and how Odysseus put out the eye of one of them—Polyphemus—with a
red-hot stake. Then comes the account of his stay with the wind-god Æolus, who
gave him the adverse winds tied up in a bag as a farewell present; his men, thinking
that the bag contained treasure, released the winds, doing themselves and their
leader little good. After that, the Laestrygones, another giant race of cannibals,
destroyed eleven of his twelve ships and ate their crews. The forlorn remainder
reached Æaea, where the witch-goddess Circe turned them all into swine—except,
of course, Odysseus, who was protected from enchantment by the herb moly, a
gift from Hermes. After a year with Circe (during which he begot a son on her,
Telegonus, who was eventually to destroy his father unwittingly) he left—his men
having been restored to human shape—to consult the seer Tiresias in Hades about
his prospects of returning to Ithaca. In Hades he saw the ghosts of many dead
heroes and their womenfolk and talked with his own mother, Anticlea. Back on the
sea again, he resisted the lethal song of the Sirens (himself tied to the mast, his men
with wax in their ears) and steered between Scylla—a mariner-eating monster in
a cave—and the whirlpool Charybdis. After so many lucky or cunning escapes, his
men now did for themselves by killing the cattle of the Sun-god Helios on Thrinacia:
such sacrilege earned them a thunderbolt, though Odysseus—who had warned
them against their crime—escaped on the wreckage of the ship to Ogygia and the
arms of Calypso.

Now comes the homecoming or Nostos. The Phaeacians take Odysseus back
to Ithaca (for their pains their ship is turned, by Poseidon, into a rock on its return)
and now the crafty Odysseus has to encompass the destruction of the suitors. The
goddess Athene disguises him as a beggar, and the faithful swineheard Eumaeus tells
him of the behaviour of the suitors. He shows himself to Telemachus (who escapes
the suitors' ambush) and together they plan a massacre. Meanwhile, two others
learn that this beggar is Odysseus—his nurse Eurycleia and his dog Argus. After
insults from the suitors and a fight with the beggar Irus, our hero learns that
Penelope is to marry the man who can string the bow of Odysseus and shoot an
arrow through twelve axe-heads. Needless to say, only Odysseus can bend the
bow and shoot the arrow, and now he stands revealed in his glory and all the
suitors quake—with justice, as it turns out, for Odysseus, Telemachus and Eumaeus

kill them all, starting with Antinous, and even hang their women. Penelope knows that this must be her husband, since he can tell her what their bedstead looks like, and so all ends, though bloodily, happily. That is how Homer tells the story.

Joyce tells it rather differently. He has eighteen chapters to Homer's twenty-four books; he misses out some of Homer's material but inserts an adventure of the Argonauts—that of the Symplegades, or clashing rocks, expanding a reference to the Planktai, or wandering rocks, in the twelfth book (line 61) of the *Odyssey*. Also, he changes the order of Odysseus' exploits and presents them all in dramatic immediacy, not in epic narration-within-a-narration. The Joycean Odyssey runs as follows:

Telemachus, like Hamlet, is sick at heart. His mother is dead, and he feels guilty about her; he has left his father's house to dwell with two companions. One of these is a foreigner, member of a race that has usurped the kingdom of his people; the other is a fellow-countryman who perpetually mocks him, de-mands money from him and even the key of the tower where they live together. He is dispossessed, bitter at the presence of the usurper. From Nestor—a sage, garrulous and reminiscent prince—he can learn nothing that will lead him back to lawful possession of his rights. He—not Menelaus—consults the sea-god Proteus, but this god changes his form perpetually, slipping out of the grasp of Telema-chus. Oracular hints have been flashed at him about his need for a spiritual, as opposed to a biological, father, but he cannot formulate this need to himself. Now, after this *Telemachia* of three episodes, we are ready for Odysseus. Joyce's hero is both an exile and at home. He has his dwelling in the west, but his heart is tugged by ancestral memories of the east, wherefrom his people have wandered. Thus his wife Penelope can take on the properties of a goddess who has seduced him into staying in exile: this is her kingdom, and her name is Ca-lypso. Odysseus goes forth, having fed her with ambrosia and nectar, and at once finds himself among the Lotus-Eaters. He passes safely through their land and proceeds, with his companions, to Hades, where he meets the ghosts of the fabled dead. Next he makes windy contact with Æolus and nearly meets Telemachus, in whom—his own son being dead—he sees the lineaments of an-other son. He wanders next among the Laestrygonians, filthy gorgers all, but is himself uneaten.

On the way to Scylla and Charybdis, a necessary passage of his journey, he espies Antinous, whom he knows to be a suitor of his wife Penelope. He does not offer fight: he is solitary; he has no son to help him. But now he sees Telemachus himself taking on with courage the perilous passage between the monster's cave and the whirlpool. Telemachus, steering through, sees this sonless father in his turn, and recalls a dream in which such a man seemed to visit him. And now both pseudo-father and pseudo-son have to face new perils: they become Argonauts and venture among the clashing rocks which hide one from the other. Then we are with Odysseus alone once more, and he is not lured by the Sirens' song away from his purpose—to do the work the gods have set him to do and, at length, return safely to Ithaca. But he ventures into territory where the Cyclops Polyphemus lurks, and Polyphemus attacks him. Odysseus gets away, but the giant hurls a heavy missile after him. It is time to seek brief shelter from the hostile world before continuing the journey. He rests in sight of the sea.

On the seashore the king's daughter Nausicaa is playing with her companions. She falls in love with the mature and weary stranger and, in a dream of abandon, gives herself to him. In a dream Odysseus takes her, but, in the convalescence of after-love, he comes to the realisation that, while he is thus dallying away from home, the suitor Antinous has prevailed in Ithaca. It is a bitter moment. Still, ever more mindful of others than himself, he sails to the island where the Oxen of the Sun-god bellow their song of fertility: the island is full of women in labour, and he knows that the wife of a companion is soon to give birth. He lands on the island, enquires about her, and is told that the hour is at hand. He sees that the young Telemachus is there, revelling with drunken companions, and Odysseus is shocked to hear blasphemy spoken against the divine gift of conception: is not this a symbolic slaughtering of the holy oxen? But Zeus hears and, as a warning, launches terrifying thunder.

Odysseus sees that Telemachus has drunk too much wine; what dangers worse than blasphemy may not befall him? He appoints himself the young man's protector and follows him to the island of Circe, where men are turned by magic into swine. The prudent Odysseus is in no danger himself, for the god Hermes has given him the protective herb moly. He sails through terrifying apparitions and phantasmagorias unscathed. As for the young hero towards whom his attitude grows ever more paternal, he too resists gross transformation and is only in danger of attack from rough men whom lust and drunkenness have turned into beasts. He is struck in the face and falls. And now it is Odysseus' duty to take this new-found son back to Ithaca, to heal him, give him opportunity to recover, and offer him the freedom—as to a true son—of his palace.

But the return to the kingdom must be made with caution. They rest awhile, taking food and drink, in the rude shelter of Eumaeus. Then they take courage and walk to the Palace, imbibing there a sacramental cup of nectar, a pledge of paternality and filiality. The young man leaves, no stranger now. Odysseus seeks his couch—he is weary; he has travelled far—and his wife Penelope finds in him a masterfulness she has not known before. The suitors may have tasted of her body, but they have not prevailed as Odysseus has prevailed: they cannot draw his long bow of cunning and knowledge of the world and the deathless gods that govern the world. And Odysseus has brought her a son to replace the true son they lost long ago to the gods of the underworld. This son, not being of her body, stands in the potential relationship of messiah and lover. She sleeps, well content.

That, briefly, is Joyce's own version of the *Odyssey*.

—ANTHONY BURGESS, "Taking Over Homer," *Re Joyce* (New York: W. W. Norton, 1965), pp. 88–93

G. M. KIRKWOOD

In Homer, though Odysseus is a brave and effective fighter, he is most conspicuous in two other realms: as the counsellor, the member of the expedition who never loses sight of the aims and the general good of the expedition; and as the under-taker of difficult, unpleasant, dangerous missions that call for skill and tact. He is the returner of Chryseis in Book 1, the recoverer of the army in the near runaway of Book 2, the leading figure in the embassy to Achilles; he shares with Diomedes the spying expedition in Book 10 and is conspicuous in the reconciliation in Book 19. The enlarged portrait of the *Odyssey* expands but does not much change these characteristics, except that there is a greater emphasis, especially in the second half of the poem, on the wiliness of Odysseus. In the *Iliad* his daring and skill in undertakings, along with his greatness as an orator and counsellor, are emphasized; in the *Odyssey* none of these qualities vanishes, but Odysseus becomes increasingly the guileful plotter: the *polymetis* must become above all the *dolometis,* to gain his ends. It was from this development of Odysseus' personality in the *Odyssey* that there sprang the picture of the unscrupulous trickster, the son of Sisyphus, that may have begun in the Epic Cycle and was prevalent in drama. In the *Odyssey* there is a delight in deception for its own sake that would readily lead to both censure and humour; already in the *Odyssey* Athena finds her protégé's skill and delight in falsehood a matter of amusement as well as admiration.

In the Odysseus of ⟨Sophocles'⟩ *Ajax* there is hardly a trace of the guileful adventurer of the *Odyssey.* The picture is drawn almost entirely from the *Iliad,* though one detail, to be mentioned below, recalls a memorable passage in the *Odyssey.* In the play as in the *Iliad* we find Odysseus undertaking a dangerous mission, this time tracking down the truth about Ajax's madness; we find him the key figure in working for the advantage of the army, both in the opening incident of discovery about Ajax, and later in preventing the vindictiveness of the Atridae from refusing to recognize the great merits of Ajax. No doubt Odysseus in some way represents the Athenian spirit of democracy, but this contemporary influence should not blind us to the extent to which Sophocles draws upon Homer for the spirit as well as the material of his portrayal. The one passage of the *Odyssey* that Sophocles seems to have had specifically in mind is the encounter of Odysseus and Ajax in the underworld, where the gentleness, reflectiveness of tone, and genuine admiration expressed by Odysseus for Ajax are like the most attractive aspects of Sophocles' Odysseus in *Ajax.* In *Odyssey,* 11, 553–60, Odysseus says:

Ajax, son of noble Telamon, would you not even in death forget your anger against me because of that ruinous armour? The gods laid sorrow upon the Argives when you, who were their tower, were destroyed; and we grieved for the loss of you as much as we did for the mighty son of Peleus, Achilles. Zeus alone, none other, was responsible; he hated the army of the Danaids exceedingly and imposed your fate upon you.

These words breathe the same spirit of reflective calm and sympathy as some of the lines that Odysseus speaks in the play:

> I pity him
> In his unhappy state, even though he is my foe;
> When I see him yoked to evil ruin
> I see his fate no more than mine.
> And I perceive that all we men who live
> Are no more than phantoms or empty shadow.   (121–6)

> Injury to a good man when he dies
> Is unjust, even though it chances that you hate him.   (1344–5)

> I am more moved by a man's worth than by hatred.   (1357)

The Odysseus of *Philoctetes* owes something to the later tradition. Homer's Odysseus would never have subscribed to the cynical opportunism expressed in *Philoctetes,* 81–2:

> Since achievement of victory is sweet, endure;
> We shall show ourselves honest another time.

Homer's Odysseus is a man of action as much as a man of words; the Odysseus of *Philoctetes* is no longer the man of action, and he has no scruples about the way he uses words. Apart from his amoral cynicism and a marked lack of disposition to engage in fighting, the Odysseus of *Philoctetes* is essentially the same figure as the hero of the *Odyssey.* He is still, as in Homer, a tireless worker for the group; he is again the undertaker of a difficult and dangerous mission; he is still the servant of deity. If we dislike the way in which he is serving deity in *Philoctetes* we should remember that some of the exploits of the *Odyssey,* for which he has Athena's firm backing, are not of an Achilles-like or Ajax-like moral forthrightness. Even in the *Odyssey* Odysseus was content to work by guile when guile was most effective. And we must never forget that Odysseus in *Philoctetes* is on the side of divine will; Philoctetes must go to Troy, and Heracles is no less emphatic in declaring that this is the will of Zeus than Odysseus is.

The two portrayals of Odysseus are two different developments of Homeric material. In both, Odysseus is the worker for the community and the worker under divine will; in both he is the undertaker of difficult enterprises. But in the one play the enterprising counsellor is also a philosopher with a broad, humane sympathy and a regard for moral values; in the other he is cynical, shifty and callous. Both are legitimate developments of the Homeric figure, however much each may owe to post-Homeric and contemporary influences.

—G. M. KIRKWOOD, "Homer and Sophocles' *Ajax," Classical Drama and Its Influence,* ed. M. J. Anderson (New York: Barnes & Noble, 1965), pp. 64–66

DERICK R. C. MARSH

The Greeks ⟨in *Troilus and Cressida*⟩ have not in general been popular with critics who look for a centre of approval in the play, but Ulysses has had some support. He demonstrates a clearer insight into human behaviour than anyone else in the play; he is shrewd, discreet, an accomplished orator, and in his speech to the Greek council, the enunciator of the need for order, one of the great recognised Shakespearean positives. He has been called wise and statesmanlike, but with little better claim to the titles than, one suspects, most of the people to whom such a combination of epithets is applied, for his wisdom and statescraft do not seem to be directed to any purpose other than the winning of a war. To the Greek leaders he offers an opinion on why Troy has resisted successfully for so long: he ascribes it to Achilles' refusal to join the battle, and prescribes a return to order and discipline in the Greek camp, not necessarily for their own sakes, but so that Achilles may be forced back into the fight. Even then, he has so little confidence in the efficacy of his own remedy, that he immediately afterwards suggests a plan to Nestor that will bring Achilles back, not by persuading him to accept his responsibilities, but by playing on his vanity. Had this plan been successful, its end would have been more bloodshed, more disorder, with only lip-service paid to the ideal on which Ulysses' eloquent discourse to the Greek generals is based. His purpose is to win the war, and he does not much care how this is done. This may show a sound practical sense, but it is hardly the sort of attitude that can be elevated to stand as a high moral positive. Thus his aims and his proposals for action form an ironic comment on the wisdom he is reputed to show, as do the circumstances of Achilles' eventual return to the battle, for when this does occur, it is not because he accepts the need for some ideal order, nor even directly because of Ulysses' attempt to work on his vanity, but because of his passionate grief and rage over the death of Patroclus.

It is undeniably true, nevertheless, that in his address to the Greek generals, and in his attempt to persuade Achilles of the need to keep his honour brightly furbished, Ulysses is given some of the most powerful poetry in the play. In the particular structure of this play, this need not be a source of confusion; no matter what ulterior motives Ulysses may have, what he says remains a valid and trenchant comment on the whole world of the play:

> Take but degree away, untune that string,
> And hark, what discord follows!   (l.iii.109)

His speech describes what the play shows, a world where everything is seen in terms of power and appetite, will uncontrolled by any operation of reason or judgement.

> Power into will, will into appetite;
> And appetite, an universal wolf

So doubly seconded with will and power,
Must make perforce an universal prey
And last eat up himself.   (I.iii.120)

This is what happens to Troilus, to Achilles, to Ajax, even to Hector and to Troy itself, but in spite of this there does not seem to be any indication that Ulysses himself is conscious of the wider implications of what he says. He is diagnosing a particular malady in the Greek camp; if he believes in order for its own sake, or allows its dictates to shape his thoughts and actions, he gives little indication of this in the course of the play. Like Isabella's "Man, proud man / Drest in a little brief authority" in *Measure for Measure,* what he says is more in the nature of a choric comment on the whole play, than a revelation of his own feelings.

His discussion of honour with Achilles,

Time hath, my lord, a wallet at his back
Wherein he puts alms for oblivion.   (III.iii.145)

despite its urging of the exercise of virtue, of the need to keep "honour bright" as the only possible defence against the jealousy of others and the erosion of time, with its destruction of reputation, works in the same way. One's reaction to it must be considerably modified by one's awareness that this is a calculated argument, and very definitely not the expression of any equivalent sentiment to Milton's "I cannot praise a fugitive and cloistered virtue, unexercised and un-breathed." Ulysses is working on Achilles' vanity, making him fear for the pre-eminence of his reputation. He is stating no absolute value, but offering a piece of carefully planned rhetoric, designed to anger Achilles, whom incidentally he despises as a mere engine of war, and to goad him back into battle. In order to do this, he makes use of the typically Trojan notion of honour, arguing for it, not as a code of behaviour, but as something to be jealously guarded and only to be retained by outdoing one's would-be emulators. The use of this argument by Ulysses, and its acceptance by both Achilles and Ajax cannot but help to reveal the deficiencies of this view of honour in Hector, who shares it with them. Thus, in the end, the role of Ulysses in the play, like that of Thersites, is one of chorus or commentator. His craft in politics is directed to the winning of the war, but the war itself is so degraded by the sordidness of the quarrel, and by the sav-agery and futility of its course, that it is impossible to see Ulysses' skill and acu-men as directed to any worthy cause. One is tempted to construct a neat antithesis by setting Hector, principle without practicality, against Ulysses, prac-ticality without principle, but to do so is to oversimplify their roles, and is in any case misleading, for Ulysses' practicality is shown to be as unsuccessful in exe-cution as Hector's principle is contaminated in the holding.

—DERICK R. C. MARSH, "Interpretation and Misinterpretation: The Problem
of *Troilus and Cressida,*" *Shakespeare Studies* I (1965): 194–95

D. J. CONACHER

In discussing Euripides' adaptation of the tale of Odysseus' adventure with the Cyclops, one must bear in mind another of the *Odyssey*'s cautionary tales: one must sail between Scylla and Charybdis in refusing either to dismiss the play (with one critic ⟨G. M. A. Grube⟩) as "a competent piece of fooling" with "no subtlety, tragic or comic,"or to regard it⟩(with another ⟨William Arrowsmith⟩) as a fifth-century parable "about a struggle for justice between two men who either distort justice or deny its existence. . . ."

The comic elements in the *Cyclops* are closer to the strong mixtures of Aristophanes than to the slick plot complexities and ironies of Euripidean romance and of New Comedy. Thus we find slapstick blended with verbal wit, comic incongruities in the placing of serious subjects in absurd contexts, and various ingenious adaptations of Homeric material to satyric situations. (The first—and major—difficulty, that of getting Silenus and the satyrs into the situation in the first place, has been easily managed in the prologue, where Silenus has told us a tale of shipwreck and capture by Polyphemus similar to that awaiting Odysseus and his men, save that the satyrs are wanted not as food but as slaves—their traditional role, as we shall see, in the satyr-play.) An excellent example of a specifically "satyric" adaptation is to be found in the absurdly Bacchic flavour which Silenus and the Chorus, dry as they are, manage to give to their pastoral duties. The approach of the satyrs with their flocks of sheep and goats reminds Silenus of the sound of feet dancing the Sicinnis (κρότος σικινίδων, 37ff.) "up at Althaea's house, with Bacchus, in the old days. . . ." Presumably the satyrs come on dancing the Sicinnis as they hail their charges with a pretty "herding" song faintly reminiscent, in its assumptions of sheepish sensibility, of the Homeric Cyclops' address to his favourite ram (*Odyssey* 9.447ff.). The song ends on a note of mock-tragic pathos (63–81) as the Chorus sadly laments (like the deprived Maenads of the *Bacchae*) the loss of Dionysus and his accoutrements of dancing, love and wine.

Especially wine: enter Odysseus with an inexhaustible flagon of the stuff. (Here we have another skilful adaptation: inexhaustibility—implied in verse 147, as well as in the subsequent action—is, theatrically speaking, a more useful kind of magic than the special strength and flavour of the Homeric potion.) The wine-bibbing is, of course, a particularly apt device for a satyr-play and Euripides extends it, beyond Homer's use of it to get the Cyclops drunk, to include full exploitation of the tippling Silenus. This provides him, first with a comic bargaining scene (which has the practical advantage of keeping Odysseus and his men outside the cave, and so on-stage, while Silenus gets the viands from within), and later with a mildly slapstick "drink-cadging" scene, in which the crafty Silenus constantly gets the better of his drunken master Polyphemus.

Other minor but amusing parodies of tragic themes are achieved by further expansions and adaptations of the traditional tale. In Silenus' absence, the Chorus quizzes Odysseus on his exploits at Troy, but all it really wants to discuss are lascivious details about the wanton Helen. This leads in turn to a parody of the potentially tragic theme of misogynism: "Would that the race of women had ne'er been born!" cry the indignant satyrs, but, unlike Hippolytus some years later, they add the satyric qualification, "... except for my use alone!" (186–87).

Odysseus' boast of his Trojan exploits brings from the Cyclops the unexpected rejoinder: "A disgraceful affair—for one woman's sake to sail against the land of Troy!" (283–84)—a charge which has already been raised, in a more sombre context, by the Chorus in Aeschylus' *Agamemnon* (e.g., at 225–26, 447–48, 799–801), and which Odysseus now dismisses with truly Euripidean cynicism: "Don't blame us *men!* It was the god's affair" (θεοῦ τὸ πρᾶγμα, 285).

In the same vein, a new twist is given to another traditional feature of the episode. As in Homer, Odysseus counts heavily, in his dealings with Polyphemus, on *Zeus Xenios,* Zeus, the protector of the suppliant stranger. (Compare *Cyclops* 353–55 with *Odyssey* ix.269–71.) Now, however, Odysseus qualifies his prayers with typically Euripidean blasphemy:

> Zeus, god of strangers, look on this!... for if you don't, then vainly (we'll conclude) we call you Zeus, who are no god at all!   (354–55)

—a remark which anticipates Amphitryon's harsh words to a much more neglectful Zeus, at *Heracles* 339–47.

So much has been said so far about adaptations and "Euripidean touches" that it should perhaps be pointed out that in its main lines, as well as in a good many details, the *Cyclops* follows the Homeric version of the adventure with remarkable fidelity. In both, Odysseus emphasizes his heroic "Trojan" renown and (as we have seen) his rights as a suppliant in the eyes of Zeus; in both, Polyphemus is equally lawless and scornful of such claims; in both, Polyphemus devours some of Odysseus' men; in both, Odysseus devises and carries out the same plan for blinding the Cyclops and escaping with his surviving comrades. Even the (to us) rather desperate "no man" joke of the *Odyssey* is faithfully preserved—though with rather less point in the necessarily changed dramatic circumstances of the Cyclops' outwitting. Indeed, it is because of, rather than in spite of, the play's faithfulness to the main lines of the Homeric account, that the Euripidean touches are so striking. Thus, in turning to the most important of these, we must bear in mind Kassel's observation that it all turns out "according to Homer" in the end.

The most original and diverting passages in the play undoubtedly occur in the first (or pre-prandial) interview between Polyphemus and Odysseus. We have, of course, been prepared for the grimmest aspect of Polyphemus by Silenus' answer to Odysseus' query about the local attitude to strangers ("They do say they are the sweetest-*tasting* men!" 125–26). However, it is truly marvellous to find a Cyclops who is so completely the amoral cannibal and at the same time so bland, so articulate, so well up in things. It is the essential aspect of the Cyclops which appears first (we will return to the Cyclops as sophist later)—in response to Silenus' barefaced false witness against Odysseus:

So! Then sharpen up the knives and light the fire ...   (241–43)

I've had my fill of lions and stags ... it's time I ate a man again!   (248–49)

[ODYSSEUS]: Now, Cyclops, listen in turn to what we strangers also have to say. It was like this. . . .   (253ff.)

The beauty of this, as of most of Odysseus' statements and arguments to the Cyclops, is the rhetorical tone of one "civilized" man (or state, even) to another. This tone is particularly marked in Odysseus' first and rather extraordinary plea for mercy (290–98) on the grounds that the Greeks have preserved the shrines of Poseidon and even the Sicilian home of the Cyclops from thieving Trojans. William Arrowsmith, suspecting an allusion to the political claims of contemporary Athens, comments cleverly:

> What Odysseus is urging here is nothing more or less than the argument which Athens had used to acquire her empire: Athens had saved Hellas and should have the rewards of her deed.

However, Arrowsmith appears to me to carry his argument too far. By cunning quotations from Thucydides' speeches, he shows the ultimate cynicism of such Athenian arguments and so concludes of Odysseus' claims: "the irony lies in the fact that an argument normally used to deny mercy to others is here being used to obtain it." Even apart from the anachronism, in the context of the critic's argument, of the Thucydidean passages which he quotes, this is surely loading Odysseus' speech with far more devious subtlety (on the poet's part) than it will bear, especially since it is this dubious part of Arrowsmith's interpretation which colours his whole view of Odysseus as an allegorical example of fifth century political depravity. Thus, Arrowsmith regards Odysseus' next plea, in the name of *nomos,* as "pure sophistry," "a mere convention of the weak to elude the strong," and Odysseus' ultimate recourse to brutal vengeance as a contradiction of that *nomos* which he has just invoked. But both the "rights-of-the-suppliant" argument *and* the ultimate vengeance of Odysseus are in accordance with the Homeric version which, in turn, is in accordance with Homeric ethics; in neither case are we meant to be shocked or outraged by this "epic" (or, possibly, "folk-tale") style of vengeance, though, like Homer's audience, we may be aware that the *lex talionis,* through the powerful agency of the Cyclops' father, Poseidon, may overtake Odysseus in the end.

The same excellences and exaggerations seem to me characterize Arrowsmith's treatment of Polyphemus himself. He rightly berates the traditional view that Euripides is simply dramatizing "Homer's parable of the civilized man and the savage," and suggests that Polyphemus is "less Caliban than Callicles, an outright exponent of philosophical egoism and the immoralist equation of might and right." This is a fair enough description of the Polyphemus of the speech at verses 316–46, which is full of splendidly expressed sophistries defending the hedonism of the belly

("*That's* the wise man's Zeus!" 337) and Cyclopeian self-sufficiency, while sneering at law and order (τοὺς νόμους, 338) as man-made embellishments. But because of such a speech to take Polyphemus so seriously as to talk, as Arrowsmith does at the end of his essay, of "a struggle for justice between two men [*sic*] who either distort justice or deny its existence . . ." is surely a distortion of Euripides' fun. At least half the time, Polyphemus is more monster than man and so is outside these solemn arguments. He is no more "all-Callicles" than he is "all-Caliban." (Can one, for example, imagine the fifth-century sophist, like a good honest cannibal, salivating and gulping, before and after taking his awful meal?) The point—and the humour— lies in the incongruity of the tone and sentiments imposed on the savage at certain moments, and this point is missed if such witty moments are prolonged and distorted to produce conclusions worthy of tragedy. It is in the speeches, not in the action, that the difference between the Homeric and the Euripidean treatment lies; hence it is a rhetorical, in places even a whimsical, difference. In terms of the action (and, if we *must* take this *tour de force* seriously, it is to the action, or plot, that we must look), Euripides' Odysseus is as guilty or as innocent as the Homeric Odys- seus, since he suffers and performs precisely the same things in the same circum- stances.

—D. J. CONACHER, "The *Cyclops*," *Euripidean Drama: Myth, Theme and Structure* (Toronto: University of Toronto Press, 1967), pp. 317–22

KARL F. THOMPSON

Shakespeare's Ulysses is the favorite spokesman for the historian of ideas interested in formulating the thought of the Renaissance. For he seems to be Shakespeare's official, public voice raised in support of the Elizabethan establishment, a wise elder statesman, ideal man of statecraft, as attractively real to scholars like Hardin Craig ("Ulysses is so statesman-like, so shrewd, so wise, and withal so kindly that he suggests one of the great statesmen for whom Elizabeth's reign was celebrated") as any of Elizabeth's competent advisers. E. M. W. Tillyard's excellent presentation, *The Elizabethan World Picture,* without the initial scrutiny and repeated citation of Ulysses' great speech on order and degree, would be a random sampling of ideas current in Elizabethan England. Similarly, in his *Shakespeare's History Plays,* Tillyard calls upon Ulysses to summarize the views of history and the state that underlie all of Shakespeare's historical drama. This is surely correct procedure, for, as Tillyard amply demonstrates, any Elizabethan statesman or writer on politics and history, given Ulysses' eloquence, would necessarily have uttered the same sentiments and employed the same imagery. A cloud of witnesses can be summoned to testify: Elyot, Hall, Holinshed, Raleigh, all of whom contribute to the picture of the world that Shakespeare suggests in Ulysses' "Take but degree away, untune that string, and hark what discord follows!"

Such interpretations of Ulysses as the wise elder statesman leave, however, a part of his character unexamined. One cannot altogether dispel the doubt that the Ulysses of the great speeches in the play is Craig's Ulysses or Tillyard's Ulysses, but is he indeed Shakespeare's Ulysses? Grant all that can be said to prove that Shakespeare's Ulysses talks in accents corroborative of the wisest and most profound Renaissance cosmology, there still remains a surplus to his character not encompassed by citation of his major formal speeches. True, Ulysses' speech on degree can be regarded as a norm, a basic philosophy of the state by which the audience can judge the other characters. Suppose, however, we measure our wise elder statesman Ulysses by that norm. Alas, according to many commentators, he falls deplorably short of expectation, and as often as not fails to practice what he so persuasively preaches. We can preserve intact our statesman Ulysses only by excising a good half of his speeches and ignoring many of his actions. For this other Ulysses is a jester, licensed commentator, sometimes indeed a buffoon, a provocateur unpleasantly reminiscent of Thersites. He is the Ulysses whom Georg Brandes (Ulysses "is as trivial of mind as the rest"), and Julius Bab (Ulysses "is above all malicious"), and Mark Van Doren (Ulysses is a "politic rogue") detest. He is the *actor* in the play, whereas Tillyard's and Craig's Ulysses is merely the *orator*. One wonders, in sum, if the critics are talking about the same play and the same character. If, furthermore, these two opposing points of view concerning Ulysses cannot be reconciled, we shall have to fault Shakespeare for giving us a divided character, an incomplete synthesis of thought and action, motive and deed, and a play fit not for harmonious instruction and delight but merely for the gratification of shallow minds and would-be wits pleased with such mocking and subverting of accepted ideas.

The eloquent dignity of Ulysses' speech on degree is manifest and needs no explication to make Tillyard's Ulysses understandable. But what does Ulysses do so reprehensible as to arouse the ire of the anti-Ulysses faction? I cite two examples as likely cases in point of Ulysses' deviation in practice from the dignity and wisdom so greatly promised in his speech on degree: his dealing with the two warrior-heroes, Achilles and Troilus. The former earns a reputation offensive to good morality; the latter is ennobled to the height of such honor as this peculiar play permits. But Ulysses, far from wisely counseling and gently persuading them, seems to do his best to betray them both.

Ulysses' labors to convert the reluctant Achilles to a proper use of his prowess for the benefit of the Greek host follow soon after his summary of the good state and what constitutes the greatest danger to it: the disruption of rank, order, and degree. Observe, however, how he proposes to restore the state. His subterfuge (there is no other word for his plan) is an acceptable enough stratagem, perhaps, considering the material (Achilles) he has to work with. But must he in order to effect his scheme behave so outrageously? Must he repeat in detail Patroclus' jeering imitations of the Greek captains (I.iii.151–184)? In this way he mocks, for his own enjoyment of their discomfiture, the Greek leaders among whom are his social and political superiors, thus giving the lie to his earlier prescriptions of observance of order and degree. Moreover, when he praises Ajax he is unpleasantly like a modern publicity agent, privately scornful of the hero he presents to the public. He enjoys his job to the point of relishing buffoonery, as when the lubberly Ajax asks (II.iii.263–264), "Shall I call you father?" and Ulysses replies, "Ay, my good son." The crowning insult, however, and one that undoubtedly capped the scene for those in the audience who got the satiric drift of the incident, is his subtle mockery of the aged Nestor:

> But pardon, father Nestor, were your days
> As green as Ajax' and your brain so temper'd,
> You should not have the eminence of him,
> But be as Ajax.   II.iii.260–263

The ending of Ulysses' labors with Achilles shows that he has had little or no expectation of persuading Achilles to engage in honorable contest again. For he hardly waits for Achilles' rejection of his pleas in the name of honor and reputation before he demolishes the hero by revealing that Achilles' wretched little secret, his love affair with the Trojan princess Polyxena, is a subject of general gossip in the camp.

In his dealing with Troilus, Ulysses is no less devious. He is responsible for Troilus' overhearing and overseeing Cressida's defection. But as he witnesses Troilus' disillusionment (V.ii) he shows no signs of sympathy for the young prince. Rather, he looks on as if relishing this vindication of his earlier judgment of Cressida. Indeed, Ulysses might well be thinking during this scene much the same thoughts as Thersites, but not perhaps in the disreputable terms that Thersites uses to deck out his opinions. Obviously, then, Ulysses takes some kind of satisfaction in seeing Troilus disillusioned. But why should he want this to happen to Troilus? The conclusion must be that Ulysses likes to disillusion people, that he derives a sardonic pleasure from making others unwittingly reveal their follies to him.

We have, thus, the two Ulysses, the statesman interested in maintaining order in the state and, on the other hand, the master of other men's secrets, the enjoyer of his own jests, the subtle revealer of others' follies. These are the extremes of interpretation, and if either is correct to the exclusion of the other, the play itself is damaged and its strength dissipated. In short, there is not room in the play for Craig's Ulysses and Van Doren's Ulysses.

There is, however, a way to combine these extremes in some sort of morally and dramatically credible character. To do so, we have first to search for Shakespeare's purpose in characterizing Ulysses. He cannot seriously have intended Ulysses as a portrait of an actual, historical statesman. Much as he may have admired Lord Burleigh, he obviously did not intend to put the real Burleigh into his play. For the humorless, dour, suspicious Cecilian mind is not evident in Ulysses. Nor does Shakespeare want to make a shambles of all notions of statecraft, as Van Doren would have Ulysses do, certainly not in the presence of the students of the Inns of Court for whom the play was probably written. Shakespeare could, however, combine the extremes in some sort of morally credible character by giving Ulysses a philosophical and an ethical being, so to speak, deriving from notions familiar to his audience, and then employing a catalyst to join them. Ulysses' political philosophy is the easily recognizable one of his degree speech; his ethics can be summarized by reference to his exhortation to Achilles to live in the present moment, to shape his conduct by the exigencies of the Eternal Now. This is, of course, Stoic doctrine, to which Ulysses further commits himself by his repeated acknowledgment that actual human nature for the most part falls short of the ideal. Why, for instance, struggle against Achilles' invincible ignorance after the hero has rejected the best and most telling arguments that can be advanced? One is reminded in this connection of a favorite theme of the classic Stoics, which they never tired of expounding and which must certainly have elicited the approving recognition of would-be sophisticates as well as the wiser sort in Shakespeare's auditory. Marcus Aurelius, for instance, admonishes himself (*Meditations,* Book II), "Say to thyself at daybreak: I shall come across the busy-body, the thankless, the overbearing, the treacherous, the envious, the unneighborly." Or Seneca's warning (*De Ira,* II.10) comes to mind that the wise man can expect to walk daily among the vicious and miserly, and among spendthrifts and profligates.

These Stoic admonitions sound for all the world like a summary description of most of the characters in *Troilus and Cressida,* and Ulysses would agree that among the Greeks and Trojans whom he knew there were many such. Neither Marcus Aurelius nor Seneca, however, found anything to smile about in their depictions of the generality of mankind, Seneca condemning alike Democritus' laughter and Heraclitus' tears. But Ulysses brands himself a somewhat less than perfect Stoic by finding his companions amusing. Here is the catalytic agent that unites Ulysses' politics and ethics and renders him fit for existence on stage. Unfortunately, the addition of this catalytic wit also gives rise to the almost incredibly different reactions of well-intentioned, serious, intelligent critics. Ulysses mingles with his Stoicism a sardonic sense of humor that, issuing in horseplay and jest which others (not only those in the play but critics too) do not fathom, enables this Stoic superiority to escape debilitating frustration. This is the unknown Ulysses who adds to his appreciation of the seriousness and nobility of statesmanship a willingness to laugh at the hazards and disappointments of the actual practice of statecraft. If we add to Hardin Craig's assertion of Ulysses' perfect statesmanship an understanding of the implications of this gift of jest, we would have indeed a sound description of Ulysses. He would then be the tangible consequence of Shakespeare's reluctance to depict a stereotype, as Ulysses would be were he simply the Statesman or the Stoic conforming to traditional patterns.

In an important way Shakespeare can tell us more of the truth about politics (or history, or sociology for that matter) than any theoretician can, for he presents not types but varied human nature encountered at first hand rather than in formulations. He does this by suggesting at first a type familiar to everyone in his audience—his Ulysses, for example, readily identifiable in the degree speech as the stereotype statesman or, in his time and honor argument to Achilles, recognizable as the high-minded Stoic. Then Shakespeare rings changes upon these familiar characterizations so as to give vitality and life to them, proof of the vitality being, indeed, reactions such as Brandes' and Bab's and Van Doren's.

Creating fiction, Shakespeare paradoxically creates truth. His dramaturgy affords insights into the true nature of men engaged in statecraft, which in its tensions of principles and practice, of ends and means, confronts us with the fundamental dilemma of human nature that, believing in ideas and states of being beyond the confines of what is here and now, must still apply transcendent beliefs to its terrestrial involvements. We can test the accuracy and pertinency of Shakespeare's depiction of political man by comparing Ulysses with the successful statesmen of actuality. We find that for the most part they too have tempered their loyalty to first principles with amusement at the obvious follies of men and an abiding patience with man's recurrent fits of invincible ignorance, witness Talleyrand's wryness, Melbourne's witticisms, Lincoln's occasional buffoonery, Disraeli's jests, Churchill's often unfair but amusing personal gibes. Among successful statesmen the name of Gladstone occurs as having won his way without the saving grace of humor. Perhaps this was so because God's mouth was so comfortingly close to Gladstone's ear. But Gladstone's character faithfully depicted upon the stage would, we can be sure, prove somewhat less than fascinating. Shakespeare's Ulysses, however, is a masterly exposition of the practical politician, for like the great ones, Talleyrand, Lincoln, even Churchill, he arouses precisely the same reactions and, like them, in their time, is "politic rogue" as well as "wise, dignified statesman".

—KARL F. THOMPSON, "The Unknown Ulysses," *Shakespeare Quarterly* 19, No. 2 (Spring 1968): 125–28

LESLIE FIEDLER

Bloom himself is not merely mythic, much less an ironic commentary on a dying myth. He is a true, a full myth, a new and living myth. He is, to be sure, based on—reflects off of—the figure of Homer's Ulysses, that Greek version of, as Joyce liked to believe and I'm prepared to believe with him, a Semitic prototype. But Bloom is Ulysses resurrected and transfigured, not merely recalled or commented on or explained. Bloom is Ulysses rescued from all those others who were neither Jew nor Greek, and who had kidnapped him, held him in alien captivity for too long. Bloom is Ulysses rescued from the great poets as well as the small ones, from Dante and from Tennyson, and—at the other end of the mythological spectrum from James Joyce—from that anti-Semite, Ezra Pound, who liked to think he was the only true Ulysses.

In fact, however, Ulysses, the old Ulysses, the remembered Ulysses, the re-evoked Ulysses, constitutes only a small part of the total Bloom, the part that the Stephen in Joyce, everything in him which was not Bloom, could most easily deal with, *had* to deal with in order to keep the tidy schematic structure which he unwisely loved, and to plant clues for future exegetes whom he unfortunately desired.

The larger part of Bloom came not from memories of Homer's Ulysses, and not from the top of the head of Joyce, the name for which is Stephen. No, much perhaps most of what constitutes the authentic figure of Bloom comes, perhaps not entirely unbidden and unconsciously, but certainly less cerebrally, from deeper, darker, more visceral sources. The myth of Ulysses lives in the head of Christian Europe, but the myth of the Jew, which is Bloom's better half, resides in the guts of Europe: a pain in the dark innards of the Gentile world, or better perhaps, an ache in the genitals, an ache in the loins of the Gentiles.

—LESLIE FIEDLER, "Bloom on Joyce; or, Jokey for Jacob," *Journal of Modern Literature* I, No. I (1970): 24

ITALO CALVINO

How many odysseys are there in the *Odyssey?* At the beginning of the poem, the story of Telemachus is the search for a story that is not there, the story that will be the *Odyssey.* Phemius, the bard at the royal palace of Ithaca, already knows the *nostoi* of the other heroes. Only one is lacking, that of his own king. For this reason Penelope doesn't want to hear him sing any more. Then Telemachus goes off in search of this story among the veterans of the Trojan War. If he finds the story, whether it ends happily or not, Ithaca will emerge from the timeless, lawless, and chaotic situation in which it has been for many years.

Like all the veterans, Nestor and Menelaus have a lot to tell, but not the story Telemachus is seeking, until, finally, Menelaus comes out with a truly fantastic adventure: disguising himself as a seal, he captured the Old Man of the Sea (that is, Proteus of the countless metamorphoses) and forced him to tell him the past and the future. Proteus of course knew the whole *Odyssey* word for word, and he began to recount the adventures of Ulysses at the same point that Homer does, with the hero on Calypso's island. Then he broke off, for at that point Homer could take over and continue the story.

Arriving at the court of the Phaeacians, Ulysses hears a bard (who is blind like Homer) singing about the adventures of Ulysses. The hero bursts into tears and then decides to take up the narrative himself. In this story he gets as far as Hades to question Tiresias, and Tiresias tells him how his story ends. Then Ulysses meets the Sirens, who are singing. What are they singing? Still the *Odyssey,* perhaps the same one we are reading, perhaps a very different one. The story of this return is already there before the return is accomplished: it exists before being acted out.

Even in the Telemachus episode we find expressions such as "think of the return," "tell of the return." Zeus did not "think of the return" of the sons of Atreus; Menelaus asks the daughter of Proteus to "tell of the return" and she explains how to force her father to do so, so that Menelaus is able to capture Proteus and say, "Tell me of the return, and how I will go on the fish-laden sea."

The return must be discerned and thought about and remembered. The danger is that it might be forgotten about before it has happened. Indeed, one of the first stages of the journey recounted by Ulysses, the episode of the Lotus Eaters, involves the risk of losing his memory by eating the sweet fruit of the lotus. It may seem strange that the test of forgetfulness occurs at the beginning of the journeyings of Ulysses, not at the end. If, after overcoming so many trials, bearing so many setbacks, learning so many lessons, Ulysses had forgotten everything, his loss would have been far graver: not to have gained any experience from what he had suffered, or any meaning from what he had lived through.

But, if we look more closely, this threat of the loss of memory comes up a number of times in books IX–XII: first in the encounter with the Lotus Eaters, then with Circe's drugs, then again in the song of the Sirens. Each time Ulysses has to be wary, lest he forget on the instant. Forget what? The Trojan War? The siege of Troy? The wooden horse? No. His home, the course to steer, the purpose of the voyage. The expression Homer uses on these occasions is "forget the return."

Ulysses must not forget the route he has to travel, the form of his destiny. In short, he must not forget the *Odyssey*. But the bard who composes by improvising, the rhapsodist who memorizes and sings passages from poems that have already been sung—they, too, must not forget if they are to "tell the return." For anyone who sings verses without the aid of a written text, "forget" is the most negative verb in existence. And for them to "forget the return" means to forget the poems known as *nostoi*, which were the warhorse of their whole repertoire.

I wrote a few comments some years ago on the subject of "forgetting the future" (in *Corriere della Sera*, August 10, 1975), and concluded as follows: "What Ulysses preserves from the lotus, from Circe's drugs and the Sirens' song, is not merely the past or the future. Memory really matters—for individuals, for the collectivity, for civilization—only if it binds together the imprint of the past and the project of the future, if it enables us to act without forgetting what we wanted to do, to become without ceasing to be, and to be without ceasing to become."

My piece was followed by an article by Edoardo Sanguineti in *Paese Sera* (reprinted in *Giornalino 1973–1975* [Turin: Einaudi, 1976]) and by a whole string of answers, his and mine. Sanguineti objected as follows:

> For we must not forget that the wanderings of Ulysses were not an outward journey at all, but a return journey. Therefore we should ask ourselves for a moment what sort of future he really has before him; because the future that Ulysses was seeking was really his past, in point of fact. Ulysses overcomes the flatteries of regression because he is totally bent toward a Restoration.
>
> We gather that one fine day, out of spite, the real Ulysses, the great Ulysses, became the Ulysses of the Ultimate Journey, for whom the future is by no means a past, but the Realization of a Prophecy—that is, a true Utopia.

Whereas the Homeric Ulysses comes to the recovery of his past as a present; his wisdom is Repetition, and we can easily realize this from the scar he bears, which marks him forever.

In reply to Sanguineti I pointed out (in *Corriere della Sera,* October 14, 1975) that "in the language of myth, as in that of folk tales and of the popular novel, every undertaking that brings justice, repairs wrongs, or relieves a miserable situation is usually represented as the restoration of an earlier, ideal order. The desirability of a future to be conquered is guaranteed by the memory of a lost past."

If we take a close look at fairy stories, we find that they present two types of social transformation, always with a happy ending: either from high to low and then again to high, or simply from low to high. In the first type a prince is by mischance reduced to being a swineherd or some such lowly station, and then regains his royal status. In the second type there is a young man impoverished from birth, a shepherd or a peasant, and maybe simple-minded into the bargain, who by his own courage or with the help of magic powers succeeds in marrying the princess and becoming king.

The same patterns hold good for tales with a female protagonist. In the first type a girl of royal, or at any rate wealthy, status falls to the condition of a derelict because of the rivalry of a stepmother (like Snow White) or her half-sisters (like Cinderella), until a prince falls in love with her and raises her to the very top of the social ladder. In the second type we have a real shepherdess or peasant girl who overcomes all the disadvantages of her humble birth and marries a prince.

One might think that it is tales of the second type that give the most direct expression to the people's desire for a reversal of social roles, whereas those of the first type reveal this desire in a more attenuated form, as the restoration of a previous, hypothetical order. But, on closer consideration, the extraordinary good fortune of the shepherd or shepherdess represents nothing but a miraculous and consolatory illusion, which in large part has been carried on by the popular romantic novel. On the other hand, the misfortunes of the unlucky prince or princess link the notion of poverty to the idea of a *right* that has been *trodden under foot,* of justice to be vindicated. That is (on the plane of fantasy, where ideas can put down roots in the form of elementary figures), this second type of story puts its finger on a spot that was destined to be fundamental to the entire development of the social conscience in the modern age, from the French Revolution on.

In the collective unconscious, the prince in beggar's rags is proof that every beggar is in fact a prince who is the victim of a usurpation and must regain his realm. Ulysses or Robin Hood, kings or kings' sons or knightly aristocrats fallen on evil days, when they triumph over their enemies will restore a society of the Just in which their true identity will be revealed.

But is it the same identity as before? It may be that the Ulysses who arrives in Ithaca as a poor beggar unrecognized by everyone is no longer the same person as the Ulysses who departed for Troy. It is no coincidence that he had once saved his life by pretending his name was Nobody. The only immediate and spontaneous recognition comes from his dog, Argos, as if the continuity of the individual could make itself manifest through signs perceptible only to an animal.

For the nurse the proof of his identity was the scar left him by a boar's tusk, for his wife the secret of the manufacture of their marriage bed out of the roots of an olive tree, and for his father a list of fruit trees. These signs have nothing regal about them; they put the hero on the level of a poacher, a carpenter, a gardener. To them are added the qualities of physical strength and pitiless aggressiveness toward his enemies, and, above all, the favor shown by the gods, which is what convinces Telemachus, if only by an act of faith.

In his turn, the unrecognizable Ulysses wakes up in Ithaca and does not recognize his own country: Athena has to intervene to assure him that Ithaca is really and truly Ithaca. In the second half of the *Odyssey* the identity crisis is general. Only the story assures us that the characters and places are the same characters and places; but even the story changes. The tale that the unrecognizable Ulysses tells the shepherd Eumaeus, then his rival Antinoüs, and even Penelope, is another and completely different *Odyssey:* the wanderings that have brought the fictitious person whom he claims to be all the way there from Crete, a story far more likely than the one he himself had told to the king of the Phaeacians. Who is to say that this is not the "real" *Odyssey?* But this new *Odyssey* refers to yet another *Odyssey,* for in his travels the Cretan had come across Ulysses. So here we have Ulysses speaking of a Ulysses traveling in countries where the "real" Ulysses never set foot.

That Ulysses is a hoaxer is already known before the *Odyssey.* Wasn't it he who thought up the great swindle of the wooden horse? And at the beginning of the *Odyssey* the first recollections of his character are two flashbacks to the Trojan War, told to each other consecutively by Helen and Menelaus. Two tales of trickery. In the first he disguises himself in order to enter the besieged city and wreak havoc; in the second he is shut up inside the wooden horse with his colleagues, and is able to prevent Helen from unmasking them by inducing them to talk.

In both these episodes Ulysses is associated with Helen—in the first she is an ally and an accomplice in his trick, in the second an adversary, who imitates the voices of the Achaeans' wives to tempt them to betray themselves. The role of Helen seems contradictory, but it is always marked by trickery. In the same way, Penelope's web is a stratagem symmetrical with that of the Trojan Horse, and like the latter is a product of manual dexterity and counterfeiting, so that the two main characteristics of Ulysses are also those of Penelope.

If Ulysses is a hoaxer, the entire account he gives to the king of the Phaeacians might be a pack of lies. In fact, these seagoing adventures of his, concentrated in four central books of the *Odyssey,* a rapid series of encounters with fantastic beings (the ogre Polyphemus, the winds bottled up in a wineskin, the enchantments of Circe, sirens and sea monsters), clash with the rest of the poem, which is dominated by grave tones, psychological tension, and a dramatic crescendo gravitating toward an end: the reconquest of his kingdom and of his wife besieged by suitors. Here, too, we find motifs in common with folk tales, such as Penelope's web and the test of drawing the bow, but we are on ground far closer to modern criteria of realism and likelihood. Supernatural interventions are concerned solely with the appearance of the Olympian gods, usually concealed in human forms.

We should remember, however, that the same adventures (especially the one with Polyphemus) are mentioned elsewhere in the poem, so that Homer confirms them. Not only that: the gods themselves discuss them on Olympus. And Menelaus also recounts an adventure of the same folk-tale stamp, his encounter with the Old Man of the Sea. We can only attribute these excursions into the realm of fantasy to a montage of traditions of diverse origins, handed down by bards and meeting up later in the Homeric *Odyssey*, which in the account given by Ulysses in the first person probably reveals its most archaic stratum.

Most archaic? According to Alfred Huebeck, things might have happened the other way around. Before the *Odyssey*—even in the *Iliad*—Ulysses had always been an epic hero, and epic heroes, such as Achilles and Hector in the *Iliad*, do not have fabulous adventures based on monsters and enchantments. But the author of the *Odyssey* has to keep Ulysses away from home for ten years, lost, unaccounted for by his family and his ex–companions-in-arms. Therefore, he must make Ulysses leave the known world, pass into a different geography, an extra-human world, a "beyond" (it is no coincidence that his wanderings culminate in a journey to the Underworld). For this excursion outside the bounds of the epic, the author of the *Odyssey* resorts to traditions (which really are more archaic) such as the feats of Jason and the Argonauts. It is thus the *novelty* of the *Odyssey* to have put an epic hero such as Ulysses at grips with "witches and giants, monsters and maneaters"— that is, in situations typical of a more *archaic* saga, the roots of which must be sought "in the world of antique fable, and even of primitive magical and shamanistic concepts."

According to Huebeck, it is here that the author of the *Odyssey* shows his true modernity, the quality that makes him so close to us, so up-to-date. Traditionally the epic hero was a paradigm of aristocratic and military virtues, and Ulysses is all this, but over and above it he is the man who bears the hardest trials, labors, sorrows, and solitude. "Certainly he draws his public into the mythical world of dreams, but this dream world becomes the mirror image of the world in which we live, dominated by need and anguish, terror and sorrow, into which man is thrust with no escape."

Elsewhere in the same volume Stephanie West, starting from premises different from Huebeck's, suggests a hypothesis that supports his argument: the idea that there had been an "alternative" *Odyssey*, another route for the return, earlier than Homer. Homer (or whoever wrote the *Odyssey*), finding this travelogue too poor and scant of meaning, replaced it with the fabulous adventures while retaining a trace of it in the voyages of the pseudo-Cretan. And, in fact, in the Proem there is a line that might be seen as the synthesis of the entire *Odyssey:* "He saw the cities and learned the thoughts of many men." What cities? What thoughts? This hypothesis would fit better with the wanderings of the pseudo-Cretan....

However, as soon as Penelope recognizes him in his reconquered marriage bed, Ulysses goes back to talking about the Cyclops, the Sirens.... Isn't the *Odyssey* perhaps the myth of every journey there is? For Homer-Ulysses, the distinction between truth and falsehood may not have existed, and he told of the same experience at one time in the language of actual experience, at another in the language of myth, just as even for us today every journey, long or short, is always an odyssey.

—ITALO CALVINO, "The Odysseys within the *Odyssey*" [1981], *The Uses of Literature,* tr. Patrick Creagh (San Diego: Harcourt Brace Jovanovich, 1986), pp. 135–45

BRIAN POCKNELL

In ⟨*La Guerre de Troie n'aura pas lieu*⟩ Giraudoux sets Hector against Ulysses, not Achilles as we find in Homer's text. Yet the reason may be found in the *Iliad.* Homer alludes to an ambassadorial visit (Book XI, ll. 138–141) which Ulysses made to the Trojan Assembly in the company of Menelaus, a tense moment in which Antimachus had suggested that Menelaus be killed on the spot. Ulysses appears to be a more appropriate match for Hector on his own rather than accompanied by Menelaus, whom Giraudoux never shows to us directly. We know from the *Iliad,* Book III, ll. 191–224 that Ulysses was the more eloquent of the two, a more fitting choice to represent the Greeks' point of view in a debate with the Trojans. Moreover, Giraudoux reserves Menelaus for a quite different purpose. Paris describes him in Act I as having his toe pinched by a crab when Helen was being carried away on Paris' horse, and he is marked on more than one occasion as the cuckolded husband, a traditional figure of fun in the French theatre. The situation of Ulysses is quite different. A family man, unlike Achilles, and attached to a faithful wife, unlike Menelaus, Ulysses resembles Hector on both counts and offers a more exact balance for him in their cleverly constructed confrontation scene. Further, Homer makes mention of Zeus resorting to the use of his golden scales only when the two parties are very closely matched; Giraudoux's choice of Ulysses for the debate is consequently consistent with Homer's procedure.

Their *pesée* or weighing scene starts with this well-matched pair of rivals standing alone on stage: according to the message that Iris brings, the gods and all other personages have withdrawn to let the two arrive at a decision; and hence a parallel occurs with Zeus' reliance on the golden scales alone for a final judgement. Hector is fearful for his chances of outduelling Ulysses if their meeting is to be a combat of words. Ulysses reassures him: "Je crois que cela sera plutôt une pesée. Nous avons vraiment l'air d'être chacun sur le plateau d'une balance. Le poids parlera...." Here the ritual begins, reminiscent of Zeus' gesture in the *Iliad.* We are further reminded of Homer's text with its repetitive use of formular language as each character advances a list of signs, with every item or group of items being introduced by the phrase "je pèse...". Hector and Ulysses see themselves as images in a series of images, relating their individual qualities to those of the nations they represent. At the outset the balance appears to be nicely struck, but the differences become marked as the ritual draws to a close:

Hector	Ulysses
1 Youthfulness (Young man; young wife, Andromache; father-to-be)	1 Maturity (Adult man; thirty-year-old wife, Penelope; father of a rapidly growing son)
2 Joyfulness	2 A taste for pleasure
3 Confidence	3 A suspicious nature
4 Hunting; courage; faithfulness; love	4 Circumspection; wariness of the gods, men and things
5 The oak	5 The olive
6 The falcon, flying in the sunlight	6 The owl
7 Joyful peasants and craftsmen; thousands of ploughs and artisan implements	7 The pitiless, uncompromising air that circulates on the Greek archipelago

The references connected to these signs give greater weight to Ulysses. Against the simpler virtues and brighter images offered by Hector, Ulysses pits subtler metaphoric signs to bring the scales down in his favour. Roy Lewis has pointed out in his commentary on the play that there are indications of Ulysses' having more than human qualities to put in the balance, for the olive and the owl are signs of Pallas Athene, ally of the Greeks and enemy of Hector. Furthermore, the penetrating insight that Ulysses shows when he is summarizing his countrymen's traits gives his side the advantage over the more limited image of the massive number of Trojans obsessed by domestic virtues. At the end of the match, both men have come to realize that the scales have pronounced a judgement:

> HECTOR: Pourquoi continuer? la balance s'incline.
> ULYSSE: De mon côté? ... Oui, je le crois.

The parallel "question-affirmation" structure of the two replies echoes the balancing process once more and serves as another allusion to Homer's formular structures in the *Iliad*.

Now the two men have carefully weighed their values, but, unlike Zeus, they are unable to ascertain the measure of their fates. Since Ulysses has won the match, he apparently has the right to make a decision. At the end of the ritual he shows himself true to his suspicious nature, for he is conscious that the real issue lies beyond his jurisdiction. Like fate in the *Iliad*, war in Giraudoux's play is considered an autonomous force:

HECTOR: Et vous voulez la guerre?

ULYSSE: Je ne la veux pas. Mais je suis moins sûr de ses intentions à elle.

If Ulysses agrees to join Hector in a bid for peace, he does so knowing that unseen forces may well be working against them. In the hope of avoiding a disaster, he will return to his ships, thereby recalling for readers of the *Iliad* Homer's first reference to the use of the golden scales which favoured the Trojans and prompted the withdrawal of Ulysses to the safety of his vessels. Ulysses in Giraudoux's play has decided to act as if the *pesée* had favoured the Trojans.

> —BRIAN POCKNELL, "Giraudoux's *La Guerre de Troie n'aura pas lieu* and
> Homer's *Iliad:* The Scales of Zeus as Dramatic Device," *Modern Drama*
> 24, No. 2 (June 1981): 138–40

CHARLES SEGAL

In order to become once more a participant in society, Philoctetes (in Sophocles' *Philoctetes*) must leave behind both the spiritual and physical contours of the savage Lemnian landscape. The task however, is not one-sided. Society must also be reshaped to receive the hero whom it once so cruelly rejected. The social order conceived by Odysseus is based on success in achieving specific goals irrespective of individual protest or suffering. This cannot be the spiritual home of the pain-wracked outcast, nor could Philoctetes accept a place in such a world.

Odysseus' concept of society rests on the subordination of inferior to superior, of individual to group. He extends his authoritarian ranking of leader and subordinate (cf. 15, 53) even to the gods, for he regards himself, self-righteously, as the "subordinate helper" (*hypērētes*) of Zeus (990). His attitude, resembling those of the Atreids in the *Ajax* and Creon in the *Antigone,* introduces conflicts similar to those of these earlier plays. In his opening lines Odysseus affirms that in abandoning the sick Philoctetes on his island he was only following orders. The spirit of this supposed justification contrasts with the heroic terms of his address to Neoptolemus (1–7):

> This is the shore of sea-girt Lemnos, untrodden by mortal men and uninhab-
> ited, where, O son of Achilles, Neoptolemus, you who had your nurture from
> the best of the Hellenes, I once cast forth Poeas' son, of Malis, appointed to
> do this deed (*tachtheis*) by those in command (*anassontōn*), his foot dripping
> with the devouring disease.

Philoctetes later takes a very different view of following orders and excuses Neoptolemus on the grounds that "he knew nothing but to do what he was ordered" (*to prostachthen,* 1010). Neoptolemus himself does not accept such an easy solution. When he disobeys military authority, he invokes Zeus in a spirit far different from the smugness of Odysseus in 990, abjuring Odyssean deceit (*dolos,* cf. 1288) by an oath to "pure reverence for highest Zeus" (1289; cf. 990).

Before this late stage in the action, there is no real alternative to Odysseus' view. In their first ode, the chorus accepts this hierarchical conception of authority. Echoing a Hesiodic sentiment, they pronounce regal authority as validated by "the rule (*anassetai*, cf. 6, 26) of the divine scepter of Zeus" (138–140; cf. Hesiod, *Theogony* 80–96). This authority they call "primordial rule" (*kraots ōgygion*), and they hold it to be the basis of their subordination and obedience (*hypourgein*) to their leader Neoptolemus (141–143). Later, they defend Odysseus in terms of his own authoritarian premises: he is but one of many, acting only under orders (*tachtheis*, 1144; cf. 6, 1010). The supremacy of the counsel (*gnōmē*, 139) of the one who possesses Zeus' regal scepter is severely shaken at the end of the play when "Zeus' purposes" (1415) are revealed as not entirely congruent with Odysseus'. The counsel (*gnōmē*) that brings the requisite return of the hero to Troy is not that of the ruler wielding the symbol of authority (139) but the counsel of friends (*gnōmē philōn*, 1467).

Neoptolemus' instinctive distaste for Odysseus' instrumental view of human relations (86ff.) opens the central conflict. Gradually this widens to a conflict between the objective needs of the society and the spiritual and emotional life of its individual members. Even in his acquiescence to Odyssean authority Neoptolemus does not see eye-to-eye with his leader. He regards himself not as a subordinate (15 and 53) but as a co-worker (*synergatēs*, 93). In the same breath he rejects Odysseus' willingness to purchase victory at the cost of baseness (*nikan kakōs*, 94), even though he acknowledges his own obligation not to be a traitor to his cause (92–93). Lured by the promise of being the vanquisher of Troy, he momentarily yields to Odysseus' characteristic argument of profit (*kerdos*, 108–120), but the tension remains.

Although Neoptolemus repeats Odysseus' lies, he expands the Odyssean view of personal responsibility (385–388):

I do not blame Odysseus so much as those in command (*tous en telei*), for the whole city and the whole army (*sympas stratos*) belong to the leaders. It is through the words of their teachers that men who behave in disorderly ways (*akosmountes*) become bad (*kakoi*).

Neoptolemus here evades the issue of Odysseus' responsibility in terms that might in fact convict Odysseus. As he finds new "teachers," he also finds a different notion of social order. There is an intermediate stage when he is torn between obedience to the army and compassion for Philoctetes. He cannot, he says, return the bow, "for justice and advantage make me heed those in authority (*tōn en telei*, 925–926; cf. 385 above). His final decision contravenes that authority and defies the whole army which Odysseus repeatedly invokes (*sympas stratos*, 1243, 1250, 1257, 1294; cf. 387).

The independent and vitriolic spirit of Philoctetes and then later the defiance of Neoptolemus force Odysseus into a harder, more brutal expression of his authoritarian views. When Philoctetes refuses to go to Troy, Odysseus curtly replies, "But I say you must; this must be obeyed" (994). With pride and accuracy Philoctetes answers that this is the relation not between free men but between master and slave (995–996). Odysseus' bullying tone undercuts his counter-argument that at Troy Philoctetes will enjoy equality with the best (*aristoi*, 997). When he leaves the stage at the end of the scene with the threat that he does not need Philoctetes at Troy, only his bow, he imposes a peremptory silence on his captive: "Answer me nothing in reply, for I am departing" (1065). The gesture repeats in microcosm his initial responsibility for Philoctetes' injury, robbing him of civilized discourse with his fellow men (see 180–190, 225, 686–695).

Odysseus takes the same high-handed tone toward Neoptolemus as the latter prepares to return the bow. First he invokes the authority of the whole army, then fear and threats of punishment (1250–51, 1258), and finally he draws his sword (1254–56). His last attempt to prevent the return of the bow is a futile reassertion of brute power: "But I forbid it," he shouts, invoking the gods and, once more, "the whole army" (1293–94). His last utterance in the play is, ironically, a threat to "ship Philoctetes off to Troy's plains by force, whether Achilles' son is willing or unwilling" (1297–98). The resort to force echoes the earlier part of the scene with Neoptolemus (1254ff.) and is equally futile. This man of guile, careful speech, and clever persuasion is reduced to angry blustering about force, which, in any case, is quite ineffectual: he retreats with prudent rapidity as Philoctetes prepares to fit an arrow to his bow.

How different are Neoptolemus' responses in the immediately ensuing lines. He invokes the gods as he begs Philoctetes not to shoot (1301) and then cites the principle of nobility which embraces both of them ("Neither for you nor for me is this noble," 1304). He can acknowledge the other's praise of his inherited, Achillean nature (1310), and then set forth with good will (*eunoia*, 1322) the advantages which Philoctetes will reap from going to Troy (1314–47). Neoptolemus' *eunoia* goes beyond the categories implied in Odysseus' outlook: superior-inferior, means-end, hunter-prey, deceiver-victim, and the use of intelligence and speech to manipulate men.

In slowly forming their bond of friendship, Philoctetes and Neoptolemus create in miniature the ties of a more wholesome and humane society. The task of recreating a valid form of society when the old is corrupt is also one of the chief concerns of Plato two or three decades after the *Philoctetes*. What Werner Jaeger has said of friendship and society in Plato can also be applied to this play:

> When society is suffering from a great organic disorder or disease, its recovery can be initiated only by a small but basically healthy association of people who share the same ideas and who can form the heart of a new organism. That is exactly what Plato meant by friendship (*philia*).

A heroic society based on good will, friendship, and respect rather than force and guile is the human precondition of Philoctetes' return and necessarily precedes the divine intervention of Heracles. A more humane and responsive social order, if only in miniature, necessarily precedes the indication of a more generous and intelligible divine order. First Philoctetes renews his trust in men; then he can once more come to trust the gods.

Like Ajax, Philoctetes embodies an older heroism which the meaner, more pragmatic, more changeable world has difficulty in assimilating. In both cases the hero rejects the society offered by the Greek army at Troy, his peers and fellow warriors. But in the *Ajax* the new society can only mourn and commemorate the hero's greatness after he is gone. Such a heroism must necessarily end in death: Ajax' society no longer has a place for his kind of intransigence. It needs compromise and adaptability rather than unbending fixity in heroic glory. In the *Philoctetes,* however, the hero is still necessary to his society. Communication between the older and newer vision of social organization is still viable. Neoptolemus performs this role, taking over the mediatory function of the Odysseus of the *Ajax,* the voice of compassion and compromise.

Yet ultimately even Neoptolemus' purely human good will is not enough. Final persuasion rests with the immortal heroism of which Heracles is the paradigm. Indeed, it is important that the symbol of that heroism is not the protagonist himself (as in the *Ajax*) but a figure outside the frame of the human action: the human hero of this play will be able to survive his heroism. Despite himself, he will prove useful to his society and to himself. The seeds of this view are perhaps present in the "enduring" (*pherein*) of Oedipus at the end of the *Tyrannus.* Its culmination is in the *Coloneus.* Oedipus there, trailing the intractable harshness of an old world of narrow, implacable domestic hatred and conflict, can create a new kind of bond, based on mutual respect and compassion, with his virtually adopted son, Theseus, in an adopted city. In like manner Philoctetes vents his destructive, hate-filled "old" heroism on the figure of his past, Odysseus, and leaves that archaic, intransigent heroism behind on Lemnos. In the more adaptable (and ultimately more pious or reverent) heroism, he can join in a new bond with his virtually adopted son, Neoptolemus. This creative power of the hero—possibly felt by Sophocles as akin to the creative power of art itself—has its roots and strength in a dark and violent part of the soul and a dark and violent past. But it will undergo transformation to help the hero shape a new world. Oedipus will leave blessings to Athens; Philoctetes will bring back to Troy the heroism which lies "dead" there now (cf. 331ff., 412ff., 446ff.). By killing Paris, the cause of the war (1426), he will definitely put an end to the ten-year struggle through which Greece has been stripped of nobility and left only with what is mean and base (412–452).

If "Odyssean" society rests on absolute obedience, subordination of individual to group, manipulation, and force, the new miniature society of Philoctetes and Neoptolemus rests on friendship (*philia*), trust (*pistis*), compassion (*oiktos, eleos*), and good will (*eunoia*). The persuasion (*peithō*) which results from this combination is very different from Odyssean guileful persuasion which seeks self-interest rather than the good of the person being persuaded. Odyssean society constitutes an ironic inversion of civilized values—ironic because Odysseus, "twisted instrument of the divine plan," is, after all, attempting to restore Philoctetes from the savagery of Lemnos to human society. Odysseus' means cancel out his ends. Undoing his earlier relegation of Philoctetes from Troy to Lemnos, he veers between coercion and persuasion or seems to use them indiscriminately (593–594). Initially unmoved at the evidence of Philoctetes' suffering (37–47), he lacks the good will to perceive, as Neoptolemus does, that the oracle means benefit to Philoctetes and not just success for the expedition.

To take the simplest of the civilized qualities to be reconstituted, friendship, *philia*, has become an instrument of Odyssean trickery. Friendless, *aphilos*, on his desert island (1018), Philoctetes welcomes with open arms the friendship he has so long lacked (509–510, 530ff., 671). Reflecting on the world he knew at Troy, he laments the disappearance of all his old *philoi*, all that was dearest to him (421ff., 434). The new *philia* with Neoptolemus is not only based, initially, on a lie but also rests on the opposite of friendship, a common hatred, alleged on Neoptolemus' part, of the Atreids and Odysseus (509, 585–586, 665–666). This mutual enmity, a "clear token" of having suffered at their hands, forms the initial bond between the two strangers (403–404). Near the end Philoctetes' offer to help Neoptolemus with his bow against the Greek army (1406ff.) is the final expression of this isolating, ultimately negative aspect of their *philia*. Olympian Heracles, however, evokes a past friendship of a more expansive and heroic nature. He can then recall Philoctetes to a comradeship rooted not in mutual hatred but in cooperation in a major enterprise of large, historical import and, we must assume, for the common good of all Greece.

Before that point is reached, Philoctetes will go through a zero point of total friendlessness, turning away from the corrupted *philotēs* of men to wild nature, the animals, and to the bow itself (*toxon philon,* 1128–29; cf. 1004). Odysseus not only uses a false friendship to entrap Philoctetes but has no scruples against abjuring his friendship with Neoptolemus: "We shall make war not against the Trojans but against you," he threatens as he prepares to draw his sword on his erstwhile ally (1253–54). But Neoptolemus, here ready to fight Odysseus, will save the life of this friend turned enemy some fifty lines later as he prevents Philoctetes from shooting the bow (1300ff.).

With the return of the bow, Philoctetes calls Neoptolemus not just friend but dearest child (*philtaton teknon,* 1301). The endearment appropriate to blood relationship expresses the newly realized spiritual kinship. Even this *philia*, however, is weaker than the bond of hatred for the Greeks at Troy (1374–85). Only the divine *charis*, kindness or grace, of Heracles can effect that change (1413). But Philoctetes' closing words show that the younger man's movement from pretended to genuine friendship has not been without its effect: in acquiescing to join the army at Troy, he now places the counsel of friends, *gnōmē philōn*, prominently beside the powers of great Destiny and the all-conquering deity.

Trust, *pistis*, undergoes a similar process of destruction and regeneration. Odysseus exploits the trustful converse, *homilia pistē*, that Neoptolemus will be able to establish with Philoctetes (70–71). In due course that trust grows between the two men and is sealed by a pledge of hand (*cheiros pistin,* 813). At this point Neoptolemus' relation of trust with Philoctetes is about to undergo a critical change. When Philoctetes sees the younger man still there after the attack of his disease, he calls it "an unbelievable housekeeping of my hopes," *elpidōn apiston oikourēma* (867–868), an untranslatable phrase which joins two basic elements of civilized association, personal trust (*pistis*) and the bonds of a house or *oikos.* Feeling himself betrayed, Philoctetes bitterly throws Neoptolemus' breach of trust in his face: "Yes, you were a trusty friend (*pistos*) but in secret full of bane" (1272). The return of the bow recreates trust. "Trust," fuller communication in words, and good will then all come together when Philoctetes, in his turn, reaches a moment of tragic decision (1350–51): "Alas, what shall I do? How can I not trust (*a-pistein*) in the words of this man who gave me counsel with good will (*eunous*)?"

—CHARLES SEGAL, *Philoctetes:* Society, Language, Friendship,"
Tragedy and Civilization: An Interpretation of Sophocles
(Cambridge, MA: Harvard University Press, 1981), pp. 328–33

JENNY STRAUSS CLAY

Language, modern linguists assure us, is an arbitrary system of signs. The Greeks were not so sure. The debate between those who maintain that language is purely conventional and their opponents who believe that language is "by nature" has a long history which cannot be traced here. But most early etymological speculation presupposes that a name and the thing denominated are closely related, i.e., that a name, correctly understood, indicates the nature of the thing named. The fact that many Greek proper names have transparent meanings (e.g., Aristodemus 'Best-of-the-people,' Telemachus 'Far-fighter,' and Patroclus 'Glory-of-the-father') lends powerful support to such a view. The more opaque names and epithets of the most mysterious of beings, the gods and the famous heroes of the past tease the ingenuity of the Greeks from the earliest times. When Sappho ponders the meaning of Hesperus, the evening star (104a L.-P.), or when Aeschylus has the Chorus of the *Agamemnon* pause to reflect on the name of Helen (689–690), or when, in the same play, Cassandra recognizes the source of her destruction in the name of Apollo (1080ff.), they are not indulging in mere punning or wordplay. Rather, they manifest a time-honored conviction that a proper understanding of a name will reveal the hidden nature of what the name designates. Such a name is called an *onoma eponumon,* a name that corresponds appropriately to the person or object designated. Homer and Hesiod offer numerous examples of this kind of etymological thinking, and it is not surprising that Homer should allow himself to speculate about the meaning of the name of Odysseus.

Our attention has already been drawn to that name indirectly through its omission in the proem, which introduced an anonymous hero whose polytropic character is revealed in his passive ability to endure great suffering and in his active role as the man of *metis*. The same double perspective is retained at the end of the poem. After Odysseus and Penelope are finally reunited and have taken their pleasure in lovemaking, they each tell their stories. Odysseus' summary of his long travels and adventures—of his Odyssey—is introduced as follows:

αὐτὰρ ὁ διογενὴς 'Οδυσεὺς ὅσα κήδε' ἔθηκεν
ἀνθρώποις ὅσα τ' αὐτὸς ὀϊζύσας ἐμόγησε,
πάντ' ἔλεγ'.

But Zeus-born Odysseus told her all—all the troubles he set
upon men, and all that he himself had suffered in misery.   (23.306–308)

Troubles inflicted and troubles endured—these are the two-fold aspects of the hero. The name itself, Odysseus, embraces both and is profoundly ambiguous in its significance.

Odysseus' naming is recounted within the framework of the famous recognition scene. The old nurse Eurycleia washes the feet of her master, who is still disguised as a beggar (19.361ff.). As she touches the old scar which identifies the stranger as Odysseus, its history is told in a leisurely fashion—how, as a youth, Odysseus visited his maternal grandfather Autolycus and took part in a hunt for a boar on the slopes of Parnassus. The boar attacked and wounded Odysseus who then succeeded in killing the beast. The sons of Autolycus healed the wound, which left the identifying scar, and then sent the young hero home with splendid gifts. The parents rejoiced at the safe and triumphant return of their son, who recounted his adventures with the boar. At this point, the narrative returns to the main story: Eurycleia touches the old scar, recognizes it, and drops the foot of Odysseus into the washbasin with a great splash. Eurycleia's joy at the return of her absent master differs from the parents' simple joy of long ago which accompanied the return of their young son (χαῖρον νοστήσαντι 19.463); hers is mixed with pain (χάρμα καὶ ἄλγος 19.471). The old woman's eyes fill with tears and she gasps, "Indeed, you are Odysseus, dear child" (19.474).

Framed within the tale of the boar's hunt and Odysseus' scar—in the manner of Chinese boxes—is the story of Odysseus' naming by his grandfather Autolycus. At first, its connection to the narrative of the scar seems tangential, if not gratuitous. The only apparent link is that the hunt was undertaken in the company of Autolycus and his sons. At any rate, we get a brief description of Autolycus and an account of his earlier visit on the occasion of Odysseus' birth. At that time, Autolycus invited his grandson to visit him when he had grown up, promising to give him many gifts. And so, years later, Odysseus came to Parnassus and earned his scar. What first appear to be purely associative and somewhat rambling digressions turn out to be an exemplary model of the characteristic Homeric technique of ring-composition, in which narrative material is arranged in the general form *A B C B A*. If ring-composition accounts for the formal structure of this digression, it does not in itself throw light on the organic interconnections of the passage on the level of content. To be sure, the story of how Odysseus acquired his scar follows quite reasonably upon Eurycleia's recognition of the scar, but Odysseus' acquisition of his name appears at first to be unrelated to the overall narrative frame.

In well-known essay, Erich Auerbach begins his study of the Western tradition of the literary representation of reality by comparing the Homeric epic with Biblical narrative. With admirable sensitivity, he contrasts the clarity, fullness, and plasticity of the epic with the inward and elliptical style of Biblical storytelling. For all his merits, Auerbach is rather unfortunate in choosing the passage involving Odysseus' scar to exemplify the epic style as "externalized, uniformly illuminated phenomena . . . in a perpetual foreground." He ,claims that "When the young Eurycleia (vv. 401ff.) sets the infant Odysseus on his grandfather Autolycus' lap after the banquet, the aged Eurycleia . . . has entirely vanished from the stage and from the reader's mind." Auerbach seems to forget that only Eurycleia, who was Odysseus' nurse and present at his naming, could pronounce the words

ἦ μάλ᾽ Ὀδυσσεύς ἐσσι, φίλον τέκος . . .

You indeed are Odysseus, dear child . . .   (19.474)

The formula in this line has occurred only twice before in the *Odyssey*. At the moment Circe recognizes Odysseus as *polytropos,* she exclaimes:

ἦ σύ γ᾽ Ὀδυσσεύς ἐσσιπολύτροπος . . .

You indeed are *polytropos* Odysseus . . .   (10.330)

The formula is to be found once more, when Telemachus *denies* that the strange beggar suddenly beautified by Athena can be his father:

οὐ σύ γ᾽ Ὀδυσσεύς ἐσσι πατὴρ ἐμός . . .

You indeed cannot be Odysseus, my father . . .   (16.194)

Yet Odysseus is indeed Telemachus' father, despite such denials; to Circe, he is the man of many turnings; but only for Eurycleia, present at his birth and childhood adventures, does he remain "dear child." Background illuminates foreground. The naming scene belongs within the context of the description of the scar. The name— and the story behind it—identifies Odysseus fully as much as his scar.

Odysseus' maternal grandfather, Autolycus, whose name suggests something like Lone Wolf, comes to Ithaca to name the infant. Eurycleia places the child on Autolycus' lap and urges him to choose a name for his grandson. Tactfully, she suggests "Polyaretus" or Much-Prayed-for. But Autolycus has other ideas:

γαμβρὸς ἐμὸς θυγάτηρ τε, τίθεσθ᾽ ὄνομ᾽ ὅττι κεν εἴπω·
πολλοῖσιν γὰρ ἐγώ γε ὀδυσσάμενος τόδ᾽ ἱκάνω,
ἀνδράσιν ἠδὲ γυναιξὶν ἀνὰ χθόνα πουλυβότειραν·
τῷ δ᾽ Ὀδυσεὺς ὄνομ᾽ ἔστω ἐπώνυμον.

> My son-in-law and daughter, give the name I say:
> for I come here a curse (*odyssamenos*) to many
> men and women all over the much-nurturing earth;
> therefore let his name appropriately be Odysseus.   (19.406–409)

Autolycus derives the name Odysseus from the verb *odysasthai,* which means 'to have hostile feelings or enmity toward someone.' The word embraces a range of meanings, including 'to be angry,' 'to hate someone,' 'to vex,' 'to trouble,' 'to offend.' A few translators have attempted to bring the play on words over into English. Fitzgerald translates: "odium and distrust I've won. Odysseus / should be his given name;" Lattimore renders it as follows: "since I have come to this place distasteful to many ... so let him be given / the name Odysseus, that is distasteful." Giving up on the pun, I have translated *odyssamenos* as 'a curse' to bring out the fact that the name Autolycus chooses is the very opposite of the one the nurse proposes. Eumaeus, the faithful swineherd, seems to allude to the ill-omened character of his absent master's name when he speaks of him to the disguised beggar:

> τὸν μὲν ἐγών, ὦ ξεῖνε, καὶ οὐ παρεόντ' ὀνομάζειν
> αἰδέομαι· πέρι γάρ μ' ἐφίλει καὶ κήδετο θυμῷ·
> ἀλλά μιν ἠθεῖον καλέω καὶ νόσφιν ἐόντα.

> Stranger, I am ashamed to name him in his absence.
> For he loved me greatly and cared for me in his heart;
> instead, I shall call him "dear friend" even if he is far away.   (14.145–147)

This interpretation of Odysseus' name is borne out indirectly by the fictitious name and lineage Odysseus concocts when he introduces himself to his aged father in the last book of the *Odyssey.* There, he calls himself Eperitus, son of Apheidon, grandson of Polypemon (24.305–306). As we might expect, all these names are significant and reveal something about Odysseus' character. Pape-Benseler gives "Strife" as the meaning of Eperitus, but offers no explanation. It seems to derive from ἐπήρεια, 'insulting treatment,' 'abuse,' and is possibly related to ἀρειή, 'menace,' 'threat,' and Sanskrit *irasya,* 'hostility,' cf. Latin *ira,* 'anger.' Homer may also have incorrectly connected it with ἐπαράομαι, 'to curse.' In any case, the name Odysseus manufactures for himself corresponds closely to the meaning of his true name. Apheidon clearly means 'Unsparing' and should, I suggest, not be connected with thrift but with ruthlessness, a quality not altogether foreign to Odysseus' character. We may remember Eurymachus' plea at the beginning of the slaughter of the suitors: "Spare your people" (σὺ δὲ φείδεο λαῶν 22.54). Mercilessly, Odysseus rejects his entreaty. Finally, Polypemon, 'Much-pain,' has the same double sense which conforms to all we have observed of Odysseus; it can mean both 'Suffering-much-pain' and 'Causing-much-pain.'

The name of Odysseus is similarly double and my rendering, 'curse,' solves the problem of whether Autolycus' *odyssamenos* should be taken as active or passive— 'angry at many' or 'incurring the anger of many.' In Greek, the verb is in the middle voice, that is, something between active and passive, which, as Benveniste defines it, is "an act in which the subject is affected by the process and is himself situated within the process." This double and reciprocal sense of incurring and dealing out enmity perfectly suits the trickster Autolycus, of whom we have just learned:

> ... ὃς ἀνθρώπους ἐκέκαστο
> κλεπτοσύνῃ θ' ὅρκῳ τε. θεὸς δέ οἱ αὐτὸς ἔδωκεν
> Ἑρμείας. ...

> ... he surpassed all men
> in thievery and equivocation; and a god gave him this talent,
> Hermes. ...   (19.395–397)

'Curse,' as I have translated *odyssamenos*, also has the advantage of having religious overtones. Such a connotation is singularly fitting, since elsewhere in Homer *odysasthai* is used exclusively to designate divine displeasure or wrath. The verb occurs four times in the *Iliad*, and its subject is always Zeus or "the gods." The most illuminating passage involving *odysasthai* appears in Book 6 within the context of the famous encounter between Diomedes and Glaucus on the battlefield, which ends with their discovery of ancient ties of hospitality between their families. The weight of mortality hangs over the meeting. Only a short time before, Diomedes had wounded both Ares and Aphrodite with Athena's help, but now he seems unsure whether his new adversary is a god or a mortal. If he should be a god, Diomedes refuses to fight with him. As an example of the dangers consequent to fighting with the gods, Diomedes then recounts the story of Lycourgus who had the temerity to attack Dionysus:

> τῷ μὲν ἔπειτ' ὀδύσαντο θεοὶ ῥεῖα ζώοντες,
> καί μιν τυφλὸν ἔθηκε Κρόνου πάϊς· οὐδ' ἄρ' ἔτι δὴν
> ἦν, ἐπεὶ ἀθανάτοισιν ἀπήχθετο πᾶσι θεοῖσιν.

> Thereafter, the gods who live easy were angered at him,
> and the son of Cronus made him blind, nor did he
> live long, since he was hated by the immortal gods.   (VI.138–140)

Therefore, Diomedes concludes, "I would not want to battle with the immortal gods" (VI.141). the enmity of the gods is aroused by Lycourgus' "contending with the celestial gods" θεοῖσιν ἐπουρανίοισιν ἔριζεν (VI.131); his punishment is blindness and premature death.

In the *Odyssey* we find—with the sole exception of the Autolycus passage—that *odysasthai* is consistently limited to the denotation of divine enmity and, more precisely, to the anger of the gods against Odysseus. It occurs in a prominent place of the poem's first scene. Speaking of Odysseus, Athena accuses Zeus: "Why are you so wroth with him?" (τί νύ οἱ τόσον ὠδύσαο, Ζεῦ; 1.62). The goddess employs a form of the same word Autolycus used in naming his grandchild. But here Odysseus is represented, not as one who provokes anger in his fellow men, but as one who undeservedly suffers the wrath of the gods.

Similar plays on Odysseus' name occur three more times in the poem. First, in Book 5 the sea nymph Leucothea takes pity on the storm-tossed hero struggling on his raft: "Poor wretch," she says, "why does Poseidon rage (ὠδύσατ᾽) at you so terribly, so that he sows many evils for you?" (5.339–340). Shortly thereafter, when the storm has subsided and land is in sight, Odysseus still fears further mishaps at sea; he says to himself, "I know how much the famous earth-shaker is angered (ὀδώδυσται) at me" (5.423). Finally, in Ithaca, during the first interview between Odysseus and Penelope, the disguised hero announces not only that Odysseus still lives, but also that he is on his way home with many treasures. But, he tells Penelope, the hero's companions have all perished: "for Zeus and Helios were angry (ὀδύσαντο) with him" (19.275–276).

The name of Odysseus, then, reveals itself to have not one but two senses. It refers both to the active Autolycan troublemaker and to the passive victim of divine wrath. As the Man of Wrath, Odysseus both causes trouble and vexation and is much vexed by the hostility of the gods. These two aspects of Odysseus as victim and victimizer coexist side by side and correspond to the same doubleness we have already observed in his identifying epithet, *polytropos*. The doubleness of Odysseus pervades the *Odyssey*.

—JENNY STRAUSS CLAY, "The Name of Odysseus," *The Wrath of Athena: Gods and Men in the* Odyssey (Princeton: Princeton University Press, 1983), pp. 54–64

GLENN W. MOST

Odysseus is introduced ⟨in Pindar's *Seventh Nemean Ode*⟩ in terms which continue the discussion of fame's surviving death, and at the same time introduce the new question of the degree of correlation between achievement and fame:

ἐγὼ δὲ πλέον᾽ ἔλπομαι
λόγον Ὀδυσσέος ἢ παθάν
 διὰ τὸν ἀδυεπῆ γενέσθ᾽ ῞Ομηρον·
ἐπεὶ ψεύδεσί οἱ ποτανᾷ ⟨τε⟩ μαχανᾷ
σεμνὸν ἔπεστί τι· σοφία
 δὲ κλέπτει παράγοιοα μύθοις. (20–23)

"It is my own opinion that the account of Odysseus was enabled by sweet-voiced Homer to become greater than his suffering, for there is a kind of irrational power to convince in his lies and winged device: for poetic skill cheats when it leads astray with fables."

Pindar begins polemically: the emphasized personal pronoun and the use of a verb, ἔλπομαι, which denotes a strong private conviction for which the grounds are not or cannot be given, presuppose the universality of Odysseus' renown precisely by calling it into question. According to Pindar, the basis in fact which alone could have legitimated genuine fame is lacking in the case of Odysseus: if his fame has exceeded that basis, it can only be due to Homer, whose sweet voice sings a sensually delightful but non-referential poetry which is able to convince irrationally, and thereby to mislead, by its verbal skills. And because this fame is not securely grounded, it is fragile, for it can always be called into question by reference to the criterion of real accomplishment; this calling into question is just what Pindar accomplishes here by the simple expression of doubt. History was to prove Pindar right: for the critical picture of an Odysseus who is all λόγος and no ἔργον, whose celebrity far exceeds any martial accomplishments he can claim, begins here in Pindar and continues, through Gorgias, Antisthenes, and the tragedians, to become one of the clichés of Western literature.

But what exactly is Pindar referring to? The proximity of these lines to the discussion of Ajax' suicide has misled some critics into thinking that here too Pindar has the judgement on Achilles' arms in mind: he would thus be saying in these lines that Odysseus' reputation for valor exceeded his achievements at Troy and that the arms were awarded to him because his lies deceived the Greeks. Such an interpretation is impossible, not only because it would require that the Greeks at Troy were deceived by *Homer* into denying Ajax the weapons but also because of the reference to Odysseus' πάθα (21), a word which in Pindar always describes a dolorous calamity which imposes itself upon a suffering subject, never a heroic success. It is apparently Fränkel who first clearly recognized that Pindar can be referring in these words only to that Odysseus who justifies the epithets πολύτλας, τλήμων, ταλασίφρων, viz. the Odysseus of the *Odyssey*, ὃς μάλα πολλὰ / πλάγχθη... / πολλὰ δ' ὅ γ' ἐν πόντῳ πάθεν ἄλγεα ὃν κατὰ θυμόν (*Od.* 1.1–2,4). Pindar would then be suggesting that the general reputation enjoyed by Odysseus among all the Greeks was not justified by the true extent of Odysseus' sufferings during the ten years after the fall of Troy; and perhaps he is referring more specifically to Odysseus' own account of his wanderings at Alcinous' court (*Od.* 9–12), for which, after all, Odysseus is the sole witness. It is worth noting in this context that Odysseus is referred to often in archaic Greek lyric and is depicted often pictorially in vase-paintings—and, in both cases, through the age of Pindar, almost invariably with reference, not to all his other adventures, but rather to the πάθαι he narrates in *Od.* 9–12.

So, Pindar may be suggesting that Homer, instead of inquiring whether Odysseus' narrative was truthful or not, simply repeated Odysseus' report in his own words; thereby Odysseus was enabled to achieve a renown among the Greeks for whose basis in fact he alone was the sole and unreliable witness; such a renown could impose upon the credulous for a while, but could not be securely enough founded to avoid being discredited eventually by a warier critic. On this interpretation, the οἱ of line 22 appears in a new light. It has often been asked whether the pronoun refers to Odysseus' lies and winged device or to Homer's. Various attempts have been made, by strategic supplementation of the missing syllable, to separate the two expressions so that they might be applied to two separate individuals: but the balance of the line makes intolerably strained any so rigid segregation from one another of the two datives: it seems unavoidable that the two be understood together as referring to the same person designated by οἱ. But perhaps the question of which man is thereby meant is ill-posed: for the fact that the four books of Odysseus' fabulations are reported in *oratio recta* means that the words they contain are simultaneously *both* Odysseus' *and* Homer's. That is why the Odysseus of these books can be referred to in terms appropriate to a poet rather than to a hero: Alcinous explicitly compares him to other bards (*Od.* 11.368). In the lines in question, the word that seems most directly to point to the activity of a poet is ποτανός, a metaphor which, going back at least to Theognis and occuring frequently in Pindar, describes not soaring loftiness but instead quite concretely the universal fame, provided by poetry, which transcends the poetic object's immediate geographic limitations and, flying over land and sea, reaches to the utmost limits of the human community. Thus a winged device is a device which gives wings, which grounds a spatially wide-ranging fame: but if the term is appropriate for Homer, it is no less so for Odysseus, whose own recounting of his adventures helped ground precisely such a fame for himself. Pindar seems to have written deliberately in a way that makes it impossible to distinguish whose lies and winged device are meant: in Homer's representation of Odysseus, the latter's lies and winged device were able to impose upon the Phaeacians; and through Homer's representation of Odysseus, the lies and winged device of both were able to impose upon the Greeks. The primordial deception at Alcinous' court was the condition and first instance of the deception which, according to Pindar, was to characterize the whole Greek reception of the *Odyssey*.

Odysseus, then, serves as an example for the way in which a deficiency of genuine practical accomplishment can be—temporarily and inadequately—compensated for by an unscrupulous poetry: because no god has guaranteed the heroic success which, as we know from the opening of this poem, alone can legitimate a poetry which recognizes its only authentic purpose in the telling of truth, Odysseus can achieve a kind of renown only through the mediation of Homer—in this regard, διὰ τὸν ἀδυεπῆ ῾Ὅμηρον (21) stands in direct contradiction to σὺν δὲ τίν (6). Homer's poetry is, to be sure, possessed of as much efficacy as any mortal's could be—otherwise it would never have imposed upon the Greek world—but it remains, precisely, a mortal's, and can consequently not provide a fame which could be proof against future disbelief. It gives a κῦδος σαθρόν (*N.* 8.34). For Homer had rejected the veridicity which characterizes poetry as a mirror, and had put all his energies into the only remaining dimension of language, its sensuous materiality (ἀδυεπῆ 21). The result is a profoundly attractive seduction, against which Pindar's wariness was to offer the first effective resistance.

The passage on Odysseus began with a mythic reference (20f.) which at once was supplied with an explanation, first in particular terms (the irrational persua-siveness of Homer's language 21–23) and then in ones of general applicability (the capacity of σοφία to cheat by deceiving with fables 23, to become thereby the ἐχθρὰ σοφία of *Olympian Odes* 9.38). This process is now reversed in the second counter-example, that of Ajax (23–30). This time Pindar begins with a general explanation in terms of human stupidity (23–25), before exemplifying that stupidity, and in the process making clear what it is that that stupidity is supposed to explain, in the Greeks' denial of the arms of Achilles to Ajax (25–30). There is a smooth transition from the backwards-looking explanation in terms of fallacious σοφία to the forwards-looking explanation in terms of human stupidity—for clearly no de-ceptive σοφία could impose itself upon men if men did not tend to be so stupid that they fall easy victims to it—yet it is important to recognize that the explanations point in two different directions: on the one hand towards the danger located in the productive side of poetry (the seductive poet), on the other towards that located in its receptive side (the unwary reader); and the Greeks who confirm the first explanation by succumbing to Homer's charm are by no means identical with the Greeks who confirmed the second explanation by failing to recognize Ajax's ex-cellence. The fact that it was Odysseus who did receive Achilles' arms makes the transition even more fluid, though Pindar is careful, here as elsewhere, to avoid making the explicit claim that Achilles' arms were awarded to Odysseus only because Odysseus deceived and cheated the Greeks: Pindar's claim is more gen-eral, that very few men are capable of seeing the truth.

With regard to the question of the award of Achilles' arms, the epic tradition knew of two indisputable facts: on the one hand, by universal consent, Ajax was considered to be the greatest Greek warrior after Achilles; on the other hand, the weapons were awarded, not to him, but to Odysseus. The apparent contradiction between these two facts presented a problem which poets were free to solve in various ways: that Trojan captives rather than Greek warriors were responsible for the choice; that the Greeks sent spies to overhear Trojan women, one of whom was prompted by Athena to favor Odysseus; that the election was fraudulent; that Odysseus was a more skilful orator than Ajax; that Ajax was a victim of the envy of the lesser Greeks. Pindar's solution in *this* poem is simply that the Greeks were stupid.

This emphasis on stupidity becomes comprehensible as soon as we recall the theme of intelligence as recognition of reality which has run through this poem since the beginning: in contrast to the βαθύφρονες Moirai, who possess a knowledge of what is and will be in a degree that far transcends human capacities, mortals can be σοφοί insofar as they have a relative and limited knowledge of the future (they can not know when they will die, but at least they can be intelligent enough not to forget that they eventually will); now we discover what was not said before, namely that such intelligence is limited to a tiny minority of mortals. The concentration of Homeric reminiscences in this passage (which incidentally suggests how very far removed Pindar is from any general indictment of Homer) lends an overwhelming authority to Pindar's claim that the denial of the arms to Ajax represented an extraordinary blindness: the fact that Ajax was, after Achilles, the best Greek warrior becomes thereby as necessary an element of the Trojan saga as Menelaus' blond hair (28), the swiftness of the Homeric ships (28–29), or indeed the whole Greek expedition to the town of Ilus (28–30). That so essential an element of the epic realia could have been overlooked attests for Pindar quite a remarkable stupidity. Pindar has chosen his example well: for on the one hand, the stupidity is demonstrated, not by people who merely read Homer (and thus might have been forgetful, ignorant or deceived), but instead by those who shared Ajax's world and received daily demonstration for ten years of his military excellence; and on the other, the peculiar privilege enjoyed in all Greek culture by the Homeric heroes (who may be assumed to be referred to here as the judges, even if Pindar does not name them) makes the claim for their stupidity even more provocative, for these are no ordinary mortals whose mistakenness is being incontrovertibly demonstrated, but instead figures whose bravery, whose beauty, whose intelligence were paradigmatic. If the Homeric heroes were incapable of seeing reality, then how much more careful Pindar's own listeners must be to avoid making a similar mistake! Thus the myth of Ajax is simultaneously a challenge and a warning, one whose full implications will be developed in the myth of Neoptolemus. Pindar is careful to qualify his warning by asserting, not that all men are blind (for in that case his own project would be hopeless) but only ὅμιλος ἀνδρῶν ὁ πλεῖστος (25): thereby he opens the possibility for his listeners of joining the tiny minority of those whose hearts are not blind and who can see the truth. But he does not offer the optimistic illusion that it is easy, and from this point on every reader must be on his guard against accepting uncritically, and thereby committing himself to, mistaken evaluations of true merit.

The immediately following lines repeat, with only slight variation, the assertion of the universality of death, couched in terms of a polar opposition, which we have encountered once already at lines 19–20: "But Hades' wave approaches common to all, and falls on both the unexpectant and the expectant" (30–31). There has been a considerable amount of discussion on the precise meaning of the words ἀδόκητον and δοκέοντα: it is uncertain whether they refer to the undistinguished as opposed to the distinguished man, or to the one who does not anticipate what will happen to him as opposed to the one who does. Although the evidence does not quite suffice to permit a final judgement, a number of considerations—the use of the words outside Pindar, and particularly the consistent theme in this poem of intelligence as awareness of what the future will bring—make the latter interpretation somewhat more probable. If that is so, the relation of this passage to lines 19–20, where the universality of death had provided the background against which the σοφοί's relative knowledge of the future was valorized, becomes even closer; and, as will become clear shortly, a coherent transition to the following section is established.

But more important than the question of the exact meaning of these two words is the fact that these lines function to remind the reader of the earlier passage. Such repetitions in Pindar have a crucial structuring purpose: they are intended, not simply in their content to remind the reader of a truth so obvious that he is scarcely likely to dispute it, nor in their generality to provide the semblance of philosophical thought, nor in their simple presence to bide for time until something more appropriate occurs to the poet, but instead, formally, to demarcate clearly the beginning and end of argumentative sections of the poem's structure as a whole. In this case the repetition unmistakeably delimits the myths of Odysseus and Ajax as belonging together to one unified passage which operates as a whole within the general organization of the poem. We thus are invited to consider the ways in which the discussions of Odysseus and Ajax can be considered together as correlates. First, the heroes themselves are understood as, to adopt Adorno's phrase, "die auseinandergerissenen Hälften der ganzen Freiheit, die doch aus ihnen nicht sich zusammenaddieren lässt. The unity, whose deficiency is common to both, is that of practical achievement and reflection in discourse whose importance the opening of the poem revealed. Odysseus is characterized by too little ἔργον and too much λόγος (20–21). Ajax, on the other hand, has more than enough ἔργον but far too little λόγος, for in the denial of Achilles' weapons to him he did not receive the discursive recognition appropriate for his practical accomplishments. Second, they partake of a purely human world with all of the vicissitudes and dangers by which that world is characterized. Nowhere is there any mention of a divine sanction for the military achievements of the two heroes, nor of any divine mediation for the discursive form of those achievements: instead, both Odysseus and Ajax inhabit a world in which only men participate. The consequence is that reality and its recognition as truth become enormously difficult to attain: the way is obstructed, from the beginning, by the inherent deficiency of human understanding, and furthermore is liable to the constant danger of deception and seduction. Poetologically, this danger can be summarized under two headings. First, productively: the poet in this realm does not necessarily operate by the criterion of truth, but instead concentrates his activity upon the elaboration of the sensual materiality to which language is reduced when, instead of being regarded instrumentally, as a tool for truth, it takes on an autonomy and a problematic self-consistency. Second, receptively: in the absence of a sure criterion for truth, most readers are incapable of discerning on their own what is real and what is not, and consequently are liable to succumb to the blandishments of an unscrupulous poetry. They notice neither the exaggeration of ἔργον in λόγος (as false praise or as empty boasting) nor the diminution of ἔργον in λόγος (as slander or as neglected praise).

—GLENN W. MOST, *The Measures of Praise: Structure and Function in Pindar's Second Pythian and Seventh Nemean Odes* (Göttingen: Vandenhoeck & Ruprecht, 1985), pp. 148–56

LINDA K. HUGHES

It is interesting that at the end of "On a Mourner" "virtue" is compared to a "household god," followed by a concluding stanza alluding to Troy and Aeneas. Perhaps this simile suggested the subject of Ulysses, but when Tennyson came to write the famous poem of that name, he ended up with something akin to and yet utterly different from "On a Mourner." The kinship between "Ulysses" and the lyric lies in Tennyson's personal participation in both forms. As Tennyson reported to James Knowles, "There is more about myself in 'Ulysses', which was written under the sense of loss and that all had gone by, but that still life must be fought out to the end. It was more written with the feeling of his loss upon me than many poems in 'In Memoriam'." I have examined elsewhere in detail the possible correlations between Tennyson's own life and "Ulysses." These include Tennyson's and the Apostles' sense that Hallam's was a "heroic" intellect and that to be associated with him was to live (in nineteenth-century terms) on a heroic plane; Hallam's and Tennyson's wanderings and adventures together on the Continent; Tennyson's own worry about becoming a mere "name" after his 1832 volume was published, and in the absence of his closest literary advisor and supporter; and the factors that would have disposed Tennyson to be ambivalent toward his own family in the aftermath of Hallam's death. Tennyson's friends, too, help us to see Tennyson's personal involvement in the poem. Some critics consider Tennyson's adoption of the "mask of age" in "Ulysses" a mere ruse, a way of hiding behind a mask so that he can say what he really wants to say, or an oblique means of expressing a death wish. Yet Robert Monteith's letter to Tennyson in December 1833 suggests that the poem's mask of age is a perfect and accurate rendering of the feelings of those bereaved by Hallam's death.

> One feeling that remains with me is a longing to preserve all those friends whom I know Hallam loved and whom I learnt to love through him. He was so much a centre round which we moved that now there seems a possibility of many connections being all but dissolved. Since Hallam's death I almost feel like an old man looking back on many friendships as something bygone. I beseech you, do not let us permit this, you may even dislike the interference of common friendship for a time, but you will be glad at length to gather together all the different means by which you may feel not entirely in a different world from that in which you knew and loved Hallam.

Monteith's letter can almost serve as a gloss on the personal elements of "Ulysses."

But if Tennyson fully exploited the dramatic monologue's recursive loop in "Ulysses," he simultaneously created an objective poem through his shaping of the poem, one that both invites the reader's participation and gives his speaker Ulysses ample rein, a separate life of his own. Scholarship devoted to "Ulysses" proves both the degree of the reader's participation in the poem and the poem's objectivity. No one has trouble agreeing what "Hark! the dogs howl!" or "On a Mourner" is all about. But many readers have taken "Ulysses" to mean quite other than what Tennyson said it meant, arguing that it is not about heroic endurance but a portrait of a Satanic egoist, a suicidal speaker, an antihero in every way. The poem in fact has been carefully shaped to leave gaps in the text, the same kind of entrances for the reader Tennyson managed so beautifully in "The Lotos-Eaters," as the poem traces the oscillations of Ulysses' consciousness in the four verse paragraphs.

In the first paragraph we see a Ulysses frustrated beyond all measure by what he feels is a kind of imprisonment, and he vents this frustration by projecting scorn on all about him—the "still hearth," the "barren crags," the "agèd wife," and the "savage race" who, he feels, force him to break up his capacity for unlimited action into discrete little parcels of acts: "I mete and dole." The second paragraph shows a shift in Ulysses' consciousness. As an alternative to his enforced idleness, he lives over again in memory his great deeds and unlimited "roaming" and imagines undertaking a new quest:

> vile it were
> For some three suns to store and hoard myself,
> And this gray spirit yearning in desire
> To follow knowledge like a sinking star. (lines 28–31)

Significantly, he does not yet say he *will* go; all is spoken in hypothetical terms: "Life piled on life / *Were* all too little"; "vile it *were.*"

His kaleidoscopic consciousness shifts once more, and he returns to the domestic sphere of the hearth, but with a difference. His frustration largely dissipated through his imaginative journeys of the second verse paragraph, he can return to his immediate surroundings in the third with an enlarged and gentler perspective. Focusing on Telemachus, he invokes to himself all that Telemachus can achieve through his patience and "slow prudence": the very impressive achievement of uplifting a people, whom he now terms "rugged" (which implies the capacity for will and endurance—Ulysses' own traits) instead of "savage." He finds that he can sympathize with both his son and his people, but in doing so is only reminded of the residual differences between himself and them. He is thus led to an epiphany from within—he is indeed different: "He works his work, I mine." He now makes his decision to move.

As opposed to the generalized statements and hypothetical voyage of the second paragraph, the last paragraph offers a concrete proposal born of Ulysses' imaginative testing. He looks directly to the port and, confident of the rightness of his quest, exhorts his mariners to "push off." And so the poem ends with its stirring lines, the emphatic vigor and stateliness of which serve to reinforce Ulysses' decision. And, I think, the reader is invited to second that decision (though many must send their regrets); for as we see the softening and enlarging of Ulysses' character as he contemplates his quest, a recognition we can come to through the gaps between paragraphs and the oscillations of his consciousness, we can see that it is right and just for him to depart.

Ulysses thus lives as a character in his own right, one with whom we can sympathize and one we can judge. Tennyson's objectivity in the poem is due partly to his having chosen just the right speaker, one through whom Tennyson could explore and filter his own feelings, yet one who has, through tradition, a story and life all his own. The result is a poem we can view, as it were, through a stereoscopic viewer. If we close one eye, we see Tennyson plain. If we close the other, we see only Ulysses. When we open both eyes we see a poem rich in resonance and depth because of the vibrations and subtle overlapping of the two intersecting images.

There is an additional reason for Tennyson to have used the dramatic monologue for "Ulysses" beyond the interplay he could achieve among poet, speaker, and reader (and text). The form of the dramatic monologue itself leads us to the very heart of the poem and its theme. Loy D. Martin has remarked that three linguistic categories—"adverbial phrases signifying temporal proximity," "present participles of non-stative verbs used as adverbs," and "verbs of progressive aspect"—act to make the nineteenth-century dramatic monologue a poetic structure "viewed from inside the time sequence in which it occurs": "The dramatic monologue, in one of its principal functions, creates a poetic moment of a certain duration which is viewed internally and which is contiguous with an implied extra-textual past and future of indefinite extent. The 'present' of the dramatic monologue is thus implicitly one open-ended fragment in a succession of fragments which do not, even projectively, add up to a bounded whole" (62, 61, 65). The dramatic monologue, again, is on the inside of time. All this matters intensely for "Ulysses" because the dramatic monologue is a means of achieving exactly what Ulysses most desires: a resistance to closure, to endings. One might say that "Ulysses" is Tennyson's "Do not go gentle into that good night"—only he is not addressing the dying or dead Hallam but that part of himself that was as one with Hallam ("I am a part of all that I have met"), crying out that this part of himself shall not be enclosed and extinguished but must go on into the future.

In the poem itself all this is translated into the linguistic forms Tennyson so masterfully chooses to render Ulysses' consciousness. The opening lines betray Ulysses' fear that he is becoming divided from a part of himself. He first refers to himself in the third person—"It little profits that an *idle king*"—and the one "I" of the first verse paragraph is hemmed in, buried in the third line after a succession of modifying phrases, and surrounded by things: hearth, crags, wife, and race. Moreover, the tense is both the simple present ("I mete and dole") and the habitual, the finite and the infinite, bespeaking Ulysses' anxiety that he is caught in a trap of external enclosure. Thus the last line of the first paragraph has three nonfinite verbs—the savage race "hoard, and sleep, and feed" unendingly—and then a finite verb that acts like the clicking of a trap: "know not me." His people are thus part of a larger process, but a process that leads only to enclosure—of Ulysses.

Accordingly, Ulysses desires precisely that "untravelled world" of ongoing present time "whose margin fades / For ever and for ever when I move." Significantly, his desire *not* to "make an end" is contrasted with diction ("hoard") that recurs to the closed lives of his people as he sees them. But he most fears closure from within, the possibility that he will "hoard myself" rather than connect with an ongoing present activity that is itself linked back with his past and forward with his future. Curiously, "To follow knowledge like a sinking star, / Beyond the utmost bound of human thought" was originally part of "Tiresias," where the latter wishes "I were as in the days of old." For Tennyson, therefore, the lines would have connoted both the future and the past.

In the third paragraph Ulysses shuts rather than opens doors on time—"I *leave* the sceptre and the isle," "When I am *gone*"—but Ulysses is accepting the only kind of closure he can accept, a closure on the closure represented by his isolation in Ithaca: "He works his work, I mine." He is then ready for the end of the poem that, in its very language, with its present-tense "are" and the succession of incompleted infinitives, opens out onto an eternal present, onto infinity: "To strive, to seek, to find, and not to yield." Each infinitive is thrown down like a gauntlet against the threat of imprisoning stasis and death, which "closes all," and, though some remark on the slowness of this last line with all its pauses, I find the sound reminds me of the successive smacks of the oars smiting "the sounding furrows" as Ulysses and his mariners set off on their voyage into a dynamic, open-ended time. Yes, Ulysses fails to say where they are going, what they are seeking or will find. But this is, in the poem's own terms, irrelevant. All that matters is to resist closure and to keep moving, no matter that eventually they will be swallowed by the ultimate closure of death, which can never be escaped. The poem is in fact startlingly amoral. So desperate is Ulysses (and, perhaps, Tennyson) to keep himself and all he has experienced on the inside of time that all other considerations are virtually mean-ingless. And to convey all this, Tennyson has chosen exactly the right form, the open-ended dramatic monologue itself situated squarely inside time.

—LINDA K. HUGHES, "Beautiful Other Worlds: The Dramatic Monologues of 1832 and 1842," *The Manyfacèd Glass: Tennyson's Dramatic Monologues* (Athens: Ohio University Press, 1987), pp. 94–99

KENNETH M. McKAY

Oenone is a reactionary overcome by her passion for the past and made danger-ous by the beauty of its sorrow in her song. In 'Ulysses,' published in 1842, Tennyson explores the deceptive character of another reactionary, one who quite explicitly would overleap the human condition, avoid the realities of the contem-porary situation, in an effort to renew the past. Impossible to realize, the heroic end projected in Ulysses' rhetoric becomes a delusive, unfixed goal masking the real consequence of the undertaking—death and damnation. In 'Ulysses,' more directly than in any other poem by Tennyson, one can see at work the meaning of Hallam's comment, quoted earlier, regarding the need to attend to the present dissociated and fallen state of man if genuine renewal is to be achieved:

But repentance is unlike innocence; the laborious endeavor to restore has
more complicated methods of action than the freedom of untainted nature.

As a poem of 'relatively unresolved antinomies,' in the words of E. J. Chiasson,
'Ulysses' has conventionally been regarded as an attempt by Tennyson to 'find
solace and understanding' upon the death of Hallam. More than *In Memoriam*,
Tennyson said, the poem 'was written under the sense of loss and that all had gone
by, but that still life must be fought out to the end.' That this is true there is no
reason to doubt; but what it means exactly when applied to the poem is, as is usual
with Tennyson's comments, much more complex and subtle than is frequently
recognized.

Like 'Oenone,' 'Ulysses' can have no substantial reference to Christianity. But
Paull F. Baum establishes the connection of the poem with Dante and anyone who
reads 'Ulysses' next to Dante will see it. The portrait drawn by Tennyson must be
seen initially as derived from that of Ulysses condemned to Hell as a deceiver. Far
from being a neutral element in the poem, as if Tennyson recalled Dante's words
without their context, the poem's language, in its underlying sense of futility and
death, directly expresses the character and situation of Dante's Ulysses. While
many readers seem to respond to Ulysses' rhetoric as the mariners in Dante's
description ('I hardly think that I could have held them in,' Ulysses recalls, *Hell*,
XXVI, 123) and while one must agree to the felt attractiveness of the language of
heroic progress, one must recognize too that the language conveys a clear sense
that the real end of the quest as undertaken must be death. However heroic their
determination, they died, according to Dante, in a storm off Mount Purgatory, on
the summit of which is the Earthly Paradise. 'On the mystical level,' writes Dorothy
L. Sayers, Mount Purgatory 'is the image of the Soul's Ascent to God ... on the
moral level the image of Repentance, by which the sinner returns to God' (*Purgatory*, I, 78–9, note). Unlike the Soul in 'The Palace of Art,' who comes to see the
need to purge herself before she can truly live in the Palace, and unlike Dante, who
must accompany Virgil through Hell and Purgatory before entering Paradise, Ulysses does not recognize the need first to die to sin, and he is destroyed with his
mariners. The sense of the heroic which he has and the language in which he
expresses it are essentially empty, of a past age; he projects an end of genial, pagan,
and heroic dimensions —

It may be that the gulfs will wash us down:
It may be we shall touch the Happy isles,
And see the great Achilles, whom we knew   (62–4)

— but he lands in the Christian Hell of Dante. If he wishes to see Achilles, he must
visit him in the second circle of the same place (Canto V). Like Cambridge, his
'manner sorts / Not with this age.' It is this which the language conveys in the
undertow of futility and in the subtle sense of bombast permeating the rhetoric of
progress. Against Ulysses' proffered justification for leaving Ithaca, that 'It little
profits' him to remain (1), one hears throughout the poem the words of Christ to

his Apostles: 'For what is a man profited, if he shall gain the whole world, and lose his own soul?' (Matthew 16:21).

For Ulysses the choice is not between life and death, though his language might leave that impression, nor is it between heroic adventure and domestic boredom. Staying or leaving, he is for death. In the sense that his youth is past and his time of heroic adventure, he is fallen; in the words Hallam uses to Emily Tennyson in the letter quoted at the beginning of this chapter, Ulysses is now 'disenchanted,' past that time when 'joy came to us not only with momentary allurement but with the full deep soul-satisfying aspect of eternal reality.' The question is whether he will, in the face of this natural loss, be inspired to see into 'the significance of life, the form of the riddle of the world,' or whether he will refuse the insight by disregarding the reality of his place in time. His choice is between a death which is the culmination and fulfilment of temporal life and a death which turns from its reality and betrays it. He chooses the latter, not recognizing that, though 'all had gone by,' in Tennyson's words, 'life must be fought out to the end.' Ulysses turns from the necessary 'complicated methods of action' by which Paradise is to be regained according to Hallam—and he fails, for 'repentance is unlike innocence.'

There is, indeed, nothing like repentance in Ulysses' mind. In this respect he is clearly a Faustian figure. As in the other poems examined, the Goethean vision of life is here seen as, at once, heroic and inadequate. Generally and positively, the Faustian strain is visible in Ulysses' obsessive striving and in the assertive smugness of such statements as 'that which we are, we are' (67); negatively, it is seen in his callous regard for wife, son, and people. Behind this, further, of course, is Ulysses' self-absorption, his abstraction from the human condition, as shown in his commitment to follow knowledge 'Beyond the utmost bound of human thought' (32) and in his failure to recognize the place of suffering in the realization of knowledge:

> My mariners,
> Souls that have toiled, and wrought, and thought with me —
> That ever with a frolic welcome took
> The thunder and the sunshine ...   (45–8)

And it is knowledge, not truth, which he pursues; certainly it is not wisdom embodied in human form.

Looking ahead, moreover, one can see that Ulysses' sense that 'It little profits' (1) him to remain in Ithaca is echoed directly in the first section of *In Memoriam*, in which the inadequacy of the Faustian vision is made explicit:

> But who shall so forecast the years
>   And find in loss a gain to match?
>   Or reach a hand through time to catch
> The far-off interest of tears?   (I, 5–8)

Further, while the metaphor is different, the sense 'That men may rise on stepping-stones / Of their dead selves to higher things' (I, 3–4), which is seen as an inadequate view in the face of actual loss, is identical with Ulysses' sense that:

> ... all experience is an arch wherethrough
> Gleams that untravelled world, whose margin fades
> For ever and for ever when I move.   (19–20)

As a Faustian figure, Ulysses is far removed from any sense of sin such as that in the Prologue to *In Memoriam* (33–6); in him it is limited to a sense of 'How dull it is to pause, to made an end' (22), that 'vile it were ... to store and hoard myself' (28–9). A man of strife, he would not appreciate Sayers' comment: 'Once lost in the Dark Wood, a man can only escape by so descending into himself that he sees his sin, not as an external obstacle, but as the will to chaos and death within him (Hell)' (XXVI, 75, note). Such a Faustian figure is attractive, of course, as he is in 'Supposed Confessions,' but in Tennyson he speaks with the accent and from the position of Dante's deceiver.

But the subtlety of the deception does not lie in the sufficiency of Ulysses' rhetoric to offset the patent folly of his proposed action; in itself the rhetoric suggests something akin to the madness of a 'Monty Python' sketch: an egotistical old man inciting other old men to row into the sunset, leaving behind them wives, country, children, the achievement and promise of life. The subtlety of Ulysses' deception lies, rather, in the ambiguity of the sense of death at its centre, one which so modulates the rhetoric as to make it *seem* expressive of a truth, for in acceptance of death as the proper culmination of the temporal human round lies the sense of real promise and hope in the poem. It is of critical poetic importance that Ulysses seem to recognize the reality of his situation at one level, for in doing so he can persuade one that he sees truly:

> Life piled on life
> Were all too little, and of one to me
> Little remains.   (24–6)

> my purpose holds
> To sail beyond the sunset, and the baths
> Of all the western stars, until I die.   (59–61)

> We are not now that strength which in old days
> Moved earth and heaven.   (66–7)

'Little remains'; 'until I die'—our sense of Ulysses' authenticity rests on these phrases and not on the earlier, assertive language; our sense that he is heroic depends on the recognition and acceptance of death which they convey. The power of the poem's close is immediately connected with the truth of the statement that they are not now what they were. Without such apparent insight, Ulysses' language could not mislead.

But it does mislead, of course, because Ulysses does not act in accordance with the truth perceived. He uses one sense of death to gain acceptance of another. Like Mariana, he stands apart from the world of meaning which he inhabits; like the

Hesperides, he would refuse the harvest, the fulfilment which is properly his. This is clear from the beginning, where the language points to the fact that his heroic sense of himself is at odds with the reality:

> It little profits that an idle king,
> By this still hearth, among these barren crags,
> Matched with an age'd wife, I mete and dole
> Unequal laws unto a savage race,
> That hoard, and sleep, and feed, and know not me.   (1–5)

The contemptuous harshness with which he represents his situation conveys his wilful self-blindness; his statement that they 'know not me' becomes a refusal to recognize that he is indeed 'matched' with Penelope, his 'aged wife.' His sense that he is unknown is a measure of his ignorance of himself, and his departure will be from the achievement and hope of Ithaca. He would, as it were, escape from the temporal cottage in the vale to live in the Palace.

This is not to deny the heroism of the past, of which, as he recognizes, he is an expression. Carried into the present, however, it is obsessively egocentric, Ulysses' description of it (6–21) being characterized by a dominating, thrusting 'I.' He does not fit and he will not be subdued to the realities of the present, which are temporal, domestic, social, and genuinely progressive. The representation of Telemachus (33–43) is at the structural centre of the poem, the leading fact of the new order's definition; Ulysses' assertion that 'He works his work, I mine' (43) establishes his own separation from the order and blurs the fact that Ulysses' own work is done, that, apart from Ithaca, his people, wife and son, he has nothing. They are life. Drawing on the sense of positive temporal effort inherent in the Telemachus portrait, Ulysses' language invests his 'work' with an equal but illusory sense of reality. Apart from the work of Telemachus, Ulysses' projected end is based on deception, on a heroism which has had its day. The larger implications of this are registered immediately in the portrait in the coolly ambivalent affirmation of Telemachus by Ulysses: 'This is my son ... Well-loved of me' (33–5); such recognition in such language echoes perversely and ironically that affirmation offered Christ in Matthew: 'This is my beloved Son, in whom I am well pleased' (17:5).

But the depth of the deception can be seen most effectively in the following lines:

> You and I are old;
> Old age hath yet his honour and his toil;
> Death closes all: but something ere the end,
> Some work of noble note, may yet be done,
> Not unbecoming men that strove with Gods.   (49–53)

'Death closes all'—on the one hand this statement recognizes death as the completion of a process of which Ulysses is a part, the culminating event in a vision of life in which even 'Old age hath yet his honour and his toil'; on the other, it points to death as the end of everything, in spite of which in old age 'Some work of noble note, may yet be done.' Turning on the ambiguity of 'closes' and 'yet,' Ulysses effects a shift from the positive vision of death at one with the temporal world of Ithaca to a negative view, in which death is a destroyer. His hubristic quest for 'Some work . . . / Not unbecoming men that strove with Gods' contrasts sharply with Telemachus' fitting or decent and specific task of paying 'Meet adoration to my household gods, / When I am gone' (41–3). That they are Ulysses' household gods is important, for his leaving them to Telemachus, as if they were cats to be fed while he is on vacation, emphasizes his separation from the realities of the present, from the underlying truth of his situation. He leaves them, not to pursue a present truth, but to maintain his past image as one who in quite a different way 'strove with Gods.' His sense of himself and his decision to leave are not decent.

But the underlying sense of the inherence of truth in change, which the poem gives, remains, as in the next sentence Ulysses' situation is fused with a vision of closing day. Remarkable in its ease and beauty, the passage becomes a touchstone of sanity in the poem:

> The lights begin to twinkle from the rocks:
> The long day wanes: the slow moon climbs: the deep
> Moans round with many voices.   (54–6)

Far from the 'barren crags' of the opening and the shrill egotism of Ulysses' recollected heroism, this Ithaca reflects the promise of his life as a fulfilment in time, in a death common, expected, and graceful. Within the natural round, the lines make clear that, in the positive sense, 'Death closes all.' It is against this promise that Ulysses' rallying his friends to 'seek another world' (57) is felt, his saying 'Push off' (58) conveying not energy simply but also a sense of strain, of falseness. He perverts the promise in seeking the wrong death. His final statement that he is a man 'To strive, to seek, to find, and not to yield' (70) is that of one who, like Faust, has a dissociated sensibility. There is now more to heroism than striving, as Dante's Ulysses, speaking from Hell, makes clear:

> No tenderness for my son, nor piety
>   To my old father, nor the wedded love
>   That should have comforted Penelope
> Could conquer in me the restless itch to rove
> And rummage through the world exploring it,
> All human worth and wickedness to prove.   (XXVI, 94–9)

Ulysses has indeed striven, sought, and found, but he yields up that truth which he lived to secure. The heroism felt as genuine in the poem belongs to the new, that embodied in Telemachus, and the poem lives in Ulysses' studied evasion of that truth within himself.

The tension between the good and the inane which characterizes 'Ulysses,' between the genuinely and falsely heroic, is an expression of Tennyson's interest in the 'abysmal deeps of personality,' as explored in 'The Palace of Art,' and the need for those like the Soul or Ulysses to pass beyond knowledge, to know despair in the experience of actual, temporal life or to 'fail and perish utterly.' More than character studies, Tennyson's poems are explorations of the ways of God, in so far as each delineates a particular will, and the will, as Hallam remarks, 'is in the power of God's election.' Between the good and the inane is a line so subtle that to distinguish it is to see into the 'riddle of the world.'

—KENNETH M. MCKAY, " 'Ulysses,' " *Many Glancing Colours: An Essay in Reading Tennyson, 1809–1850* (Toronto: University of Toronto Press, 1988), pp. 115–22

THEOHARIS CONSTANTINE THEOHARIS

Ulysses also displays its heroes recovering from the most dangerous crises of their lives, pulled back from catastrophe at the extreme moment. Bloom has not had complete sexual intercourse with Molly for "10 years, 5 months and 18 days," or complete mental intercourse for "9 months and 1 day." The separation results in Molly's adultery on June 16, the worst psychological blow Bloom has yet encountered. Like Odysseus, Bloom never forgets his spouse or stops loving her; like Dante, who did forget Beatrice's example, Bloom is himself responsible, as Odysseus is not, for the trouble he's in vis-à-vis his isolated lady. Odysseus' ten-year struggle to return to Penelope results from accidental interference, not from unwillingness on his part, whereas Bloom's ten-year-plus (trust Joyce to improve all his analogies by detailing them so specifically) alienation from Molly, while it is brought on by the accidental death of Rudy, contains no struggle for sexual reunion and is in fact acquiescence, symptomatic of a drifting will as calamitous as Dante's. While Bloom's wandering Dublin on June 16 recapitulates Odysseus' errant detour home, it also reenacts Dante's purposeful doubletracking through the afterlife. Bloom's reconciliation to Molly, like Dante's to Beatrice and the Divine love she leads him to, is a reeducation of the will, unlike Odysseus' homecoming, which depends not on his moral education along the way, but entirely on his prudence and perseverance. Homer's hero returns because he has faith and reason marshaled; Joyce's Bloom possesses these virtues, but he also needs to face, as Dante does, the failure in his soul that has put him at such a distance from happiness.

Bloom cannot stay home to forestall his cuckoldry; things have gone too far, as he knows, for that to prevent the inevitable result of his middle-aged failure. His return, like Dante's, starts with recognition of the desperate situation he is in, realization of the full sundering he has brought about between himself and his love. Unable to move simply, directly out of the wilderness he has drifted into, Bloom must wander in circles all over Dublin, analyzing himself and those he encounters, identifying the failures and successes of a world in which he is as alien as the living Dante is in the afterlife. In Dante's poem a living soul learns its nature from the dead;

in Joyce's crisis narrative two living souls, Bloom and Stephen, are sent out to recover themselves by observing the world of generation alien to them. In both epics the heroes recover only after they travel through a world more real than the one their mistakes have trapped them in. Dante sees the absolute, permanent life of the dead; Bloom and Stephen see the perpetual transformations of generation and decay, from which they are cut off through sexual isolation. Dubliners, like the dead, are good and evil, and like the dead they show Bloom and Stephen truths that fit the two Irish pilgrims for the symbolic deliverance Dante earned on his Odyssey—the chanting of Psalm 114.

Stephen's error is simple to identify: he's loveless and so lifeless. June 16 finds him in extremis, with no home, no job, no direction, no hope until Bloom comes on the scene. The older man's kindness can retrieve Dedalus from the fatal consequences of the adolescent funk that he has been nurturing and can direct his artistic genius to mundane affairs, the only satisfying subject for artists, the only possible one. Stephen is found by Bloom as Dante is by Virgil, helpless, aware of his mistakes but ignorant of their remedy. He faces his danger in this passage from "Scylla and Charybdis": "Fabulous artificer. The hawklike man. You flew. Whereto? Newhaven-Dieppe, steerage passenger. Paris and back. Lapwing. Icarus. *Pater, ait.* Seabedabbled, fallen, weltering, Lapwing you are. Lapwing be." The answer to Stephen's cry "Pater, ait," comes in Bloom's goofy solicitude, in the practical rescue of Dedalus from Nighttown, and in the symbolic proferring of personal and artistic maturity to Stephen during the late-night conversation in "Ithaca." As guardian and instructor of an artist recovering himself, Bloom recapitulates Virgil's assistance to the pilgrim. And Stephen repeats Dante's circling through the afterlife to recoup moral and creative force, as he circles through Dublin retrospectively analyzing his own will's errors by observing humanity at large.

Bloom's error is more difficult to pin down, since he is, as Joyce wanted him to be, a good man, the normative man, Odysseus. The adulterous violation of his marriage is the last consequence of the error, the event that forces him to discover what has been wrong for ten years and what needs to be done for any reconciliation with Molly to be possible. The mistake of course is abandoning Molly sexually; what caused the deprivation is never entirely clear. Rudy's death is the efficient cause, but Bloom's personality, his response to the loss, is the material and final cause, and Joyce is not explicit about what went wrong in Poldy. The most plausible explanation, psychologically, is that Bloom fell into guilty despair when Rudy died, believing he was responsible for his son's death. Two passages from the novel suggest this. In "Lestrygonians," Bloom thinks, "Could never like it again after Rudy." In "Hades," after seeing a child's hearse pass, Bloom remembers his son. "A dwarf's face, mauve and wrinkled like little Rudy's was. Dwarf's body, weak as putty, in a whitelined deal box. Burial friendly society pays. Penny a week for a sod of turf. Our. Little. Beggar. Baby. Meant nothing. Mistake of nature. If it's healthy it's from the mother. If not from the man. Better luck next time." Having failed nature's fundamental requirement (reproduction) by creating a diseased, preempted extension of himself, Bloom simply drops out and gives up his natural privilege as sire, convinced he cannot enjoy it. Life has demonstrated his insufficiency, Bloom feels: there is no point in challenging the hideous evaluation nature made of him when Rudy died. Unwilling to deprive Molly utterly of sexual life, the options for Bloom are to substitute annoying peculiarities or to force her into adultery, both of which he takes, neither of which satisfy her.

Bloom has wandered for ten years in the chronic delusion that his marital responsibilities ended with Rudy's death. Until June 16, Bloom has been acting as if serving Molly breakfast in bed suitably substitutes for what nature requires she should receive there. Boylan's presence shocks Bloom into understanding that such an arrangement will not do and forces him to discover how he might put his house in order. Unlike Odysseus, Bloom recovers his wife psychologically without ousting her lover from their bed. In the course of his wandering Bloom redefines the meaning of husband, which he has distorted for ten years, so that it denotes not sexual possessiveness (a hopeless aspiration, as the passage from "Ithaca" about the series of violators indicates), but intimate understanding and delight with a lifelong companion. That discovery does little for Bloom's sexual inertia. He still has nothing better than a proximate erection at the end of this day, and that after kissing Molly's unfertilizable, diversionary bottom. She will continue seeing Boylan, plans the liaisons that night in "Penelope," but those plans do not affect Bloom's superior place in her affections, the place Bloom has resecured for himself that day by understanding the importance and insignificance of her infidelity. Given this shift in their emotional balance, given Bloom's continued sexual appetitiveness, and the confidence he has gained by surrogate fatherhood with Stephen, the possibility that Bloom could renew a full sexual life with Molly, and try for another son, seems not inconceivably remote. In that possibility Bloom enacts Odysseus' recovery of his patrimony. The difference between the two accomplishments makes for the comedy, joy, and acute psychological realism of Joyce's art and thought.

Bloom's psychological mastery of adultery is not an evasive rationalization of the crisis he has brought on but the only possible successful resolution of it. Bloom nullifies the suitor's assault on his happiness when he reaches equanimity about Molly's adultery, and in the process undoes the worst effects of his despair, the cause that forced that violation. Before Boylan, Bloom did not need to understand what his failure meant to Molly, and so compounded its damage, behaving all the while as if his marriage was safe. After Boylan, Bloom knows what his failure has meant, and what it hasn't, and through that knowledge ends the drifting anxiety he has been lost in for the entire day (and, one assumes, for ten years previous to it). Walking through Dublin, reevaluating himself and his love for Molly as those subjects are recalled to him by the chance encounters of the day, Bloom puts his house in order by reforming his will, understanding his negligence vis-à-vis his wife, and accepting its consequences (finally in "Ithaca") without evading or exaggerating them. The long sundering is reconciled that day, although the sexual alienation that has been its chief symptom persists.

Like Dante, and unlike Odysseus, Bloom returns to his lady after educating his will, because he has changed himself. The return, like Dante's, is more psychological than physical. Beatrice is dead, after all, and Dante's love for her cannot be more than spiritual. The marriage Bloom saves, like Dante's to Beatrice, lives in spiritual devotion more than in bed, where it has been lost for over a decade (the time Dante has been separated from Beatrice, according to *Purgatorio* 32, the time Odysseus has been wandering home to Penelope). Bloom's error and Dante's are sexual failures brought on by the deaths of loved ones. Whereas Dante's sin was licentiousness and promiscuity (so the *Commedia* suggests in *Purgatorio* 29–31), Poldy's is sexual negligence. Both heroes recover their happiness not by direct assault on their problems, but by understanding how they came to be through observation of the full range of the soul's actions, Dante on a detour through the next world, Bloom on a detour through Dublin. Bloom, like the Greek king, regains his marriage couch, but its fullest pleasures are not immediately (or even certainly) restored to him, as Odysseus' and Penelope's were.

—THEOHARIS CONSTANTINE THEOHARIS, "Recasting an Epic Journey of the Soul,"
Joyce's Ulysses: *An Anatomy of the Soul* (Chapel Hill: University of
North Carolina Press, 1988), pp. 126–30

George de F. Lord

THE *ODYSSEY* AND
THE WESTERN WORLD

Mr. Eliot's recent article, "Vergil and the Western World" (*Sewanee Review,*
Winter, 1953), has redefined for us the Christian-like qualities of the *Aeneid* and
its hero. Virgil is seen as a sort of prophet, perhaps unconsciously inspired by Judaic
thought, who anticipated some of the values of the Christian world. The *pietas* of
Aeneas requires his acceptance, at the cost of his personal feelings, of a mission on
which a future civilization depends, and this acceptance requires the subjection of
his own will with all humility to the will of the gods. Aeneas' mission is everything,
its fulfillment ordained by destiny, and yet destiny does not relieve him of moral
responsibility for its fulfillment. Thus Virgil fills "a significant, a unique place, at the
end of the pre-Christian and at the beginning of the Christian world."

Mr. Eliot's description of the unique place which Virgil fills in the evolution of
Western culture seems to me invaluable for a proper understanding of the *Aeneid.*
But the occasional comments that he makes on the *Odyssey* in the course of de-
fining the spiritual qualities of the *Aeneid* give, I think, a wrong impression of
Homer's poem. His discussion of Aeneas as "an analogue and foreshadow of
Christian humility" is brilliant in itself, but when he tries to show the superiority
of Virgil's hero to Homer's heroes he misconceives or underestimates the character
of Odysseus and the part it must have played, consciously or not, in the Roman
poet's conception of Aeneas. The *Odyssey* presents through the experiences of its
hero the birth of personal and social ideals which are remarkably close to those of
the Christian tradition and repudiates the old code of the heroic warriors at Troy
as resolutely as does the *Aeneid.* In the *Odyssey* we can witness the origin and
evolution of values which made the Roman ideal possible. Aeneas could not have
been without Odysseus, and the drama of Odysseus lies in his struggle out of chaos
toward an order which we can still respect. The conflict between Aeneas and
Turnus in the final books of the *Aeneid* epitomizes the victory of the new hero, the
builder of a civilization, over the old—one might say obsolete—warrior hero with

From *Sewanee Review* 62, No. 3 (July–September 1954): 406–27.

his narrow tribal loyalties, his jealous personal honor, and his fierce passions, who is, whatever his motives, the foe of reason, order and civilization. Virgil, in Mr. W. F. Jackson Knight's words, "made the contrast between right reason and the dark instinct, as of Turnus devil-possessed, secure, and shewed the pitilessness, and the frightful havoc, of mass impulse, knowing it strangely well." (*Roman Vergil,* p. 135) Like Achilles, possessed with *ate,* Turnus fights for glory, while Aeneas fights for a future. Aeneas can only assume the burden of his great mission when he has renounced personal glory and desperate courage, which are the chief virtues of the old warriors of the *Iliad.* His victory over Turnus at the end of the poem is only possible because of his victory over the Turnus in himself at the beginning of the poem.

The *Odyssey* mediates between these two concepts of the hero—the old and the new. Odysseus grows in the course of his experiences from the shrewd "sacker of cities" to the wise restorer of Ithaca. His success at the end of the poem is not accidental, but founded just as surely as Aeneas' on the subjection of his angry or amorous passions to reason, on his recognition and acceptance of his divine mission, and on harmonizing his own will with the divine will. The gods of the *Iliad* may be, as Mr. Eliot claims, "as irresponsible, as much a prey to their passions, as devoid of public spirit and the sense of fair play, as the heroes," but the gods of the *Odyssey* are just and responsible, and the ideal of the poem is "a more civilized world of dignity, reason and order" like that of the *Aeneid.* Odysseus, admittedly, has a less impressive and consequential mission than Aeneas'. He is not destined to found a world which history shows is our own. But cannot rocky Ithaca be a type of that world? And cannot Odysseus be thought of as having demonstrated in the restoration of his little country virtues which anticipate Aeneas' as a founding father?

The distinction which Mr. Eliot draws between Aeneas and Odysseus in the following passage in my opinion badly misrepresents the meaning of the *Odyssey.* If Odysseus is the irresponsible and lucky hero he describes, the *Odyssey* is of little interest to us except as an adventure story:

> Aeneas is the antithesis, in important respects, of either Achilles or Odysseus. In so far as he is heroic, he is heroic as the original Displaced Person, the fugitive from a ruined city and an obliterated society, of which the few other survivors except his own band languish as slaves of the Greeks. He was not to have, like Ulysses, marvellous and exciting adventures with such occasional erotic episodes as left no canker on the conscience of the wayfarer. He was not to return at last to the remembered hearth-fire, to find an exemplary wife awaiting him, to be reunited to his son, his dog and his servants.

Since Mr. Eliot is only incidentally concerned with the *Odyssey,* and since his comment on Aeneas is so perceptive, the whole matter could well be ignored except for the fact that this misreading of the *Odyssey* is widely held and, I am convinced, blocks the way to one's full understanding and enjoyment of the poem.

Three or four years ago, in the course of studying Chapman's translation of the *Odyssey*, I found a remarkable and apparently little-known book which helped me to understand Chapman's approach while it illuminated the central themes of Homer's poem more fully and convincingly than anything else on the subject I have encountered. Denton J. Snider's *Homer's* Odyssey: *A Commentary*, published in 1895, is a brilliant demonstration of the spiritual evolution of Odysseus, the moral character of his universe, and the pre-eminence of freedom and moral responsibility throughout the poem:

> The theme . . . deals with the wise man, who, through his intelligence, was able to take Troy, but who has now another and greater problem—the return out of the grand estrangement caused by the Trojan expedition. Spiritual restoration is the key-note of the *Odyssey*, as it is that of all the great Books of Literature. (pp. 7–8)

Much of what I have to say about the *Odyssey* in the following pages is built upon or developed out of Snider's insights, and I hope that this discussion will send readers on to a unique work of Homeric criticism.

The history of criticism of the *Odyssey* from Hellenic times to the present reveals two principal and unreconciled positions. The allegorical interpreters such as Heraclitus,[1] Natalis Comes and Roger Ascham were impelled to defend the poem on ethical grounds by presenting Odysseus as a *persona* of reason, virtue, and endurance triumphing over enticements to lust, luxury, and greed. The allegorists concentrated on those adventures most susceptible of their sort of interpretation—especially the hero's encounter with Circe or with the Sirens. The fabulous experiences which Odysseus recounts in books nine to twelve were treated as if they were the whole poem, and those episodes in which the hero was least successful in dealing with temptations or obstacles to his return were either neglected or forced quite arbitrarily to reflect the preconceptions of the interpreters. In most of the allegorical accounts one finds a monotonous determination to demonstrate Odysseus' moral perfection on every occasion. Comes' popular compendium of mythology is typical of them all:

> Who then is Ulysses, if not Wisdom, which intrepidly passes through every danger unconquered? And who are Ulysses' companions but the passions of our hearts?

The allegorists' interest is centered on the *Odyssey* as a moral lesson, and the poem is ignored. They tended to find a simple identification of characters and objects with moral abstractions like wisdom, temperance, lust, and passion. The other school, which has prevailed in the last two hundred years, is "realistic" in its approach and refuses to see any ethical significance at all in Odysseus' career. The realists insist on the primitive nature of Homer's characters. Thomas Blackwell was among the first to propose the historical *apologia*, still current, that although Odysseus was a pirate, piracy was considered respectable in those benighted days: "living by Plunder gave a reputation for Spirit and Bravery." This view supposes that whatever the hero does is endorsed by the poet, just as the allegorical view does. Mr. Eliot's own strictures belong to this tradition, and he would, I suppose, approve of the position taken by Mr. C. S. Lewis:

> There is no pretence, indeed no possibility of pretending, that the world, or even Greece, would have been much altered if Odysseus had never got home at all. The poem is an adventure story. As far as greatness of subject goes, it is much closer to *Tom Jones* or *Ivanhoe* than to the *Aeneid* or the *Gierusa- lemme Liberata. (A Preface to* Paradise Lost, p. 26)

In the adventure story what happens to the hero is accidental, and the action is largely external. The interest lies in a series of hair-breadth escapes brought about by the hero's cleverness, stamina, and good luck. The *Odyssey* unquestionably provides this sort of interest, but that is not all.

The conception of the *Odyssey* as an adventure story is, I am convinced, as great an obstacle to understanding it as to see it simply as moral allegory. The first view removes it from serious consideration as one of the world's greatest poems; the second ignores its status as a poem altogether. A third view is required that will recognize the *Odyssey*'s great spiritual significance at the same time that it recog- nizes Odysseus as a complex and typically human character. Odysseus' vicissitudes are intimately related to his varying attitudes toward himself, his fellow man, and his gods. Odysseus' "mission" is the greatest known to man—to discover himself and his world and to act effectively in accordance with these discoveries. Such a view as this sees the goal of his return as more than a geographical one and recognizes both the established moral order of the *Odyssey*'s universe and the hero's gradual discovery of that order through suffering and error. If the *Odyssey* were as Hera- clitus or Comes or Lewis or Eliot represented it, the poem would not have the enduring hold on men's spirits that it has. A morally perfect hero excites no more sympathy than one whose adventures are amoral and therefore accidental and meaningless.

Primary Epic, in Mr. Lewis's terms, is distinguished from Secondary Epic by the absence of "the large national or cosmic subject of super-personal interest." "That kind of greatness," he continues, "arises only when some event can be held to effect a profound and more or less permanent change in the history of the world, as the founding of Rome did, or still more, the fall of man." (*A Preface to* Paradise Lost, p. 28) This distinction as to kinds is undoubtedly a valid one. But the historical consequence of the subject is relatively unimportant if the theme of the epic is typical and universal. Rocky Ithaca may be the type of Rome and Odysseus the prototype of Aeneas. The *Odyssey* has a great design, despite Mr. Lewis, and it cannot be described by "the mere endless up and down, the constant aimless alternations of glory and misery, which make up the terrible phenomenon called a Heroic Age," any more than it can by Mr. Eliot's conception of it as an alternation of marvellous and erotic adventures that leave the hero essentially unchanged.

The chief obstacle to understanding this revolutionary and evolutionary char-

acter of the *Odyssey* is the spareness of direct comment or abstract moral statement in the poem. Aeneas' destiny is stated in the invocation, and his moral
struggles are unmistakably presented in the encounter with Dido and the intervention of the gods, in his foolhardy last-ditch stand at Troy and the admonitory or
prophetic visions of Hector and Iulus, and in the similes which compare him and
his companions in their rage to ravening wolves and serpents. (See II, 370ff.) The
Odyssey never explicitly associates the hero's return with his moral and spiritual
stature in the way that the *Aeneid* identifies the founding of Rome with Aeneas'
pietas. Homer, furthermore, externalizes psychological and emotional developments in action. Odysseus is not introspective or reflective in the way that Aeneas is.

The best way I know to illustrate the ideas I have been discussing is to focus
on one of the great turning-points in Odysseus' career—his experiences from the
time of leaving Calypso in book five to the beginning of his narrative to the
Phaeacians in book nine. This passage introduces the hero after our curiosity about
him has been wrought to the highest pitch in the four books of the Telemachia, and
it marks his escape from the fabulous world in which he has wandered for ten years
since leaving Troy into what we may call the real world. This crisis in Odysseus' life
is announced by a council of gods in which Zeus gives orders that the hero is to be
released from the island of Calypso and permitted to sail for home. The divine
decision has its counterpart in Odysseus' own choice. Calypso offers him immortal
life with her, and he rejects the offer in favor of mortal life with Penelope:

> Great goddess, do not be angry with me for this. I know myself that wise
> Penelope cannot compare with you in beauty or figure, for she is mortal, you
> immortal and unaging. Nonetheless, day after day, I long to reach home and
> see the day of my return. And if some god strikes me on the wine-dark sea,
> I will take it, for I have a heart inured to affliction. In days gone by I have
> suffered and toiled greatly in the sea and in war; let this come too. (V, 215–24)

The divine machinery which sets Odysseus free through the agency of Hermes, as has often been noted, can stand for, or, perhaps more accurately, is
accompanied by, the hero's effective resolution to accept his human lot and leave
Calypso's paradise. For many years he has longed to depart, yet the intervention of
the gods at this moment is not simply a heavenly rescue party, a Euripidean *deus
ex machina.* The elementary resources needed to build and equip the raft have
been available on Calypso's island all the seven years Odysseus has been there.
What he lacked for a time was the courage to commit himself once more on the
deeps to the strenuous dangers attendant upon such a journey, a journey which,
Zeus specifies, must be made "with guidance neither of mortal men nor of gods."

The voyage to Phaeacia turns out to be the hardest of all. Odysseus' last
encounter with the wrath of Poseidon literally beats him to his knees and drives him
once and for all out of the attitude of cocky self-sufficiency which characterized him
earlier. The epithet *polutropos*—shifty and resourceful—does not carry unqualified

approval, especially when it applies to Odysseus' rugged individualism. The extremities Odysseus suffers after his raft is wrecked compel him to turn to the gods for help. The stages by which he is forced to this final resort dramatize the hero's characteristic reluctance to depend on anyone but himself. When the sea nymph Ino Leucothea out of pity offers him a miraculous veil, he suspects that "one of the immortals is once again weaving a snare for me in bidding me to leave my raft," and determines to cling to the wreckage as long as he can. He still thinks of the gods' hostility as purely arbitrary. A tremendous wave finally forces him to use the veil. But when, after two days and nights in the sea, he comes in sight of the Phaeacian shore, there is nothing but fatal reefs and cliffs beaten by a violent surf. When he tries to cling to rocks he is torn away by the waves and nearly drowned. At last he finds a river-mouth with a shelving beach and makes a spontaneous prayer to the river-god in the name of wanderers and suppliants, who are all sacred to Zeus. At this the river's current is calmed, Odysseus wades ashore, sinks down among the reeds and kisses the earth.

From this moment Odysseus encounters only human foes and human temptations. There are no more one-eyed giants or monstrous sea-goddesses or sorceresses who can turn men into pigs. Nor are there any further conflicts with nature—storms, shipwrecks, whirlpools, or threatening starvation. When he falls asleep in the olive-grove by the Phaeacian shore, the wrath of Poseidon is done with Odysseus, and he awakes into a world of purely human values. The change is marked by a striking simile at the very end of book five, when Odysseus sees the grove and feels an impulse of joy and relief:

> he lay down in the midst and heaped over him the fallen leaves. And as a man hides a brand beneath the dark embers in an outlying farm, a man who has no neighbors, and so saves the seed of fire that he may not have to kindle it at some other source, so Odysseus covered himself with leaves. And Athene shed sleep on his eyes that it might cover his lids and quickly free him from toilsome weariness. (V, 487–93)

The simile represents the hero's loneliness, exhaustion, and sense of relief as well as his striking capacity for self-preservation in any fatigue or danger. It suggests further than this that here is the essential Odysseus, the very spark of his spirit which no hardships have been able to quench. The realistic detail of the anxious farmer on his lonely farm emphasizes at this stage of the hero's experience the emergence of realistic human adventures.

The phase of supernatural dangers and of the hostility of physical nature which comes between the departure of Odysseus from Troy and his arrival in Phaeacia divides two vastly different human worlds: that of the Trojan war dominated by the heroic code of men and that of family and community life whose values are centered in several extraordinary women—Arete, Nausicaa, Penelope. The great importance of these women in the *Odyssey* has often been discussed. I need not refer the reader to Samuel Butler's facetious thesis that the *Odyssey* must have been written by a woman or to Bentley's remark that the *Iliad* was written for men and the *Odyssey* for women. It can be shown, I think, that the domestic and social values embodied in or emanating from these women act as a critique of the code of the male warrior just as much as the actions of Turnus or Nisus or Euryalus or of Aeneas on the night that Troy fell reveal Virgil's view of the inadequacy of the heroic code. The behavior of warriors is subjected to a searching and critical scrutiny in the *Odyssey,* although not by much direct comment. Its weaknesses are dramatized in Homer's characteristically subtle fashion. It is extremely significant, I think, that Odysseus enters the world of natural and supernatural disasters after committing an act of violence that becomes, because of the formulaic manner in which it is related, the typical crime of the *Odyssey.* In all his pseudo-autobiographies in the last books of the poem, Odysseus describes his troubles as having originated with a piratical raid against unwary townsmen in which the men were slain, the women and children taken as slaves, and a quantity of plunder carried off. In each case the leader is unable to control his men, who become drunken and careless, and an unexpected counterattack takes it toll of the invaders.

Odysseus' unprovoked attack on the town of Ismarus following his departure from ruined Troy is typical of the acts which cast him out of the world of men, if we except his followers, for ten years. This aggression, which, I am told, Grotius cites as the earliest recorded violation of international justice, is not mitigated in Homer by any mention of the Cicones' alliance with the Trojans. Odysseus relates it in laconic fashion at the beginning of book nine:

> From Ilios the wind bore me to the Cicones, to Ismarus. I sacked the city and slew the men, and from the city we took their wives and a store of treasure and divided them among us, so that as far as lay in me no man might go defrauded of an equal share. Then I gave orders that we should flee with all speed, but my men, in their folly, did not listen. (IX, 39–44)

Odysseus loses six men from each ship to the counter-attacking Cicones and is then driven into a world of fantastic terrors, which he describes for four books, by a twelve day's storm. He raises land at the Lotus-Eaters', but it is ten years before he sees a human being again, except for his own companions. In his twelve fabulous adventures with monsters, nymphs, demigods, sorceresses, and ghosts he some-times encounters, as Snider argues, the monstrous personifications of inhuman facets of his own nature, like Polyphemus and the Laestrygonians. In one way or another all these encounters jeopardize his human individuality, or at least that of his followers. His men who eat the lotus lose all memory of home, as he himself does when he hears the Sirens' song:

> Whosoever in ignorance draws near them and hears the Sirens' voices never returns to have his wife and little children stand at his side rejoicing; but the Sirens beguile him with their clear-toned song as they sit in a meadow, with

all about them a great heap of bones of mouldering men, and round the bones
the skin shrivelling. (XII, 41–46)

Circe transforms men into pigs who yet retain the same minds they had before. (Is
this satirical?) Calypso promises to make him immortal and ageless if he will only live
with her forever. But after seven years the delights of this naturalistic paradise have
palled to the extent that he is willing to endure any hardship in order to reach home
and Penelope. Odysseus' recognition at this point that his innermost identity is
inseparably bound up with his home and wife is the key to his escape from the
fantastic world, just as his unprovoked attack on society, as represented by Ismarus,
opened the door to his entrance into it.

The subject of the *Odyssey* is the return of Odysseus to his home and his
reunion with his family. Such a subject, as Chapman remarks in his preface, may
seem "jejune and fruitless enough." If, however, the hero can return home and
rejoin his family only in the course of discovering his proper relation to the gods
and to his fellow men, no greater subject could be imagined, for the familiar and
common situations in which these discoveries are made are an earnest that the
pursuit of *these* heroic ideals is the right and duty of all men and not the privilege
of any particular caste.

Mr. L. A. Post, in his recent book *From Homer to Menander,* makes this
point in general terms when he speaks of "new resources or a new attitude in
himself" which Odysseus must find "before he can win happiness." But I cannot
agree with Mr. Post when he says that after many years with Calypso on her
island Odysseus "has nothing new to learn. He must merely display his qualities
of craft and courage and restraint." It is true that Odysseus behaves with much
more self-control in the second half of the poem. The ordeals he undergoes as
a beggar appealing to the hospitality of his wife's suitors—the blows and insults
he must suffer without answering their violence—require a self-mastery that he
has not shown before. Epictetus and Plutarch found in Odysseus aspects of the
Stoic. But Homer's interest in his hero extends far beyond the Stoical qualities of
endurance and restraint to pursue the dynamic origins of these and other moral
virtues in the human spirit.

The chief importance of the Phaeacian experience lies in its dramatizing a
new attitude in Odysseus. His emergence from the supernatural world of Lotus
Eaters, Cyclopes, Circe, and Calypso has involved, as I have shown, a recognition
of the conditions of being human: mortality, limited power and wisdom, and the
need for divine assistance. Odysseus' ready acceptance by Alcinous, Arete, and
Nausicaa depends on his acceptance of their own social, religious, and political
ideal. Phaeacia has all the earmarks of an ideal civilization with just enough defects
to make the whole picture plausible. The Phaeacians are conspicuously peace-
loving. They do not use warfare and migrated long ago from a land beset by the
godless Cyclopes to this remote place. The gods, they say, are in the habit of
visiting them without disguise. They are charitable to strangers. They excel in the
arts of peace—in shipbuilding, sailing, spinning and weaving, and so forth. The

queen Arete is the real ruler of the kingdom and settles the disputes of her subjects to the invariable satisfaction of both parties. Odysseus kneels to her for permission to sail for Ithaca and by this action pays tribute to the domestic ideals which Arete stands for. Arete is, perhaps, almost impossibly wise and competent, but Nausicaa stands in the foreground as an extraordinarily real young girl. As Mr. Post says, "It is here that the climax of temptation comes for Odysseus. It is characteristic of Homer to make his good woman more tempting than any bad woman could be."

For Odysseus Nausicaa serves as an enchanting vision of the new ideal, just as fading Helen, with her ornamental distaff and her anodynes, provided Telemachus with a *fin de siècle* vision of the heroic past. Nausicaa appeals to Odysseus by virtue of qualities which make his surrender to her impossible: by her hospitality and charity and courage and deep loyalty to the civilized institutions to which he is now dedicated. In her consuming interest in marriage and in family and household affairs he may well see an image of his own wife. Thus he treats her with unwonted tact and restraint. His manner is a judicious mixture of the gallant and the paternal. With the immortal Circe and Calypso Odysseus had no age, but with Nausicaa he is a mature man. Much of the humor in their encounter stems from this discrepancy of ages which attracts them to each other and yet helps to keep them apart. His famous words on their first meeting, when he emerges so delightfully from the underbrush naked and holding an olive-branch modestly before him, set the tone of the whole episode:

> Show me the city and give me some rag to throw about me. . . . For thyself, may the gods grant thee all thy heart desires—a husband and a home and oneness of heart—great gifts. For nothing is finer than when husband and wife live in one house in one accord, a great grief to their foes and a joy to their friends. But they themselves know this best. (VI, 178–85)

This note is struck again in that exquisite farewell interlude in which Odysseus gently deflects Nausicca's growing love for him by pretending not to understand her Desdemona-like hints:

> Now when the maids had bathed him and rubbed him with oil and had cast a fine cloak and tunic about him, he came from the bath and went to join the men at their wine. Nausicaa, gifted with beauty by the gods, stood by the doorpost of the hall and watched Odysseus with wonder and spoke to him with winged words:
> "Farewell, stranger, and hereafter even in thine own native land remember me, for to me thou owest thy life."
> Then the wily Odysseus answered her:
> "Nausicaa, daughter of great-hearted Alcinous, may Zeus, the loud-thundering lord of Hera grant that I reach my home and see the day of my return. Then I will pray to thee as a god all my days, for thou, maiden, hast given me life." (VIII, 454–68)

If Odysseus' rejection of Calypso's offer of immortality was a rejection of a sort of eternal and monotonous existence approximating death, the endless cycle of instinctive gratifications which left the spirit unsatisfied, his rejection of Nausicaa represents, paradoxically enough, his acceptance of a way of life which is more than mere existence. He now sees his own identity bound up with Penelope's. Away from home he is not himself.

I do not think it is doing violence to this crucial phase of the *Odyssey* to see in the Phaeacian visit a sort of spiritual and ideological revolution in the hero. This involves his reorientation in regard to the dominant values of the poem—the domestic and social values of which I have been speaking. Nor do I think it extravagant to insist that these values which center on the family, on the pre-eminent virtue of hospitality, and on the just administration of the state are shown throughout the poem as superior to what might be loosely designated as the heroic values of the *Iliad.* (In saying this I do not mean to imply that Homer gives unqualified assent to these values in the *Iliad.*) What threatens these domestic values is the old ideal of military glory and honor as man's noblest goal—the individualistic quest for eternal fame in battle. The *Odyssey* never disdains true honor as such, and in the slaughter of the suitors it recognizes that the most extreme punitive measures may sometimes be needed to protect society, but it submits what passes for honor to a searching inspection and shows that heroic deeds are often motivated by greed, accomplished with terror, and indistinguishable from piracy. In this poem Odysseus' career evolves from one set of values toward the other, from the narrow concepts of heroic honor to the broader concepts of the civilized man in a post-war world. Odysseus is not given to introspection, and his change of view is presented in a series of episodes that are emblematic of inner developments. Of these there are three main kinds: (1) a divine visitation; (2) an unexpected emotional response; and (3) a speech in which the hero analyzes his experiences in a way that lets us see implications of which he is only partly aware.

After his first meeting with Nausicaa on the shores of Phaeacia Athene transforms Odysseus, we are told, into a handsome man with hyacinthine locks. He has just bathed in the stream where Nausicaa and her maids have been doing the washing to rinse away "the scurf of the unresting sea." This bath is a spiritual as well as physical cleansing, for

> Athene the daughter of Zeus made him taller to look upon the mightier, and from his head she made the locks flow like hyacinth flowers. Just as when a smith overlays silver with gold, a cunning workman whom Hephaestus and Athene have taught all manner of craft, and his work is full of grace, even so the goddess shed grace upon his head and shoulders. Then he went apart and sat down on the shore gleaming with beauty and grace ... (VI, 229–35)

The passage can of course be interpreted to some extent in purely naturalistic and psychological terms: Odysseus looks better after a bath and makes more of an impression on Nausicaa when duly washed and combed than did the uncouth and worn figure who emerged from the underbrush. But the fact that Athene is said to work this transformation is more than a mere *façon de parler,* for this is the first time, chronologically speaking, that she has had anything directly to do with her protégé in more than nine years. This miraculous change occurs at one other critical point in the poem, furthermore, and that is when Odysseus, having accomplished the destruction of the suitors and the purification of his halls, is transfigured before his meeting with Penelope. Both examples mark a rapprochement of the hero and his patroness, and the one under discussion signalizes Odysseus' reunion with all that Athene represents. It is important in this connection that Homer stresses Athene's role as patroness of domestic arts—that Arete and Penelope, for example, are said to be under her peculiar protection: "for Athene had given to them above all others skill in fair handiwork and an understanding heart" (VII, 110–11). It is even more important that the goddess of wisdom, whom the hero offended at Troy, gives at this point a particular mark of her favor.

Secondly, the fact that Homer has chosen Phaeacia as the setting for the hero's narration of what has happened to him in the last decade has more than structural significance. The peace-loving and hospitable Phaeacians who listen to his story serve as mute critics of his behavior. On the third day of his stay at Alcinous' court Odysseus asks the singer, Demodocus, to tell of his greatest exploit, the device of the wooden horse. There could be no more impressive build-up to revealing himself as the great "sacker of cities."

> "But come now, change thy theme and sing of the building of the wooden horse, which Epeius made with Athene's help, the horse which Odysseus once led up into the citadel as a thing of guile, when he had filled it with the men who sacked Ilios. If thou dost tell me this tale aright I will declare to all mankind that the god has with a willing heart granted thee the gift of divine song."
>   ... And he sang how the sons of the Achaeans poured forth from the horse, and leaving their hollow ambush, sacked the city. Of the others he sang how in various ways they wasted the high city, but of Odysseus, how he went like Ares to the house of Deiphobus together with godlike Menelaus. There it was, he said, that Odysseus braved the most terrible fight and in the end conquered by the aid of great-hearted Athene. (VIII, 492–98; 514–20)

Odysseus reacts in a totally unexpected manner to this account of his exploits. His pride in his heroic accomplishments is suddenly transformed into pity for his victims. The moment of self-revelation is presented in a remarkable simile:

> And as a woman wails and flings herself about her dead husband who has fallen before his city and his people, seeking to ward off the pitiless day from his city and his children; and as she clings to him shrieking while the enemy behind her strike her back and shoulders with their spears and lead her to captivity to bear toil and woe, while her cheeks are wasted with most pitiful grief, even so did tears of pity fall from Odysseus' eyes. (523–31)

The moment of compassion includes for the first time those heretofore excluded from compassion on the grounds of being the "enemy." Until this moment the formalism of war prevented Odysseus from recognizing and feeling the humanity of his foes. Perhaps the effective man of war cannot afford too much imaginative and sympathetic identification with his victims, and must often pay for his effectiveness as a soldier by seeing the enemy as an abstraction or by denying them human status. This is what Odysseus has done up to this moment, and now all the sympathies suppressed or denied flood back upon him. The brutal side of heroic action is suddenly revealed in the question which the simile dramatically presents: does not the warrior's code destroy more than it creates? The question is raised elsewhere in the poem—by the disintegration of post-war Ithacan society under the lawless instincts liberated by the absence of the ruler, by the most sympathetic representation of enslaved or alienated or displaced people like Eumaeus, and by other dramatic incidents, pathetic, like this one, or ironic, like the question Polyphemus addresses to the tiny warriors in his cave: "Are you travelling on business or do you wander at random over the sea like pirates who risk their lives to bring evil to men of other lands?"—to which Odysseus answers proudly that he and his men are the followers of Agamemnon, whose fame is the greatest under heaven because of the city he sacked and the great numbers of people he killed.

The judgments which the *Odyssey* makes on the hero's behavior must often occur in this form. A community or an individual incorporates certain values beside which Odysseus is implicitly judged. Peripheral or minor characters are more frequently praised or condemned. Zeus himself expresses loathing for Aegisthus, and his attitude is reflected in the words of right-thinking characters such as Nestor, Telemachus, and Menelaus. Explicit evaluations of this third kind applied to Odysseus are so rare that they carry extraordinary force. An outstanding example is Circe's rebuke when Odysseus has angrily expressed his intention of defending his men against Scylla by force:

> "Rash Man! Is thy heart still set on acts of war and on trouble? Wilt thou not yield even to the immortal gods? She is not mortal but an immortal bane, dreadful, sinister, fierce and not to be fought with. There is no defense; to flee from her is bravest." (XII, 116–20)

It is significant that Odysseus forgets this warning as he threads the straits and arms himself to the teeth without affecting the outcome. Circe's outburst exposes the excessive self-reliance which Odysseus must lose and does lose, as we have seen, before he is saved at Phaeacia from his long battle with the sea.

Even less frequent is the self-critical, introspective speech. In his autobiographical narrative. Odysseus does not consciously relate his behavior over the past ten years to any principles, moral or otherwise. We find in his account examples of unregulated pride, brutality, and lust among moments of vision and restraint, and they are defined as such by the religious, social, and political idyll of Phaeacia, as well as by the principle of contrast in the individual adventures. Though Odysseus never sums up with a *mea culpa*, he emerges from the telling at harmony with himself and with human, natural, and supernatural elements of his universe. The final stamp of approval on the rehabilitation he has undergone is given in his reunion with Athene in book thirteen. Here he meets his divine protectress undisguised and face-to-face for the first time since the fall of Troy. His words at this moment verge on the analytical, moral judgment:

> It is hard, goddess, for a mortal however wise to know thee, for thou changest thy shape at will. But this I know well—that long ago, while we were fighting at Troy, thou wast kind to me. But when we had sacked Priam's towering city, and had gone away in our ships, and a god had scattered the Achaeans, I have never seen thee since, daughter of Zeus, nor marked thee boarding my vessel to ward off sorrow from me. (XIII, 312–19)

One short step further and Odysseus would realize the connection between his past acts and the alienation of Athene. *We* realize it, but Homer prefers the dramatic to the analytical method.

This moment of reunion marks the beginning of Odysseus' role as judge and restorer of Ithaca. The goddess who left him when he sacked her shrine at Troy watches over him throughout the greatest of all his enterprises. Odysseus plays his part through most of the second half of the poem not as a king or a warrior but in the disguise of an abject old beggar. The significance of this disguise is almost inexhaustible. It enables him to test the charity of the suitors, and charity is one of the essential virtues in the world of the *Odyssey*. It suggests the fundamental weakness of all men and their dependence on their brothers. It dramatizes divine immanence in human affairs in accordance with the idea that the gods often take upon themselves the basest and poorest human shapes. It is a further demonstration that human worth is not graded according to rank or position or power. It represents the theme that all men are beggars, outcasts, and wanderers in some sense at one time or another, a theme that is traced through the fugitive Theoclymenus and such displaced persons as Eurycleia and Eumaeus. It is, finally, a test of Odysseus' own inner strength—his patience and self-restraint. As Odysseus experiences the insults and cruelties of some of the suitors and some of his own servants, as he witnesses from the depths of his own experience the blasphemous frivolity of Antinous and Eurymachus, he imposes on himself the hardest task of all for such a passionate and action-loving nature. He holds his peace and leaves the satisfaction of his cause to be determined by the gods. As the beggar who continually appeals to the suitors for alms in the name of Zeus, to whom strangers and refugees are sacred, and in the name of common humanity, which unites men in the experiences of hunger, vicissitude, and humiliation, he displays a courage more difficult for him and more valuable for civilization that he did in the wooden horse. When Ctesippus hits him with the cow's hoof, or Antinous throws a stool at him, he stands "firm as a rock . . . shaking his head in silence, and pondering evil in the deep of his heart." In the midst of these provocations to violence he remains just

and does all in his power to save some of the better men among the suitors by
appeals to their wisdom and sense of justice. Amphinomous has shown him charity,
and Odysseus' plea to him is the most explicit statement in the *Odyssey* of a moral
theme and at the same time Odysseus' clearest evaluation of his own experience:

> Of all things that breathe and move on the face of the earth there is none
> feebler than man. For he thinks that he will never suffer evil in time to come
> as long as the gods give him prosperity and his knees are strong; but when the
> blessed gods decree sorrow for him he bears it reluctantly with an enduring
> spirit, for our outlook on earth depends on the day to day fortunes which the
> father of gods and men brings upon us. For I too once prospered among men,
> but I did many wicked deeds, yielding to my strength and trusting in the power
> of my father and brothers. Therefore let no man ever be lawless, but let him
> keep silently whatever gifts the gods give. (XVIII, 130–42)

This shift from power, which is accidental, to the principle of justice, which is in the
reach of every man, marks the extraordinary moral revolution which occurs in the
Odyssey and in the character of its hero. Without this principle the best that life has
to offer is "the human and personal tragedy built up against the background of
meaningless flux," which C. S. Lewis wrongly finds in the *Odyssey* as well as the
Iliad. The power and excitement I find in the *Odyssey* stem in large measure from
its testimony to the birth of civilization in the emergence of charity and law and
order out of the flux of passion and aimless brutality.

If one thinks of the *Odyssey* as the rehabilitation of a veteran after a long and
terrible war in the course of which the justice of the cause has been betrayed, as
is so often the case, by the methods of the crusaders; if one sees the hero's long
voyage home as an exploration of his identity as man; if one feels that he cannot
arrive home in the profoundest sense until he has discovered the metaphysical
order of the human community, the deepest significance of this great poem will not,
I am convinced, be violated. The historical circumstances of Odysseus' situation are
so like ours that his restoration of the waste land within and outside him has the
deepest relevance for ourselves.

NOTES

[1]Author of *Allegoriae Homericae*, which apparently belongs to the Age of Augustus. Reprinted in
Leipzig (1910) as *Heracliti Quaestiones Homericae*.

G. E. Dimock, Jr.
THE NAME OF ODYSSEUS

"There is no way to stand firm on both feet and escape trouble."

—*Odyssey* 5.413–4

In a way, the whole problem is the *Odyssey* is for Odysseus to establish his identity. "After all, who knows who his father is?" says Telemachus in the first book. "My son, if he really ever existed," says Laertes in the last. To establish his identity Odysseus must live up to his name.

This is not a new idea. A nameless ancient commentator has puzzled editors by glossing *hēbēsas* in line 410 of the nineteenth book with *odyssamenos*. *Hēbēsas* means "when he has grown up," a meaning with which *odyssamenos* has nothing to do; but as we shall see, the scholiast means that for Odysseus to grow up, to achieve his full stature, will be for him to "odysseus"—to live up to the meaning of his name, whatever that may be.

"To odysseus" (*odyssasthai* in Greek) is usually said to mean "be wroth against," "hate," and to be connected with Latin *odisse*. Historically speaking, this may be true. For the *Odyssey*'s poetical purposes, however, the verb denotes a more general sort of hostility, which Homer is at pains to define. In the fifth book the nymph Ino explains it as "planting evils," without specifying what sort of hostility is in the mind of the planter. It is true that Poseidon, who happens to be the planter in this case, is angry; but Zeus, who also odysseuses Odysseus, is not. In the nineteenth book Odysseus' grandfather Autolycus indicates that it is not a question of anger; asked to name the baby, he replies,

"I have odysseused many in my time, up and down the wide world, men and women both; therefore let his name be Odysseus."

Now, all we know from the *Odyssey* about Autolycus' career is that he was the foremost liar and thief of his day. Most naturally, by "odysseusing many" he means

From *Hudson Review* 9, No. 1 (Spring 1956): 52–70.

that he has been the bane of many people's existence. The secret of his palpable success would seem to be that he has never given a sucker an even break, and he wants his grandson to be like him. In the career of Autolycus, and in the attitude which it implies, we are much closer to the *polytropon* "crafty" of the *Odyssey*'s first line, than to the *mēnin* "wrath" of the *Iliad*'s. So let us think no more of "wrath," which implies provocation and mental perturbation, but rather of a hand and mind against every man, by nature, or as a matter of policy. Autolycus' own name does not suggest "Lone Wolf" for nothing. These considerations, and others, lead me to think that in the *Odyssey odyssasthai* means essentially "to cause pain (*odynē*), and to be willing to do so." We need not draw the line between subjective and objective here, any more than we need do so in the case of the word "suffer." Where did Odysseus "suffer" the "woes" of the *Odyssey*'s fourth line: "on the high seas," or "in his heart"? Just as "suffer" brings to mind both the external and internal aspects of being a victim, so "odysseus" implies subjectively and objectively what it is to persecute. For what it is worth, the seven-odd instances of the verb outside the *Odyssey* show nothing inconsistent with this meaning.

Autolycus, then, we discover in the nineteenth book, intended Odysseus to be a causer of pain. He has been one all along, of course. Perhaps the most prominent fact about him is that more than any other man he was responsible for taking Troy; and what it means to sack a city, we know from the simile at the end of book eight. Odysseus

> wept as a woman weeps when she throws her arms around the body of her beloved husband, fallen in battle before his city and his comrades, fighting to save his town and his children from disaster. She has found him gasping in the throes of death; she clings to him and lifts her voice in lamentation. But the enemy come up and belabor her back and shoulders with spears, as they lead her off into slavery and a life of miserable toil, with her cheeks wasted by her pitiful grief.[1]

Less than a hundred lines later, at the beginning of his tale, Odysseus will say,

> "The same wind as wafted me from Ilium brought me to Ismarus, the city of the Cicones; I sacked the place and killed the men; their wives, together with much booty, we took out of the city and divided up."

As has been well observed, the Sack of Ismarus is the Sack of Troy in its predatory essentials, with the glamor stripped off. This attitude Odysseus will maintain to the end. "The cattle which the suitors have consumed," he says in the twenty-third book, "I will for the most part make up by raiding on my own; the Achaeans will give others." Perhaps worse than this, Odysseus' going to Troy caused Telemachus grievous mental suffering, wasted Penelope's nights in tears, and reduced Laertes, his father, to misery and squalor; his absence killed his mother, Antikleia.

So conceived, Odysseus is not an attractive character. In fact the poem implies a good deal of criticism of the Autolycan attitude. As Mr. H. N. Porter once pointed out to me, one of the first things we hear about the hero is his predilection for poisoned arrows. Athene, disguised as Mentes, tells Telemachus,

> He was on his way from Ephyre, where he had stayed with Ilus Mermerides—he went there in his fast ship to get a mortal poison to smear his bronze-tipped arrows with. Ilus wouldn't give it to him in fear of the eternal gods. But my father [Zeus?] gave him some. He was terribly fond of him."

Much better, one would think, for Autolycus to have adopted Eurycleia's suggestion of Polyaretus as a name for the baby: "He's our 'Answer to Prayer' (*polyarētos*)," she remarked as she put the child on his grandfather's lap. But Autolycus preferred a name that most would regard as ill-omened.

For in spite of the fact that Odysseus is so obviously a causer of pain, the name which Autolycus wished on him strikes one as ironical. Up to the nineteenth book, Odysseus has been referred to as odysseused rather than odysseusing: "Why do you odysseus him so, Zeus?" Athene asks, before the poem is well under way; Ino and Odysseus both say that Poseidon is odysseusing him; finally, as we read the Autolycus passage, we are aware that Odysseus has just told Penelope that Zeus and the Sun-god odysseused her husband. In the *Odyssey's* proem itself, the hero seems essentially the sufferer: he is the *polytropos* man, the Autolycan rogue who treats the world as his enemy, but who sacks Troy only to be driven far astray thereafter, and take a beating. In the process, we are told, he is to win his *psychē*, which means loosely his life, and more properly the image of life after the liver is gone—in other words something very like identity—but the whole business seems unpleasant, to say the least.

To understand the satisfaction involved in injuring and suffering and the connection between them, we must return to the nineteenth book and the scholiast's note. The giving of the name is coupled with the adventure in which Odysseus first lives up to it. *Hēbēsas* is in fact *odyssamenos*. "When he has grown up," the hero, as though undergoing an initiation, wins Autolycus' favor and recognition by going on a boar hunt; as causer of pain he kills the boar; as sufferer he is slashed by it, thus acquiring the scar important in identifying him later. The pain given and received results in joy:

> Autolycus and the sons of Autolycus
> Efficiently healed him and loaded him with presents;
> Rejoicing they dispatched him rejoicing to his beloved
> Ithaca. His father and his good mother
> Rejoiced at his return, and asked for each particular
> Of how he got his scar.

The suffering results from the doing, and is inseparable from it in the recognition and satisfaction produced by the exploit. Not simply "how he killed the boar" but "how he got his scar," is for Odysseus' parents the measure of their son.

To be Odysseus, then, is to adopt the attitude of the hunter of dangerous game: to deliberately expose one's self, but thereafter to take every advantage that the exposed position admits; the immediate purpose is injury, but the ultimate purpose is recognition and the sense of a great exploit. Odysseus killed a boar to win his name; he went to Troy to enlarge it; in order to keep it, he will presently kill 108 suitors in as cold blood as he can manage.

In the adventure with the Cyclops, Odysseus inflicts pain in order to identify himself, and in so doing challenges the hostility of the universe. Polyphemus' pain is obvious. Even Euripides could not have dwelt more explicitly than Homer on the boring of the red-hot stake into the great eyeball, the sizzling of the eye's fluid, and the crackling of its roots. By virtue of this deed of horror, Odysseus, until now *Outis* "nobody" as far as Polyphemus is concerned, puts himself in a position where he can tell the monster who he is, can cry his name aloud to the Cyclops' face. This cry of defiance is thought to be foolish of the wily Odysseus, no less by his crew than by the critics, but it is in reality, like the boar hunt, a case of deliberate self-exposure for the purpose of being somebody rather than nobody.

To blind the son of Poseidon, and then to defy him, is both to challenge nature to do her worst, and to demonstrate her ultimate impotence to crush human identity. It is challenging nature in the sense that the sailor does, every time he goes to sea. The hero's colonizing eye as he approaches the Cyclopes' island, the remark that they have no ships or shipwrights, the shipbuilding technique employed in blinding Polyphemus and the mention of axe, adze and auger, the tools which enabled Odysseus to leave Kalypso and set sail on his raft, all this sounds very much as though Odysseus' crime against Poseidon were the crime of all those who go down to the sea in ships. But Poseidon will not get his revenge. In the *Odyssey* navigation is a practical possibility; the elements are conquered. So to blind Polyphemus is to convict savage nature of impotence and blindness. She is indiscriminate in her blows. Her most hostile efforts, like the rocks thrown by Polyphemus, are as likely to wash the hero to safety as they are to drive him into danger. Thus the power of the elements does not render Odysseus' identity meaningless. Rather he makes sense, and the elements do not. This, I think, is the significance of the general assumption in the *Odyssey* that Poseidon will give Odysseus his bellyful of trouble before he reaches his home, but will not kill him.

Polyphemus and Poseidon, however, are more than the hostility of inanimate nature. There is no "inanimate nature" in Homer anyway. They prefigure all the overt savagery which the universe presents, human and divine. This savagery is as able to breach the conventions, hospitality and the rest, among the civilized suitors in Ithaca, or the hypercivilized Phaeacians (remember Euryalus), as it is among the cannibal Laestrygons, or among the Cyclopes. If Poseidon and Polyphemus are the hostile aspects of this world, it is not foolish for Odysseus to cry his name in defiance of them, and so be subject to Polyphemus' rock-slinging and his curse; or rather, the foolishness or good sense of the action is not the point. To pass from the darkness of the cave into the light, to pass from being "nobody" to having a name, is to be born. But to be born is to cast one's name in the teeth of a hostile universe; it is to incur the enmity of Poseidon. In such a world, what better name could be found than Odysseus, "Trouble"? ("Trouble" is perhaps as good a translation of Odysseus' name as any. When a character in a western movie says, "Just call me Trouble, stranger," we take him to be a hostile type who makes trouble for other people, and so presumably for himself also.)

That braving Polyphemus is being born is not my metaphor; it is Homer's. In the nineteenth book Odysseus hints to Penelope that her husband has undergone a birth somewhere overseas:

> He put in at Amnisus, where the cave of Eileithuia is, in a difficult harbor; he barely escaped the gales.

Eileithuia is goddess of childbirth. But in the nineteenth book this is merely a way of reminding us of the Polyphemus adventure and possibly of Kalypso as well. In the ninth book, as Polyphemus is in the act of rolling the stone from the mouth of the cave, we are told of his anguish for the second time. We already know how his eye hurts, but this time we hear that he is "travailing in pain"; ōdinōn odynēsi are the words used. Whether or not we hear in them the name of Odysseus, we should not fail to reflect that ōdinō means essentially "to be in labor of childbirth." We are born for trouble, the adventure of the Cyclops implies, yet to stay in the womb is to remain nobody. There is security of a sort in being nobody, but as the Cyclops promises, Nobody will be devoured in the end, though last of all.

For there are more insidious threats to identity in the *Odyssey* than those which Polyphemus represents, the dangers and sufferings consequent upon taking on the world as one's enemy. Trouble is difficult and dangerous, but it can lead to identity. Security, on the other hand, is inevitable oblivion. The narrative proper of the *Odyssey* begins as follows:

> By now all the others, as many as had escaped sheer destruction, were at home. Odysseus, alone of all, wanting his home and his wife, a queenly nymph held prisoner, Kalypso, divine goddess, in her hollow cave, begging him to be her husband.

This is the state of affairs which the fifth book will develop. He wants home and a wife. He has a cave and a goddess. Why do all the gods but one pity him for this? Odysseus has realized the tired soldier's or sailor's dream, an immortality of comfort and physical satisfaction, with no troubles. But Odysseus would rather die, as Athene says. Everybody sees this paradox and understands the flaw in this paradise: such an existence has no meaning. But it adds something, I think, to see life on Ogygia in terms of identity and nonentity. Kalypso is oblivion. Her name suggests cover and concealment, or engulfing; she lives "in the midst of the sea"—the middle of nowhere, as Hermes almost remarks—and the whole struggle of the fifth book, indeed of the entire poem, is not to be engulfed by that sea. When the third great wave of book five breaks over Odysseus' head, Homer's words are: *ton de mega kyma kalypsen*—"and the great wave engulfed him." If this wave had drowned him, it would have been a "vile death," surely, as Odysseus remarks at the beginning of the storm. Much better, he says, to have died where "the spears flew thickest" at Troy; then he would have had "recognition," *kleos*. People would know about him and his death. Odysseus does not wish he were back with Kalypso. Though she offered immortality, not death—an immortality of security and satisfaction in a charming cave—it is still an immortality of oblivion, of no *kleos,* of nonentity. Leaving Kalypso is very like leaving the perfect security and satisfaction of the womb; but, as the Cyclops reminds us, the womb is after all a deadly place. In the womb one has no identity, no existence worthy of a name. Nonentity and identity are in fact the poles between which the actors in the poem move. It is a choice between Scylla and Charybdis—to face deliberately certain trouble from the jaws of the six-headed goddess, or to be engulfed entirely by the maelstrom. One must odysseus and be odysseused, or else be kalypsoed.

Odysseus did not always live up to his name. There was one occasion when oblivion seemed almost preferable to trouble. His name seemed to have lost its magic. Hence his failure with the Laestrygonians, and the necessity of winning back his identity in the Circe episode.

While we remember Polyphemus ("Much-fame") in connection with Odysseus, we are very apt to forget Antiphates ("Against-renown"), the Laestrygonian king. In the Laestrygonian affair Odysseus himself avoids the encounter, and loses his whole fleet. In this, his least creditable adventure, he never makes his identity felt. The Laestrygonians don't know who he is, or care. Yet Odysseus survives. With poetic rather than nautical logic, he escapes by virtue of having left his ship in an exposed position, while the rest of the fleet trusts itself to the security of the fiord and is lost.

Odysseus in the land of the Laestrygonians is not the Odysseus whom we saw with the Cyclops, though in both cases he has to do with cannibal giants. Avoiding the encounter here is perhaps as sensible as avoiding the Planctae, but there are other reasons why Odysseus is not up to it. In the interim, as we have said, his name has lost its magic. "Trouble," intended to mean success, has seemed to be failure. Aeolus has listened with interest to the tale of prowess at Troy and has sent Odysseus on his way, insuring that he will have, for once, a remarkably painless trip. But in sight of the goal, trouble strikes. Aeolus, seeing in this a sign that heaven is inveterately hostile to Odysseus, banishes him from his sight. Such trouble means to Aeolus not identity, but oblivion. Odysseus himself has nearly reached a similar conclusion. Since leaving Troy he has sacked Ismarus in characteristically ruthless fashion and rejected the passive peace of Lotos-land. By handling the situation in a manner worthy of Autolycus, he has been able to cry his name in defiance of Polyphemus. He has come within sight of his home. He has done all this only to find his achievement undone at the first relaxation of his mistrustful watchfulness. Small wonder that success on these terms should seem impossible. As the winds sped Odysseus out of sight of Ithaca, "I debated," he says, "whether to leap from my ship and end it all in the sea" (embracing thus the "vile death" of the Kalypso episode), "or whether to bear my misery and remain among the living." He adopts a sort of compromise: "I endured and I remained: *kalypsamenos* I lay in my ship," he puts it, meaning that he had wrapped his head in his cloak. This is the Odysseus who fails to confront Antiphates.

After the discouragement of the Aeolus episode, it is natural that life's difficulties should appear as insuperable as the Laestrygonians; but Odysseus will find the courage to go on. After the Laestrygonian experience his depression is shared by his men. Two days they all lie in weariness and woe on Circe's beach. But against this sea of troubles Odysseus takes arms, a spear and a sword. As he once killed a boar, he now kills a stag. This puts heart in Odysseus' men: "dis-kalypsoed" (*ek de kalypsamenoi*) they revive. Odysseus now makes a remarkable speech:

> "Friends, we don't know where the darkness is, or where the dawn; where the sun that shines for mortals rises, or where it sets. Still let us quickly consider whether any resource can still be found. I for one don't think so."

The point, as Odysseus goes on to suggest, is whether they must indeed make themselves known and ask the inhabitants of the island for their route, perilous though it has proved to confront Polyphemus and Antiphates. In other words, shall they turn their backs on the comparative security of their present oblivion? Characteristically, this wider implication is stressed by a pun—a blatant pun which has been used before, in the Cyclops passage. "Whether any resource can still be found," sounds in Greek almost precisely like "Whether any of us is going to go on being nobody." "I for one don't think so," is Odysseus' comment. They have been "nobody" for some time, in fact ever since Aeolus refused to recognize their claims as human beings. This cannot go on, as the pun implies. The time has come when Odysseus must stand and be recognized.

Without taking account of the pun, critics have interpreted this passage as Odysseus at the end of his human resources, about to apply for divine aid. The moly plant, soon to be granted, becomes for them almost a symbol of grace. This is fair enough in its way. Identity in the *Odyssey* is in some sense a gift of the gods. But "from the gods who sit in grandeur, grace comes somehow violent."[2] Odysseus doesn't pray for grace; he exacts it, first by killing the stag and then by threatening Circe and forcing her to swear to do him no harm. Hermes, Autolycus' patron, puts him up to the threatening, but it is quite in accord with Odysseus' name and nature anyhow. We remember the oaths exacted from Helen and Kalypso. In the present instance Odysseus remains nobody, a denatured wolf or lion like Circe's other victims, until sword to throat, he makes her recognize him and speak his name. Prior to this, despite the introductory formula "he took my hand and spoke my name," Hermes had not named the hero; he only named his passive aspect, *O dystēne* "poor wretch." But with the gift of moly, "black at the root, but with a flower like milk," Hermes seems to restore the magic of the name of Odysseus. However black its first effects, it will ultimately flower with balm and solace. Though she "struck [him] with her rod and named" him, Circe gives Odysseus no name at all until the hero seems "like one eager to kill her"; once having recognized him as "Odysseus *polytropos*" however, she uses his name every chance she gets, four times with full titles: "Zeus-sprung son of Laertes, expedient Odysseus." By choosing to live up to his name with Circe, Odysseus restored its magic; he had to in order to get anywhere, and so to be anybody, at all.

For Odysseus to choose to pursue the path of his painful identity as he did on Circe's beach, is to win power over, and recognition from, that ambiguous daughter of Sun, the life-giver, and Ocean, the all-engulfing. It is also to accept pain as the only real basis of meaning in this life or the next. This is the secret of Teiresias.

To achieve the goal of recognition and identity, and to learn the secrets of the abyss, are equally to row upon the sea of trouble. This is the meaning of the apparently witless question, "What ship brought you to Ithaca, for I do not think you came on foot," and of Antikleia's first words to her son in the underworld:

> "My child, how did you come beneath the misty dark, alive as you are? It is hard for the living to get a sight of all this. For in between are great rivers and dreadful streams, first Ocean, which there is no way to cross on foot, if one does not have a well-built ship."

But with Aeolus the question arose, is such sea-faring endurable? To ask this question is "to enquire of Teiresias" (*Teiresiēs* in Homer); for Teiresias' name is the weariness of rowing. *"TEIReto d' andrōn thymos hyp' EIRESIĒS alegeinēs,"* Odysseus says of his crew after Aeolus denied them: *"Worn* was my men's spirit by the woeful *rowing."* To enquire of Teiresias is to ask the meaning of trouble.

This is why Odysseus is not so much interested in what the prophet has to say of the troubled future—"You seek homecoming sweet as honey, noble Odysseus; heaven will make it hard for you"—as he is in recognition, in the meaning of his own painful and pain-producing existence:

> "Doubtless the gods had all that in store for me. But tell me: I see here the shade of my dead mother; she sits in silence near the blood, and has not the strength to look her son in the face or speak to him. Tell me, lord, how might she recognize the man I am?"

His mother's recognition contains a blow. It was Odysseus' sweet nature, she says, that killed her. Thus it appears that even in his gentlest aspect, Odysseus gives pain. He is, after all, soft as well as hard. The predatory brooch, dog throttling fawn, pinned on him by Penelope as he left for Troy, is coupled with a second mark of identification, equally important: the shirt which gleamed on his body

> like the skin of a dried onion—so gentle it was to the touch, and at the same time bright, like the sun; many were the women who admired it.

Yet Odysseus' soft side can be as painful, or as fatal, as his hardness. The love, not the hate he inspired, killed the dog Argus and wasted Penelope's nights in tears. Antikleia recognized at least part of her son's nature by dying for the love of him.

Agamemnon, dead by no sweet nature, but rather by the treacherous hand of his wife, also recognizes Odysseus; despite Penelope's virtue, he had better not, Agamemnon thinks in contrast to Antikleia, tell his wife everything. Neither of these recognitions, neither the first, evoking the hero's sweetness, nor the second, calling upon his guile, can bring Odysseus much comfort as to the value of life as Trouble. Achilles on the other hand makes it clear that it is something to be alive at all, and furthermore his concern for his son's prowess reminds us that Telemachus too, promises to become a credit to his father. Still, neither simple existence, nor existence continued through a worthy son, is of the essence. Ajax' silence, though eloquently expressive of the power of Odysseus as injurer, is discouraging; but the climax of recognition is reached when Heracles, whose "seeming" is hell's own picture of hostile ferocity, but whose reality "dwells in bliss among the immortals," equates Odysseus to himself:

> "One look was enough to tell Heracles who I was, and he greeted me in mournful tones. 'Zeus-sprung son of Laertes, expedient Odysseus—unhappy man! So you too are working out some such miserable doom as I was slave to when the sun shone over my head. Son of Zeus though I was, unending troubles came my way . . . a master far beneath my rank . . . sent me down here to bring away the Hound of Hell. And under the guiding hands of Hermes and bright-eyed Athene, I did succeed in capturing him and I dragged him out of Hades realm.' "

Not just Heracles, but all these people (except Ajax) explicitly recognize Odysseus; still excepting Ajax, all but Antikleia, who appropriately calls him "my child," use Odysseus' full titles. Each sees him differently, and to a greater or less degree, truly. To all of them he means, in one way or another, pain. To Antikleia he is the pain of a lost child; Agamemnon connects him with the pain and betrayal that marriage may bring; Achilles is reminded of the ultimate pain of being dead, Ajax of wounded honor. Heracles sees in him the "unending troubles" of life under the sun. For the secret of life which Odysseus has come to the realms of the dead to discover is the necessity of pain, and its value. The generations of woman ("and each proclaimed her bringing-forth") may be for good or ill, involving Zeus or Poseidon indifferently. Man's fate may seem to be Tantalus' endless craving, never satisfied; or Sisyphus' endless striving, never successful; life's basis may even be Tityus' vultures, a great gnawing in a great belly, as Odysseus several times suggests (7.216–21; 15.343–4; 17.286–9; 18.53–4). Yet Minos continues to pass his judgments, and Orion to pursue his quarry. Heracles has his heavenly, as well as his hellish aspect—and so does Odysseus, "Trouble." Ajax feels only Odysseus' hellish side, but Heracles implies that a life of pain, given and received, snatches something from Death himself. This is the secret of Teiresias, the answer to the weariness of rowing. To know himself as Trouble, and to be so known by others, is the only way for Odysseus to possess his identity.

There is no human identity in other terms than pain. To escape Kalypso, Odysseus needs a ship (4.559–60, 5.16–7), and so must accept the weariness of rowing. To see life in any other way is to live in a dream-world, as the Cyclopes do, and the Phaeacians. To avoid trouble, the Phaeacians withdrew, we are told, from their ancestral conflict with the Cyclopes. The conflict is indeed ancestral, for the Cyclopes are as savage as the Phaeacians are civilized; but both are out of touch with reality. Polyphemus thinks he can act with impunity, "for we are much mightier than the gods," but he succumbs to Trouble in the shape of a clever "weakling" and a skin of wine. The Phaeacians on the contrary trust in their piety. Nausicaa thinks that no one could possibly come "bringing enmity, for we are dear to the gods." This she says of Odysseus, Enmity himself. To her, he is either an object of pity or a dream come true:

> "Doubtless she has picked up some castaway from his ship [she thinks of someone as remarking of her], a foreign man, since there is nobody like that nearby [or "those nearby are nobodies"], or else in answer to her hopes a god, long prayed-for (*polyarētos*), has come down from heaven to keep her all her days."

Eurycleia's "Polyaretus" fits Odysseus in the sense that his return to Ithaca in his hostile might is something to pray for, but he is not what Nausicaa would pray that he be. Nausicaa is victimized by her too trusting love for him, and his visit is ultimately disastrous for her people. The *Odyssey* has its dream-worlds, and, "near to the gods," Scheria is one of them. Its queen, "whose name is Prayed-for" (*Arētē d'onom' estin epōnymon*), suggests her antonym, Odysseus, who, the poem later tells us, might have been Polyaretus, but was not. "So let his name be Trouble" (*to d'Odysseus onom' estin epōnymon*), Autolycus will say in the nineteenth book.

Odysseus no more can exist in the dream-world of Alcinous and Arete, where woman rules man and rowing is no trouble, than he can with Kalypso. In a world without trouble love must be as little serious as the affair of Ares and Aphrodite. With Nausicaa there is no scope for the relationship which Odysseus describes to her:

> "There is nothing nobler or more admirable than when two people who see eye to eye keep house as man and wife, *confounding their enemies* and delighting their friends, as they themselves know better than anyone."

How can love be really felt, without pain? Therefore, after arriving exhausted, naked, and unknown on Scheria, Odysseus must somehow so impress the inhabitants that they will send him on his way, neither killing him as enemy nor overmuch befriending him and settling him down with Nausicaa. This he accomplishes primarily by means of his well-advertised Tale of Woe. It is received with mingled horror and fascination. Avid for its miseries the Phaeacians certainly are. This supports our impression that their dream-world, lacking pain, is human life *manqué*. On the other hand, after the smile of the woman led into captivity, it is easy to assume Phaeacian feelings of horror at Odysseus' brutal account of the Sack of Ismarus. The recognition accorded the tale is equivocal: "Phaeacians," Arete asks during the intermission, "what do you think of this man, his size and strength and wit?" A dubious answer is implied in Alcinous' polite comment:

> "O Odysseus, when we look at you we don't find you a bit like a liar and thief, [or "your *Outis* looks to us like a liar and thief"] such as the black earth produces in such far-flung numbers—thieves piling lie on lie, and where they get them all from nobody knows; your words are charming, there is good sense in them, and you tell your story as skillfully as a bard, the grim sufferings of yourself and all the Argives."

After all Odysseus has shown himself to be a pirate, and it is worth noting that Alcinous' remarks occur half-way through the story of the underworld, before the value of pain is established. But for the Phaeacians this is never established. Their rowing is without drudgery, for all their sea-faring. At the end of the table Alcinous will tell the guest he once thought of as a son-in-law that he is sure he will never come back. One doesn't quite know whether the Phaeacians are bestowing on Odysseus more wealth than he won at Troy in recognition of his exploits, or as an invitation to leave the country; for it was Odysseus' stated willingness to stay a year that brought forth Alcinous' remarks about liars and thieves. In Odysseus the Phaeacians enjoy Trouble vicariously, but ultimately dismiss him. We may be pretty sure that, for their "painless escorting of strangers," Poseidon's threat to "surround (*amphikalypsai*) their city with mountains" will come off. Just as he turned their ship to stone, he will bar them from the sea, and therefore from any chance of future identity. The price of no trouble is oblivion.

Teiresias implies three modes of pain: first, pain administered, like the slaying of the boar and stag, or the blinding of Polyphemus. Odysseus, Teiresias predicts, will kill the suitors. Second, there is the pain of the resisted impulse. Odysseus must restrain his predatory impulses when he comes upon the cattle of the Sun. Third, to plant the oar, the symbol of the weariness of rowing, among those "who do not know the sea, nor eat their food mixed with salt, nor know of red-prowed ships, nor balanced oars, which are a vessel's wings" is to introduce the idea of trouble to those who, like the Phaeacians, are not sufficiently aware of it. In establishing his identity, Odysseus must use these three modes of pain.

It is sufficiently clear how administering pain by killing the suitors and threatening their kinsmen with annihilation serves to establish Odysseus in Ithaca. The second mode is subtler. It would seem a denial of Odysseus' name for him to boggle at a little cattle-rustling. That he does so leads some to suppose that his adventures are intended to purge him of the brutalizing effects of the Trojan campaign and bring him home readjusted to civilian life. But the temptation of the cattle of the Sun is more like the temptation of the Lotos than like the Sack of

Ismarus. It is a temptation not to crime but to oblivion. To fall for it is the typical weakness of the "innocent" crew, as the proem suggests. Faced with the Planctae, the Reefs of Hard Knocks, they drop their oars. Knowing the mortal danger in eating the Sun's cattle, they do not know it thoroughly enough to forego the immediate satisfaction of eating when they are hungry. Forgetful of homecoming and identity itself, they eat. Of all that band only Odysseus can resist such impulses and hang on interminably, as he does clinging to the fig tree above Charybdis, refusing to drop and be comfortably engulfed.

Odysseus is a master of the delayed response, of the long way round, of the resisted impulse. That is the reason he is able to keep his identity intact. It is courting oblivion to rush blindly into love, as Nausicaa did, and as Penelope, even when reunited with her husband, did not. In Circe's bed, Odysseus would have become just another denatured wolf or lion, if he had not first with a show of hostility made sure of his integrity. As in love, so with eating. Man is a predatory animal; to eat he must kill; but he must know what he is doing. He must not, like the crew and the suitors, take life as a table spread before him, insufficiently aware of the presence of enemies.

He must not even take life as a song, though the episode of the Sirens suggests that this is the most irresistible of impulses. The Phaeacians are certainly not proof against it. Alcinous may think that the meaning of life's pain is that

> "the gods were responsible for that, weaving catastrophe into the pattern of events to make a song for future generations,"

but pain must be experienced, not just enjoyed as after-dinner entertainment. Therefore the Phaeacians are victimized by Odysseus' Tale of Woe. Odysseus on the other hand is proof against the Sirens and their singing of "all things that happen on this fruitful earth," just as he is against the Lotos and against Circe. He is steadfast in enduring Teiresias' second mode of pain, the pain of the resisted impulse.

"The steadfast," says a priest in *Murder in the Cathedral*, "can manipulate the greed and lust of others, the feeble is devoured by his own." This leads us from the second mode of pain to the third—introducing the idea of trouble to those insufficiently aware of it. Odysseus in his steadfastness knows the pain of the thirst for life, the danger it leads to, and the trouble involved in successfully gratifying it. He knows it so well ("he saw the cities of many men, and knew their mind"), that he can use this knowledge in manipulating others, for the purpose of getting himself recognized as Trouble. One picture of this is Odysseus in the underworld, sword in hand, controlling the access of the ghosts to the blood. Manipulating the Phaeacians chiefly through their itching ears, he introduces himself to them as Trouble, and wins survival and homecoming. In the second half of the poem, using his lying tales, his wife, and the good things of his house as bait, he maneuvers the upholders and the defilers of his household alike into a position where, bow in hand and arrow on string, like Heracles in the underworld, he can make himself really felt.

For Odysseus to establish his identity at home, manipulation is necessary, manipulation even of those who favor him. It is difficult to get people to accept pain. Even the suitors do not dispute that he was a good king; unfortunately this is not enough to maintain his position in Ithaca. He must get both his pleasant and his hostile aspect recognized at the same time. When they finally are, near the end of the last book, this is signalized by the curious salutation of Dolius, the last to join forces with him: *oule te kai mala chaire,* he says, "hail and rejoice!" But *oule* is an exceedingly rare word, and its auditory suggestions of *oulos* "baneful," and *oulē,* the famous scar, will be felt—something like "Bane and Weal!" For the scar which the boar gave him is in particular the mark of Odysseus as Trouble. Antikleia ("Opposed-to-fame"), in her recognition of her son in the underworld, did not seem to understand the scar's full meaning, but it is easy for Eurycleia ("Far-fame") to accept it. After touching the scar as she washed his feet,

> joy and pain seized upon Eurycleia at the same time; her eyes filled with tears, and the voice caught in her throat. Touching his chin she said to Odysseus: "Surely you are Odysseus, dear child—and I didn't know my master until I had felt all of him!"

Eurycleia knows both aspects. It is she who has to be restrained from howling in triumph over the dead suitors. Telemachus is not much of a problem either. "I am no god," Odysseus says, "Why do you think I am an immortal? No, I am your father, for whom you groan and suffer so much pain, accepting the insults of your fellows." Telemachus' difficulty is to determine whether Trouble is a miserable wretch in filthy rags or a very god for splendor. We have met this ambiguity before in the double nature of Heracles.

Penelope's recognition is harder to win. She knows Odysseus' soft garment, and her own hands pinned on him the badge of the dog and fawn; but the predatory side of him she cannot accept. Troy is to her not a great and necessary exploit, but something he merely "went to see," and for this she cannot forgive him. To her Troy is not a source of renown, but "Evil Ilium, not to be named." If Odysseus' manipulation, or his knowledge of the mind of man ever fails, it is with her. In their false-recognition scene, his riddle-name is *Aithōn,* the "blaze" which melts her (19.204–9) but which she cannot face (19.478). In spite of all the help her disguised husband can give her, she reacts to her dream of the eagle, Odysseus, killing her geese, the suitors, not by preparing for his "return," but by deciding, at last, to give him up for good. After the suitors are dead, and Odysseus has had his bath, she still holds out. Even the appeal to her desire as a woman, effective though it was with Kalypso, Nausicaa, and Circe, doesn't work; Odysseus, it appears, will have to sleep alone. In exasperation he asks who moved his bed. In spite of all he has done to make permanent their marriage and the symbol of it, he still cannot tell, he admits, "whether it still stands or whether by now someone has moved it elsewhere, and cut through the trunk of the olive." By this bed and by this exasperation she knows him; flinging her arms around his neck, "Odysseus, don't scold me," she cries, giving him his true name at last. Later, she will accept trouble in more detail. The "immeasurable toil" still to come, none other than the planting of Teiresias' oar, she elects to hear of immediately, though in the first book, after ten years, she could not bear to hear the bard singing of the return from Troy. In the end she takes delight in hearing "all the woes Zeus-sprung Odysseus inflicted on others, and all he himself toiled and suffered." She has accepted the meaning of the name of Odysseus.

Teiresias implied that to win identity one must administer pain, resist all impulses to ignore it, and plant the idea of it in the minds of others. Hence the curious behaviour of the hero in making himself known to Laertes. Checking his own tears and resisting the impulse to "kiss his father and embrace him, and tell him all, how he had come and was back at home," Odysseus instead teases the suffering old man with the pain of the loss of his son. This is the pain which killed Antikleia, but it now serves to make clear to Laertes and Odysseus what they mean to each other.

Laertes knows Odysseus by his scar, but also by some fruit trees, given to Odysseus as a boy, which the old man is still tending for him. There is something obviously fruitful in the pain of this relationship between father and son, and the sense of the boar-hunt exploit is there too, especially when later the old man delights to see "son and grandson vying in prowess" in the fight with the suitors' kinsmen. The fruitfulness of trouble has been hinted all along, particularly by the image of the olive. There is the double olive thicket which shelters the hero, naked and alone on Scheria; the green olive stake which puts out Polyphemus' eye; and notably the great olive trunk which makes one corner of Odysseus' bed. The recurrent phrase, *kaka phyteuein* "to plant evils," points to the same fruitfulness. Therefore we can be sure that the life of pain contemplated in the *Odyssey* is fruitful, not sadistic. The ultimate object is recognition and the sense of one's own existence, not the pain itself. The pain necessary to win recognition may be as slight as the show of anger to Penelope, or as great as the blinding of Polyphemus, but in some degree pain will be necessary. Nothing less than the death of 108 suitors (to say nothing of the faithless maids), and the readiness to kill the suitors' kinsmen, will get Odysseus recognized in Ithaca. Once recognition is achieved, however, pain is pointless. At the very end of the poem, Odysseus "swooping like an eagle" on the fleeing ranks of the suitors' adherents, "might have killed them all." Then, "Zeus-sprung son of Laertes, expedient Odysseus, stop!" Athene cries, ". . . lest Zeus be angry at you." The daughter of Zeus herself, as Circe and others have done before her, now hails Odysseus with the rolling epithets of his full titles. Killing beyond the point of this recognition would anger Zeus, would violate the nature of things. But has Zeus not been angry all along at the hero "who received so many buffets, once he had sacked the sacred citadel of Troy?" No. The universe is full of hostility, it includes Poseidon, but it is not ultimately hostile. Zeus has been showing Odysseus not anger, but a terrible fondness, to echo Athene's words quoted early in this paper.

It is thus that the *Odyssey* solves the problem of evil, which it raised at line 62 of the first book. "Excessive suffering," says Zeus, or words to that effect, "is due to folly." "So it is," replies Athene; "but what about Odysseus? Why do you odysseus him so, Zeus?" It is a good question; Zeus admits that Odysseus is the wisest of mankind; yet he permits Poseidon to persecute him. It is a good question, and it contains its own answer. In exposing Odysseus to Poseidon, in allowing him to do and suffer, Zeus is odysseusing Odysseus, giving him his identity. In accepting the implications of his name, Trouble, Odysseus establishes his identity in harmony with the nature of things. In the ultimate sense he is "Zeus-sprung," one whose existence is rooted in life itself.

NOTES

[1] This quotation is from E. V. Rieu's excellent translation. So, in whole or in part, are many of the passages which follow.

[2] Aeschylus, *Agamemnon* 182–3 (Lattimore's translation).

Hugh Kenner

HOMER AND HAMLET

... Couldn't you do the Yeats touch?
He went on and down, mopping, chanting with waving graceful
arms:—The most beautiful book that has come out of our country in
my time. One thinks of Homer.   *Ulysses* (U213/207)[1]

Ukalepe. Loathers' Leave. Had Days. Nemo in Patria. The Luncher
Out. Skilly and Carubdish. A Wondering Wreck. From the Mermaids'
Tavern. Bullyfamous. Naughtsycalves. Mother of Misery. Walpurgas
Nackt.   *Finnegans Wake,* 229.

The myths endure. In years of exile from Ithaca, observing many cities—Paris,
London, Trieste, Pola, Rome, Zurich—enduring troubles and hardships in the struggle to save fellow-citizens who were determined to perish of their own madness,
Joyce could not have failed to see his own plight and that of Ulysses repeated in the
situation of any man of good will in Dublin. Ulysses had been his favourite hero in
a classroom essay of his Belvedere schooldays; he had thought of writing a story,
"Ulysses", about the wanderings of a citizen named Hunter, for the *Dubliners* series
but the project "never got any forrarder than the title"; at another time he had
intended to call the collection of stories *Ulysses at Dublin,* and even accumulated
some Homeric parallels, but he lost interest in what was proving a none too
satisfactory structural device half way through the writing of a book that was
assuming what we have seen to be a compulsive unity of its own.[2] His homage to
the *Odyssey* was not to be performed for another ten years, though he had
vaguely realized from the time he completed *Chamber Music* that the *Odyssey*
held the clue to much of his job.

His error in starting to hang the stories in *Dubliners* from a string of incidents

From *Dublin's Joyce* (London: Chatto & Windus; Bloomington: Indiana University Press, 1956), pp.
179–97.

in Homer had been to suppose that the *Odyssey* was a book to be *used*. Its function was to give him, the writer, a scaffolding. He was building (was he not?) an ordered book out of chaos, and needed a plan. It was only after the image of artist as imposer of order, lawgiver to his limp materials, had been lived to the dregs and discarded (*Exiles*) that he could understand with his whole mind how Homer could control the *treatment* of Dublin material because it illuminated the *subject;* because there was a subject to illuminate, not just a jumble of impressions. *Dubliners* was saved by Joyce's willingness to abandon a contrived order the moment he realized that he understood it only as contrivance; *Ulysses* was made a monument and a triumph through his determination to stay with the idea of a Homeric parallel until he saw why it had been right.

For it had been a sound intuition. Homer afforded a situation through which Joyce could control the whole of Dublin's daylight life. It is to this situation that the title of *Ulysses* points; to the situation the elaborate paralleling of incidents and characters is firmly subordinated.

This has never been gotten into focus. The most qualified readers have been put off by a misleading critical tradition. *Ulysses* is habitually regarded as a photograph of Dublin, 1904. Homer's world is somewhere else, in another book; and it is with the greatest impatience that one remarks Joyce or his exegete Mr. Gilbert making incidents tally off. To accustom ourselves to the idea that the Homeric situation—Homer's world—is *in Joyce's text,* because Joyce found it in Dublin, we may consider the implications of one of his letters to Harriet Weaver: T. S. Eliot had just written, "Instead of narrative method, we may now use the mythological method.... It has the importance of a scientific discovery."[3]

> I suppose you have seen Mr. Eliot's article in *The Dial.* I like it and it comes opportunely. I shall suggest to him when I write to thank him that in alluding to it elsewhere he use or coin some short phrase, two or three words, such as the one he used in speaking to me, "two plane". Mr. Larbaud gave the reading public about six months ago the phrase "interior monologue" (that is, in *Ulysses*). Now they want a new phrase. They cannot manage more than one such phrase every six months—not for lack of intelligence but because they are in a hurry.[4]

The subsequent history of *Ulysses* criticism consists in the fact that the requisite phrase—"double-writing", perhaps—was never coined, nor put in circulation. So the public and their middlemen moved only as far as "interior monologue", and stuck fast. The Homeric substructure has been either haggled over in detail, or brushed aside as a nuisance, by readers settling down, cutlery in hand, to a slab of bleeding realism. That the fundamental correspondence is not between incident and incident, but between situation and situation, has never gotten into the critical tradition.

Joyce is exploring a situation full of quite serious analogies with the Homeric situation. The action of *Ulysses* is an action of emerging intelligibility, progressive epiphanization, to which the doings and details of the characters are subservient. The main situations—the intelligible forms—of the two books coincide. The details are freely disposed, never without point. Joyce doesn't even confine himself to the corresponding Homeric episode for materials; for the Sirens, for instance (Homer's Book X) he borrows the singing minstrel from Book VIII.

The Situation

The basic analogies are clear enough by the end of the first episode. Ireland is the kingdom usurped. It is usurped by Buck Mulligan, as stage Irishman vis-à-vis the autochthonous wit of Simon Dedalus' now ageing and dying generation, and as priest of the body vis-à-vis folk wisdom (the milk-woman) and spiritual order (the artist and the priest of God). No. 7 Eccles Street, correspondingly, is usurped by the merry adulterer, Blazes Boylan. The avenger, the dispossessed paternal principle, point d'appui of hierarchic order, has been absent, tossed about by the sea-god (Ireland's difficulties in Joyce's generation were in part due to the long struggle with the politics and commerce guaranteed by English sea-power). Odysseus' enemy is Poseidon; the Poseidon of *Ulysses* is the *dio boia* presiding over the sea of matter in which Bloom is tossed all day, nearly submerged, clinging to enthymemic planks and clambering onto occasional treacherous rocks or into situations (the newspaper office, the tavern, the lunch-house) that merely delay and betray. The quest for the father is the quest for the masculine and rational, of which Bloom is a paradigm at one level, though hopelessly inadequate on several others.

The detailed correspondences are largely comic—Mr. Bloom's "knockmedown cigar" brandished, like Odysseus' sharpened and heated club, in the Cyclops' face; Nausicaa's cartful of laundry and Gerty MacDowell's airing and blueing of her "four dinky sets" of undies; Corley recommended to apply for the master's job in Deasy's school, and Melanthius castrated for dog-meat.

The larger correspondences are more usually serious, in the sense that they recognize Homer's registration of a permanent mode. Navel-gazing in a bath-tub *is* Lotus-eating. They are two metaphors for one psychological state. Aeolus the wind-god makes an apt counterpart for the journalist, and it is the sort of figure that illuminates wherever explored. (Compare Bacon's way of exposing, in *The Wisdom of the Ancients,* the configurations of Elizabethan polity in classical myths.)

Finally, Homer is constantly employed in a critical mode. He provides a measure of what the Dubliners *don't* do. The new Penelope isn't faithful, Telemachus doesn't refuse to cast out his mother for fear of being haunted by her curses, Nausicaa's father isn't a king but a drunkard and she doesn't take Ulysses home with her, and so on. Both Mr. E. B. Burgum's statement that "it is not simply a parallel but a parallel in reverse—the opposite of everything that happens in *Ulysses* happens in the *Odyssey*"[5] (Dublin unequivocally inverting an ideal order) and Mr. Stuart Gilbert's timid acknowledgment that Bloom "is no servile replica of his Homeric prototype, for he has a cat instead of a dog, and a daughter instead of a son"[6] (Joyce playfully altering a few trifles in the interests of variety) deflect attention from the fundamental seriousness with which the main analogies are to be regarded. The variations exist within a norm; they are neither capricious nor mechanical. The awakening of Telemachus at the opening of Homer's Book II ("He dressed himself, slung a sharp sword over his shoulder, strapt a stout pair of boots on his lissom feet, and came forth from the chamber like a young god")[7] reminds us that Stephen has his ashplant, Mulligan's castoff shoes, and his weary walk: an ineffectual artist, a comically inadequate Telemachus, but reduced to a plight that genuinely images the status of the arts in our time. When these perspectives are grasped, the numerous corroborative details such as Antinous Mulligan sponging "twopence for a pint" from Telemachus, the only person in the tower with any money, drop into place as echoes of a situational correspondence, not as a structure of links on the accretion and cohesion of which the entire parallel depends.

Many Dimensions

It is impossible to draw a reliable map. Joyce uses and reuses the same Homeric material at various levels. At the end of Book IV of the *Odyssey* we read about Telemachus' enemies:

> But the plotters embarked and sailed over the waters, with foul murder in their hearts for Telemachus. There is a rocky islet between Ithaca and the cliffs of Samos, quite a small one, called Asteris, and harbours in it for ships on both sides; there they lay in wait for him.

The primary correspondence is with Stephen's appointment to meet Mulligan, Haines, & Co. in a significantly-named tavern: "—The Ship, Buck Mulligan cried. Half twelve", U24/20. If Stephen had not evaded this ambush, as he did by sending a mocking telegram, U197/188, he would have been relieved of his money, gotten drunk by early afternoon, and (for what the encounter is worth) never met Bloom. That is one part of Joyce's use of the Homeric passage. At the end of his Telemachia (Part I), however, he uses it again in another mode (it occurs at the end of the Telemachia of the *Odyssey*). Stephen is about to leave the beach:

> He turned his face over a shoulder, rere regardant. Moving through the air high spars of a threemaster, her sails brailed up on the crosstrees, homing, upstream, silently moving, a silent ship. U51/47.

This is, as we later discover, "the threemaster Rosevean from Bridgwater with bricks", U609/587. It is part of the pattern of usurpation; it comes from the usurping land, bringing yet more matter to obliterate the soul of Dublin. *This* ambush is not to be evaded; the bricks are discharged, the bricks will constitute yet another patch of ignobility on the betrayed realm. And there is yet another parallel: with the ship that brought Telemachus' father back to Ithaca. The *Rosevean* bears W. B. Murphy,

Ulysses Pseudangelos, the garrulous sailor of the cabman's shelter, to his native shore.

At no time is Joyce crossing off common factors as he disposes of them. In the Proteus section, for instance, the principal perspective comes from Homer's characterization of Proteus as a source of universal information: hence "signatures of all things I am here to read", and the philological art of reading the Book of Nature in search of clues to the intelligible order abolished after Eden. (Telemachus went to Lacedaemon to seek clues to the whereabouts of his father; the missing father, Ulysses, is at one level God, at another the rational principle of social, aesthetic, and philosophical order.) The binding of Proteus as accomplished by the artist compels intelligible form out of the flux of things: "He will turn into all sorts of shapes to try you, into all the creatures that live and move upon the earth, into water, into blazing fire; but you must hold him fast and press him all the harder": the intense contemplation by which the epiphanic insight is wrested. Telemachus doesn't wrestle with Proteus, nor in any significant sense does the egocentric Stephen; his skirmish with appearances does yield an enigmatic poem,

> On swift sail flaming
> From storm and south
> He comes, pale vampire,
> Mouth to my mouth.   U131/123.

—which images the return of the father who will take revenge on him (for his adoption of a feminine role of egocentric pathos) rather than on the suitors.

As usual, Joyce employs the Homeric episode at many levels. The wrestler with Proteus in the *Odyssey* is Menelaus, who finds out from him how to get home, what has happened to his companions, and the nature of his own end. The Dublin Menelaus is Kevin Egan, like his prototype a cuckolded exile, whose tales of the revolutionary movement—"Of lost leaders, the betrayed, wild escapes. Disguises, clutched at, gone, not here"—imply that he has been engaged in furthering, not binding, the Protean (in the absence of coherent principles, political activity in Ireland increased rather than dissipated confusion). Egan, a Menelaus in reverse, has helped unbind Proteus, cannot get home, knows the fate of his companions as he knows nothing else ("How the head centre got away, authentic version", U44/40) and already inhabits a mockery of the "Elysian plain at the end of the earth where golden-headed Rhadamanthys dwells ... for you are Helen's husband."—"Loveless, landless, wifeless. She is quite nicey comfy without her outcast man, madame, in rue Gît-le-Coeur, canary and two buck lodgers." Proteus' prophecy to Menelaus is fused with Tiresias' to Odysseus in Stephen's reflections on "sea-death, mildest of all deaths known to man." Odysseus went to Hades to see Tiresias, and Bloom is at this moment in the cemetery; but a Tiresias is the one Homeric figure he does not meet there. No external wisdom guides him. As his mutations of sex in Circe's palace imply, he is Tiresias himself, an Eliotic Tiresias foresuffering all.

Bloom's relations with Odysseus are complex. In the second book of the *Odyssey* the soothsayer rehearses his prediction, that the hero will wander 19 years, that all his companions will be lost, and that no one will know him on his homecoming. Bloom's day lasts 19 hours, the litany of his lost comrades—"Martin Cunningham (in bed), Jack Power (in bed), Simon Dedalus (in bed)... Paddy Dignam (in the grave)"—resounds at the end of the day, U689/665, and his adopted son knows him not. Odysseus, as Zeus acknowledged, is the wisest man alive; Bloom is the incarnation of contemporary lore and know-how. But Odysseus is thwarted by the sea-god Poseidon because he blinded the Cyclops. Bloom, analogously, is a wandering Jew because of his role in the denial of Christ. (His unintentional pretensions as secular Messiah—blinding of Cyclops—enrage the eponymous Citizen, U339/329.) The curse God has laid on the Jewish people, according to Jacques Maritain, is immersion in matter: the correlative of their very efficiency in practical affairs. The equation of the sea with matter is one of the master keys in the analogical structure of *Ulysses*.

As Odysseus leaves the island of Calypso, Poseidon lashes the waves in a furious tempest. In the Calypso episode of *Ulysses,* the storm is reduced to a little cloud covering the sun, but the effect on Bloom is not less marked: his mind turns to the Dead Sea, he thinks "No wind would lift those waves, grey metal, poisonous foggy waters.... Grey horror seared his flesh", U61/54 This evocation of the Dead Sea, the Cities of the Plain, utter exhausted sterility, is both a counterpoint to Poseidon's bracing tempest and an epiphany of the plight of Dublin, a sea-evocation proper to the sea in which the modern Ulysses is cast adrift.

It is unnecessary to heap up detailed parallels for the reader who can extract them from the text or from Mr. Gilbert's commentary; our object is to indicate their multivalent modes of functioning. Sometimes they are jokes: in line with Joyce's Aeolus symbolism, we find Odysseus satisfying Aeolus' thirst for news with a full account of what happened in Troy. Sometimes they are comic inversions: Penelope recognizes Ulysses by the secret of the marvellous bed's construction, but the secret of Bloom's bed is known to all Dublin—it jingles. Sometimes they are correspondences of fact inflected with a pathetic divergence of intention: Odysseus the disguised returned avenger takes pleasure in Penelope's behaviour, "to see how she attracted their gifts, while she wheedled them with soft words and had quite other thoughts in her mind", while Bloom's pathetic pride in Molly's charms for other men (he displays her picture at any opportunity, U636/614) somehow assuages the fact that whatever other thoughts she has in her mind they are not of him. Sometimes they are bits of symbolic opportunism; Odysseus when young was wounded in the thigh by a boar, which image, with its Freudian overtones of castration complex, is applied to Shakespeare (another Ulysses avatar) by Stephen, U194/185, and has obvious relevance as well to Bloom's unprotesting effeminacy. Sometimes, finally, they are structural: as Homer, for instance, has the story retold in Hades from the viewpoint of the suitors, Joyce retells it, in analogous coda, from that of Penelope.

The Character of Ulysses

Butcher and Lang's *Odyssey*, not only "not Homer" but not even "a very pretty poem", registers the Odysseus whom representative nineteenth-century minds perceived in the Greek: a sort of Tennysonian Arthur, "ideal manhood clothed in real man." Every translation is a contemporary poem, and the contemporary poets of that age were Tennyson and, say, Lewis Carroll. So the Victorian Ulysses is an important part of Joyce's subject-matter.

It is useful to think of Joyce as a sort of twentieth-century Homeric translator, at least to get one's lines of sight pegged down. A twentieth-century perspective on Odysseus is given by Mr. Pound—no irreverent Homerist, as Canto I and the opening of Canto XLVII testify—in his correspondence with Dr. W. H. D. Rouse concerning that scholar's remarkable translation:

> As to character of Odysseus. Anything but the bright little Rollo of Chamber's Journal brought up on Sam Smiles. Born un po' misero, don't want to go to war, little runt who finally has to do all the hard work, gets all Don Juan's chances with the ladies and can't really enjoy 'em. Circe, Calypso, Nausicaa. Always some fly in the ointment, last to volunteer on stiff jobs.[8]

This Odysseus resembles a demi-god much less than he resembles the irreducible ethical structure of Mr. Bloom:

> Decent quiet man he is. I often saw him in here and I never once saw him, you know, over the line.
> —God Almighty couldn't make him drunk, Nosey Flynn said firmly. Slips off when the fun gets too hot. Didn't you see him look at his watch? Ah, you weren't there. If you ask him to have a drink first thing he does he outs with the watch to see what he ought to imbibe. Declare to God he does.
> —There are some like that, Davy Byrne said. He's a safe man, I'd say.
> —He's not too bad, Nosey Flynn said, snuffling it up. He has been known to put his hand down too to help a fellow. Give the devil his due. O, Bloom has his good points.... U175/166.

Thus the Bloomesque *ethos;* it is in the mode of *pathos* that Mr. Bloom is un-Homeric, that he exhibits a sordid shapelessness that *is* continuous with the poetic world of Butcher and Lang. Bloom combines permanent virtues with a nineteenth-century sensibility.

Here, for comparison with Mr. Pound's, is Joyce's image of Odysseus (the interlocutor is Frank Budgen):

> "Your complete man in literature is, I suppose Ulysses?"
> "Yes," said Joyce.... "Ulysses is son to Laertes, but he is father to Telemachus, husband to Penelope, lover of Calypso, companion in arms of the Greek warriors around Troy and King of Ithaca. He was subjected to many trials, but with wisdom and courage came through them all. Don't forget that he was a

war dodger who tried to evade military service by simulating madness. He might never have taken up arms and gone to Troy, but the Greek recruiting sergeant was too clever for him.... But once at war the conscientious objector became a jusqu'auboutist. When the others wanted to abandon the siege he insisted on staying till Troy should fall."

I laughed at Ulysses as a leadswinger and Joyce continued:

"Another thing, the history of Ulysses did not come to an end when the Trojan war was over. It began just when the other Greek heroes went back to live the rest of their lives in peace. And then"—Joyce laughed—"he was the first gentleman in Europe. When he advanced, naked, to meet the young princess he hid from her maidenly eyes the parts that mattered of his brine-soaked, barnacle-encrusted body. He was an inventor too. The tank is his creation. Wooden horse or iron box—it doesn't matter. They are both shells containing armed warriors."[9]

Joyce, it is evident, had no difficulty in evading the nineteenth-century illusion of the Achaean hero's inviolable grandeur. That there is an impassable gulf of 3,000 years between Bloom and Odysseus is the error of a reader who has had the *Odyssey* served up to him as something archaic and alien, invested with the glamours of an infinite remove: the Greek Dream. Joyce placed in his text, as point of reference, a reader precisely so blinded; Buck Mulligan, for whom poetry means "Swinburne", hankers after "the Attic note. The note of Swinburne, of all poets, the white death and the ruddy birth." In 1920, when about half of *Ulysses* had appeared in *The Little Review,* Mr. Eliot wrote,

We need a digestion which can assimilate both Homer and Flaubert.... We need an eye which can see the past in its place with its definite differences from the present, and yet so lively that it shall be as present to us as the present. This is the creative eye....[10]

Homeric Exegesis

"My Ulysses," Joyce told Frank Budgen, "is a complete man as well—a good man. At any rate, that is what I intend that he shall be."

Joyce's habitual Aquinatian view of evil as privation opens into less formularized issues. Both Bloom and Odysseus contain all the natural virtues in some sort of laudable balance (much of Bloom's ignobility is a function of the ignoble materials with which his prudence, charity, temperance, fortitude, justice, etc. are engaged). There is a sort of decorum, furthermore, in both men's ready perception of the applicable means and stratagems for every situation. It is as gadgeteer that Bloom fulfils the nineteenth-century epithet, "man of many devices" ("He was an inventor too," Joyce slyly remarked of Ulysses). In his public actions Bloom fulfils Dr. Rouse's translation of the same epithet, quite literally "never at a loss": unhesitatingly adaptable to such varied demands as guiding the blind stripling through traffic, helping to arrange the speedy payment of Mrs. Dignam's insurance, or rescuing Stephen from Nighttown, with admirably unselfconscious tenacity and prudence. It is only in the managing of his interior life that his gestures become absurd. Lenehan's tribute isn't at all ironical:

> —He's a cultured allroundman, Bloom is, he said seriously. He's not one of your common or garden ... you know. ... There's a touch of the artist about old Bloom. U231/222.

Homer was the educator of Greece primarily because his poems provided a lexicon of states of moral and emotion being, and of modes of prudence in exemplary action. Respect for the completeness of Odysseus' paradigm of civic and domestic prudence is echoed by commentators of almost every generation from the age of Plato to that of Pope. Pope's preface to the *Odyssey* throws valuable light on the continuity of this tradition: he remarks, quite in the mediaeval way, on Homer's competence as historian, antiquary, divine, and professor of the arts and sciences.

The analogy with Joyce's arts, symbols, and bodily organs is obvious. *Ulysses* is an epic in the Renaissance sense, a manifestation of every province of rhetoric and a compilation of every form of learning. Commentators too often forget that allegorical exegesis of Homer was not a Blavatskyesque underground but the central and most respected tradition of poetic studies from Theagenes of Rhegium (fl. 525 B.C.)[11] through the middle ages to Chapman's explicitly allegorized translation of the *Odyssey* (1615) and beyond. Homer was thought of as presenting a multi-faceted solid whose planes had only to be projected to make contact with every portion of the surrounding empirical, moral, and metaphysical world.

Via the Cynic moral exegesis the figure of Ulysses assumed an important role in education; after a millennium and a half Shakespeare, presenting him in the conventional Renaissance light, gives us an incarnation of copiously eloquent wisdom and prudence, yet another version of the Ciceronian ideal orator. At one point in their conversations Joyce drew Mr. Budgen's attention to the Ulysses of Shakespeare; the major difference is that Bloom's endless encyclopaedic monologue is heard by no one. There was nothing accidental in Joyce's choice of the *Odyssey* as theme for a brightly keyed compendium of twentieth-century folklore, know-how, art and wisdom.

Odyssey as Comedy

> I come from Wonderland, where I have good estate, and I am the son of my lord Neverstint Griefanpain; my name is Battledown.

From *Ulysses*, somewhere in the Cyclops episode? It is not. It is from Homer himself (*Od.* xxiv, 304) as rendered *ad verbum* by Dr. Rouse. The usual practice of translators is to leave these proper names impenetrable: Alybas, Apheidas

Polypemonides, Eperitos; they sound so much more majestic, and the whimsical etymologies are (surely!) a mistake. But Dr. Rouse (in an essay appended to his *Odyssey*) introduces much evidence that Homer's diction is colloquial and often ingeniously comic. The decorum of the stock epithet is often comic (refusal to believe that this can be so accounts for the frequent assertion that the epithets are often introduced without regard for context). Thus "I cannot help thinking that the company laughed when he introduced Eumaios as δῖος ὑφορβός, pigman by divine right." Homer, it appears, did his share of guying the epic conventions; Dr. Rouse calls attention to the battlefield epithet by which the pigherd is made to chop wood with a pitiless blade. It has not, of course, been possible for anyone to suppress the pun by which Odysseus deceives the Cyclops; Dr. Rouse indicates many more; Athena makes one to sting Zeus (*Od.* i, 62). Finally, he fills three pages with examples of words, often used only once like much of Joyce's vocabulary, as colloquial as the Dublin "gave me the wheeze" and "chucking out the rhino".

Thus Joyce in the Cyclops episode offers an explicit critique of Homer-as-he-is-read:

> And lo, as they quaffed their cup of joy, a godlike messenger came swiftly in, radiant as the eye of heaven, a comely youth, and behind him there passed an elder of noble gait and countenance, bearing the sacred scrolls of law and with him his lady wife, a dame of peerless lineage, fairest of her race.

> Little Alf Bergan popped in round the door and hid behind Barney's snug, squeezed up with the laughing ... I didn't know what was up and Alf kept making signs out of the door. And begob what was it only that bloody old pantaloon Denis Breen in his bath slippers with two bloody big books tucked under his oxter and the wife hotfoot after him, unfortunate wretched woman trotting like a poodle. U293/283.

The first version is a fair pastiche of Butcher and Lang; we may be sure that if Homer had used an epithet meaning "trotting like a poodle" a scholiast would have been found to explain it as a stock metaphor meaning "fairest of her race". (Hasn't the significance of "ox-eyed Hera" been lost in purple clouds of "poetic" preconceptions? "Stupid bitch Hera has her bull eyes", Mr. Pound remarks apropos of Homer's epithetic rightness). Joyce had no difficulty exhibiting the relation of the slack poetizing of Idyllized Homer to the never-never Celtic twilight, U288/279, Yeats-Blavatsky spiritualism, U296/286, pseudo-Ossianics, U291/281, journalistic pathos, U301/291, etc. There isn't really a great deal of difference between this, from one of the parodies:

> The *nec* and *non plus ultra* of emotion were reached when the blushing bride elect burst her way through the serried ranks of the bystanders and flung herself upon the muscular bosom of him who was about to be launched into eternity for her sake, U304/294,

and this, from Butcher and Lang's *Odyssey:*

> But the daughter of Cadmus marked him, Ino of the fair ankles ... and sat upon the well-bound raft and spake: "Hapless one, wherefore was Poseidon, shaker of the earth, so wondrous wroth with thee? ..."

Dr. Rouse's version of the latter runs,

> "Poor Odysseus! You're odd-I-see, true to your name! Why does Poseidon Earthshaker knock you about in this monstrous way?"

On surge-and-thunder principles, naturally, the pun on Odysseus and ὠδύσατο had to be overlooked. *Ulysses* is at this level a comment on the age that had allowed its perception of Homer to get into such a state.

Pope, who predicted the Universal Darkness in which the contours of Homer were blotted out, affords valuable evidence of the persistence of stylistic discrimination from the age of the Alexandrian scholiasts to the early eighteenth century; the reader who imagines that Dr. Rouse, abetted by the irreverent Mr. Pound, is just a cynical modern making things up should check Pope's account of the matter. Pope quotes Longinus' statement that the *Odyssey* is partly comic, Ulysses being shown not in the full light of glory but in the shade of common life. The Cyclops, he adds, is explicitly comic, and Calypso and the suitors "characters of intrigue" (a cross-light on stately, plump Buck Mulligan thus comes from Restoration comedy). The themes, as he lists them, are strikingly Dublinesque: banquets, sports, loves, and the pursuit of a woman. With a glance at *Don Quixote,* he notes that the perfection of the mock-epic is the employment of pompous expressions for low actions. And finally, with his usual prescience, Pope hands us the key to Arnold's Homer lectures, Lang's translations, Tennysons' *Idylls,* all the tushery of the century that was to follow: the sublime style, he says, is of all styles the easiest to fake.

The moment we stop thinking of Homer's sweaty and quarrelsome Achaeans as unrelaxingly heroic posturers, much comes into focus. As Mr. Pound does Propertius, so Joyce presents Homer as a modern and in some respects comic poet. Odysseus, like Bloom, it is not always realized, contends with his milieu as much as he illustrates it. His men are constantly hanging back, running out, falling asleep, getting drunk, and letting the winds out of the bag.

Once more, Joyce is in a tradition coterminous with the disciplines of the trivium. He sees Homer much as Pope saw him, and much as did Pope's predecessors for over two thousand years. The immediate source of his Homeric insight is a mystery. He didn't know much classical Greek, though he was fairly fluent in modern Greek (it was always *spoken* languages that interested him). From schoolroom days, he had no difficulty seeing the *story* in modern terms (he first read it in Charles Lamb's version), and as for the language, he was perfectly capable of looking up a few etymologies. Victor Bérard's researches, as Mr. Gilbert copiously if somewhat over-solemnly demonstrates, made it easy to smell out the (Phoenician: hence Semitic) seafaring yarns underlying the epic, and the Joyce who had hung around the quays of Dublin and Trieste had ample experience of the conversation of sailors. Whatever crib he employed had disappeared by the time the relics of his working library were catalogued in 1949. We have here, it would seem, another instance of the kind of poetic insight that was manifested when Mr. Pound wrested his wonderful *Cathay* from a somewhat unreliable crib to ideograms he couldn't at that time make a pretence of reading.

Hamlet

The stories of Dedalus and Hamlet reinforce the Homeric situation, just as such local analogies as the Parnell case and the biography of Shakespeare furnish modes of special emphasis in line with the main form of the book.

Dedalus, of course, had engaged Joyce's attention for many years. In *Les Dieux antiques,* a translation and adaptation of George Cox's small English handbook of mythology, Stéphane Mallarmé gives a note on his name:

> What does his name signify? Simply the wise or resourceful workman: and the same idea occurs in the epithet, πολύμητις, which is constantly applied to Odysseus.... The wisdom of Dedalus is in fact only another form of the wisdom of Phoebus or Odysseus. As for Icarus, behold in him a feeble reflection of his father, as Phaethon is of Helios, and Telemachus of Odysseus.[12]

That Icarus might be the son of Ulysses is implicit, that is, in the very etymology of his surname, Dedalus. A feeble reflection of one father, imagining that the situation will better itself if he hunts out another: that is Stephen. Having employed the Dedalus situation throughout the *Portrait,* Joyce simply switches its materials onto a main-line track of the same gauge.

As for the *Hamlet* situation, it is easy to see how it reinforces that of the *Odyssey:*

Hamlet	Stephen	Telemachus	Dispossessed heir
Ghost	Rational Principle	Ulysses	Ghost through death or absence
Claudius	Mulligan, Rome	Antinous	Usurper
Queen	Ireland	Penelope[13]	The usurped
Ophelia	Stephen's sister		Drowned innocent[14]

The shift from the *Odyssey* into *Hamlet* is accompanied by a great increase in psychological intensity: the shift, between Classic and Renaissance, from the civic to the personal (a similar theme underlies Mr. Pound's first thirty *Cantos*). There is also a displacement of centre, from errant father to tortured son. *Hamlet* is in this sense simply the *Odyssey* narrated from the viewpoint of an introverted Telemachus. (There are fragmentary allusions in Joyce's text to *Don Giovanni;* Mozart's opera repeats the same plot from the point of view of the doomed usurper). Hence, although Bloom is allowed at one point to declaim, "Hamlet, I am thy father's spirit", U150/141, the *Hamlet* correspondences centre on Stephen. The scene in the Tower begins, like Shakespeare's play, on the upper platform. The mummers then descend the stairs and Mulligan plays Claudius, twitting Stephen on his black costume and delivering sententious wisdom on the inevitability of death ("I see them pop off every day in the Mater and Richmond and cut up into tripes in the dissecting room. It's a beastly thing and nothing else.") The Ghost beheld by Stephen is that of his mother, "her wasted body within its loose brown graveclothes giving off an odour of wax and rosewood". Having planted the correspondence firmly in the first episode, Joyce drops its detailed development and shifts his attention to the character of Stephen/Hamlet.

His projection of Hamlet seems significantly related to the meditations of two French poets, Mallarmé and Laforgue. Mallarmé's phrase, quoted to Stephen by Mr. Best, "Il se promène, lisant au livre de lui-même", U185/175, comes from a page on *Hamlet et Fortinbras* which deserves further quotation:

> ... he walks, that is all, reading the book of himself, a high and living Sign; he scorns to look at any other. Nor will he be content to symbolize the solitude of the Thinker among other men; he kills them off aloofly and at random, or at least, they die. The black presence of the doubter diffuses poison, so that all the great people die, without his even taking the trouble, usually, to stab them behind the arras. Then, evidently in deliberate contrast to the hesitator, we see Fortinbras in the role of general, but no more efficaciously lethal than he; and if Death deploys his versatile appliances—phial, lotus-pool, or rapier—when an exceptional person flaunts his sombre livery, that is the import of the finale when, as the spectator returns to his senses, this sumptuous and stagnant exaggeration of murder (the idea of which remains as meaning of the play, attached to Him who makes himself alone) so to speak achieves vulgar manifestation as this agent of military destruction clears the stage with his marching army, on the scale of the commonplace, amid trumpets and drums.[15]

Mallarmé's insistence on Hamlet's otherness runs counter to the English Romantic critical tradition of "Hamlet is ourselves". Hamlet is alien to the namby-pamby "so French, don't you know" world of the Dublin aesthetes, but equally alien to the rational masculine world epitomized by his own father. Hamlet, furthermore, is the very incarnation at once of creativity and of death. And Hamlet, like Stephen, reads no book but his own nature, his soul in some manner all that is, the form of forms, U27/23.

Stephen is continuous with Dublin, as his relation of sonship with Bloom emphasizes; Fortinbras, the conquering general, is a vulgarized Hamlet, that is all. Hamlet's kingdom is not of this world. Stephen's image of himself as a destroying force ("Shatter them, one and both. But stun myself too in the blow", U238/229) is allied to Mallarmé's emphasis; English criticism has given the gloomy prince a contrary build-up as Thinker. The propensity for slaughtering suitors, it is worth noting, is transferred from Ulysses to Telemachus by this Hamlet interposition.

Stephen has lethal thoughts all day ("Hired dog! Shoot him to bloody bits with a bang shotgun, bits man spattered walls all brass buttons", U43/38); Bloom rejects them ("Assassination, never") but does toy with "Exposure by mechanical artifice (automatic bed) or individual testimony (concealed ocular witness)", U718/694. The lines from *Don Giovanni* that he hums after lunch belong to the marble avenger in the opera: *a cenar teco m'invitasti.* An X-ray version of "exposure" is comically juxtaposed: "have to stand all the time with his insides entrails on show. Science", U177/168.

As for Laforgue's Hamlet, he is introduced to us in *Moralités Légendaires* high in a tower by a stagnant arm of the sea (cf. the opening of *Ulysses*) contemplating his own soul and his Works. The castle is hung with "completely accurate views of Jutland", Academy Art at which Hamlet invariably spits as he passes. He is very much the Artist Manqué, exhibited as comic adolescent. He is also a homicidal maniac. His longing is "To be the hero of a play! And to reduce all of the other plays to little curtain-raisers!" He dazzles, or imagines he has dazzled, the self-sufficient little actress Kate with visions of a flight to Paris "this evening under the extremely lucid moonlight", pauses to gather from his father's grave "a flower, a simple paper-flower, which will serve us as a bookmark when we interrupt the reading of my drama to kiss each other", encounters Laertes, and dies with a Neronic *"Qualis ... artifex ... pereo!"*[6]

The comic dimensions of Joyce's treatment of Stephen are aligned with Laforgue's. Laforgue's genius was for the exposé, and in his *Hamlet* he exposed the self-sufficient posturings of Romantic aestheticism, and its lethal substratum. The difficulty the reader experiences keeping Stephen in focus depends, as a look at Laforgue may convince us, on the fact that the arty adolescent, incapable of sepa-rating with exactness his *persona* from himself, can't keep himself in focus; he resembles the kind of picture puzzle in which the perspective suddenly snaps into reverse and foreground becomes background.

In so far as he is a serious figure, Stephen's alignments are with the Hamlet of Mallarmé; in so far as he is the object of satire, they are with the Hamlet of Laforgue. A final dimension comes from the *Odyssey.* As Mr. Deasy brings forward the Parnell case, U35/32, so Nestor in the third book of Homer relates the betrayal of Agamemnon by his wife. What he presses on Telemachus, however, is the role of Orestes the avenging son. Homer is evidently quite aware of the parallel be-tween the situations of Telemachus and Orestes. There is, so to speak, a Hamlet in the *Odyssey,* and a successful one.

NOTES

[1]References to *Ulysses* are to the Modern Library edition and then the John Lane/The Bodley Head edition.
[2]Such is my reading of the facts set forth by Richard Levin and Charles Shattuck in their article, "First Flight to Ithaca" (*Accent,* Winter, 1944, reprinted in *James Joyce: Two Decades of Criticism,* ed. Seon

Givens (Vanguard Press, N.Y.), 47–94). They attempt to force the parallel to the end, though admitting that it falters. It seems to me to have been sustained by Joyce about as far as "Clay".

[3]T. S. Eliot, "Ulysses, Order, and Myth", *The Dial*, Nov. 1923. Reprinted in Givens, 198–202.

[4]Joyce to Harriet Weaver, Nov. 19, 1923. Transcript in Slocum collection.

[5]E. B. Burgum, "Ulysses and the Impasse of Individualism", *Virginia Quarterly Review*, xvii–4 (October 1941), 561–573.

[6]Stuart Gilbert, *James Joyce's* Ulysses (Knopf, N.Y., and Faber and Faber, London).

[7]All Homeric quotations from the translation of Dr. W. H. D. Rouse.

[8]*The Letters of Ezra Pound*, ed. D. D. Paige.

[9]Frank Budgen, *James Joyce and the Making of* Ulysses (Grayson and Grayson, London), 16–17.

[10]*Selected Essays:* "Euripides and Professor Murray."

[11]Sandys, *History of Classical Scholarship*, I, 7.

[12]Mallarmé, *Oeuvres*, Pléiade, Paris, 1945, 1244. (My translation.)

[13]Queen Gertrude who gives in and Queen Penelope who doesn't comprise Joyce's familiar bipolar feminine, just as the Ghost and the triumphant Ithacan give us the bipolar masculine. The tensions between Shakespeare's and Homer's worlds are exploited as much as the analogies.

[14]"She is drowning. Agenbite. Save her. Agenbite. She will drown me with her, eyes and hair", U239/230. As the "agenbite" and the emblematic "salt green death" imply, sister Dilly is simply Stephen's mother over again. Ophelia in the same way repeats the spiritual death of the Queen. The death of Stephen's mother parallels that of Ireland.

[15]Mallarmé, *Oeuvres*, 1557. Joyce was digging in the very apparatus criticus of the *Divagations* volume (1897) when he found this. It was a paragraph contributed to *La Revue Blanche*, salvaged by Mallarmé in the "Bibliographie" of *Divagations* because, as he says, he wasn't able to work it into his main Hamlet essay. The most evident failure of my translation is its omission of the multiple senses of "autour de Qui se fait seul." French word-order permits this to mean both "Him who makes himself alone" and "Him who alone makes Himself". Hamlet the epitome of Life and Death, Creator and *dio boia*.

[16]*Six Moral Tales from Jules Laforgue*, ed. and trans. Frances Newman, N.Y., 1928, 140, 190, 200.

George Scouffas

KAZANTZAKIS: ODYSSEUS AND THE "CAGE OF FREEDOM"

Although its initial edition, published in Athens in 1938, numbered only three hundred copies, *The Odyssey* by Nikos Kazantzakis attracted immediate attention. As a literary work, it was declared a daring sequel to the Homeric epic in a genre usually thought unsuitable to modern taste. Thematically, it was taken as Kazantzakis' master statement of his view of modern man. In Greece itself it aroused fierce controversy, strong echoes of which still reverberate. The academicians attacked its form, its idiomatic styling, and what they considered its heterodoxy.

The poem did not come as a complete surprise. Before its publication, it was well known that Kazantzakis had been preoccupied with it since 1925. Moreover, by 1938 the direction of his thinking and the versatility of his genius were familiar; novels, prose and poetic dramas, travelogues, philosophic disquisitions, and even translations of such works as Dante's *Divine Comedy* and Goethe's *Faust* had anticipated *The Odyssey*. As also had the known facts of his life, private and public. For Kazantzakis' own experience in many ways prefigured the adventures of his picaresque hero. When he had completed his formal education, having taken the degree of law from the University of Athens, Kazantzakis became a chronic traveller, restlessly moving through Europe, Asia, and Africa, in the process learning five modern languages to add to his Latin and modern and ancient Greek. Yet he also felt the need for withdrawal and contemplation, at one time spending two ascetic years on Mount Athos. And he was willing to submit to public life when his country needed him, by taking on the duties of Director General of the Ministry of Public Welfare at the end of World War I. Later, after the appearance of *The Odyssey*, he was to become for a brief, stormy period Minister of National Education; and in 1947 he was Director of Translations from the Classics for UNESCO.

The English reading public knew little or nothing of Kazantzakis before 1953, when his novel *Zorba the Greek* was published in English. *The Greek Passion* followed in 1954, and two years later came *Freedom or Death*. Although the last

From *Accent* 19, No. 4 (Autumn 1959): 234–46.

was considered disappointing, taken together the novels revealed a major talent and set the stage for the publication in 1958 of *The Odyssey*, translated into English verse by Kimon Friar. The American reader, accustomed to leanness and directness even in his more "symbolic" or esoteric reading, is likely to approach the poem with awe and resistance, for its sheer bulk alone is formidable. Once engaged, however, he will discover a remarkable range of knowledge and depth of insight controlled by a disciplined mind.

The poem consists of 33,333 lines, is opulent in style and lavish in its use of fable, dream, and digressive incident; yet, the main narrative action is relatively simple. Odysseus, having set Ithaca in order, leaves again with a small band of companions. His destination is Sparta, where his friend Menelaus and the beautiful Helen rule. Abducting Helen, who is obviously bored with her royal domestic life, he takes her to Crete, where he loses her to a "blond barbarian," member of the new Doric race. From here Odysseus goes to Egypt, engages in an unsuccessful revolt, then sets out to trace the Nile to its source. After crossing a wilderness, he builds a Holy City, which is destroyed soon after its inauguration. Now completely alone and aged by his experience, Odysseus travels southward through Africa. When he reaches the sea, he builds himself another boat and sails to the polar regions. There he meets his death. This sequence of adventure is paralleled by the spiritual growth of Odysseus, who recognizes seven stages in man's progress from bestiality to pure soul; hence one of his epithets: "seven-souled."

In his comprehensive introduction to *The Odyssey*, Friar states that the work, like Joyce's *Ulysses*, is "concerned with the modern man in search of a soul." He isolates the active agent in this search by quoting W. B. Stanford: "In fact, psychologically, [Kazantzakis'] epic is an exploration of the meaning of freedom." Since Kazantzakis brings to bear on his subject a lifetime of study in philosophy, anthropology, history, religion, and literature, the result is that the basic terms of the exploration become a catalogue of the central motifs and dilemmas of modern Western literature. For it is his purpose to expose Odysseus to all the strains and counter-strains that beset modern man, to guide him to a revelatory synthesis that can give him clarity of understanding and ultimate peace, and to do this without depriving him of his status as man. Whatever spiritual heights Odysseus ascends, he is to remain deeply rooted in nature. He is to grow downward as he reaches upward.

To launch himself in his search, Odysseus must become the self-exile. The Ithaca he has found after twenty years' absence and delivered from its oppressors quickly palls, becomes confining. He feels the limitation of order, and against the advice of the elders, who believe in the sacredness of boundaries, he will "concede no boundaries." It is significant that Odysseus is out of place, "hung" between generations, for he sees in both his father, Laertes, and his son, Telemachus, a strong predisposition for discipline and order. He is the lost generation. At the death of Laertes, he is especially conscious of this:

> Watching his son before him run to find a bride,
> feeling his father's body rot in the grave behind him,
> and he at the dead center, bridegroom both and corpse,
> he shuddered, for his life now seemed the briefest lightning flash.

This feeling has it historical counterpart, for Odysseus sees himself at the end of the Homeric era. As a Cretan bard puts it, " 'Athena's helmet . . . has now been smashed to bits. . . .' " Typically Odysseus interprets his position in time as advantage: " 'Blessed be that hour that gave me birth between two eras!' " This historical position Kazantzakis exploits fully throughout the work, for wherever Odysseus goes on his travels—Sparta, Crete, Egypt—he finds decay and the seething of revolt. Although for Menelaus' sake he helps suppress the attempted overthrow of Sparta, he plays a leading role in the revolts against Crete and Egypt. The view expressed or demonstrated by Odysseus emphasizes the cyclical inevitability of cultural decline and death. Moreover, for him this is a "long" or infinite view that sees civilizations forever toppling and gods continually discredited.

Acutely sensitive to instability and change, Odysseus measures the validity of experience only in terms of flux. In a life that offers an infinitely multiple choice, man must maintain his freedom to choose. But since choice itself stops the flow, it becomes an agony and a confinement. Odysseus' reaction to this dilemma is essentially romantic, based on what may be called the "open end" concept. Choice is tentative in time and one must expose himself eternally to change if he is to fulfill his existence. When Odysseus declares, " 'If only the soul of man had myriad forms to serve it. . . ,' " he is expressing not only romantic insatiability but also the poignancy of the dilemma itself. Nevertheless, he must pursue experience, he must make a cult of change, for to his temperament fixity of choice is death. Thus he is obsessed with and tortured by the multiplicity of "roads" open to him, and the "road" metaphor as an expression of the pursuit of freedom is dominant, especially in his earlier wanderings. Even the conservative Menelaus, when he is under the influence of Odysseus, dreams of freedom as a seeking of "all roads." It is, on one level, this open pursuit of experience that Odysseus is expressing when he says, " 'My soul, your voyages have been your native land!' " For he seems to be most at ease with himself when he is saying farewell. Yet, caught in the eternal current, Odysseus remains very much aware of the paradoxical limits imposed on man by the infinity of choice. In one of his anguished moments, he sees earth as always "over-reaching" him, life always "cheating" him by "changing face so often my mind can't grasp it all."

Closely allied to this determined exposure to experience is the Odyssean dread of Paradise that is rooted in his strong sense of the relativity of time and in his earth-centeredness. This is a side of the hero that is implicit in the beginning lines of the poem: "Good is this earth, it suits us!" Earth is man's source and earth is the arena of his struggle. But since the earthly is imperfect and man is bedeviled by the dream of perfectibility and immortality, he is constantly trying to escape his origins.

Odysseus expresses all stages of this dilemma through a recall of three of his Homeric adventures: his meetings with Calypso, Circe, and Nausicaa. The sexual union with Calypso transformed flesh into spirit. But this he recognized as a dangerous state, for it dehumanized him, left him "without man's springing heart." On the other hand, Circe, obviously representing the bestial in man, threatened his potential divinity. With Nausicaa, the ideal balance was apparently struck:

'She neither raised me to the empty sky nor hurled
me down to Hades, but we walked on earth together....'

However, this state also is untenable. More than that, it is the most treacherous of the three "temptations" ("'...most deadly forms which Death assumed...'"). Significantly, it is Nausicaa whom Odysseus chooses as the proper wife for his stay-at-home son, Telemachus, whose limited ambition to be a good king of Ithaca he scorns. For Odysseus' own vision of perfectibility, grounded in matter yet dynamically pursued by time and change, will never permit a utopian synthesis. Ironically, Odysseus himself is deceived into illustrating this in the pivotal action that Books XIV through XVI describe. In Book XIV, in many ways the most moving of the entire work, Odysseus establishes his position in man's and nature's evolutionary scale. After seven days of reflection on a mountain top, for the first time he holds in suspension a universal view of creation with himself playing an integral role. His vision is remarkably like that of Whitman in its emphasis on the archetypal and representative *I*, the sense of the unbroken, upward continuity of creation, the mystical association with all creatures and plants accompanied by a deep feeling of love, all climaxed by the exhilaration of freedom. There is also an abiding satisfaction that comes with the belief that he is, to use Whitman's words, the "acme of things accomplish'd."

Odysseus systematically assesses his ancestral past, strains out its value to him, and then rejects it ("He felt himself at length freed from the snare of race"). He next turns to a consideration of all races and discovers a kinship with all men. Finally, he accepts all creation, "welcomes" all beasts, and through this acceptance he realizes that nature is his intimate ally, his "co-worker." By the end of Book XIV he has reached the stage of love, expressed in "wedding couplets" that again recall Whitman:

'Open all doors and windows now, break all the locks,
O bride, receive the bridegroom, shepherd of all flocks!
. . . .
Today the sky and the day glow, with love, my Love,
today in blazing light are wed the eagle and the dove!'

When Odysseus returns from the mountain with his new-found secret (the "palpable partridge warm and slain"), he is inspired to put his knowledge to action. The result is the enthusiastic planning and building of the Ideal City. Even during the inauguration ceremonies, however, there are evil omens, and soon after the city's completion it is destroyed by earthquakes and volcanic eruptions. Odysseus' atti-tude throughout this ordeal makes it clear that he has been almost wilfully self-deceived in his hope for an Edenic creation. Though man's efforts are foredoomed, nevertheless he must build. At this stage of his development he fights necessity with action. This is not the typical mood or motivation of the teleological mind. During the early warnings of disaster, Odysseus rails at his "devouring god" like a Captain Ahab, asserts the importance of man's own drive toward creative order, and once again defies necessity.

What is most paradoxical in the entire episode is that it seems to betray all that Odysseus to that point has represented. His presence everywhere has meant disruption: he is the destroyer of cities, the "god-slayer," the "soul-snatcher." Mene-laus reacts with characteristic fear of Odysseus when he thinks:

'Fate has in him grown proud, the holy measure is smashed
that balances the good and evil powers within us.'

For Odysseus moral absolutes are impossible; he feels too strongly the dualistic relativity demanded by experiential growth; like an existentialist he accepts the "moral" value of evil itself ("'Alas for him who seeks salvation in good only!'"). Although his cosmology does not permit an Edenic myth, his humanistic view of man implicitly supports the doctrine of the "fortunate fall" (i.e., man is properly man only in his imperfection). In fact, as Friar interprets it, the destruction of the city is necessary to the completion of the spiritual development of Odysseus, for it is only through fall and betrayal that man grows. And, in a sense, man must provide his own betrayal, assert his own antitheses. Nowhere is this more explicitly and ve-hemently stated than during the Mosaic flight through the wilderness preceding the building of the city. When Odysseus surprises one of his followers attempting to plant a flower in the desert, he becomes enraged. The immediate reason is his fear of stability ("'... for then the heart takes root and never again will leave!'"). But this quickly leads to the expression of a doctrine of wholesale perversity: "'To all laws I'll erect contrary secret laws.'" Sometime later he defines his stand in terms of the necessity of suffering: "'To climb and hunger...; this is my God's feast....'"

The destruction of the city thus becomes on one level grist for Odysseus' spiritual mill. Indeed, the shock of the experience turns his hair completely white and sets the final stage of his exploration of freedom, the freedom from hope itself ("'Dear heart, you've flown beyond the final labor, Hope'"). From this point on, The Odyssey settles into an extended Wagnerian embellishment of the theme described by Stanford as the abandonment of the "cult of doing for the cult of being."

In its total effect, then, the building of the city operates as an illustrative exercise in tragic irony. And as such it serves as a means of clearing the hurdle of naturalistic determinism. From the beginning Odysseus is in the anomalous position of being victimized by necessity, yet, although constantly railing against it, being himself its instrument. In this respect the new Odysseus is very much his Homeric self, for he is unmatched in his devious ability to survive, both physically and psychologically. He plunders his own stores to escape from Ithaca; he unhesitatingly betrays his good friend Menelaus when he abducts Helen, and this after he has by a ruse preserved Menelaus' kingdom against incipient revolt; he craftily plans the destruction of Crete; and when circumstances demand it, he kills without sentiment. He is feared as much for his treachery as for his boldness of thought and purpose. Odysseus' view of man as half-beast, half-god, as the battleground of antithetical forces, supports him in this role. Yet, in Book VIII, after the brutal Cretan revolt, when Odysseus begins to eat, he notices a huge locust settled on his bread and glaring at him "wrathfully with crystal eyes." For the first time he knows fear, and in revulsion he surrenders his bread to the locust.

In Book XIV Odysseus works out a complex dialectical and psychological escape from the naturalistic trap. The key to the basic method, as given him by Mother-Earth, is an identification with earth-bound creation, an unreserved affirmation of the primordial and instinctual. To accomplish this, mind, source of abstract concept, must be forced into abeyance to permit the life-stream, represented by heart, to run free. This does not mean the total rejection of reason. Odysseus never loses his respect for it. One of his epithets is "Archer of the Mind," and a full study may be made of the many references to and images involving the mind that occur throughout the poem. A significant level of tension dramatizes the eternal conflict between mind and feeling, reason and intuition, and man's need to reconcile the two. In this preoccupation, also, Kazantzakis is exploring an urgent modern problem, the "dissociation of sensibility." At this particular stage in his growth, Odysseus is in effect testing out a possible resolution of this conflict by subjecting reason to instinct. He hopes that when he blows the "murky brain away," the "dark inhuman powers may change to God." This "grounding" of high-flying reason is expressed in a sexual metaphor:

'The time has come to stretch blue-eyed Idea down
on earth like a chaste bride and fill her full of seed!'

Thus the city, product at this act, becomes both a memorial to his apparent success in the resolution of the conflict, and a sacrifice to its failure.

The ulterior motives behind Odysseus' affirming of instinctual nature may perhaps be best explained by the principle of purgation. Odysseus is using this means to free himself from the limitations of nature. Hence his ecstatic joy when he feels that ". . . he'd become all earth from his loins down," or when ". . . he shot his deadly arrows happily everywhere / till his hands filled with pulsing forms, with bloodstained wings," is in the nature of exorcism, about which more will be said later. Through his participation in nature's atavistic struggle he rises above it. The working of this principle is illustrated in his inner dialogue with his God. When Odysseus asks his God, " 'What hunter so pursues you that you gasp and groan?' " the answer is:

'I climb my own dark body, Son, to keep from stifling.
Trees and beasts smother me, and your flesh chokes me, too;
I fight to flee you, not even your soul can hold me now.'

During the actual building of the city Odysseus' motivation becomes even clearer. In a sermon to his workers, he describes the naturalistic immanence of his new-found God. Soon after, he organizes the citizens into distinct classes of workers, soldiers, and intellectuals, and establishes a communal society: no private property, no marriage or family unit, compulsory death for the old. And one day he is inspired by the fierce, destructive mating of a colony of termites to the announcement of the city's fundamental law:

'Whatever blind Worm-Mother Earth does with no brains
we should accept as just. . . .'

Here is the acceptance of determinism. Yet, when Odysseus chisels on stone his ten commandments, the final one reasserts the search for freedom as the " 'greatest virtue on earth.' " And thus the destruction of the city through the working of the very law on which it was founded itself becomes a crucial stage in the search. Odysseus now breaks clear of naturalistic necessity and participation. This freedom is anticipated just before the inauguration of the city, when his bow crumbles and he renounces his role as hunter. And it is summarized after the destruction as a salvation from the needs of "castle" and "tent," hunger and thirst.

Bereft of all companions and thwarted in his supreme effort to objectify love in a stable form, Odysseus now goes through the change that prepares him for the only companionship left him, that of death. In this final stage Friar describes him as concerning himself "more and more with the outer world," and he points up the basic contradiction in the means Odysseus uses to arrive at his ultimate understanding of life and his relation to it by stating that "It is when he turns ascetic that Odysseus becomes most materialistic." *The Odyssey* from Book XVI to the end, however, actually "documents" the stratagems which the romantic sensibility employs to circumvent its dilemmas.

From the beginning, Odysseus has stressed the demands and needs of the self. Typically romantic is the fascination with the prospects of the limitless potentiality of the individual ego and the urge to explore this potential without reservation at whatever cost. In other words, the travels of Odysseus are an interior voyage, and the subjective level of his adventures is made unmistakably explicit by Kazantzakis. This is such a prominent feature of *The Odyssey* that a most fruitful study may be made of its "interior landscapes." The sea speaks of itself as an "inner sea" and the sun, matrix of symbol and metaphor in the book, describes itself as "Sun of an inner sky and sea, peak of an inner world." When Odysseus reaches the Nile, he characteristically internalizes it, chiding his companions for not seeing its true significance: " 'Blockheads, you see but river! It never swipes your brain / our soul's the river. . . .' "

So that the self may remain free to fulfill itself, Odysseus maintains a policy of non-commitment. Very early in the work, he reveals this stand to his father: " '. . . my warp is No, my woof is Yes, / and what I weave all day I swift unweave by night.' " This is an ironic play on the trick Penelope played to hold off her suitors, ironic because it is precisely this side of Odysseus that she now fears. The theme of non-commitment is constant throughout: Odysseus, just before his death, passes between the twin peaks of Yes and No. Moreover, it operates on all levels. In a dream Odysseus is accused by a General of refusing to take sides during a battle (is called the "left-right-handed man") and is ordered to serve both armies. That there are political connotations here is clear. There is esthetic non-commitment in his reaction against the effete Pharaoh who believes in the immortality and absoluteness of Art. And humanistic non-commitment in the paradoxical side of Odysseus " 'that loves all things on the bright earth yet sticks to none.' "

Inevitably the worship of self leads to the negation of all external authority (cf. Odysseus as "god-slayer"). When he is still in Ithaca, Odysseus makes a point of drinking to "man's dauntless mind" instead of to the gods. Orpheus, the piper, early sings of man's constant outwitting of his God, who is pictured as an arrogant and jealous murderer. And later, when Odysseus fashions a god out of a log to deceive the African natives, he refers to " 'God as good merchandise . . . sales without end.' " The total discrediting of external divinity is expressed by him when he asserts that " '. . . God is clay in my ten fingers, and I mold him.' " Simultaneously he identifies God with earth-bound man, as has already been discussed. The ten commandments for the city are founded on this identification.

With the destruction of the city begins the final stage in Odysseus' assumption of divine authority—the apotheosis of the ego. Odysseus, "desolate, lone, without a god," sinks into the "terror of thought" and emerges with a new identity, the fulfillment of a wish he had even as as child (" 'O God, make me a god!' "). This experience is dramatized in a demonic rite of self-communion, in which he bends and bites his heel and ecstatically declares:

'I'm both the brain-begotten god and the anti-god,
I'm the warm womb that gives me birth, the grave that eats me!
The circle is now complete, the snake has bit its tail.'

Thus is the psychological circuit closed and all antinomies resolved. Although there are mystical implications in this ultimate state, there is an important difference from the Buddhistic mysticism which at one time strongly attracted Kazantzakis. The most obvious result of mysticism is the utter abasement of self, but antithetic to this is self-enlargement—out of nothingness, the great *I*. Odysseus' ascetic enlightenment leads to this latter victory of self. In a sense, he has fought his own Armageddon and has emerged the victor over the opposing powers. He is presumably freed from time, from the confining pressures of moral, esthetic, and philosophic absolutes, and from the need of salvation, for he is now " 'the savior, saved from his salvation. . . .' "

Henceforth the "world-creator" (his new epithet) with "self-lighted head," Odysseus now juggles reality to suit his whim. Inevitably, however, he must also be the destroyer, for his hierarchy of self has been founded on a systematic annihilation of nature, including his own material existence. Creation, "sucked down in the great ascetic's gyre," is "swallowed all" in his "black wells." In a passage that describes his joy in his epiphany this necessary annihilation is described as a "dislodgement" of creation. And, again, in lines that aptly express Kazantzakis' thematic method throughout and perhaps reveal his relation to his art:

> ... his hands rejoiced in fondling all the upper world
> and yet his mind rejoiced to scatter it far and wide.

Transferred to the psychological level this impulse strips away the self: " 'I am the savior, and no salvation on earth exists!' " Thus is God likewise destroyed and supplanted by the dynamic urge toward freedom: " '... by God is meant to hunt God through the empty air!' "

In his new role Odysseus freely indulges himself, but since, as he well knows, reality still involves necessity and the pressure of time, he takes refuge in irony. Indeed, it is only through irony that he can hold his high ground of detachment and maintain the suspension of contraries. Irony also prevents his becoming victimized by his self-created illusion, for the contraries still exist and are potent. Thus it is ironic insight that prompts Odysseus to laugh down the inner Tempter who tries to flatter him into believing he has reached the finality of truth.

But irony can be dangerous and fickle. Properly used it operates as a catalyst, and as such it frees and illuminates. When it assumes an intrinsic value, it can destroy. It can dehumanize, enervate, and annihilate. Or it can become simply a stance, a superficial imposition on experience that hampers meaning. Or, being what it is, it can turn on itself. The shrewdness of Odysseus makes him sensitive to most of these dangers. In a dream-fable which re-plays his own changes, a young king in search of meaning arrives at the secret that the " 'mind's a lamp with little oil,' " breaks out into apparently releasing ironic laughter, only to be caught short by the smell of death. This forces him back to a re-affirmation of material reality. In another dream Odysseus kills a deer, re-asserts the naturalistic doctrine (" 'A great and mighty tiger rules the living world' "), awakens to fashion a new bow, and so re-enters nature as a participant.[1] Still another time he berates a lord who defines his freedom in terms of ironic self-indulgence, who stripped off "the veil from life," saw her nude, then tasted "'all things indifferently with mocking skill." Finally, Odysseus is appalled at the supreme irony of having himself deified and worshipped by others, for this he recognizes as enslavement for all concerned.

This final irony, however, suggests a disturbing area of blindness in Odysseus which is inherent in the basic theme of The Odyssey. Although Odysseus sees in his own deification by others all that he has from the beginning struggled to escape (man's chronic surrender to form and ritual), Kazantzakis himself describes him in his final state as having been "drained pure till life turned to immaculate myth." The key word is immaculate. Most obviously it refers to the ultimate stage of man's seven-stepped spiritual evolution. A brief summary of Kazantzakis' views on the relation between experience and art, however, will reveal other implications. In *Zorba the Greek,* which of the translated novels is closest in thematic details to *The Odyssey* and is thus very helpful in illuminating the latter work, the narrator's many statements on life and art may be considered Kazantzakis' own. Taken together they define art as exorcism. As such, "Art is, in fact, a magic incantation" that purges man of "obscure homicidal forces" and "deadly impulses," which are "cast out by the all-powerful exorcism of the word." The narrator thus uses his writing to overcome and drive out the influence of Buddha ("I must throw over him the net of images, catch him and free myself"). He even goes so far as to attempt a "writing-out" of the temptation of "a woman's body soaked by the rain." On the level of experience this process is necessary for the freeing of self from the bonds of materiality. One devours life to cleanse himself of it. This is especially evident when the narrator says that the "belly is the firm foundation . . . it is only with bread, wine and meat that one can create God." On re-reading Mallarmé, he is repulsed because he believes that his poetry did not begin with these essentials. That is, it was not the product of a systematic process of exorcism. Then he summarizes what he considers the proper relation of art and experience:

> The human element is brutish, uncouth, impure—it is composed of love, the flesh, and a cry of distress. Let it be sublimated into an abstract idea . . . let it be rarefied and evaporate.

It is this sublimation that Odysseus has achieved:

> The archer has fooled you, Death, he's squandered all your goods,
> melted down all the rusts and rots of his foul flesh
> till they escaped you in pure spirit . . .

Yet when Odysseus, as "immaculate myth," cannot subscribe to Christianity because only " 'That man is free who strives on earth with not one hope' "; or when, in response to a request for his "wisest word," he says, " 'I've gone beyond the Word . . . and fling you, for profound reply, a wordless smile,' " he is driving myth not toward but out of meaning. Like Coleridge the romantic may awake to find his dream a reality. The result can be and has been great art. Driving reality into dream-annihilation, however, is another matter. And herein lies a level of irony to which Odysseus seems insensitive.

It is not that Kazantzakis has dared too much in his complete exploration of the meaning of freedom, but that, in a sense, he has exposed the subject beyond most profitable return in terms of meaning. Odysseus insists so obsessively on freedom that it becomes cleansed of definition. His spiritual progression certainly provides a significant model for man's possible development in an Einsteinian universe, and it does function effectively as the inner structure of *The Odyssey,* but its meaning is hampered by the context in which it operates. For example, the fundamental fact and experience of death dominates the poem from beginning to end;

but despite Odysseus' elaborate preparations for his own death in the concluding books—described with grandeur and a passionate sense of loss—there is finally little offered toward the illumination of the experience beyond its incontrovertible necessity. As a matter of fact, Odysseus' ultimate annihilation of reality—including both its generative contraries and its illusions—makes death something gratuitous. One recalls that Kazantzakis is faced by a similar dilemma in *Freedom or Death,* where Captain Michales, driven by a "pure" sense of pride, in effect forces his foes to kill him, because for him freedom is finally synonymous with death. In the experience of life itself, as in the art that renders it, freedom like all else must have its measurement. It cannot simply be asserted as an absolute. And this suggests the greatest irony of all in *The Odyssey.* Friar, in his Synopsis of the work, touches on it when he describes Odysseus' death as freeing his mind from its "last cage, that of its freedom." Odysseus has been imprisoned in an abstraction and a category.

But this, too, should be a part of the story of modern man's quest and perhaps Kazantzakis has been truer to his subject than at first seems apparent. If so, his irony has still another layer, subtler and more devastating, which makes of *The Odyssey* a dramatization of the effects of a modern brand of *hubris* generated by man's being forced to make of himself the absolute measurement of his life and experience and destiny. Then, the final utterance of Odysseus, with its Tennysonian heroics, becomes almost unbearably poignant: " 'Forward, my lads, sail on, for Death's breeze blows in a fair wind!' "

NOTES

[1] This re-entrance is important, also, because it partially saves the irony in *The Odyssey* from the self-conscious pose of "ironic laughter." Too often the reader is reminded of the "laughter of the gods" that the latter-day Romantic, Lord Dunsany, was addicted to.

W. R. Elton

SHAKESPEARE'S ULYSSES AND THE PROBLEM OF VALUE[1]

While Shakespeare's *Troilus and Cressida* (ca. 1601–2) remains perhaps the most enigmatic play in the canon, its very genre being still in question, its language has been shown to contain an unusually frequent and pervasive series of references to value.[2] Terms and concepts, that is, relating to exchange, commerce, estimation, worth, price, buying and selling, trading, and so on, seem central to at least one meaning-level of the play. As a mode of entry into that level, I have chosen to examine the "value" speeches of Ulysses, who appears to represent the "establishment," or hierarchical position of the state, and whose famous "degree speech" is often taken to be an expression of Shakespeare's, or at least the play's, orthodox conception of order.[3]

I

Since Ulysses' speeches occur within a dramatic sequence of dialogue and action, their comprehension should benefit from a contextual glance at the play's other references to value. For, as Hobbes reminds us, "they that insist upon single texts, without considering the main design, can derive nothing from them clearly."[4]

At the start, Shakespeare's "arm'd" Prologue to *Troilus and Cressida*, entering "not in confidence / Of Authors pen ..." (ll. 24–25), suggests a reply, it is generally held, to Ben Jonson's armed Prologue in *Poetaster* (1601). There, with "well erected confidence" (l. 13), Jonson's Prologue asserts,

> put case our Authour should, once more;
> Sweare that his play were good ...   (11.15–16)[5]

Jonson's self-proclaimed "goodness" is again asserted in *Cynthia's Revels* (1600–1), whose Epilogue concludes authoritatively with a quotation from the writer himself:

From *Shakespeare Studies* 2 (1966): 95–111.

By (—) 'tis good, and if you lik't, you may.   (l. 20)

In contrast, Shakespeare's Prologue invokes *his* audience to less absolute judgments, concluding,

Like, or finde fault, do as your pleasures are,
Now good, or bad, 'tis but the chance of Warre.   (ll. 31–32)

This less "confident" conclusion seems to imply, contrary to Jonson, that "good" and "bad" are not fixed or absolute values, but are subject to "pleasure," alternations of time and chance, vacillating like the fortunes of war. Against Jonson's claim to judge absolutely, Shakespeare's Prologue appears to relinquish such judgment to the variable "liking" of an audience. *Troilus and Cressida*'s opening thus seems to lead us into questions of relevance to the play: Is there a relationship between "pleasure," or the hedonistic criterion, and good and bad? Is war, or its analogue, "liking," a mere matter of chance? And is the Trojan War, claimed on both sides to be chivalric, patriotic, and honorable, to be viewed in a context of hedonistic relativism? Despite his high council schemes, for example, Ulysses' strategies are eventually consummated through the low angry passions of an unchivalrous Greek bereft of his lover.

As we turn from the Prologue to Scene One, we find that the question of value-relativity is carried forward into the discussion between Pandarus and Troilus regarding the merits of the absent Cressida. While Scene Two informs us that she knows her own value to be relative (l.ii.290–299), the first scene suggests that her "fairness" is a function of the competing perspectives of uncle and lover. In addition, it seems to be related to Pandarus' kinship-partiality (l.i.78–79), to the day of the week (l.i.79–80), and to the terms or standards of comparison. As most of the first scene is comprised of such evaluative discourse, the audience is led into Troilus' soliloquizing regarding a supposed universal standard of "fairness:"

Helen must needs be faire,
When with your blood you dayly paint her thus.   (l.i.95–96)

If these lines suggest that the standard of value may herself not be certain, they may also imply that her "fairness" is related to her being "painted;" and that the pragmatic test of value being ironically invoked, her "beauty" is shown by its deadly effects. Indeed, Troilus' choral exclamation introducing these lines, "Fooles on both sides" (l.i.95), also undercuts the rightness of Trojan and Greek cause, while it throws "fairness" itself into question as a relevant criterion.

In addition, Troilus' soliloquy also sets up a series of character-evaluative metaphors: demanding of Apollo the identity of Cressida, Pandarus, and himself, he proposes that the ocean between him and the Indian "Pearle," Cressida,

> ... be cald the wild and wandring flood,
> Our selfe the Merchant, and this sayling *Pandar*,
> Our doubtfull hope, our conuoy and our Barke.   (I.i.107–109)

Like the

> Pearle,
> Whose price hath launch'd aboue a thousand Ships,
> And turn'd Crown'd Kings to Merchants   (II.ii.83–85)

in Troilus' unconsciously ironic later remark, Cressida is the pearl which, by his dangerous quest, Troilus the merchant has highly priced. Emphasizing the joys as well as the distance of vicariousness, the "sayling Pandar," as well as the vicariously experiencing audience—finally addressed by him as fellow panders—evidently participates in the pricing. Between value and action, Shakespeare interposes the questionable evaluator with his problematical set of norms.

Scene One thus introduces a major principle of the play's evaluative technique: the interposition of a gap or indirection in the materials and process of valuing. Here, for instance, Cressida's absence from stage limits the spectators' opportunity to judge Pandarus' and Troilus' evaluations. Through this distancing method in the course of the play, characters and events are discussed at second- and third-hand, allowing room for the intervention of subjectivity and relativism. In the process, which also tends to "de-empathize" the audience from the character and situation, what is revealed is not only the mind of the valuer, but also the subjectivity of valuation itself. Indeed, the entire war plot hangs on the relative valuation of one woman's "fairness," for whom many men absolutely die.

Troilus and Cressida thereby elevates to our view an issue complementarily self-reflexive to that of the nearly contemporaneous *Hamlet,* with its theatrical problem of action: how do we "know" the characters, how do we evaluate and identify them? And ultimately, what is the value of the valuing process? In contrast to *Hamlet, Troilus and Cressida* holds the mirror not only up to nature, but equally self-reflexively, up to the nature of evaluation itself.

Scene Two, complicating the method of Scene One, involves the absent Troilus' evaluation by Cressida, who in the process is herself thus valued. Moreover, having just witnessed Troilus, the audience has an additional perspective. Since the vacillating and love-sick Troilus observed in Scene One is comically different from the hero of perfection here described by Pandarus to his niece, we can more readily measure the disparity between Pandarus' praise and Cressida's mockery. As before, Scene Two throws the bases of judgment into question. Whereas in the first scene it could be demanded what objective standard existed for Cressida's "fairness," here Cressida herself helps undermine Pandarus' claim for Troilus' "complexion" (I.ii.94–107). That passage reveals Shakespeare's progression into further complexity: whereas in Scene One Pandarus set Cressida's beauty against Helen's, while Pandarus himself as judge was not evaluated, here Cressida, the evaluator, is herself evaluated by reference to Helen as judge of male attractiveness (I.ii.94–107). Such increasing modes of evaluative recourse may serve to intensify the impression of distortive relativisms. In addition, the terms of comparison themselves appear more questionable. For in Scene One, such honorifics as "white" and "soft[ness]" (I.i.60–63) were not themselves at issue, while In Scene Two the very terms "browne" and "not browne" are thrown into question (I.ii.94–99). In the scene's descriptions of the Trojan heroes, further, the same man, Troilus, depending on the perspective, produces opposite descriptions: that "sneaking fellow" (I.ii.228) and "the Prince of Chiualrie" (I.ii.231–232).[6]

In addition, paralleling Troilus' soliloquy in Scene One, Cressida, the mistress of love's market, concludes Scene Two by describing the seller's complementary viewpoint to Troilus' buyer's attitude. Where Troilus was interested, at all costs, in grasping his beloved object, Cressida's interest is in holding off, to raise the price (I.ii.290–299). Herself a commodity, she must be noticeably on display, as Ulysses disparagingly later observes (IV.v.65–74). And while Troilus is a buyer who will not exchange

> Silkes vpon the Merchant
> When we haue spoyl'd [Q soild] them;   (II.ii.71–72)

the "spoyl'd [soild]" merchandise herself is not averse to exchanging the buyer. Together, Troilus and Cressida are matched in a perfect if transitory transaction, providing an amatory microcosm to a market universe.

Since *Troilus and Cressida* may now be understood to advance by a process of multiplying perspectives, each feeding into the next, in Scene Three, the scene dominated by Ulysses, we are in fuller possession of our critical viewpoints and techniques. We are prepared, that is, to observe a world where, it becomes increasingly evident, evaluation, knowledge, and even identity are far from fixed and objective. "To say the truth," as Cressida summarizes Pandarus' judgment, "true and not true" (I.ii.99). If the internal evidence of the play has thus revealed its values to be fluctuating and relative market-place ones, what then may be said for the larger issues of the state, for which Ulysses appears to speak? How is he to supply a necessary standard to order, or at least stem, this potential anarchy of values?

II

Although scholars have abundantly indicated the traditional analogues of Ulysses' "degree speech" (I.iii.81–144) and their relation to orthodox Elizabethan political thought,[7] they seem not to have emphasized the ironies of its dramatic context, nor sufficiently analyzed the passage's ironical implications. To rehearse: up to this point, *Troilus and Cressida,* somewhat anticipating Pirandello's *Right You Are If You Think You Are,*[8] has operated self-reflexively to expose an analogue of theatrical illusion: the relativity of value, the difficulty of knowledge, the consequent

confusion of identity. If value, knowledge, and identity appear relative, what principles of order must a politic spokesman for the state espouse?

In a speech whose ironies cut both ways, Ulysses claims that, while degree is
necessary to prevent chaos, members of the degree, or hierarchical, system would,
if masked, be indistinguishable (I.iii.89–90). Degree thus emerges as an external
criterion. Anticipating the extremity of the mad Lear's "A dog's obey'd in office"
(IV.vi.161), Ulysses' "great image of Authority" (*Lear*, IV.vi.161) is a matter of
necessary form. As Achilles later observes, the place makes the man—in effect, a
version of Troilus' view, *"Who's* aught, but as he's valew'd?":

> And not a man for being simply man,
> Hath any honour; but honour'd for those honours
> That are without him; as place, riches, and fauour.   (III.iii.85–88)

If, according to Ulysses,

>   Degree being vizarded,
> Th' vnworthiest shewes as fairely in the Maske   (I.iii.89–90)

then "shew" becomes, *faute de mieux,* the symbol of worth. Degree is also, Ulysses
observes,

> . . . the Ladder to all high designes   (I.iii.108)

an external device which encourages, or allows, men to climb. The self-reflexive
question concerning the relation of degree to the manner by which men

> . . . stand in Authentique place   (I.iii.114)

is thus broached. If degree were removed.

> Force should be right, or rather, right and wrong,
> (Betweene whose endless iarre, Iustice recides)
> Should loose her names, and so should Iustice too.   (I.iii.122–124)

Not only is degree's value the negative one of restraining men from devouring each
other (I.iii.122–130)—a worthy purpose, no doubt, but hardly the sanctified message hailed by many critics of the play—but it is also related to a nominalistic
conception of right, wrong, and justice. Mere names, these are, like degree, modes
of restraint against chaos, and hardly first and enduring principles. Supreme prag-
matist rather than pious traditionalist, Ulysses summons up "specialty of Rule"
(I.iii.84) as a practical military device, rather than as high moral doctrine: because of
neglect of "speciality of Rule," the Grecian tents are hollow, and Troy continues to
survive (I.iii.81–86,144). The dramatic position of Ulysses' degree speech, in Scene
Three, following the indications of the Prologue and the first two scenes, suggests
that, if values are relative, and standards are lacking to preserve hierarchy, the last
resort is the qualified one of degree. Hitherto, a chain of relationships based on a
more-than-secular "bond," *nexus et naturae vinculum,* it now becomes an arbitrary

alternative to flux. From one perspective, indeed, the passage suggests an inversion of traditional dependence: the "primogenitiue, and due of Byrth," as well as "Prerogatiue of Age, Crownes, Scepters, Lawrels," require the formality of degree to "stand in Authentique place" (I.iii.112–114). In a world of self-devouring force, degree must be observed for fear of worse.

In addition, Ulysses' speech contains built-in elements of self-parody. We may consider, for example, his reference to the General:

> Great *Agamemnon:*
> This chaos, when Degree is suffocate,
> Followes the choaking:
> And this neglection of Degree, it is
> That by a pace goes backward in a purpose
> It hath to climbe. The Generall's disdain'd
> By him one stop below; he, by the next,
> That next, by him beneath.   (I.iii.131–138)

The ludicrous profusion of steps, the repetition of the idea associating degree with "climbing" and above all the recognition of the General as the prime factor, if not the prime mover, in the overall debacle, make the passage noteworthy. For it is to Agamemnon, shown shortly to be indistinguishable by Aeneas from his inferiors (I.iii.223–265), that Ulysses addresses himself. If the General is a fool, then he is hierarchically the most influential fool in a ladder of fools. In a kind of judgment-by-parody of the degree-principle, following his vision of dissolution ("did not the General run, were not that a botchy core?" II.i.6–7), Thersites later remarks:

> *Agamemnon* is a foole to offer to command *Achilles, Achilles* is a foole to be commanded of *Agamemnon, Thersites* is a foole to serue such a foole: and Patroclus is a foole positiue.   (II.iii.59–62)

Rather than unalterably sacred, "degree" may also be relative to the position from which one views it.[9] Under the guise of platitudinous orthodoxy, Ulysses' degree speech suggests, from one point of view, a relevant commentary on a contemporary social setting, torn between possibly questionable authority figures and asocial individualism.

In summary, this paper has thus far examined the dramatic sequence and ironies which seem to indicate the relativistic value perspectives of *Troilus and Cressida*. Ulysses' position, in particular, has been shown, through internal inspection of the play, to be meaningful when viewed through such a perspective. In order to confirm these conclusions, I have chosen to compare Ulysses' value speeches with the views of a recognized seventeenth-century exponent of value-relativism.[10] If, then, both internal and external evidence coincide in establishing Ulysses' value attitudes, the case for Ulysses' relativistic views will be further strengthened.

III

To understand the value-context of Shakespeare's play, it may be useful to glance at the transformation of value philosophy between such significant figures as Thomas Aquinas and Thomas Hobbes. For Aquinas, the basis of value is "being," which man does not create.[11] Indeed, all existent things possess value, whether humanly perceived or not, value being in the object independently of one's acting for it or valuing it. Although between the valuing or appetitive man and the valued object, there results a kind of fusion, value is involved with the object, with being, and is incomprehensible apart from it. In the act of valuation, the subject changes, but not the object: ". . . appetibile apprehensum est movens non motum, appetitus autem movens motum" (*Summa Theologica,* I, q.80, a.2). Mankind thus does not create, but discovers, value. Whereas, therefore, the Thomistic view would hardly have accorded with Troilus' notion, "What's aught, but as 'tis valew'd?" (II.ii.54), Hector's reply, which may also suggest a contextualist attitude, qualifies the idea of his brother:

> But value dwels not in particular will,
> It holds his estimate and dignitie
> As well, wherein 'tis precious of it selfe,
> As in the prizer.   (II.ii.55–58)

For Hobbes, however, born in 1588 and sharing with Shakespeare the skeptical heritage of the sixteenth century—of such writers, for example, as Machiavelli and Montaigne—value is not only relative: it is quantified.[12] Succeeding to Montaigne's relativism and Machiavelli's *sang froid* "realism," Hobbes considers with them both not how men ought to live, but how they do live. He follows also Machiavelli's realistic substitution, for traditional contemplative virtue and abstract excellence, of political virtue and patriotic pragmatism.[13]

Value, Hobbes holds, is relative to a market-situation:

> The *value,* or WORTH of a man, is as of all other things, his price; that is to say, so much as would be given for the use of his power: and therefore is not absolute; but a thing dependant on the need and judgment of another.[14]

Value, moreover, is changeable and relative to individual human appetites:

> . . . because the constitution of a man's body is in continual mutation, it is impossible that all the same things should always cause in him the same appetites, and aversions: much less can all men consent, in the desire of almost any one and the same object.   (III, 40–41)

Like Troilus, Hobbes reverses the traditional notion of the *bien en soi:*

> But whatsoever is the object of any man's appetite or desire, that is it which he for his part calleth *good:* and the object of his hate and aversion, *evil.* . . .

there being nothing simply and absolutely so; nor any common rule of good and evil, to be taken from the nature of the objects themselves.[15]

In keeping with Hobbes's quantified view of value, throughout *Troilus and Cressida* market-price recurs as a value consideration.[16] Agamemnon, for example, says of Achilles,

> if he ouerhold his price so much.
> Weele none of him.   (II.iii.134–135)

And he warns that the hero's market-value may go down, as the product remains unbought and deteriorates; being not for all markets, he must sell when he can:

> yet all his vertues
> ....
> Doe in our eyes, begin to loose their glosse;
> Yea, like faire Fruit in an vnholdsome dish,
> Are like to rot vntasted.   (II.iii.118–122)

Elsewhere, while Pandarus is busy "selling" his niece, her father Calchas floats a plan whereby Antenor ". . . shall buy my Daughter" (III.iii.31). As in Jonson's *Volpone,* a member of a family is priced and marketed. At another point, where the lovers must separate, Troilus, who had earlier imported merchants and merchandise into the sacred garden of love (I.i.108; II.ii.72, 85), laments the market-drop at which Cressida and he must sell cheaply what they bought dear:

> We two, that with so many thousand sighes
> Did buy each other, must poorely sell our selues,
> With the rude breuitie and discharge of our [Q one].   (IV.iv.38–40)

Previously, Paris replies to Diomedes' disparaging evaluation of Helen by projecting onto him a commercial intent:

> Faire *Diomed,* you doe as chapmen doe,
> Dis praise the thing that you desire to buy:
> But we in silence hold this vertue well;
> Weele not commend, what we intend to sell.   (IV.i.84–87)

In addition, Thersites taunts Ajax with the charge that he is "bought and solde" (II.i.44). Achilles tells Hector,

> I will the second time,
> As I would buy thee, view thee, limbe by limbe.   (IV.v.262–263)

And far outdoing the bustling Pandarus, whose business it is, the supreme statesman Ulysses is the supreme manipulative merchant of human flesh:

> Let vs (like Merchants) shew our fowlest Wares,
> And thinke perchance they'l sell   (I.iii.373–374)

Revealing that there are merchants, as well as fools, on both sides, Ulysses thus seems practically to violate "degree" in the same scene in which he appears to defend it.

Since a major concern of *Troilus and Cressida* is the accumulation of honor, it is useful to glance at Hobbes's notion of honor as a relative commodity:

> The manifestation of the value we set on one another, is that which is commonly called honouring, and dishonouring. To value a man at a high rate, is to *honour* him; at a low rate, is to *dishonour* him. (III, 76).

Human value and honor are the consequence of a market-situation:

> And as in other things, so in men, not the seller, but the buyer determines the price. For let a man, as most men do, rate themselves at the highest value they can; yet their true value is no more than it is esteemed by others. (III, 76)

In terms comparable to Hobbes's, Achilles senses his own market-depreciation:

> What am I poore or late?
> 'Tis certaine, greatnesse once falne out with fortune,
> Must fall out with men too: what the declin'd is,
> He shall as soone reade in the eyes of others,
> As feele in his owne fall. (III.iii.80–84)

Like Hobbes, whose language conveys such relativistic concerns (e.g., "To honour those another honours, is to honour him," III, 78), Achilles recognizes honor as not intrinsic, but rather as an external, subjective, often accidental attribute:

> And not a man for being simply man,
> Hath any honour; but honour'd for those honours
> That are without him; as place, riches, and fauour,
> Prizes of accident, as oft as merit. (III.iii.86–89)

Achilles' illustration of externally acquired honors, "place, riches, and fauour," is echoed in Hobbes's list of powers men desire to acquire, "riches, place...., favour" (IV, 38). To the same list Hobbes adds "good fortune," just as Achilles in his same speech remarks, "Fortune and I are friends ..." (III.iii.94). Despite Achilles' sense, as one of the *fortunati*, of his own merit—most men, as Hobbes noted, "rate themselves at the highest value they can," and Ulysses earlier mentioned Achilles' "Imagin'd wroth [i.e., Q worth]" (II.ii.175)—the Greek hero is perturbed by the changed evaluation he now senses. He is confused by

> these mens lookes: who do me thinkes finde out
> Something not worth in me such rich beholding,
> As they haue often giuen. (III.iii.96–98)

In reply, Ulysses, who has already rigged the honor-market against Achilles, provides a market-diagnosis. It recalls the pragmatic-operational test of virtue set forth at length by Agamemnon and Nestor in I. iii—the "protractive trials" of virtue in adversity. Bringing to mind Hobbes's injunction, "For let a man, as most men do, rate themselves at the highest value they can; yet their true value is no more than it is esteemed by others," Ulysses asserts that no man can claim to judge his own values privately, apart from social valuation:

> man, how dearely euer parted,
> How much in hauing, or without, or in,
> Cannot make boast to haue that which he hath;
> Nor feeles not what he owes, but by reflection:
> As when his vertues shining vpon others,
> Heate them, and they retort that heate againe
> To the first giuer.   (III.iii.103–109)

"Reflection" is the term Hobbes, too, uses regarding the relativity of human qualities, not "honourable" in themselves alone: ". . . *nobility* is honourable by reflection, as a sign of power in the ancestors" (IV, 39). Ulysses provides, in addition, a further elaboration of the operational or pragmatic theory of value:

> no may [i.e., Q man] is the Lord of any thing
> . . . .
> Till he communicate his parts to others.   (III.iii.121, 123)

Even knowledge or self-knowledge is operational:

> Nor doth he of himselfe know them for ought,
> Till he behold them formed in th' applause,
> Where they are extended.   (III.iii.124–126)

Following Achilles' recognition that his market value may now resemble that of "beggars" in relation to "mysers" (III.iii.149), Ulysses launches into his famous speech on Time—itself an omnivorous and ungrateful beggar with "a wallet at his backe" into which "he puts almes for obliuion" (III.iii.152–153). In Hobbesian value terms, this speech fits perfectly the cruel and fickle fluctuation of the world's "honor-market." Thus Ulysses, grand manipulator of the market in honor, can explain to the "dishonored" Achilles that "good deedes past"

> are deuour'd
> As fast as they are made, forgot as soone
> As done.   (III.iii.155–157)

In this world, there is no reified, platonic value status for virtues, but only, at best, an unceasing series of nominalistic recognitions. Not merely mutability is the theme here, but also a continuous market-fluctuation, where virtuous deeds are immediately quantified and at once forgotten. Only a ceaseless "perseurance" keeps "honor bright" (III.iii.157–158). The good action does not even linger in its own right, but in a rapid flux is "deuour'd as fast as . . . made" (III.iii.156). "O let not," Ulysses advises,

> vertue seeke
> Remuneration for the thing it was,   (III.iii.176–177)

With an irony that points forward to the frailty of Cressida, Ulysses summarizes:

> The present eye praises the present object.   (III.iii.186)

Ulysses further admonishes that not even the highest virtues, such as love and friendship, survive the flux:

> Loue, friendship, charity, are subjects all
> To enuious and calumniating time.   (III.iii.179–180)

For example, Troilus with love and friendship had supported his brother Paris' claim to Helen; yet Paris' response to Troilus' plight in having to relinquish Cressida, while temporal, is hardly reciprocal:

> There is no helpe:
> The bitter disposition of the time will haue it so.   (IV.i.55–56)

Apropos, it is friendship, so highly esteemed in Shakespeare's age, that Hobbes relates to "enuious and calumniating time." For friendship is also a fluctuating commodity in time. Among the "causes for which men come together, and delight in each other's company," Hobbes distinguishes

> a certain market-friendship, . . . which hath more of jealousy in it than true love . . . whence [a man] . . . may . . . by comparison of another man's defects . . . pass the more current in his own opinion. (II, 3–4)

If, as Ulysses and Hobbes suggest, all values, including honor, are quantified, and virtues are evaluated in pragmatic and operational terms, we enter a ceaseless realm of competition in time, a Hobbesian *bellum omnium contra omnes* for the commodity, "honor." For, as Ulysses advises Achilles, who had recently "Made emulous missions 'mongst the gods themselues" (III.iii.195),

> emulation hath a thousand Sonnes,
> That one by one pursue; if you giue way,
> . . . .
> Like to an entred Tyde, they all rush by,
> And leaue you hindmost.   (III.iii.163–167)

Emulation is defined by Hobbes as close to *envy:*

> *Grief,* for the success of a competitor in wealth, honour, or other good, if it be joined with endeavour to enforce our own abilities to equal or exceed him,

is called EMULATION: but joined with endeavour to supplant, or hinder a competitor, ENVY. (III, 47)

Emulation is shared by other glory-seekers in the play, including Diomedes, who speaks of "mine emulous honour" (IV.i.34). Yet it is this *emulation* that Ulysses, in his degree speech, diagnoses as related to *envy* and as the enemy of "degree." It is "this neglection of Degree," Ulysses argues, that leads to emulous disorder:

> so euery step
> Exampled by the first pace that is sicke
> Of his Superiour, growes to an enuious Feauer
> Of pale, and bloodlesse Emulation.   (I.iii.134–141)

For Ulysses, then, as also for the play, human society resembles a battleground where individuals fight each other for "honor," which, in Hobbes, is quantified into power:

> *Honourable* is whatsoever possession, action, or quality, is an argument and sign of power . . . Dominion, and victory is honourable; because acquired by power . . . honour consisteth only in the opinion of power. (III, 79–80)

Such quest for honor, notes Hobbes, is without limits:

> For every man looketh that his companion should value him, at the same rate he sets upon himself: and upon all signs of contempt, or undervaluing, naturally endeavours . . . (which amongst them that have no common power to keep them in quiet, is far enough to make them destroy each other), to extort a greater value from his contemners, by damage; and from others, by the example. (III, 112)

If "honor" is a sign of "power," and "power" involves material values, the competitive quest for such values results in inevitable social hostilities:

> the most frequent reason why men desire to hurt each other, ariseth hence, that many men at the same time have an appetite to the same thing; which yet very often they can neither enjoy in common, nor yet divide it; whence it follows that the strongest must have it, and who is strongest must be decided by the sword. (II, 8)

This passage may be read as a description of Helen and the Trojan War in Hobbesian—and we may now agree—quasi-Shakespearean terms: ". . . many men have an appetite to the same thing; which [recalling Priam's admonition to Paris on Helen: "You haue the Hony still, but these the Gall," II.ii.151] they can neither enjoy in common, nor yet divide it." For in Shakespearean-Hobbesian terms, *Troilus and Cressida is* a study of appetites in society—indeed, a dramatic exploration of an appetitive war for a "thing" many men desire, and none "can enjoy in common nor yet divide."

If, politically, a competitively anarchic power-struggle results in which each man hostilely seeks his own ends, "All society," as Hobbes remarks, being "either for gain, or for glory" (II, 5), then the "State" must intervene for the preservation of the individual. For the sake of survival, the individual must renounce, in favor of the state, his disruptive right to private value-judgment and behavior. Such individualism is exemplified not only in Troilus' anarchic "What's aught, but as 'tis valew'd?" (II.ii.54), but also in his intemperate behavior. "And we haue made a god of our owne blood," as the Nuncius observes in Samuel Daniel's *Philotas* (1623, p. 251; three acts of this 1604 political play were written in 1600). Moreover, as characterized in Act IV from the viewpoint of his dramatic foil, the politic statist, Ulysses, the "plaine and true" Troilus (IV.iv.114) emerges as rashly chivalrous and open:

> For what he has, he giues; what thinkes, he shewes   (IV.v.117)

the very opposite to all Machiavellian counsel. Checking with his *nomos* or legal convention, Troilus' youthful *physis,* or natural force, Ulysses, who "knows all," while counseling restraint, also maliciously manipulates Troilus into a torturous view of his own betrayal. Although, in one sense the *hypocrite* Ulysses is Troilus' relativistic *semblable* and *frère,* Troilus' rebellious antinomianism is thus coupled with his practical folly. Ulysses, like Hobbes, would have remarked in Troilus a symptom of

> the *diseases* of a commonwealth, that proceed from the poison of seditious doctrines, whereof one is, *That every private man is judge of good and evil actions.* This is true in the condition of mere nature, where there are no civil laws . . . But otherwise, it is manifest, that the measure of good and evil actions, is the civil law. (III, 310)

It follows from this that there is, in Hobbes as in Ulysses, no pretence at absolute good or evil, but only an attempt at expedient restraint for the peaceful operation of the state. Peace, and freedom from fear of "sudden death" are gained by subjection to "degree" in Ulysses' terms, or to the monarch in Hobbesian terms.

Not surprisingly, therefore, Ulysses emerges as a pragmatic spokesman for state-values—for *raison d'état* and *mystère d'état,* and it is thus no accident that two of his major speeches concern the interests of the state. In addition to his degree speech, which has been discussed, we may glance at his speech on "mystery of state"—a semi-divine attribution of mysterious unsleeping and omniscient power—a secularized version of the eye of providence. In terms which suggest a religious absolute, Ulysses describes this "mystery of state":

> The prouidence that's in a watchfull State,
> Knowes almost euery graine of Plutoes gold;
> Findes bottome in th'vncomprehensiue deepes;
> Keepes place with thought; and almost like the gods,
> Doe thoughts vnuaile in their dumbe cradles:

There is a mysterie (with whom relation
Durst neuer meddle) in the soule of State;
Which hath an operation more diuine,
Then breath or pen can giue expressure to.   (III.iii.205–213)

In addition to recalling the medieval religio-political idea of "mystery of state," a concept of monarchical sacred omniscience,[17] Ulysses' comment, like his degree speech earlier, opposes the interests of state to individualism. In view of the speaker and the occasion, as well as of possible overtones of the Elizabethan practice of informing,[18] the lines suggest, as in the degree speech, an *ad hoc* adaptation of a traditional notion. For "mystery of state" gave sanction to "reason of state," a much discussed notion in the second half of the sixteenth century. "Reason of state" allowed the prince, in Montaigne's words, "for state matters, to breake his . . . faith . . . It is no vice . . ."[19] Such relativistic apologies for Machiavellian *Staatsräson* were canvassed broadly in Shakespeare's time. For example, Don Quixote discusses with his friends "esto, que llaman razon de Estado,"[20] while, partly because of its title, Giovanni Botero's *Della ragion di stato* (Venice, 1589) enjoyed much success in several languages.[21] In *Troilus and Cressida*, it is now evident, Ulysses speaks for reason of state. Contrasting a Ulysses-Hobbesian patriotic pragmatism with the asocial individualism of Troilus or Achilles, Shakespeare's balanced irony reflects a political issue which would have engaged his Elizabethan audience.

In summary, this paper has attempted to show, contrary to the views of some critics, that Ulysses' "value" speeches suggest a relativism consistent both internally with the evidence of *Troilus and Cressida* and externally with the recognized relativism of a seventeenth-century philosopher. Yet it is not Ulysses, master manipulator of values, but Pandarus who significantly has the last word, drawing the spectators in his epilogue familiarly into the play's own circle of flesh-peddlers and tradesmen. As kinsmen, he addresses them even as members of his own family: "Brethren and sisters of the hold-dore trade" (V.x.54), a recognition which may be a little more than kin and less than kind. If, finally, in Shakespeare's plays, all the world's a stage, in *Troilus and Cressida*, where Everyman is Pandarus' "trader in the flesh" (V.x.49) and human values are transient and quantified, all the world becomes a market place—"a great Market," as *Poor Robin's Visions* (1677) calls it, "in which every thing is sold; *as large consciences, fair Misses with foul Bodies, Wit, Vanity, Knavery, Mens lives, and their Reputations, and the welfare of their Families thrown in to boot*" (p. 123).

NOTES

[1]Portions of this paper were presented at the Tenth International Congress of the Fédération Internationale des Langues et Littératures Modernes, held in Strasbourg, August, 1966; and at a Faculty Colloquium of Brown University, February, 1967. The paper (for suggestions on which I am indebted to S. F. Johnson, S. I. Mintz, and E. A. Snow) is part of a book nearing completion interpreting *Troilus and Cressida* in the light of its linguistic, rhetorical, and intellectual contexts.

²See, e.g., Una Ellis-Fermor, "Discord in the Spheres: The Universe of *Troilus and Cressida,*" in *The Frontiers of Drama,* 3rd ed. (London, 1948); Wolfgang Schmidt, "Die Wertlehre in *Troilus und Cressida,*" *Neuren Sprachen,* XLVII (1940), 181–188. Economic aspects are discussed in Raymond Southall, "*Troilus and Cressida* and the Spirit of Capitalism," in *Shakespeare in a Changing World,* ed. Arnold Kettle (London, 1964), pp. 217–232; and Margaret Schlauch, "*Troilus i Kressyda* Szekspira i Chaucera— Jezyk Metaforyczny w Świetle Przemian Spoŀeczynch," *Kwartalnik Neo-filologiczny,* I, no. 3–4 (1954), 3–20.

³See New Variorum Edition of *Troilus and Cressida,* ed. Harold N. Hillebrand and T. W. Baldwin (Philadelphia, 1953), pp. 52–59, 389–410. All future references are to this text.

⁴*The English Works of Thomas Hobbes of Malmesbury,* ed. William Molesworth (London, 1839), III, 602; references to Hobbes will be to this edition.

⁵Jonson references are to *Ben Jonson,* ed. C. H. Herford and Percy Simpson (Oxford, 1932), IV.

⁶Cf. a similar irreconcilability in Troilus' later view of Cressida: "This is, and is not Cressid:" (V.ii.171).

⁷See New Variorum ed., pp. 389–410; Robert Kimbrough, *Shakespeare's* Troilus and Cressida *and Its Setting* (Cambridge, Mass., 1964); Virgil K. Whitaker, *Shakespeare's Use of Learning* (San Marino, 1953), pp. 195–199, which regards the degree speech as paralleled in idea but surpassed in style by Richard Hooker's *Of the Laws of Ecclesiastical Polity.* See also Whitaker's "Philosophy and Romance in Shakespeare's 'Problem' Comedies" (In *The Seventeenth Century: Studies ... By Richard Foster Jones and Others ...* , Stanford, 1951, p. 342), relating the "degree" speech to Hooker's views; and Hiram Haydn's *Counter-Renaissance* (N.Y., 1950), p. 297, asserting that in the "degree" speech "Ulysses is spokesman not only for the world but for the ages as well." See E. M. W. Tillyard, *Shakespeare's History Plays* (London, 1948), pp. 10–20; and especially his influential *Elizabethan World Picture* (London, 1943), pp. 7–15, 82–84.

⁸Luigi Pirandello's *Cosí è (se vi pare),* recalling Shakespeare's *Sein und Schein* problem, implies that truth, knowledge, and identity depend on the observer—*esse est percipi.* In Pirandello's play, a woman is irreconcilably regarded, depending on the perceiver, as Ponza's second wife, and as Signora Frola's daughter. As the woman remains veiled at the end, the play, in respect of identity, offers no resolution. Closer to Shakespeare's time, Cervantes anticipates Pirandello's *teatro dello specchio,* questioning whether Don Quixote's romantic fantasy regarding identity is any less "real" than Sancho Panza's "realism." Shakespeare's general background in this regard may include Montaignian and pyrrhonist influences; cf. Wolfgang Clemen, *Schein und Sein bei Shakespeare* (München, 1959), pp. 44–46, for some relevant Montaigne citations. Cf. Richard H. Popkin, *The History of Scepticism from Erasmus to Descartes* (Assen, Neth., 1950); and see, for relations between "illusionism" and baroque, Jean Rousset, *La Littérature de l'âge baroque en France* (Paris, 1954). The familiar appearance-versus-reality relativity recurs, e.g., in the "fair without—foul within" pattern in *Troilus* (cf. V.vi.39–41 and V.viii.2–3).

⁹Further support of the view questioning Ulysses' degree-speech orthodoxy is found in a note complementary and corroborative to the present paper: Johannes Kleinstück, "Ulysses' Speech on Degree as Related to the Play of *Troilus and Cressida,*" *Neophilologus,* XLIII (1959), 58–63. Seeking success rather than eternal truth, Ulysses, the author remarks, violates degree by preferring Ajax to Achilles, and thereby breeds the emulation his degree speech deplores. In regard to another problem, he observes that the characters constantly belie their words by thought or action: e.g., Pandarus refuses to woo for Troilus, then goes to it; Troilus announces his refusal to fight for Helen, and goes out to fight for her. The crux of Hector's sudden change (Ii.ii.196–200) after having adduced reasons against championing Helen may thus be understood as part of a general pattern of inconsistency—or, to employ the present writer's approach, relativity—between word and action. Relativity, it may be added, affects "truth" throughout the play, truth being subject to time and circumstance. Further, Troilus' "What's aught, but as 'tis valew'd?" (II.ii.54) reaps its ironical reward in the relativistic behavior toward truth of Cressida, and in her betrayal.

¹⁰Although A. E. Taylor has opened the question of whether Hobbes was in all respects a complete relativist, that debate need not concern us here insofar as we are not involved in interpreting the *general* philosophic position of Hobbes, but rather the particular and relativistic statements which we quote. See Keith C. Brown, ed., *Hobbes Studies* (Cambridge, Mass., 1965), containing both Taylor's view and refutations of it.

¹¹See, for fuller discussion, Sister Mary Dominica Mullen, *Essence and Operation in the Teaching of St. Thomas and in Some Modern Philosophers* (Washington, 1941), pp. 66–74. The citation below is from S. Thomas Aquinas, *Summa Totius Theologiae* (Antwerp, 1575), I, 234. It echoes Aristotle, *De Anima*

(iii.10: "that which moves without itself being moved is the realizable good, that which at once moves and is moved is the faculty of appetite . . ."; *The Works of Aristotle*, ed. W. D. Ross, Oxford, 1931, III, 433b).

[12]The development of ideas of value in the Shakespearean era remains to be traced. Of possible interest may be: Franz Joachim von Rintelen, *Der Wertgedanke in der europaïschen Geistesentwicklung* (Halle, Saale, 1932); Oskar Kraus, *Die Werttheorien: Geschichte und Kritik* (Brünn, 1937); Everett W. Hall, *Modern Science and Human Values* (Princeton, 1956); Rudolf Eisler, *Wörterbuch der philosophischen Begriffe* (Berlin, 1927–30), *s.v.* "Wert." See also particular studies, e.g., Johannes Binkowski, "Die Wertlehre des Duns Skotus in ihrer Bedeutung für die Gegenwart," *Wissenschaft und Weisheit*, III (1936), 269–282. A useful formulaic summary of Hobbes and some modern value theories appears in Elie M. Adams, *Ethical Naturalism and the Modern World-View* (Chapel Hill, 1960), p. 37. See also John Laird, *The Idea of Value* (Cambridge, Eng., 1929).

[13]Although Hobbes's serious publication began later, he was, of course, subject to some of the early currents which might even, distantly, have influenced Shakespeare. Interestingly, a recent study has shown the likely influence on Hobbes of a work published about the time of the composition of *Troilus and Cressida*: Pierre Charron's *De la sagesse* (Bordeaux, 1601). In "Pierre Charron: Precursor to Hobbes," *Review of Politics*, XXV (1963), 212–224, Paul F. Grendler concludes that Hobbes knew the work of Charron (1541–1603), a follower of Montaigne, and that they share not only a worldly pyrrhonism and distrust of the people, but also similar views with regard to a strong state as a barrier against the "restless souls of men." Like Hobbes, Charron bases his views on human nature; and observation had taught him that tradition and custom were "very relativist" (p. 220).

[14]III, 76. In " 'Opinion' and 'Value' in *Troilus and Cressida*," *Essays in Criticism*, IV (1954), 282–296, Winifred M. T. Nowottny almost uniquely ventured a citation from Hobbes, in relation to Troilus. In his reply, "Opinion, Truth and Value," *Essays in Criticism*, V (1955), 181–187, Frank Kermode, although identifying Ulysses with Hobbes (p. 183), declared it was dangerous to bring Hobbes into the argument (p. 181).

[15]III, 41. Hobbes's statement involves a libertine *topos*. See the present writer, *King Lear and the Gods* (San Marino, 1966), pp. 128n–129n; in addition, cf. William Wycherley, *Complete Works*, ed. Montague Summers (London, 1924), IV, 123 (no. cxxxii), as well as the tradition running beyond Protagoras' *homo mensura*. Cf. Montaigne, *The Essayes*, tr. John Florio (London, 1928), I, 269–291 (Bk. I, ch. xl). "That the Taste of Goods or Evils Doth Greatly Depend on the Opinion We Have of Them." On the connection between relativism in value and nominalism, and the recognition of conventionalism in language, cf. Samuel I. Mintz, *The Hunting of Leviathan* (Cambridge, Eng., 1962), pp. 25–26. Cf. the summary of attitudes in Aristotle, *Ethiques* (1547), sig. [Cvii^v–Cviii]: "The wyll is the ende or the intente . . . & where it semeth to some men that to be good which please them, other there be to whom it semeth that all is good that the most would have commonly: but according to the truthe it is not so, but good is that whiche seemeth good to them that be good, that judge thinges as they bee, and judge as doth the whole man, that judgeth that swete, which is swete, and that bitter, which is bitter. But the sicke man doth al contrarye, for he judgeth bitter to bee swete, & the swete bytter, and so unto an evel man that which is good seemeth evell, and that is evyll good . . . there be manye sicke of this naughty syckenes, because the woorkes good and evell be in their jugement."

[16]The transformation between "use value" and "exchange value" which is reflected in the Renaissance context of this play should be noted, but requires a separate and fuller treatment. Regarding socio-economic setting, cf. the stimulating but controversial work of C. B. Macpherson, "Hobbes's Bourgeois Man," in *Hobbes Studies*, ed. Keith C. Brown (Cambridge, Mass., 1965), pp. 169–183; and his book, *The Theory of Possessive Individualism: Hobbes to Locke* (Oxford, 1962). For economic controversy about the time of *Troilus and Cressida*'s composition, including debate over individualism versus state interest, see: Thomas Milles, *The Customers Apology* [n.p., 1599?; Folger STC 17928.5]; John Wheeler, *A Treatise of Commerce* (Middelburgh, 1601), ed. George B. Hotchkiss (New York, 1931); Gerard de Malynes, *A Treatise of the Canker of Englands Common Wealth* (London, 1601), and *Saint George for England* (London, 1601). In 1601, during the last three months, Parliament met, and in that time debated individual versus state interest, especially with regard to monopolies. See John E. Neale, *Elizabeth I and Her Parliaments*, (1584–1601) (London, 1957), pp. 376–393; and the detailed parliamentary records of Heywood Townshend, *Historical Collections* (London, 1680), and Simonds d'Ewes, *The Journals of All the Parliaments during the Reign of Queen Elizabeth* (London, 1682).

[17]See Ernst H. Kantorowicz, "Mysteries of State: An Absolutist Concept and Its Late Mediaeval Origins," *Harvard Theological Review*, XLVII (1955), 65–91; he does not include this play's instance. Cf. also

"mysteries of state" in Daniel's *Philotas* (1604; three acts written in 1600), Chorus ending Act I (1623, p. 203).

[18]Cf. M. W. Beresford, "The Common Informer, the Penal Statutes and Economic Regulation," *Economic History Review*, ser. 2, X (1957–1958), 221–237; G. R. Elton, "Informing for Profit: A Sidelight on Tudor Methods of Law-Enforcement," *Cambridge Historical Journal*, XI (1954), 149–167; William F. Friedman, "Shakespeare, Secret Intelligence, and Statecraft," *Proceedings of the American Philosophical Society*, CVI (1962), 401–411.

[19]Montaigne, *The Essayes*, tr. John Florio (London, 1928), III, 18. "Honor" thus seems relative to the interests of the state. In addition to such positive studies of honor as Curtis B. Watson's *Shakespeare and the Renaissance Conception of Honor* (Princeton, 1960), see G. A. Borgese, "The Dishonor of Honor from Giovanni Mauro to Sir John Falstaff," *Romanic Review*, XXXII (1941), 44–55. See also Alice Shalvi, " 'Honor' in *Troilus and Cressida*," *Studies in English Literature*, V (1965), 283–302. Robert Ashley's *Of Honour*, ed. Virgil B. Heltzel (San Marino, 1947), pp. 35, 70, 80, treats "honor" as related to "degree," and a safeguard of order.

[20]*Segunda Parte del Ingenioso Cavallero Don Quixote de la Mancha* (Madrid, 1615), fol. Iᵛ.

[21]See Botero, *The Reason of State*, tr. P. J. and D. P. Waley (New Haven, 1956). See also Heinrich Lutz, *Ragione di Stato und christliche Staatsethik im 16. Jahrhundert* (Münster i. W., 1961); George L. Mosse, *The Holy Pretence: A Study in Christianity and Reason of State* ... (Oxford, 1957); Rodolpho de Mattei, "... Origini e fortuna della locuzione 'Ragion di Stato,' " *Rivista Internazionale di Filosofia del Diritto*, XXVI (1949), 187–202; Roma Gill, "Necessity of State: Massinger's *Believe as You List*," *ES*, XLVI (1965), 407–416; Augusto del Noce, "La crisi libertina e la ragion di stato," in *Cristianesimo e ragion di Stato* ... *Atti del II Congresso internazionale di studi umanistici* (Roma, 1953,), pp. 35–47. A standard work on reason of state and Machiavelli is Friedrich Meinecke, *Die Idee der Staatsräson in der neueren Geschichte* (München, 1925). For background on "policy" see Napoleone Orsini, " 'Policy' or the Language of Elizabethan Machiavellianism," *Journal of the Warburg and Courtauld Inst.*, IX (1946), 122–134.

R. F. Storch

THE FUGITIVE FROM THE ANCESTRAL HEARTH: TENNYSON'S "ULYSSES"

We commonly underestimate the vulgarity of great poems, the coarseness of appetite with which they incorporate a mixture of ideas and feelings that cannot be harmoniously connected. E. M. Forster's "only connect" is the watchword of a finely discriminating, critical mind; but our civilization, our life-style, may contain unresolvable and conflicting attitudes, and may indeed be given a characteristic imprint by them. It is true that poets have often addressed themselves to the rectification of moral confusion—and in the very act revealed rather uncivilized motives. Dr. Johnson found "Lycidas" offensive for the intrusion into the elegiac occasion of egocentric concerns, for the mixture of pastoral convention, private anxieties and public issues. Similarly, Tennyson's "Ulysses" has given offense with its coarseness of sentiment at the beginning and stridency of tone at the end. The hero's plainness of speech in leaving behind "an aged wife" and "a savage race / That hoard, and sleep, and feed, and know not me" has in recent years been judged harsh and irreconcilable with the noble aspirations voiced at the heart of the poem. The modern critic knows, however, to guard his sensibility and the poet's reputation against such painful incongruities. He dissociates Tennyson as well as himself from the hero's coarseness by detecting in the poem ironic characterization. Tennyson, we are told, deliberately made the opening sentences morally coarse in order to characterize Ulysses as an egotistical brute as well as a dreamy adventurer. We are offered, then, the moral refinements of irony and denied the image of a hero who has both nobility of aspiration and coarseness of feeling. The poem has become "... a dramatic portrayal of a type of human being who held a set of ideas Tennyson regarded as destructive of the whole fabric of society."[1] Other modern critics note another incongruity in the poem: the voice of Tennyson's personal experience of desolation, withdrawal and melancholy ("The long day wanes; the slow moon climbs, the deep / Moans round with many voices") and the voice of public morality ("To strive, to seek, to find, and not to yield"). These critics do not,

---

From *Texas Studies in Literature and Language* 13, No. 1 (Summer 1971): 281–97.

at any rate, impute to the poet a deliberate and ironic contrast in voices. But their assumption that the voice of desolation is more autobiographical, more private than the voice of moral exhortation, and that there is necessarily an unpoetic discrepancy of tone here, needs surely to be examined.

Victorian readers do not seem to have been disconcerted by a lack of harmony in the poem. John Sterling, one of its earliest reviewers, singles out for praise its unity and consistency of tone: "There is in this work a delightful epic tone, and a clear impassioned wisdom quietly carving its sage words and graceful figures on pale but lasting marble."[2] It is true that Sterling was somewhat obtuse regarding Tennyson's choice of Ulysses rather than "Columbus, Gama or even Drake" for his subject. Sterling's response to the poem takes in only heroism; there is no question of coarseness, and therefore no occasion for ironic dramatization. He is alive to irony in "St. Simeon Stylites," which he calls "a kind of monological personification of a filthy and mad ascetic. We find exhibited with the seriousness of bitter irony, his loathsome, yet ridiculous attempts at saintship." Sterling sees ironic possibilities in certain situations and characters which he here formulates with remarkable gusto. But regarding other situations and characters ("How different, how superior is *Ulysses*") he is immune to the moral discriminations that bother later readers. He was a leading member of the Apostles, that group of intense and sensitive spirits to which Tennyson also belonged, and was therefore as close as any one was likely to be to the moral tone of the poem.[3] He saw in it no conflicting voices or ideas destructive of society. Nor is he alone in this tone-deafness. One reviewer of 1844 praises "the mild dignity and placid resolve."[4] R. H. Hutton in 1888 clinches the argument: "His *St. Simeon Stylites* is his hostile picture of the fanatic, just as his *Ulysses* is his friendly picture of the insatiable craving for new experience, enterprise, and adventure, when under the control of a luminous reason and a self-controlled will."[5] We cannot dismiss Hutton as an insensitive or careless reader, for he notes "the scorn of Ulysses for the petty drudgery of his Ithacan household and government" and approves of Ulysses' refusal "to shut himself in between the narrow walls of humdrum duties." Tennyson's contemporaries saw in the poem all the ingredients we see in it, but unlike us they discovered no discrepancies of attitude and had no difficulty in "connecting"—or saw no need to connect. Their culture seems to have been tolerant of incongruities which we find morally inadequate. The poet and his readers were immersed in a conglomeration of feelings that made up their program of a rewarding life; and only by stepping outside the Victorian world do we become aware of unresolved, unconnected attitudes. Victorian readers were not more obtuse to the gamut of feeling-tones in the poem than we are. They accepted what we feel to be disharmony because their moral sensibility moved along other lines, and not the line of spiritual danger inherent in Ulysses' rejection of family and social responsibilities. Ulysses' cry for self-fulfillment rang out so powerfully that it rearranged the pattern of Victorian moral perceptions. Today the noble and heroic dimensions of Tennyson's Ulysses are being questioned. But it is still possible for a sensitive reader to see in the poem the portrait of a culture hero without irony. "In 'Ulysses' the sense that he must press on and not moulder in idleness is expressed objectively, through the classical story, and not subjectively as his own experience. He comes here as near perfection in the grand manner as he ever did; the poem is flawless in tone from beginning to end; spare, grave, free from excessive decoration, and full of firmly controlled feeling."[6]

Tennyson's Ulysses is a culture hero because he embodies certain unresolved conflicts that are cardinal to our civilization. The poem contains counterpoints of feeling that belong not only to Tennyson and his age, but to the secular tradition of the greatness of soul that is traceable to Dante, Virgil, Homer, and ultimately to the family situation.

By setting out westward in his insatiable thirst for knowledge Tennyson's Ulysses is breaking with the Christian geography of salvation, as it is for example described in John Donne's "Good Friday, 1613. Riding Westward." The truth lies in the East and the motion proper to the soul is toward that point of heaven. But our souls become captivated by ambitions and desires not their own:

> Subject to forraigne motions, lose their owne
> And being by others hurried every day,
> Scarce in a yeare their naturall forme obey:
> Pleasure or businesse, so, our Soules admit
> For their first mover, and are whirld by it.
> Hence is't, that I am carryed towards the West
> This day, when my Soules forme bends towards the East.[7]

The conflict is simple enough: spirituality and business pull in opposite directions. The conflict is too simple, for the business of the world, though it may deflect us from the East, is also sweetened by familial duties and loyalties toward fellow men. Would Donne have called the tending of the ancestral hearth and the taking up of civic life, pleasure, business, or the soul's natural form? The motions proper to the soul are not in our civilization linear but circuitous:

> in strange way
> To stand inquiring right, is not to stray;
> To sleepe, or runne wrong, is. On a huge hill,
> Cragged, and steep, Truth stands, and hee that will
> Reach her, about must, and about must goe;
> And what the hills suddennes resists, winne so.[8]

To leave behind the domestic and civic sanctities in the quest for spirituality is too simple a solution and alien to our tradition, because it leads to stagnation both in spirituality and in worldly business.

Tennyson's Ulysses therefore offends against two kinds of sanctity, by rejecting his family and his kingdom, and by turning toward the West instead of the East. This is no doubt the strongest undercurrent of feeling we bring to the poem; but it is an

undercurrent that is hidden or submerged by a contrary motion, namely the feeling
that it is heroic to separate oneself from family and community and to find salvation
in a solitary struggle. Tennyson's poem has these countermotions and contains
them by a comprehensiveness: Ulysses' words point one way—his is the rhetoric
of heroism—but his sadness reminds us of what he sacrifices. He voices high
aspirations, restless striving, courageous independence, responsibility toward selfhood and its perfection. ("The grand leading principle ... is the absolute and essential importance of human development in its richest diversity," to quote the
epigraph to J.S. Mill's *On Liberty.*) With these noble aspirations domestic and civic
duties are irreconcilable. Ulysses' voice is tired with distaste for such ties, or harsh
with contempt. But there is the other current of feeling, creating the dominant tone;
the restlessness is permeated with the fear of death. Ulysses' spiritual search must
end in disaster, because immortality is unattainable:

> To follow knowledge like a sinking star,
> Beyond the utmost bound of human thought.

The keynote of the poem is a sinking feeling; the exultation is attended by a
profound melancholy. Fear of desolation, of death, cannot be hidden by a restlessness that never quite becomes the certainty of faith:

> but every hour is saved
> From that eternal silence, something more,
> A bringer of new things.

Restlessness and desolation are the two countermotions in the poem. The rejection
of civic duties, the note of defiance toward the family, and the urgent claims of
self-cultivation are intensified through the sense of loss and dereliction, and so is the
fear of death with its concomitant hunger for immortality. Compared with the
counterpointed ideas and feelings of "Ulysses," Donne's poem has the clarity of a
linear argument, but also a sparseness of feeling in spite of its brilliant paradox. Its
feeling is engaged on one side only: the rejection of the world without experiencing
the loss of what is being rejected. For Donne the business of the world does not
contain domestic life; for Tennyson it does.

    The conflict between the freedom of the soul and family ties is part of the
European tradition, and may already be sounded in Homer's Odysseus. It is certainly active in Plato's mind. "And what is proper to the soul?" asks Diotima in the
Symposium, and answers, "Why, Thought and all the other virtues of which poets
and such craftsmen as may be considered inventors are progenitors. But by far the
greatest and noblest aspect of Thought, which is called self-control and justice, is
that which regulates both civic and domestic affairs." In these words Diotima might
be rebuking Ulysses for his abandonment of Ithaca; but she concludes her discourse
in a very different vein: "Do you not understand that only he who perceives beauty
with the eyes of his soul can bring forth veritable Virtue and not its image? For it
is not the image but the truth that he grasps. And he that brings forth and fosters

veritable Virtue will be beloved of the Gods; and he, if any of the sons of man, will become immortal." Ulysses, too, seeks immortality through a beauty and virtue lying beyond the horizon of mere images of ordinary business and pleasures. But at the very moment of asserting the freedom of his soul from the business of this world, his voice carries the pain of leaving Ithaca for the solitude of the unknown. His heroic fortitude is inseparable from melancholy fears; desolation will make itself heard through the self-assertion. The cost of independence is guilt and the fear of death. That is the whirlpool Ulysses is drawn into.

A whirlpool is least like the tidy unfolding of an argument: literary criticism may have to put aside its predilection for consistency of thought or characterization according to some simple abstraction. Poetry can reflect intricacies that to the tidy mind look like confusions but are in truth the incised patterns in a way of life. The Common Reader is often nearer to the truth because he is immersed in the pattern that offends the philosophic mind. To see the "inconsistencies" in our own culture we have to step outside it in order to get a larger view of the terrain. If we can no longer respond naively, then we have to come to an understanding of our cultural landscape by seeing it with the eyes of a stranger.

It is by now a commonplace that a writer's ideas and language contain more meaning than he consciously controls; and that his mind is inhabited by a personality that is largely a stranger to our world of rectitude and decency. Depth-psychology has enabled us to see individual experience through the eyes of that stranger. We have further come to understand that not only the individual but a whole culture contains organizations of experience for which that culture has no language in its ethics or politics. There are handed down from age to age ways of getting through life with the optimum gratification of needs and desires we are hardly aware of having. Only a stranger to our culture would see those uncharted highways, which are often at odds with our rules of conduct. Anthropology has alerted us to the hidden landscape and helps us to map it. When literary interpretation acknowledges that our rules of conduct, our standards of decency, do not suffice in giving an account of a literary work of art, it can lean on depth-psychology and on anthropology to make plain what is strangely hidden. In Tennyson's "Ulysses" the hidden landscape makes itself powerfully felt, but our neat ethical language can describe it only as confused or contradictory; it cannot describe its power.

Depth-psychology and anthropology are combined in a book that sees Western man through the eyes of a complete stranger, whose customs and beliefs are so alien that they can open our eyes to aspects of our own culture for which we otherwise cannot find a language. O. Mannoni's *Prospero and Caliban* is ethnography of Madagascar and psychology of the European mind. The author explains that his investigations of the two mentalities acting upon each other led him to describe "the human personality and its development in universal terms."[9] The inhabitants of Madagascar, the Malagasi, are Orientals and their ways of satisfying those hidden needs and desires are very different from ours. Their ways are strange to us because we have disavowed them, at least with one half of our being.

The Malagasi seek not self-fulfillment through independence, but submergence in the community; they want to be dependent rather than self-reliant, responsible individuals. When the worst that can befall a Westerner is to be inferior, or be surpassed, or be counted irresponsible, to lack achievement, the worst fear of the Malagasi is abandonment: he wants above all to feel dependent and secure. This need is the prism through which all his experience is refracted; it determines the tone of his every gesture and action. It makes inconceivable Ulysses' setting out into the unknown—self-sufficient, striving, seeking—because the cost would be too great. For the Malagasi there is no East or West of salvation; the distinction between the West of pleasure and business and the East of the soul's proper home is meaningless to him, because both directions would mean a journey, which would be pointless since meaning is only found at home. The truth is not to be searched for in suffering or through conflicting goals, but lies safely buried in the ancestral ground.

By comparing the Oriental and the Western attitudes, Mannoni is able to disentangle some of the strands that tie us to our cultural inheritance. He shows that the restlessness (which we find in Ulysses) is both an act of rebellion, an assertion of individual liberty, and a symptom of the attendant guilt. Western man has deified free will so that he can practice obedience to divine authority. He has projected his father image onto a God who has liberated his conscience from the power of his father and his community. The Malagasi on the contrary sees the ultimate lawgivers in his ancestors, the great community of the dead and the living, of which the dead are the more powerful. For the tribal man everything has been laid down from time immemorial: the ancestors are guardians and censors, watchdogs that safeguard the old customs. One's own father lacks awfulness, because he too is subservient to the ancestors. The tribal chief becomes interpreter and custodian of communal life, of which the center is the ancestral hearth. In the midst of the living family or clan the life-giving pieties are cultivated. It is they which give meaning to life, and not a man's strivings or achievements. His spirit is cradled in the security of unquestioned traditions.

I have used the term ancestral hearth, although it is not quite appropriate to Madagascar in the literal sense. It belongs to the world of Homer and Virgil. The ancestral hearth plays such an important part in the European epic because it is one of the two poles between which the hero must find a balance. One is the pole of faithful adherence to ancient traditions watched over by the ancestors. The other pole is individual destiny and achievement, which we call heroism and which we intuitively know to lead to infringements of the ancestral laws. In Virgil the cultural tension between ancestral pieties and individuality achieves the finest pathos: it accounts for the high note of sadness, of civilized nostalgia, the *lacrimae rerum,* which attracted the succeeding ages. Aeneas is *pius:* he carries his father on his shoulders out of the flames of Troy, and it is his decreed task to find a new place for the ancestral hearth. But this can no longer mean simply maintaining things as they are. The home has been burnt down and the hero has to set out, to travel across the known world until that landfall, in a place unknown, which will again become the place for the old pieties. The West will become the East, and end of Troy the beginning of immortal Rome. His task calls for heroic independence and responsibility. It is true that in the middle of the tale (Book Six) the hero has to descend into the underworld for ancestral wisdom. But at other times his is the individual mind pitting a sense of responsibility and independence against the temptations of settling down too early. His guiding spirit is a goddess, and ultimately Jupiter. Dido cannot hold him. In the most poignant account of his struggle to tear himself away from her, the call of his destiny is louder than his longing for security and the past. Dido is a link with the past, first because she is a woman, second because of her history, and then more allusively because on the walls of her palace Aeneas sees paintings commemorating the war of Troy. For a moment he is overcome by the recognition of the transience of life, but immediately rallies his comrades with an appeal to fame. Similarly Tennyson's Ulysses exhorts his mariners:

> The long day wanes; the slow moon climbs; the deep
> Moans round with many voices. Come, my friends.
> 'Tis not too late to seek a newer world.

Nevertheless, the temptation to stay at Carthage is given its full attraction. Only because Aeneas has projected his self-assertion into an empyrean god can he rededicate himself to the task. The god now sends a message and reminder of the task to be fulfilled, *urbs condita est;* the city is yet to be built and the restlessness must not be abated, however great the anguish at his parting with Dido. That pious Aeneas is the great prototype of the master builder is a platitude one never tires of contemplating. He exemplifies the glory of individual responsibility and achievement, as well as the cost in suffering.

Whatever may have been the pristine message of Christianity, the history of Christendom is rich with ambiguity in regard to the spiritual states of dependence and responsible striving. The psychology of salvation alone shows a tragic tension between a trust in passive reception of grace and strenuous works. The teaching of Jesus is of the wisdom of dependence on divine will and love, but this is a very different kind of dependence from that enjoyed by the Malagasi in his great community of ancestors. The Christian is a pilgrim as well as a member of a flock. In the Gospels he is exhorted to put his absolute trust in the divine Father and at the same time to leave his home and relations in search of Him. The household gods are cast out and cold ashes lie on the domestic hearth. The spirit must find another home. Instead of the security of ancient customs there is faith and hope, and in place of submergence in the tribe there is love between individual souls, souls who moreover cannot belong to this world because it is the Adversary's. But such spiritual heroism is given to few, and the pristine vision soon precipitates homelier virtues. Paul, with sombre and solitary grandeur, exalts the freedom of the spirit and denounces bondage to the old ways, but he also has to make concessions and show tolerance to the established law. The ties of nature reassert themselves beside the heroic and solitary quest for God. The need for dependence can never be totally subjugated.

Dante is the poet of Christendom, but in his *Inferno* the conflict between the ties of nature (the duties to the domestic hearth) and the searching, questing soul is portrayed with all the pathos of secular experience. His Ulysses, in Canto xxvi, is generally thought to be one of the pinnacles of his poetry. He was also the chief literary source for Tennyson's poem. The link between Dante and Tennyson raises two questions: Is Tennyson's Ulysses in a kind of hell, and does Dante's poetry really persuade us that his Ulysses belongs in hell? Dante placed Ulysses in hell because (and here he followed the medieval schema) the Greek had given bad counsel and stirred up civil discord. Together with Diodemes he planned the Trojan Horse (and therefore brought about the fall of Troy) and was responsible for at least two other instances of deception. For such conduct he finds himself in nether hell, next to the lowest pit. For the modern reader the shock of finding Ulysses' lost soul suffering for actions which nowadays we lack conviction to call sins, let alone heinous ones, is severe enough. But the shock is transformed by Ulysses' speech into something even more difficult to bear, a feeling more poignant and ambiguous, of elevation, even exaltation, not unmixed with an ultimate hopelessness. When Ulysses tells the story of his last journey, his heroic intrepidity, aspirations, freedom of spirit, and even his putting aside the pieties of tradition and custom, all this exacts from us powerful though conflicting responses. In Canto xxvi of the *Inferno* we recognize once more an intricacy of feeling, nourished by literary traditions and raised by the poet's art to a great representative moment in Western culture. Dante's culture made him exquisitely sensitive to the beauty of Ulysses' freedom of spirit, as well as to the tragic cost this entails for others and for the adventurer himself.

Dante's portrait of Ulysses is not all of a piece; a distinction has to be made between the conventional account of him by Dante's guide, Virgil (who represents the classical and medieval traditions), and the self-portrayal in Ulysses' speech, in which Dante's own imagination is fully and personally engaged. That Ulysses is found in nether hell is explained by the medieval characterization of him as one who gave bad counsel, sowed discord, and criminally neglected the ties of nature. According to the Aristotelian division of sins such conduct was malicious, abused the specifically human faculty of reason and therefore was far worse than incontinence or even bestiality. Only violence was a more heinous crime. Malice was subdivided into fraud and violence, according to Cicero's *De Officiis*. In the *Inferno* there is then only one pit deeper than Ulysses', namely the place for instigators of civil violence. Ulysses' tortures are not to be compared with those of Bertrand de Borne (Canto xxviii, bolgia ix) and Ugolino (Canto xxxiii). In the very maws of the devil the worst horrors are suffered by Brutus and Cassius in company with Judas Ischariot himself. The Romans are traitors to the founder of the Imperium, whereas Judas has betrayed the founder of the Church. There is no distinction here between the envy of Cassius and the nobility of Brutus' love of freedom and republican virtues. They are both traitors to the master and benefactor. The formula is simple: it has the uncomplicated logic of the Malagasian need for secure dependence. Nature has established and sanctified ties of loyalty and trust, the disruption of which is the worst imaginable treason (Canto xi). No consideration of individual aspirations or freedom of the spirit can be allowed. Ulysses' crime was not quite so heinous, because it was destructive of domestic rather than communal or civic ties: "Fraud, which gnaws every conscience, a man may practice upon one who confides in him; and upon him who reposes no confidence. This latter mode seems only to cut off the bond of love which nature makes; hence in the second circle nest hypocrisy, flattery, sorcerers, cheating, theft and simony, panders, barrators, and like filth" (Canto xi).[10]

The classification of Ulysses' crimes belongs to what we may call the tribal aspect of the situation, which considers above all the welfare of the community by imposing an inflexible law. But when Dante begins to imagine Ulysses' punishment with poetic concreteness, the schematic simplicity is complicated by a variety of feelings. The poet's sorrow in seeing the hero in hell has a personal edge to it, for the ingenious adventurer used his imagination very much the way a poet does. Dante remembers: "I sorrowed then, and sorrow now again when I direct my memory to what I saw; and curb my genius more than I am wont, lest it turn where Virtue guides it not; so that, if kindly star or something better have given to me the good, I may not grudge myself that gift" (Canto xxvi). The Italian *ingegno* stands for both ingenuity and the poet's genius—"e piu lo'ngegno affreno chi'i'non soglio." The affininity between Ulysses the explorer and Dante the poet is deeply felt and colors the whole Canto.

The description in the eighth bolgia is lyrical. The flames of the tortured souls appear like swarms of fireflies at the height of summer. A peasant is imagined resting from his labors and looking down a valley of olives and vines. The simile is made especially splendid by naming summer "the time that he who lights the world least hides his face from us." Following this idyllic moment there comes a comparison of the sinners enveloped by flames with the fiery chariot of Elijah ascending to heaven. The comparison explicitly rests on the point that both Elijah and the lost souls are hidden by flames; but it has a half-hidden extension, for just as Elisha asked for a double portion of Elijah's spirit, so Dante asks this of Ulysses. For what the poet needs is the intrepidity of the explorer, to leave home and security in his quest for the truth which will make him immortal. And so Ulysses' speech, giving an account of his last journey, is entirely Dante's invention, indeed might be spoken by the poet himself.

When I departed from Circe, who beyond a year detained me there near Gaeta, ere Aeneas thus had named it, neither fondness for my son, nor reverence for my aged father, nor the due love that should have cheered Penelope, could conquer in me the ardour that I had to gain experience of the world, and of human vice and worth; . . .

Setting sail again, Ulysses and his small company pass through the Pillars of Hercules and face the Atlantic.

> "Oh brothers!" I said, "who through a hundred thousand dangers have reached the West, deny not, to this the brief vigil of your senses that remains, experience of the unpeopled world behind the sun. Consider your origin: ye were not formed to live like brutes, but to follow virtue and knowledge."

They voyage on for many days and nights until they sight a mountain.

> We joyed, and soon our joy was turned to grief: for a tempest rose from the new land, and struck the fore-part of our ship. Three times it made her whirl round with all the waters; at the fourth, made the poop rise up and prow go down, as pleased Another, till the sea was closed above us.

At the beginning of his speech Ulysses frees himself from the spiritual indolence of Circe. But instead of renewing natural ties with his family and treasuring the pieties of the domestic hearth, he sets out, hungry for experience, on a journey of discovery. His sinful neglect of primary loyalties is not expatiated upon; the terms Ulysses utters are resonant with feeling and speak for themselves: *dolcezza, pietà, debito amore.* And yet Dante's heart and imagination are with the voyager, the free spirit in search of knowledge, braving the unknown and equating life with endless striving. Ulysses' call to his fellow mariners echoes and also significantly adds to the Virgilian sentiment in Book I of the *Aeneid,* in which the hero exhorts and heartens those who with him survived the storm. Where Ulysses speaks of discovering more experiences, Aeneas merely asks for endurance, the sheer living through hardships and the fulfillment of the task imposed upon him "Durate et vosmet rebus servate secundis." The only comfort he can offer is that later they will perhaps remember these things with pleasure: "forsan et haec olim meminisse juvabit." Ulysses' speech is more heroic and is borne aloft by a finer pathos inherent in the twin condition of man—his longing for experience and the ensuing cost of disloyalty, isolation, and destruction in the whirlpool. The whirlpool, with its meaningless sound and fury, the energy of madness, is a more finely appropriate punishment for the overweening voyager than is the enveloping double-headed flame.

It is true that before Dante there had already accumulated around the figure of Ulysses many legends quite unconnected with Homer's hero. He had become the exemplar of curiosity, an explorer of mankind, their cities and customs. (See Horace *Epistles* I.ii.17–22 and Cicero *De Finibus* V.18 and 49; and also many medieval tales.) But it was Dante who first gave noble expression to the liberal aspirations which lie behind the restless search for knowledge, as well as to the threat of mortality giving poignancy to the search, and to the price to be paid for the *extravagant* hunger for knowledge. Dante's imagination is rich in sympathy as well as dread; conscious of the beauty of the ancient *sapientia,* waiting upon the wisdom of God, he is equally fascinated by *experientia.* And yet Ulysses' end in a whirlpool suggests that Dante saw an ultimate futility in the secular hunger for

variety of experience. He maintained a fine balance of feelings between dependence and freedom of the will. Dante felt the affinity between the poet's imagination and Ulysses' hunger for virtue and knowledge; that is why he invented
Ulysses' last voyage and filled it with such passionate intensity.

The affinity between the explorer's restlessness and the poet's imagination is
also felt in Tennyson's poem. Ulysses' voice is at least in part Tennyson's. But
whereas Dante speaks clearly of fondness, reverence, and due love for son, father,
and wife, Tennyson's poem leaves such feelings unacknowledged. Dante's hero
knows that he is committing a heinous crime, and to him the contrary attractions
of the domestic hearth and unbounded experience are unmistakable. Tennyson's
Ulysses apparently does not see, or does not wish to acknowledge, the sinfulness
of his action, though he unwittingly reveals his remorse in a pervasive melancholy.
The drama of Tennyson's Ulysses does not shape itself into Aristotelean virtues and
vices which are amenable to rational appraisal. Tennyson's poem does not establish
the moral categories which would make Ulysses' rejection of wife, son, and nation
a crime. The ingredients of experience that Dante was willing to sort out into social
and antisocial, virtuous and criminal, are in Tennyson's poem left as feeling-tones:
energy, lassitude, anger, self-pity, longings, and apprehensions.

Tennyson's poetic exploration of moods has provoked some critics to impugn
his intelligence. But a comparison with Dante's more intellectually clarified poetry is
not all to Tennyson's disadvantage. Although Tennyson's poem without a doubt is
a descent onto an emotional ground and works through images weaving together
feeling-tones without the bracing effect of intellectual clarification, in one respect it
comes closer than does Dante's poetry to our notion of poetic essence. It conveys
the actual sensation of guilt, what it feels like to have one's whole life enveloped by
a guilt that is not even conscious, let alone understood: where every moment is
infected by melancholy, even those impulses of courage and desire for achievement; when the call to fellow adventurers, memories of comrades in arms, threatening seas, fear of death, urgency to crowd remaining years with action, beauty,
knowledge, and fame—when all these impulses are fed by the invisible and un-
mentionable remorse. Dante's schema of virtues and vices gives us the exalted
pleasure of *comprehending* Ulysses' character and experience; Tennyson makes us
share the lifelike mixture of anguish and aspirations without understanding them.
Ulysses' speech in the *Inferno* is not his complete history; it has to be linked with
the earlier descriptions of the setting, and with the moral classification of the
offenders. Tennyson's poem is complete, containing within itself all the ingredients
of a rounded-off aspect of experience, as long as we do not look for moral
judgment.

It remains to describe the emotional ground to which Tennyson descends or
withdraws. His Ulysses separates himself from the rest of mankind. Noting the
"sphere / Of common duties" and the "household gods" he yet claims to be standing
outside civic and religious obligations. He has "become a name." His people are
savage, unable to understand, value, or indeed to love him; they "know not me."

The "still hearth" is devoid of life for him. Those who loved him and in whose company he enjoyed greatly and suffered greatly were not his family, or even his countrymen, but peers on the battlefield and fellow mariners. They make up the band of congenial spirits who have isolated themselves from their country and the commonalty of men. Free from all ties they oppose "Free hearts, free foreheads" to thunder and sunshine. This freedom is also a self-imposed exile. Ulysses enacts the emotional condition that our civilization, with its conflicting demands of self-fulfillment, self-reliance, and achievement on the one hand, and of family and civic loyalties on the other, has built into our existence. It sharpens itself to that point where dependence on the ancestral hearth and flight from it, become irreconcilable alternatives. When the father's rule is denied through an act of rebellion, which need not be carried out but be only a mental presence, the rebel feels abandoned, cast out. Although logically rebellion and exile are contradictions, spiritually they are like the two ends of a seesaw pivoting on guilt. Rebellion produces guilt and calls for punishment. A need for adequate punishment can produce violent fantasies, of which exile from the revered and sheltering hearth is in our civilization the most purposeful. Or, to reverse the seesaw motion, if one feels rejected and abandoned, this seems to ease the burden of guilt because one can project it on to the other, and one can even assume moral superiority by rejecting the other instead of feeling rejected: I am now cutting myself off voluntarily because the ancestral hearth does not provide conditions for self-fulfillment. Unfortunately the severing of ties raises the specter of mortality and creates an unquenchable thirst for ultimate truths.

Tennyson's biographers have not found it difficult to describe and account for the sense of abandonment, desertion, and betrayal in much of his poetry. The loss of Hallam awakened memories of childhood experiences that overshadowed the adult man. But the private tragedy reflects in an intense form a broadly cultural situation. Every ingredient in the poem makes general sense and is an accurate reflection of part of our reality. The contradictory impulses, the harshness of tone, are not offensive to the Common Reader. Tennyson has planted the necessary clues: no profits, idleness, a lifeless hearth, the land and the aged wife barren, the people savage. No Victorian reader could hope for self-fulfillment in such a place. The private history of Tennyson's suffering is therefore re-enacted at the level of Victorian culture, so that Ulysses becomes a culture hero. But it was above all the Victorian poet for whom Ulysses spoke. If Tennyson the man lived under a sense of personal dereliction, Tennyson the poet was equally dismayed at the age in which he wrote. Outside the band of chosen spirits he saw an indifferent or hostile world. Ulysses is the spokesman not merely of an individual fate, but also of a type of exile who in the nineteenth century becomes nearly identical with the figure of the poet, who spurns "a savage race / That hoard, and sleep, and feed, and know not me." Such bitterness is not unusual in Victorian literature. It is often exceeded in the writings of Carlyle, Dickens, and Ruskin when they revile the world of Mammon. The poetic imagination rejects the crassness of the times and in turn feels rejected by it. The poet exiles himself and in his voyaging through unknown seas his vision becomes more and more dreamlike. Ulysses is self-exiled and rejecting, or so he vigorously asserts; but the poetry lies in his feeling abandoned. The reader responds to the tension between these two states. The poet accuses his age of not knowing him and forcing him into exile, at the same time that he has reviled his age for being unworthy of his art. In this manner he becomes the rebel and the self-pitying exile in one and the same breath.[11]

By the beginning of the twentieth century the connection between art, rebellion, and exile rose to the surface of literary consciousness, most dramatically in James Joyce's life and writing. In *A Portrait of the Artist as a Young Man* Stephen has to discover "the mode of life or art whereby your spirit could express itself in unfettered freedom." A voice speaks softly to his lonely heart: "Away then; it is time to go." Commonsensical Cranly is mistaken when he says "you need not look upon yourself as driven away if you do not wish to go or as a heretic or an outlaw." Stephen must see himself as an exile, because he feels guilty: he despises his father and his people, and he cannot become reconciled to his mother by making his Easter Duty. The neglect of these pieties and loyalties is the condition of his uneasy freedom. In Joyce's *Ulysses* Bloom returns to Penelope, while Stephen turns his back upon the proffered hearth. The roles of father and son have become reversed.

If Victorian readers found Tennyson's Ulysses plausibly heroic, what makes more recent critics pull back from him in dismay? The Victorian experience of individualism, with its hidden tensions between self-assertion and isolation, is no longer the mode that produces distinctive poetry. In the poetry of Yeats and of Eliot the yearning for the ancestral home is dominant and unambiguous. In "Ash-Wednesday" *experientia* still beckons—"The white sails still fly seaward, seaward flying / Unbroken wings"—but the poet's prayer is to the "Blessèd sister, holy mother, spirit of the fountain, spirit of the garden" for *sapientia:*

Teach us to care and not to care
Teach us to sit still
Even among these rocks,
Our peace in His will
And even among these rocks
Sister, mother
And spirit of the river, spirit of the sea,
Suffer me not to be separated.

In Eliot we find again the ancient skepticism regarding the value of self-assertion and achievement. He looks to the dead for wisdom; he discovers in "Little Gidding" at the moment of returning home that "the communication / Of the dead is tongued with fire beyond the language of the living." In his poetry there reigns disillusionment but also a renewed spiritual effort. Richard Blackmur summed it up as "A summoning of human strength and effort to extinguish both hope and despair in the

face of death."[12] One might add—in the face of life, and the temptation to with-
draw from it.

Self-reliancy and self-fulfillment were trumpeted by Victorian prophets all the
more vehemently because the contrary attractions of the ancestral hearth, with its
pieties and above all its security, were always present. "Ulysses" remains a moving
and important poem because it embodies tensions between these two poles that
are likely to continue as long as Western civilization survives. Much of our literature
was energized by the same tensions. And they do not have to be intellectually
defined, or morally categorized. The emotional ground of a style of civilization may
embody experiences that to analytic reason must be contradictory. One is therefore tempted to make moral judgments, either by diagnosing confusion or by
reading into the poem ironic distancing (implying a moral judgment). But a great
poem like "Ulysses" can encompass wide fluctuations of feelings including logical
contrarieties that do not rise into awareness but are part of our most intense life.

NOTES

[1] E. J. Chiasson, "Tennyson's 'Ulysses'—A Re-interpretation," *Critical Essays on the Poetry of Tennyson*,
ed. John Killham (New York, 1960), pp. 165–167. Tennyson's artistic control over his material, for
example by ironic distancing, has become a critical focus. See especially Jerome H. Buckley, "Tennyson's
Irony," *The Victorian Newsletter*, 31 (Spring, 1967), 7–10, though "Ulysses" is not mentioned. Elton E.
Smith, on pages 1–4 of the same issue, traces our growing awareness of Tennyson's polarizations of
experience, but does not say whether the polarities are unified by a comprehensive vision ("Tennyson
Criticism 1923–1966: From Fragmentation to Tension in Polarity"). On this point we are left in doubt.
John Pettigrew's very thorough analysis ("Tennyson's *Ulysses*: A Reconciliation of Opposites," *Victorian
Poetry*, 1 [1963], 27–45) argues that the admirable and the offensive character traits are deliberately
placed side by side in order to convey complexities of experience. But it remains obscure how the
reconciliation of opposites, "the larger synthesis," is effected within the poem. Robert Langbaum's *The
Poetry of Experience* (New York, 1957) contains the most helpful account of how we respond to
offensive character traits in Victorian dramatic monologues. He notes "the effect created by the tension
between sympathy and moral judgment." He also observes that "most successful dramatic monologues
deal with speakers who are in some way reprehensible" (p. 85): "Sympathy adapts the dramatic
monologue for making the 'impossible' case and for dealing with the forbidden region of the emotions"
(p. 93). But surely these hidden regions surfacing in the monologue also belong to the moral realm. It
is shirking the critical issue to say that we sympathize and therefore refrain from moral response. We
have to face the fact that the monologue and the reader can accommodate certain contradictory moral
positions.
[2] John Sterling's review of *Poems* (1842) in the *Quarterly Review* (September, 1842), 385–416; quoted
in John D. Jump, *Tennyson: The Critical Heritage* (London and New York, 1967), p. 120.
[3] The poem was written after the death of Hallam, the most brilliant of the Apostles, and out of
Tennyson's sense of loss. See Jump, p. 172.
[4] Ibid., p. 163.
[5] Ibid., p. 356
[6] Basil Willey, *More Nineteenth Century Studies* (London, 1956), p. 71.
[7] John Donne, *Complete Poetry and Selected Prose*, ed. John Hayward (London, 1949).
[8] "Satyre III," ibid.
[9] *Prospero and Caliban* (London, 1956; first published in Paris, 1950, under the title *Psychologie de la
colonisation*), p. 205.
[10] John Aitken Carlyle, tr., *Dante's Divine Comedy: The Inferno* (London, 1848).
[11] The poetic imagination is not the only way of dealing with the sense of abandonment and guilt:
commercial enterprise and scientific discipline are equally favored in our civilization. Robinson Crusoe

leaves home in order to better his economic condition. "Something fatal in that propension of nature" calls him to sea and adventure, and away from "settling to busieness" in the station to which he was born. Later he comes to understand this lack of "confined desires" and his dissatisfaction with "the state wherin God and Nature has placed" him—it is his original sin, his "secret burning lust of ambition for great things." His means of salvation will be "unwearied diligence and application." But Tennyson was not an artisan or shopkeeper, and could not make wealth his aim; on the contrary, by his time Mammon was the chief adversary. Ulysses flees his guilt, but his restless strivings have vague, dreamlike goals; inevitably, because reality lies in the situation from which he is fleeing. There remained science. After Hallam's death Tennyson drew up an elaborate program o;f scientific studies. This may be compared with the Cartesian spirit as it is analyzed in Mannoni's book; having been abandoned by his parents, Descartes learned to turn directly to a God both abstract and remote, the bulwark of science, and the guarantee of an independent intellect: a God who would ensure progress provided the individual soul were armed with firm resolve. Descartes overcame his feeling of insecurity by deliberately placing himself in a position of abandonment and then denying it. Mannoni sees the Cartesian spirit as embodying enterprise and independence at a turning point of the Western world.

[12] R. P. Blackmur, "T. S. Eliot—From 'Ash Wednesday' to *Murder in the Cathedral*" in *Language as Gesture* (London, 1954), p. 169.

Michael Beausang

SEEDS FOR THE PLANTING OF BLOOM

The seed-bedding of *Ulysses* attempted here provides, like Bloom's garden, for a number of scarlet runners: (1) Odysseus is a vegetation-hero or divine king; (2) Bloom stems from the same mould, and the correspondence between *Ulysses* and the *Odyssey* makes more sense, once this is accepted; (3) Joyce's treatment of the father-son theme, and the subservience of Bloom to Molly, are both conditioned by the status of the year-king under matriarchal rule; (4) the main characters, the legendary figures, and the motif of rivals (Bloom-Boylan, Stephen-Mulligan), all relate to the divine king and his ritual functions.

I. Odysseus the Year-King

"At a certain stage of early society," writes Frazer, "the king or priest is often thought to be endowed with supernatural powers or to be an incarnation of a deity, and consistently with this belief the course of nature is supposed to be more or less under his control, and he is held responsible for bad weather, failure of the crops, and similar calamities ... if drought, famine, pestilence, or storms arise, the people attribute the misfortune to the guilt of their king, and punish him, accordingly, with stripes and bonds, or, if he remains obdurate, with deposition and death."[1] The view that kings are responsible for food supply is upheld by Homer in the *Odyssey:* "Your fame has reached heaven itself," Odysseus tells Penelope, "like that of some perfect king, ruling a populous and mighty state with the fear of god in his heart, and upholding the right, so that the dark soil yields its wheat and barley, the trees are laden with ripe fruit, the sheep never fail to bring forth their lambs, nor the sea to provide its fish—all as a result of his good government—and his people prosper under him."[2] All of these attributes, as A. M. Hocart has pointed out,[3] compose an inventory of the responsibilities of divine kingship

The year-king's term of office has been variously estimated. For Frazer, the

From *Mosaic* 6, No. 1 (Fall 1971): 11–22.

king's rule in early Greece followed an octennial cycle because this is the shortest period at the end of which sun and moon come together. Francis Cornford postulates a lunar or solar year or a longer period of two, four or eight solar years. "During this period," he adds, "long or short as it might be, the tenant of the office represented, or rather *was*, the power which governed the rains of heaven and the fruits of earth; at the end of it he was either continued for a new *eniautos*, or violently dispossessed by a successor. Further, since the *eniautos* itself could be concretely conceived as a daimon carrying the horn of plenty—the contents and fruits of the 'year' in the more abstract sense—we may think of the temporary king as actually being the eniautos-daimon or fertility-spirit of his year. When the year is fixed by the solar period the single combat appears as the driving out of winter or of the dying year by the vigorous spirit of the New Year that is to come."[4]

For Gilbert Murray, Odysseus manifests major traits of the divine king. These would be even more apparent, he believes, were it not that Homer excised all, or nearly all, vestiges of beliefs offensive to Achaean sensibility from the mass of epic material he transformed in the *Iliad* and the *Odyssey*. Many of the expunged allusions concern the gods and goddesses of Homer's predecessors and bear upon "the divine king who embodies the life of his tribe, and who must be born anew at fixed periods lest that life should grow weak." "This figure," adds Murray, "is generally called a vegetation spirit, since the welfare of the trees and crops is the first need of an agricultural tribe. But he affects not only the fruits of the soil, but also the flocks and human beings. So it is better to consider him as embodying the life, or the vital force of the community."[5] Odysseus is such a figure, argues Murray, and despite Homer's work of expurgation, elements of pre-Hellenic kingship survive in his story. In particular, his return to Penelope, on the last day of the nineteenth year when the New Moon coincided with the New Sun of the Winter Solstice, shows that he originally personified the divine king whose life was governed by solar and lunar cycles.

The identification of Odysseus as a divine king by scholars like Murray and J. A. K. Thomson[6] represented the culmination of the efforts of successive generations of nineteenth-century mythologists to interpret Homer's epic as an allegorical version of the adventures of the sun. To George Cox, for example, Odysseus "fought the battle of the children of the sun against the dark thieves of night," and though his adventures are interwoven with wonderful skill "they may each be traced to some simple phrase denoting originally the phenomena of the sun's daily or yearly course through the heavens."[7]

Is this kind of interpretation merely fanciful nonsense? Not entirely, submitted Murray: "Can we be surprised to learn that Odysseus has just 360 boars, and that one of them died every day? Or can we any longer neglect the other solar characteristic that seems to cling about Odysseus: that the sun is his rival and enemy; he goes under the world in the West, visits the realm of the dead and comes up in the East where the daughter of Dawn has her dwellings and her dancing-floors and the Sun his uprising . . . that he is brought back home asleep in a magic boat, like the Sun in Mimnermus by Phaiakes (Dark Ones?) who do even the farthest journey in twenty-four hours . . . ; that he lives in an island in the sea, "low-lying, apart from others, furthest of all towards the sun-set . . . a description that cannot be twisted to suit Ithaca; that he is a Far-Darter of arrows, that his death comes to him out of the sea; and that like most Year-Kings, he is doomed to be slain by his son?"[8]

II. Bloom the Year-King

The transition from Odysseus, the solar year-king and daemon of vegetation, to his modern counterpart, Bloom, is facilitated by Murray's discussion of the vegetation-spirit in *Euripides and His Age.* To the ancients, vegetation was not an abstract noun, but an anthropomorphized figure dying periodically and returning in triumph: "His death was as our own deaths, and his rebirth a thing to be consciously sought with prayers and dances. Every year," Murray adds, "he waxes too strong and commits "Hubris" and his sin has its proper punishment . . . 'The sun shall not transgress his measures,' says Heraclitus; 'if he does he shall be punished by Erinys, till justice be refulfilled,' It is the law of all existing things. And *the history of each year's bloom* was an example of this refluent balance. The Year Daimon, Vegetation Spirit or Corn God or whatever we call him—waxes proud and is slain by his enemy, who becomes thereby a murderer and must in turn perish at the hands of the expected avenger, who is at the same time the Wronged One re-risen."[9]

The phrase "the history of each year's bloom" is underlined here, not so much to suggest that Joyce may have taken the surname of his protagonist from Murray's observations on the vegetation spirit, though indeed this is possible, but in order to underline the adroitness with which Bloom is integrated into the year-king scheme of *Ulysses.* One may argue, of course, that when he chose "Bloom," Joyce had in mind nothing more than a fairly common Jewish surname, but the argument is a weak one, since Bloom's pseudonym, "Henry Flower," and his original family-name (Virag is Hungarian for "flower") make the association with vegetation even more explicit. So do the punning references: *"Leopoldo or the Bloom is on the Rye"*[10] (p. 233), "There is a flower that bloometh" (517), and the "Sirens" threnody: " 'Tis the last rose of summer left blooming alone.' "

By comparison with Murray's year-king, Odysseus, Bloom's solar attributes and associations may appear modest. Yet, they are tangible enough. The sun's vicar in 7 Eccles St. is haunted by "parallax," a concept linking him in cosmic fashion to the Earth-mother, Molly. Leaving his house in the morning, he sets off "in the track of the sun" (57), oblivious that "What went forth to the ends of the world to traverse not itself. God, the sun, Shakespeare, a commercial traveller, having itself traversed in reality itself, becomes that self" (505). Framed in "the disc of the soapsun" in "Circe," Sweeny, the druggist, announces: "We're a capital couple are Bloom and I; he brightens the earth, I polish the sky." But Bloom is a bit of a polisher himself, it seems, for in their litany the "Daughters of Erin" ask him to pray for them as a

"Wandering Soap" in his own right. In the course of "Circe" Virag identifies him with the "nightsun" (515), and at the end of "Ithaca" Bloom goes to bed as "Darkinbad the Brightdayler" (737), a description completed in early editions by the apposition of a black sun at the foot of the episode. As a night-bird, Bloom's weather is described as "a sunburst in the north-west" (482). Of his hobbies, his favorite is astronomy, on which he is a recognised authority: "Bloom was pointing out all the stars and the comets in the heavens ... the great bear and Hercules and the dragon and the whole jingbang lot" (234). At home he keeps "astronomical kaleidoscopes exhibiting the twelve constellations of the zodiac from Aries to Pisces" (683). In the "Oxen of the Sun," notes William York Tindall, "Bloom ranges the zodiac (a cycle of beasts controlled by sun and earth) pausing at the signs of Taurus and Virgo, descending to Martha-Milly."[11] But Joyce himself apprised us of the kind of cosmic parallels to look for in *Ulysses* when he observed that in "Ithaca" Bloom and Stephen become heavenly bodies, wanderers like the stars at which they gaze. And if Odysseus' return to Penelope takes place at a midwinter meeting of sun and moon, Bloom's reinstatement alongside Molly occurs on the morning of June 17th, just three days away from that other astronomical marker, the summer solstice. But, it may be asked, what's the summer solstice to Bloom? Is he even aware of it? The answer would seem to be that he is, and that it matters to him a great deal. In fact, he appears to regard it as a turning-point in his fortunes. His opinion of Stephen's "Parable of the plums" is that it should appeal to all those who, like himself, are "tacitly appreciative of successful narrative and confidently augurative of successful achievement, during the increasingly longer nights gradually following the summer solstice on the day but three following, videlicet, Tuesday, 21 June (S. Aloysius Gonzaga), sunrise 3.33 a.m., sunset 8.29 p.m." (685).

Though a solar hero, Odysseus finds, in the words of *The Rise of the Greek Epic,* "that the sun is his rival and enemy." Bloom makes something of the same discovery in *Ulysses.* No matter where he goes, "Blazes" awaits him. "Gold watch," "white disc of a straw hat flashing in the sunlight," and "skyblue brow and eyes," Molly's lover exemplifies the dazzling ubiquity of the sun that troubled Odysseus. "Blazes'" excursion to Eccles St. is the mock-heroic sortie of Phaeton: "By Bachelor's walk jogjaunty jingled Blazes Boylan, bachelor, in sun, in heat, mare's glossy rump atrot, with flick of whip, on bounding tyres: sprawled, warmseated, Boylan, impatience, ardentbold" (269–70). This ouranian brashness and self-confidence is accentuated to the point of parody by "a suit of indigo serge," "a skyblue tie," and "a red carnation ... between his teeth" (228).

But it is his full name, Hugh "Blazes" Boylan, which most clearly reveals him as bright, rival sun to Leopold Bloom. "Hugh" comes from the Gaelic for "fire," "Blazes" speaks for itself, and Tom Rochford's punning remark "Tell him I'm Boylan with impatience" (232) shows that the surname is intended as a play on the Dubliner's pronunciation of "Boiling."

By contrast Bloom, dressed in black like Stephen, is a rather sombre character.

But then he is specifically identified with the "nightsun" in "Circe," whereas Boylan lords it over the day. In essence the rivalry between the men is an extended nature-allegory in which "Blazes," the hot June sun, provokes a drought, and withers up "Bloom" in the process.

III. Year-Twins: Stephen and Malachi

The king is the central figure in ritual. His eclipse and renewal, or his replacement by a new fertility representative, are of crucial importance to primitive society. In the ancient Near East the king each year met and "defeated" a seasonal antagonist in mock-combat. His success signified the victory of life and fertility over death and infertility. As Frazer reminds us, this kind of seasonal contest often takes the form of a battle between actors incarnating Winter and Summer. "This clear distinction and opposition of the two spirits is easy," observes Cornford, "because, in the succession of the seasons, each in turn has his separate reign, the period during which he triumphs over his rival."[12]

" 'Why was it,' Stephen asked himself, 'that when he thought of Cranly he could never raise before his mind the entire image of his body but only the image of the head and face? . . . the face of a severed head or deathmask . . .' " In his opening diary entries in the *Portrait* he explains why: Cranly, his rival, is "the child of exhausted loins." The exhausted loins are those of Elizabeth and Zacchary. Then, concludes Stephen, "he is the precursor. Item: he eats chiefly belly bacon and dried figs. Read locusts and wild honey. Also, when thinking of him, saw always a stern severed head or deathmask . . . Decollation they call it in the gold." As this commentary shows, Cranly is the precursor; the severed head, that of St. John the Baptist.

But St. John's feast-day falls on June 24th or Midsummer, and St. Stephen's day on December 26th or Midwinter. In other words the key *agōn* of the *Portrait* opposes "St. John" Cranly and "St. Stephen" Dedalus, twins of the summer and winter solstices.

At the beginning of *Ulysses,* Buck Mulligan suddenly links his arm in Stephen's and walks him round the tower. Stephen's reaction is immediate: "Cranly's arm. His arm" (7). Cranly and Mulligan are linked in Stephen's mind. But why, and in what capacity? So far as concerns the *agōn* of *Ulysses,* Stephen's dislike of Mulligan parallels his resentment of Cranly because Mulligan, like Cranly, is geared to the Baptist archetype. The evidence? Mulligan's full name, given only once in the entire book, is "Malachi Roland *St John* Mulligan" (417). Again, the model for Mulligan, as Joyce delighted in underlining, was *St. John* Gogarty. That other John—Eglinton— also prompts Stephen to make the association with Cranly: "Smile Cranly's smile" (184), at the beginning of "Scylla and Charybdis." And, finally, the connection between Mulligan and John is restated in the person of John Mulligan, manager of the Hibernian bank, whose cast-off coat Tom Kernan wears in a somewhat strained parallel with Stephen's donning of the Buck's shoes.

In summary, the rivalry between Stephen and Mulligan is a restatement of that between Bloom and Boylan. Stephen's preoccupation with the summer solstice is no less marked than Bloom's. Early on in the novel he joyfully anticipates the coming events: "Tuesday will be the longest day. Of all the glad new year, mother, the rum tum tiddledy tum. Lawn Tennyson, gentleman poet. Giá. For the old hag with the yellow teeth" (50). Tuesday sets a term to the energies of his usurping twin, Mulligan, who thereafter loses the upper hand little by little. Malachi epitomizes the waxing sun: "Tripping and sunny like the Buck" is his own way of putting it. In "Telemachus" Stephen links him to yet another John—Chrysostomos, author of *De Solstitiis et Aequinoctiis,* and exegete of Malachi's Old Testament prophecy: "The Sun of righteousness shall rise with healing in his wings." By a double irony, in his role of Malachi, Mulligan heralds the coming of "Elijah" Bloom, and as St. John, the precursor, he prefigures the manifestation of Stephen-Christ. In *Ulysses,* as in the *Portrait,* the St. John archetype covers the bright part of the year, Stephen the dark. The bright twin (Mulligan) covers the period from winter to the summer solstice (St. John's day), a time of waxing light. The dark twin (Stephen) begins to re-assert himself following the longest day of all the glad new year, mother, and rules up to December 26th when, as "Bloom's Boys" testify in "Circe," "The wren, the wren, The king of all birds, Saint Stephen's his day, Was caught in the furze" (481).

IV. A Time of Crisis: The Wasteland

Stephen and Bloom are presented as the victims of usurpers. Stephen is Mulligan's prisoner in the tower and Bloom is cuckolded by Boylan. The condition they have in common is that of dispossessed men struggling to re-assert themselves. But their "outcast" state and their supersession by "pretenders" are a function of what Gogarty and Shakespeare call "that time of year." Midsummer day is the hub of all their fortunes. At that time Molly must decide whether to take a new year-king from among her suitors or whether to keep on with the old (Bloom) for another term, and from that day on, Mulligan's hold over his dark rival diminishes little by little. This is why June 16th, a pre-solstitial date, is nonetheless a time of "exile" for Leopold and his adopted son.

June 16th is also a time of crisis. The country is in the grip of a devastating drought. Seed won't sprout, and fields are barren. An outbreak of foot and mouth disease threatens all livestock, and cattle are due to be slaughtered in great numbers. All of these problems are a reminder that "the fertility of men, of cattle, and of the crops is believed to depend sympathetically on the generative power of the king."[13] But in *Ulysses* the generative power of the king is open to question: Bloom has no male heir, and Stephen's search for a father has its complementary aspect in Bloom's quest for a son.

At this level, it is clear that *Ulysses* and Eliot's *The Waste Land* draw upon the same back-ground of myth and ritual and evoke the medieval image of the young knight succoring the Fisher-King on whose well-being the land depends for its revival. To recapitulate: in Cornford's definition of the year-king, the tenant of the office is identified with the "power which governs the rains of heaven." The power which governs the rains of heaven is certainly an important power in *Ulysses*. "Blazes" has baked the earth dry and dried out every "bloom" in sight. "I thirst," (50) says Stephen in "Proteus." "Clouding over. No black clouds anywhere, are there? Thunderstorm." In "Calypso" Bloom meets a man with a "Watering cart. To provoke the rain. On earth as it is in heaven. A cloud began to cover the sun wholly slowly. Wholly. Grey, far" (61). In the same episode, Molly, the earth-mother, announces: "I'm parched." In "Hades" a raindrop falls on Bloom's hat and Power volunteers that it's "wanted for the country" (90).

But the cloud of Polonius, "very like a whale" (40), seen by Stephen in "Proteus," and which "began to cover the sun slowly" is no doubt the same as that seen by Bloom. Indeed, it seems to be directly related to Bloom's efforts as year-king to revive a flagging nature. At the beginning of "Ithaca" Leopold's collapse is attributed by Stephen, not to excessive drinking, but to the reapparition of a matutinal cloud. In spite of Bello's criticism: "A downpour we want, not your drizzle" (541), the thundershower he does produce anticipates the resuscitation of nature and the revival of many a wilted "Bloom."

Hopes for a real cloudburst rise with the announcement in "Lestrygonians" that "Elijah is coming." Elijah, like Zeus, controlled atmospheric phenomena and brought rain to Palestine. In the Old Testament his contest with the priest of Baal occurs after a long drought, and his success is signalled by "a little cloud out of the sea, like a man's hand." In *Ulysses* only the sex has changed—the matutinal cloud appeared "at first no bigger than a woman's hand" (667), and undoubtedly its import is much the same. Elijah Bloom ascends heavenward amid "clouds" of angels in "Cyclops"; two episodes later, the long-awaited downpour takes place. Again, it is the "pillar of cloud by day," not the fire symbol, which is featured in the "Aeolus" evocation of Moses with whom Bloom is also identified. Indeed, what Elijah and Moses have in common in *Ulysses* may be guessed at from Lord Raglan's coupling of them in *The Hero:* "Moses is successful in a series of magical contests in which rain-making is included; and Elijah defeats the prophets of Baal in a rain-making contest." "Power over the elements is," as the same writer asserts, "the most unvarying characteristic of the divine king."[14]

Another gauge of the state of the reigning king is the condition of cattle. Here again nature is in poor shape. The distemper is a subject of concern in Dublin, entering into the thoughts of professional men like Deasy, Bloom and Stephen, as well as preoccupying the farmers and jobbers. As a former actuary with Joe Cuffe, the cattle salesman, Bloom is quite conscious of the threat to the meat-trade, but he is also aware of the threat to himself; if foot and mouth disease is not stamped out, the blame will fall squarely on his shoulders. However, just as the thundershower foreshadows an end to the drought, the birth of a child under the aegis of Dr. Horn and the oxen of the sun presages the return of animal and human fertility.

The meeting between young knight and Fisher-King, between Stephen, "the bullock-befriending bard" and Bloom, the bull-king, is the covenant of this general renewal.

V. The Question of Hamlet

"The original Hamlet," argues Gilbert Murray in "Hamlet and Orestes," "is in the line of vegetation-kings or year-daemons. There are two ways of reckoning the year-kingship: you can reckon by seasons or half-years, by summers and winters; or you can reckon with the whole year as your unit. On the first system a Summer-king or Vegetation-Spirit is slain by Winter and rises from the dead in the spring. On the second, each year-king comes first as a wintry slayer, weds the queen, grows proud and royal, and then is slain by the Avenger of his predecessor."[15] The Hamlet saga begins, therefore, "in that prehistoric and world-wide ritual battle of Summer and Winter, of Life and Death, which has played so vast a part in the mental development of the human race."[16] The original Prince of Denmark personified Winter in a year-king ritual, and traces of this are still visible in Shakespeare's tragedy: "Hamlet is no joyous and triumphant slayer. He is clad in black, he rages alone, he is the Bitter Fool who must slay the King."[17] Indeed, like Hamlet, Stephen rages alone, plays the bitter fool, and is clad in black; but unlike Hamlet, he avoids bloodshed. "In here it is," he mutters, tapping his brow in "Circe," "I must kill the priest and king." This does not prevent the "mother-murder" from haunting him as much as it does the prince. Other interesting similarities between Stephen and Murray's Hamlet worth noting are: feigned madness, dirtiness and disorder in dress, cynical opinions about women (see Stephen on Ann Hathaway), the hero away from home when the main drama begins, and an escape from a ship (Stephen's telegram to Mulligan). Finally, Murray's observation that the world-wide ritual of the Golden Bough Kings, of whom Hamlet is one, also forms the basis of the traditional Mummer's play[18] furnishes a pertinent explanation of why Stephen should be both mournful and the "loveliest mummer of them all."

What Hamlet and Odysseus have in common is that they are year-kings. And what Hamlet, the Odyssey and Ulysses have in common is that they all focus on a certain crisis in kingship. For Murray, Odysseus' winter-solstice return to Ithaca marks the end of cyclically determined tenure of the kingship, and in the suitors he identifies candidates for Odysseus' office. Joyce reproduces this pattern in Ulysses. Stephen, as his name (Stephanos = "crown") implies, is one of the heirs apparent to the kingship. So, too, is Boylan, backer of a horse called "Sceptre." Bloom, strangely enough, is marked down as an outsider in the contest, and identified with an unfancied runner, "Throwaway," which proves the winner. A further competitor is Mulligan ("O won't we have a merry time/On coronation day"), related in Stephen's monologue on the beach to all of the pretenders in history, and in particular to Perkin Warbeck and Lambert Simnel, "All king's sons."

But as with everything else we have discussed, Hamlet leads back ultimately to

Molly. The Danish queen-mother retains many traits of the earth-goddess bound up in the primitive ritual of fertility marriages. Yet, according to Murray, the poet or dramatist who "tries to realise the position and feelings of this eternally traitorous wife, this eternally fostering and protecting mother, cannot but feel in her that element of inward conflict which is the seed of great drama. She is torn between husband, lover and son."[19] This, of course, is Molly's position in *Ulysses* in respect of Bloom, Boylan and Stephen and shows the strength of the archetype as well as the particular impact of the Great Goddess figure on Joyce's version of the *Ewig Weibliche*.

VI. Father and Son

The pre-Hellenic religion blotted out by Homer in composing the *Odyssey* was organized around a mother-goddess who, in Murray's opinion, is simply the Earth as female. The year-king had his role in this scheme, but lived a subordinate existence in the shadow of the female deity—an existence such as Bloom enjoys *vis-à-vis* Molly. Within the matriarchy the reigning representative of the goddess was free to choose king and lovers as she saw fit.

But the marital privilege of the queen is not the only consequence of matriarchal rule reflected in *Ulysses*. Just as central to the plot, and in particular to the relationship between Stephen and Bloom, is the fate of the father. He is overlooked, unidentified. In the pre-Hellenic system when the mother required protection she turned to her brother, and the children came under the influence of their maternal uncle. In *Ulysses*, accordingly, Stephen ignores Simon Dedalus, and in the course of "Proteus" envisages a visit to "Nuncle Richie," his maternal uncle, whom his father cannot abide. But eclipse of the male parent, his "non-existence," raises the question of identity, and the search for a compensatory image of paternity; and if Stephen leaves home, it is partly for the express purpose of finding a substitute father in Leopold Bloom.

The core of Stephen's Hamlet address is an attack on the notion of physical paternity. As he proclaims,

> Fatherhood, in the sense of conscious begetting, is unknown to man. It is a mystical estate, an apostolic succession, from only begetter to only begotten. On that mystery and not on the madonna which the cunning Italian intellect flung to the mob of Europe the church is founded and founded irremovably because founded like the world, macro- and microcosm, upon the void. Upon incertitude, upon unlikelihood. *Amor matris*, subjective and objective genitive, may be the only true thing in life. Paternity may be a legal fiction. Who is the father of any son that any son should love him or he any son? (207)

This reasoning has many points in common with that of the Trobriand islanders visited by Malinowski in his investigation of kinship and descent in matriarchal society. For them, as for Stephen, the child is of the same substance as the mother. The relationship between father and child is non-existent, i.e. void. In the eyes of the Trobriander, the "father" merits social definition, nothing more; "he is the man married to the mother who lives in the same house with her and forms part of the household."[20] This relatively modest status of the father is the outcome of ignorance in relation to the procreative role of the male. Like Stephen, the Trobrianders argue that conscious begetting is unknown to man, and not even Malinowski succeeded in convincing them of the contrary. Their word for "father"— "Tomakawa," meaning "stranger" or "outsider"—is also a just measure of Simon Dedalus' significance for his son.

In *The Rise of the Greek Epic,* Murray contrasts the tribal matriarchy of the early Greeks with the stolid patriarchal system reflected in the *Odyssey.* His conclusions, with their implications for the Christian ideal, form a remarkable anticipation of Stephen's eulogy of mother-love. We speak, he says, of the moral concepts of the patriarchal Aryans as the most noble yet devised, yet we overlook the moral import of the relation between mother and child, which is probably the "deepest," "most influential," "most holy," of all human relationships. No form of worship is "more intense, more human, more likely to achieve its end, than the supplication which rises from all parts of Southern and Eastern Europe to that most ancient and many-named Madonna, who has sat throned upon her rocks and been a mother of many erring children from thousands of years before the coming of Christianity . . . The religious system connected with the matriarchal household, based on the relation of mother to child and no other must be counted, I think, among the great civilizing and elevating influences of mankind."[21]

"Amor matris," says Stephen, "subjective and objective genitive, may be the only true thing in life" (207). With his own mother dead, it is natural for him to direct his attention sooner or later to Molly Bloom, the Magna Mater presiding over *Ulysses.* But Molly is something more than a mere mother-substitute. She symbolizes the erring flesh, the claims of nature, and human love. Stephen's gravitation toward her is symptomatic of his disenchantment with all forms of patriarchal pressure, whether in the form of political authority, or the hirsute Nobodaddy of the Old Testament. She is the stabilizing moral goal towards which he is drawn as a result of his rebellion against the church. As Murray explains: "If a man, who believes somehow in the reality and ultimate worth of some religion of gentleness and unselfishness, looks through the waste of nature to find support for his faith, it is probably in the phenomena of motherhood that he will find it first and most strikingly."[22]

Stephen's heresiarchs, Arius, Photius, Sabellius, are all perverters of the relationship between father and son, and he himself is of their number. The explanation for this is simple: the patriarchal concept constitutes an essential part of the Christian message. The Trobriand islanders knew nothing of the doctrine and ideal of paternity up to the arrival of Christian missionaries. "If we consider," writes Malinowski, "that the dogma of God the Father and God the Son, the sacrifice of the only Son, the filial love of man for his Maker—that all of this falls somewhat flat in a matriarchal society, where the relation between father and son is decreed by tribal law to be that of two strangers, where all personal unity between them is denied, and where the only deities are associated with the mother line, we cannot wonder that Paternity must be the first new truth to be inculcated by proselytizing Christians."[23] Stephen, of course, is moving in the opposite direction, living apart from his family and making of the timeless mother an icon for his inchoate moral ideal. The family is the Christian cell, and Stephen will have no more of it for that reason. "The whole Christian morality," as Malinowski observes, "is strongly associated with the institution of a patriarchal family, with the father as progenitor and master of the household."[24] In breaking with home and father, Stephen cuts the last tie with Christianity itself and accedes to a difficult new freedom.

But the father-son relationship must also be placed in the context of year-king and successor, and in Murray's statement that Odysseus, like most year-kings, is doomed to be slain by his son, we can discern the basis for that somewhat troubled relationship linking Stephen to his spiritual father, Bloom. If Stephen denies a fatherhood of "conscious begetting," he admits one that is a "mystical estate, an apostolic succession." The apostolic succession is that of the year-kingship; "father" is dispossessed by his "son;" the old year-king is slain and succeeded by the new. But such is not the denouement in either the *Odyssey* or *Ulysses*. Telemachus refuses to draw the bow, though it seems within his capacity to do so. Stephen, too, expressing his hatred of bloodshed, refuses to enter into the ritual role expected of him, and Bloom, the incumbent king, gets another lease of life.

VII. Queen Molly and Her Suitors

"The tribal nymph, it seems, chose an annual lover from her entourage of young men, a king to be sacrificed when the year ended; making him a symbol of fertility rather than the object of her erotic pleasure. His sprinkled blood served to fructify trees, crops and flocks."[25] Robert Graves' account of the lot of the year-king under matriarchal rule helps us put Penelope's "suitors" in perspective. The movement of the *Odyssey* is towards a wedding-feast prepared for by "the traditional prenuptial contest" of bow-stringing. But bow-bending or stringing of this type is an ancient Indo-European rite associated with the conferring of kingship.[26] Odysseus' going to bed with Penelope "in the place or rite (*thesmon*) of their ancient bed," one post of which is the trunk of an olive tree, testifies in Clarke's words, "to the stability and union of marriage,"[27] but also preserves traces of the ritual coupling of earth goddess and priest-king.

In *Ulysses* the ritual marriage receives its fair share of attention. Stephen taxes Ann Hathaway with being an all-powerful matriarch. Shakespeare did not make a mistake: "He chose badly? He was chosen, it seems to me. If others have their will Ann hath a way.... The greyeyed goddess who bends over the boy Adonis, stooping to conquer, as prologue to the swelling act, is a boldfaced Stratford wench who tumbles in a cornfield a lover younger than herself" (191). Having delivered himself of this judgement, Stephen wonders: "And my turn? When?" The symbolic marriage-threat concerns Molly who in "Penelope" remarks of Stephen: "he was on the cards this morning when I laid out the deck union with a younger stranger" (774). Mulligan's mockery of John Eglinton: "*John Eglinton, my jo, John./Why won't you wed a wife?*" (215) is in the same vein. Shakespeare himself makes a lightning appearance in "Circe" to remind us of the player-queen's connubial philosophy: "Weda seca whokilla farst" (568) or, in the original: "None wed the second but who killed the first"—as good a motto as can be found for the promiscuous mother-goddess.

As the modern equivalent of Penelope's confrontation with one hundred and eight young men, Joyce gives us a Dublin woman's sexual fantasies in relation to twenty-five possible "suitors." But the queen's prerogative is to choose. Odysseus/ Bloom's meeting with his rivals takes place, not in a great dining-hall, but in the fluid dimension of his wife's stream of consciousness, and without his even being aware of it. Molly's fickle fancy, flitting from candidate to candidate with the inconstancy of a butterfly from bloom to bloom, engrosses all other criteria as the absolute standard for his reinstatement as year-king. Midsummer is near, the time of decision is upon her. Like Penelope, she finally decides to renew her ties with her returning husband, her closing thoughts leading her to recall "the day I got him to propose to me" (782). Her reply to his proposal, her wedding response, and Penelope's answer to the triumphant Odysseus are all one and the same: "yes I said yes I will Yes."

NOTES

[1] James G. Frazer, *The Golden Bough,* abridged version (London, 1963), p. 221.
[2] Book XIX, 109ff. Trans. E. V. Rieu (Harmondsworth, Middlesex: Penguin Books 1969, c 1946).
[3] A. M. Hocart, *Kingship* (Oxford, 1927), p. 9.
[4] Francis Macdonald Cornford, "The Origin of the Olympic Games" in Jane Ellen Harrison's *Themis* (Cleveland and New York, 1962), p. 223.
[5] Gilbert Murray, *The Rise of the Greek Epic* (London, 1907), p. 135.
[6] See J. A. K. Thomson, *Studies in the* Odyssey (Oxford, 1914), pps. 11–12 and 144–145; and for a summary of related German views, Dr. J. Menrad, *Der Urmythus der* Odysee *und seine dichterische Erneuerung: Des Sonnengottes Erdenfahrt* (Leipzig, 1910).
[7] George Cox, *Mythology of the Aryan Nations* (London, 1870), Vol. 2, pp. 171–172, 175.
[8] Murray, p. 212.
[9] Gilbert Murray, *Euripides and His Age* (New York and London, 1913), pp. 61–62.
[10] Page references are to the Modern Library Edition (New York, 1934, re-set 1961).
[11] William York Tindall, *A Reader's Guide to James Joyce* (New York, 1959), p. 200.
[12] Francis Macdonald Cornford, *The Origin of Attic Comedy* (New York, 1961), p. 12.
[13] Frazer, p. 354.
[14] Lord Raglan, *The Hero* (New York, 1956), p. 190.
[15] Gilbert Murray, "Hamlet and Orestes" in *The Classical Tradition in Poetry* (Cambridge, Mass., 1927), pp. 228–229.
[16] Ibid., p. 234.
[17] Ibid., p. 235.
[18] Ibid., p. 228.

[19] Ibid., p. 233.

[20] Bronislaw Malinowski, *The Father in Primitive Psychology* (New York, 1966), p. 14.

[21] Murray, *The Rise of the Greek Epic,* p. 79.

[22] Ibid., p. 79.

[23] Malinowski, p. 58.

[24] Ibid., p. 59.

[25] Robert Graves, *The Greek Myths* (London and Baltimore, 1955), Vol. I, pp. 14–15.

[26] Ibid., Vol. 2, p. 161.

[26] Howard W. Clarke, *The Art of the* Odyssey (New Jersey, 1967), p. 78.

John Freccero

DANTE'S ULYSSES:
FROM EPIC TO NOVEL

In antiquity, history seemed to be made in the image of man. Civilizations, like men, succeeded one another according to the life cycle: a coming-to-be and a passing away to which men and all things of men, as well as the universe itself, seemed forever subject. Time seemed to move in an eternal circle, with repetition as its only rationale. In the face of inexorable destiny, man's only hope for permanence, or at least for its pale reflection, resided in his aspiration to worldly glory and human renown.

For St. Augustine, the advent of Christ changed all of this by introducing into history an absolutely new event. In the twelfth book of the *City of God* he asserts that the "circles have been shattered" for all time. The coming of the Redeemer seemed to cut through the circle of time and to establish a fixed point, making of the circular flux a linear progression toward that new and eternal event. Time seemed at last to have been moving toward its consummation, the fullness of time, which in retrospect gave to all of history a meaning, as a target gives meaning to the flight of the arrow. Christ seemed to have wrought a change not only in universal history, but in the history of the individual soul as well, whose story could no longer be reduced to the curve extending from birth through maturity to death, but was rather a continuous trajectory toward the target: a death that would give meaning to life. It was this new linear conception of time that some have claimed as the ancestor of our own idea of progress.

Whatever the accuracy of such a dichotomy, the circle and the straight line, time as continued repetition and time as a progression toward an apocalyptic goal, these do seem to be logically opposite poles of historiography. They are at the same time logically opposite poles of the narrative art, insofar as that art gives a picture, however idealized, of human existence. Homer's *Odyssey*, for example, seems to reflect in the spatial circularity of the journey's trajectory a temporal

From *Concepts of the Hero in the Middle Ages and Renaissance*, edited by Norman T. Burns and Christopher J. Reagan (Albany: State University of New York Press, 1975), pp. 101–19.

circularity as well. The gem-like episodes are strung together as on a necklace, one set of events succeeding another quite independently while the strand measures ten years of the hero's life—Ulysses leaves Ithaca, has his adventures, and to Ithaca he returns. What gives meaning to the adventure is the portrait of the hero in an epic world where there are great dangers and great challenges, but scarcely ever any doubts. The hero may not know what fate has in store for him, but he has no illusions about fate itself or about the limits of his own mortality in dealing with it. Whether the gods are benevolent or malign, their behavior is predictable and the punishment for offending them is equally clear. There can be misfortunes or di-sasters, monsters and sirens, but from beginning to end the game is fixed and both the reader and the protagonist, confident by tradition about the eventual outcome of the adventure, are more concerned with the "how" of it than with the "why" of the universe in which it is enclosed.

Ulysses' journey was widely read in antiquity as the spatial allegorization of circular human time; Ulysses' *return* to his homeland served as an admirable vehicle for Platonic and gnostic allegories about the soul's triumph over material existence, its gradual refinement back to its pristine spirituality. The return of Ulysses to Ithaca by force of his own wits, the most important element of the story, was taken to represent the most important event of man's spiritual odyssey: the return of the soul to its heavenly *patria* by the exercise of philosophical wisdom. All of human existence seemed to be strung out between the point of departure and the point of return, the homeland of philosophers as well as heroes.

Nothing could be further from the modern form of narrative, the novel, in which linear temporality is of the essence. In any linear narrative, there arises one fundamental doubt that is enough to call the whole world of the novel into ques-tion: assuming that there is a goal, will it be reached or not? and the question cannot be answered until the story is fully told. It becomes desperately important to know the outcome because the rules of the game are no longer fixed simply by the character of the protagonist. At any stage along the way, the freedom of the protagonist or the inscrutability of the laws to which he is subject can combine to stop the evolution for reasons which seem not at all to spring from any inner exigency. The reader is often tempted to skip ahead, to ignore the incidental excursions which are the stuff of epic, in order to arrive at the conclusion, awaited with anxiety and suspense. To be sure, a faith in God and the supernatural limited the anxiety that concerned the exterior events, but this had the effect simply of shifting the suspense to a different plane, not of eliminating it: death ceases to be the end of the trajectory and is replaced by the question of the meaning of death—salvation or damnation in medieval language—the definitive ending of any story. Death within a Christian context seems threatening, not because it is the end of life, but because it enters the sphere of human responsibility as the most important moment in life. Like the syntactic silence that ends the sentence and gives meaning retrospectively to all that went before, it is the moment of significance. In the absence of that significance, as in the modern novel, the irreversible linearity of time is perceived, even when its terminal points are shrouded in obscurity, even when the novelist finds himself powerless to improve on the idiot's tale, signifying nothing.

György Lukacs suggested that Dante wrote the last epic and the first novel, so that in the matter of literary genre, as well as in the history of western culture, he bridges the gap between the Middle Ages and the modern world. On one hand, we know from the beginning that Dante's story will have a reassuring ending. In the first sentence, the narrator says "I," an unmistakable sign that he has returned from his adventure in order to tell us his story. At the same time, however, the pilgrim's terror en route, his bewilderment in the world of the beyond, cannot be dismissed simply as dramatic coyness—it is real fear, remaining however in the past. The terror of the pilgrim is gradually refined away until it becomes the confidence of the author who has been with us from the beginning. To understand the *Divine Comedy* simply as a religious epic is to dismiss the transformation of the pilgrim as unimportant. To call it a novel, on the other hand, is to miss the confidence of the poet's voice, perhaps the narrative's most constant theme. Epic and novel exist, side by side, linearity with circularity, in this poetic synthesis which has always been considered a genre unto itself.

As in Homer's epic, so in Dante's story the journey of Ulysses stands as an emblem of human time, but the Homeric story is glossed from a linear, Christian viewpoint, which is to say from the perspective of death. It is for this reason that Dante's Ulysses ends as a shipwreck rather than at home with Penelope. In spite of the fact that, as Benvenuto da Imola tells us, even unlearned people in Dante's day knew that Homer's hero returned safely to Ithaca, Dante has him die within sight of the Mount of Purgatory. This startling transformation of one of the world's most famous stories is the mandatory Christian corrective of the ancient view of human destiny. It is as if the poet had accepted the ancients' allegorical reading of Ulysses' trajectory as a spatialization of human temporality and then had transformed the circularity of the literal journey in order to have it correspond to a linear reading of human time under the aspect of death. The transformation of Ulysses' circular journey into linear disaster is a Christian critique of epic categories, a critique of earthly heroism from beyond the grave.

Death in hell is the determining factor, the moment of significance that defines a human soul, not according to an overall evaluation of life on earth, but rather according to life's last term. For this reason the perspective of Hell very often seems to invert the world's perspective, represented by the perspective of the pilgrim, transforming some of the world's greatest heroes into villains. So it is with Ulysses, whose last voyage is an emblem of his life. In the twenty-sixth canto of the *Inferno,* Virgil does not ask the tongue of flame to recount any of his adventures, the sort of question to which Homer's poem represents the definitive response, but asks instead about the final moment: ". . . ma l'un di voi dica / Dove per lui perduto a morir gissi." In effect, Virgil asks a novelistic question, left unanswered by Homer.

Such a question can be answered only in the afterlife, from the vantage point of death. Ulysses can speak with authority about his life only because, like all drowning men, he has seen it panoramically in retrospect, from the ending. This is the privilege, the only privilege, of the souls of the damned. The central fiction of the *Inferno,* the descent into Hell, amounts to Dante's claim to the same vantage point while still in this life. At the simplest level, it is clear that Dante can hear Ulysses because they are in the same place; what separates them is the fact that Dante will return to tell us the story. The descent into Hell, in other words, represents a discontinuity in Dante's life that provides him an Archimedean point from which he can comprehend his own experience as though it were concluded, as though he had in fact survived his own death. Dante's voyage is linear, as are the spiritual odysseys of all men in the Christian view, yet his return as poet enables us to hear of his experience. The paradox of continuity and discontinuity in the midst of life, a spiritual death and resurrection, finds its formal reflection in the poem that is at once novelistic and epic, a linear trajectory that ends with the possibility of a poetic beginning.

Because it provides us with an antitype of Dante's experience, the Ulysses episode is one in which Dante is intimately involved, for all of the pilgrim's silence. Ulysses' itinerary is clearly set forth as an ancient analogue of Dante's adventure: it is for this reason both an episode in the *Inferno* and, unlike any other, a constant thematic motif referred to several times throughout Purgatory and even at the last stage of the journey in Paradise.

It is as a metaphoric shipwreck at the foot of a mountain that Dante begins his poem:

> E come quei che, con lena affannata,
>   Uscito fuor del pelago a la riva,   (*Inf.* I. 22–23)

[like one breathless, coming forth from the open sea to the shore.]

Furthermore, Dante refers to that sea as a

> passo che non lasciò gia mai persona viva,   (*Inf.* I. 27)

[a pass never left behind by living man]

and when he at last reaches the mountain in sight of which Ulysses drowned, he refers to the shore as a

> . . . lito deserto,
>   Che mai non vide navicar sue acque
>   Omo che di tornar sia poscia esperto.   (*Pur.* I. 130–32)

[a desert shore, whose waters were never navigated by a man capable of returning.]

The waters *are* finally crossed by the angel's bark, bringing the souls of those who are saved to the mountain of their purgation. The implications of this dramatic

theme would seem to be that one can indeed return home from such an exploration, provided that one can experience a death and resurrection. Exactly the
same point was made by Augustine, in the same terms, in the *De Beata Vita,* as I
have tried to show in a previous essay.¹ The point I wish to make here is that the
tragic death of Ulysses seems to have as its counterpart the survival of Dante's hero.
The poem is in this sense the view of his own life grasped by a drowning man who
somehow survives to tell his life story. In other words, the *morphosis* of the soul,
the circular return to the truth read into Ulysses' ancient trajectory, becomes a
metamorphosis, a death and resurrection, in Dante's poem. What separates Ulysses' definitive death by water from Dante's baptism unto death and subsequent
resurrection is the Christ event in history, or grace, the Christ event in the individual
soul.

In Dante's story, as well as in literary tradition, Virgil's Aeneas mediates between Homer's Ulysses and Dante's pilgrim. The pilgrim begins his journey with a
metaphoric survival of shipwreck within sight of the mountain in the first canto of
the *Inferno,* at a point, that is, where Ulysses met his death. It happens that Aeneas
too begins his journey with a quite literal near-shipwreck. It must have been clear
to Dante that his readers would assume that only a providential stroke, "com' Altrui
piacque," separated the fate of Dante's Ulysses from the landing of Aeneas in Book
One of the *Aeneid.* Recently Robert Hollander has examined the first scenes of the
Inferno with Book One of the *Aeneid* in mind and has come up with some
remarkable parallels, although he acknowledges a great difference in tone between
the two episodes.² The providential stroke, of course, was the election of Aeneas
and his men for the foundation of Rome. It is clear to every reader of the *Aeneid,*
however, that Virgilian providence does not extend to the fate of individuals, who
die as everyone must, finding whatever solace they can in the collective survival of
Rome. To return to the dichotomy with which we began, we may say that Virgil
seems to exempt only Rome from the circular epic destiny. Aeneas' trajectory is
linear, but his descent into Hell ends not in survival, but in Anchises' funereal
reminder of the fate that still awaits individual men:

> manibus date lilia plenis,
> purpureos spargam flores animamque nepotis
> his saltem accumulem donis, et fungar inani
> munere.   (*Aen.* 6. 883–886)

[Give lilies with full hands; let me scatter bright flowers and let me at least heap
these gifts for my descendant's soul and perform an empty tribute.]

No reader of Dante need be reminded of the fact that Aeneas' descent into
Hell was the model for Dante's. The difference is in the kind of Hell presented in
each poem. The descent into the underworld is signaled by the most famous of
classical similes indicating a cyclic view of human destiny. As Aeneas and his guide

prepare to cross the River Styx, the amassing of souls on the bank recalls to the poet the Homeric comparison of generations of men to falling leaves:

> huc omnis turba ad ripas effusa ruebat,
> matres atque viri defunctaque corpora vita
> magnanimum heroum, pueri innuptaeque puellae,
> impositique rogis iuvenes ante ora parentum:
> quam multa in silvis autumni frigore primo
> lapsa cadunt folia, aut ad terram gurgite ab alto
> quam multae glomerantur aves, ubi frigidus annus
> trans pontum fugat et terris immittit apricis.   (*Aen.* 6. 305–12)

[Hither all crowded and rushed streaming to the bank, matrons and men and high-hearted heroes dead and done with life, boys and unwedded girls, and children laid young on the bier before their parents' eyes, multitudinous as leaves fall dropping in the forests at autumn's earliest frost, or birds swarm landward from the deep gulf, when the chill of the year routs them overseas and drives them to sunny lands.]

The presence of this simile should suggest that, whatever the difference between the linear nature of Aeneas' journey and that of his ancient rival, the two views of individual destiny are the same. For all the eternity of Rome, death remains the common goal for all men, including the poet himself. This elegiac note in Virgil sets the poet off for a brief poignant moment before he too must enter into the cycle which is the extinction of the individual for the sake of the species—a pathos tempered, perhaps, by a collective survival. This ubiquitous tone in the *Aeneid* finds its exact dramatic counterpart in the pathos of the figure of Virgil in the *Divine Comedy,* lighting the way for others, yet unable to help himself. As Rome was the *praeparatio* for Christianity, so Virgil was Dante's poetic *praeparatio,* and his own reward, in the fiction of the poem, is simply the respite from Limbo for the duration of the journey, just as the historic Virgil, presumably, found a respite from the circle of time for the duration of his authorial voice in the poem.

In the poem, Virgil stands between Ulysses and Dante above all as poet and it is as a poet that he addresses Ulysses. It is clear that the two ancient figures speak the same language, right from the beginning of their encounter. Dante wishes to question the flames of Ulysses and Diomed, but his guide says:

> Lascia parlare a me; ch' i' ho concetto
> Ciò che tu vuoi. Chè sarebbero schivi,
> Perchè fuor Greci, forse del tuo detto.   (*Inf.* 26. 73–75)

[Let me speak, for I know what you wish. Because they are Greeks, they would perhaps be disdainful of your speech.]

"Speech" in this context is by no means "language"—naive commentators in the past have attempted to gloss this passage by saying that it means simply that Virgil could understand Greek, while the poet could not—but Dante's text shows that

such a reading is a misunderstanding, for in the next canto, the soul of Guido da
Montefeltro, who, we presume, has overheard Virgil dismissing Ulysses, not only
has understood their language, but claims to identify a Lombard accent:

... O tu, a cu' io drizzo
La voce, e che parlavi mo Lombardo,
Dicendo: "istra ten va, più, non t' adizzo,"   (*Inf.* 27. 19-21)

[O you, to whom I direct my voice, who spoke lombard just now, saying, "you
can go now, I won't urge you on any more ...."]

In other words, the language that Virgil and Ulysses share is a common style, the
high style of ancient epic, whose qualities are unappreciated in the vulgar company
of Hell, where the language is the *sermo humilis* of Christian *comedia*. Virgil implies
as much when he turns to the pilgrim, disdaining to answer Guido, and says

... 'Parla tu, questi è Latino,'   (*Inf.* 27. 33)

[You speak, this one is Italian.]

In part, of course, Virgil's disdain for this sinner, who is guilty of the same sin as that
of Ulysses, is a biting commentary on false counselors in Dante's world, and particularly in the papal court. The suggestion of the episode is that at least in antiquity,
when men were evil counselors they were still capable of a certain heroic stature
and magnanimity, whereas the meanness and base quality of this thirteenth-century
evil counselor puts him beneath Virgil's contempt. At the same time, there can be
little doubt that Dante meant to draw the parallel between Guido and Ulysses as
closely as possible, even to the navigational figure. As Guido recounts his attempted
false conversion to make up for a sinful life, he describes his approaching old age
in terms of that figure:

Quando mi vidi giunto in quella parte
    Di mia etade ove ciascun dovrebbe
    Calar le vele e raccoglier le sarte,
Cio che pria mi piacea allor m' increbbe,
    E pentuto e confesso mi rendei,
    Ahi miser lasso! e giovato sarebbe.   (*Inf.* 27. 79–84)

[When I reached that stage in life when one ought to lower the sails and coil
up the ropes, what had pleased me before I regretted, and I commended my
soul to God, contrite and shriven. Alas, it might have worked....]

The major difference between Ulysses and Guido da Montefeltro, therefore, is
neither in their material guilt nor in their language, but quite simply in their style.
    Virgil's style in his conversation with Ulysses is elevated and rhetorical, begin-
ning with the traditional *Apostrophe,* containing at least one antithesis, and passing
quickly to a *captatio benevolentiae* [S' io meritai di voi assai o poco] (*Inf.* 26. 81).
Ulysses' tongue of flame flickers with equal oratorical and tragic fervor, and when
he addresses his men, he too begins with the traditional *captatio* and manages at

least one famous Virgilian figure as well as several lesser oratorical flourishes. Ulysses' speech to his men is of course modelled on Aeneas' speech to his men in the first book of the *Aeneid*, beginning "O Socii" (*Aen*. I. 198–207), and it is even conceivable that Dante might have known from a remark in Macrobius that the "O Socii" speech was itself modelled on a Homeric original, as David Thompson has suggested,[3] so that Dante came as close to recapturing Ulysses' original speech as anyone could come who had never seen Homer's text. The speech has been universally admired and widely discussed from the Renaissance to our own day and I have little to add to the sensitive readings it has received, except to insist that, thanks to a series of echoes and parallelisms, there seems to be no difference between the rhetoric used by the character of Virgil and that of Ulysses.

At the same time, there is no doubt that Ulysses is portrayed as an anti-Aeneas, who is mentioned in passing, for he lacks the essential quality of *pietas:*

> Nè dolcezza di figlio, nè la pieta
>   Del vecchio padre, nè 'l debito amore,
>   Lo qual dovea Penelopè far lieta,
> Vincer poter dentro da me l' ardore   (*Inf*. 26. 94–96)

The essential characteristic of Ulysses' rhetoric is that it is completely self-serving, dedicated to a heroic enterprise, without any sense of moral duty. In his speech to his men, the comfort he offers them is their own manhood and stature:

> Considerate la vostra semenza:
>   Fatti non foste a viver come bruti,
>   Ma per seguir virtute e canoscenza.   (*Inf*. 26. 118–20)

[Think of your ancestry. You were not made to live like brutes, but to seek virtue and understanding.]

By contrast, the comfort that Aeneas offers his men is the foundation of Rome, the eternal consolation for individual suffering. Aeneas is portrayed in the *Divine Comedy,* as he is in the *Aeneid,* as the man who is constantly receptive to his providential destiny, who is elected to greatness by God. His descent into Hell was, like Dante's, willed in Heaven, and is by no means simply a consequence of his heroic stature.

The contrast between Aeneas' humility and Ulysses' pride is at least in part the contrast between Greek and Roman ideas of the uses of rhetoric. In a passage in the *De Inventione*, Cicero describes the corrupt orator in terms that serve very well to describe the figure of Ulysses:

> Postquam vero commoditas quaedam, parva virtutis imatrix, sine ratione officii, dicendi copia consecuta est, tum ingenio freta malitia pervertere urbes et vitas hominum labefactare assuevit.   (1. 2.3)

[When a certain agreeableness of manner—a depraved imitation of virtue—acquired the power of eloquence unaccompanied by any consideration of moral duty, then low cunning supported by talent grew accustomed to corrupting cities and undermining the lives of men.]

Dante seems to accept Cicero's judgment about the social function of eloquence when he condemns Ulysses by showing that his objective was to find virtue and understanding outside of himself, in a world without people ("il mondo sanza gente").

The providential course of history is represented in the *Divine Comedy*, as it is in the *Aeneid*, by the trajectory of the sun from East to West. Once it is established that this is the linear course of history, then it is clear that the proud man who, in his excess, would outstrip history, or grace, dies a shipwreck even if enfolded in the arms of Penelope. In other words, Ulysses' journey in the *Divine Comedy* exists on exactly the same plane of reality as does Dante's: a journey of the body which stands for a journey of the soul. If it were otherwise, then it would be difficult to understand why Dante would use the figure as a moral *exemplum* as he does in the very beginning of the canto:

Allor mi dolsi, e ora mi ridoglio,
   Quando drizzo la mente a ciò ch'io vidi;
   E più lo 'ngegno affreno chi'i' non soglio,
Perchè non corra che virtù nol guidi;   (*Inf.* 26. 19–22)

[I was grieved then and I grieve now, when I fix my mind on what I saw, and I rein in my genius more than is my wont, lest it run where virtue does not guide it. . . .]

It cannot be coincidental that in the previous canto, Dante's poetry has reached the heights of virtuosity with the double metamorphosis of the thieves, a display of his poetic powers that led him first to challenge Ovid and Lucan and then finally to repent for letting his pen run away with him. The episode of Ulysses thus provides a moral *exemplum* metalinguistically as well, as a poetic representation of such gravity that it both warns against and atones for a poetic excess beyond the poem's didactic needs. Dante's warning to himself at the same time furnishes one more indication of the way in which Ulysses stands for a kind of writing as well as for a habit of mind.

The navigational image serves admirably as a metaphor both for the journey of the mind and the progress of the poem. The metaphoric use of the image is what accounts for the close analogy that we feel between the figure of Ulysses and Dante himself. We have already seen several examples of its use as a figure for the pilgrim's journey, but equally obvious is the use of the figure in the *exordia* of the *Purgatorio* and the *Paradiso*, Dante's adaptations of an epic *topos* studied in detail by Curtius.[4] The "bark of genius" (navicella del mio ingegno, [*Pur.* I. 2]) sets sail in Purgatory just as the pilgrim reaches the shore of the mountain. The use of the word "ingegno" associates the journey with the poem—both are in a sense itineraries of the mind. At a deeper level, the journey is the poem, the writing of it, for that is the ultimate objective of the pilgrim, to become the poet that we have been reading from the beginning. In the beginning of the canto of *Ulysses,* it is as an admonition to his *ingegno* that Dante introduces the episode:

> "E più lo 'ngegno affreno ch'i' non soglio."   (*Inf.* 26. 21)

> [I rein in my genius more than is my wont, lest it run where virtue does not guide it.]

For this and other reasons, it seems safe to presume that the figure of Ulysses, for all of its apparent historicity, is at the same time a palinodic moment in the *Divine Comedy,* as Bruno Nardi once suggested, a retrospective view of Dante himself both as poet and as man, when with confidence and *ingegno* he embarked upon the writing of the *Convivio,* a work never completed, which began by stating that all men desire to know and that ultimate happiness resides in the pursuit of knowledge. Ulysses would then stand for a moment in the pilgrim's life. In the recapitulation of salvation history, that is, the history of the Christian soul, Ulysses would stand for the disastrous prelude to the preparation for grace, a disastrous guide before the encounter with Virgil. Whatever the validity of the suggestion, it goes a long way toward explaining at once the greatness of the figure and the harsh judgement upon him implied by his position in hell.

The distance that separates Ulysses' point of shipwreck from the pilgrim's survival, or, for that matter, the *Convivio* from the *Purgatorio,* is measured by the descent into Hell. This is literally true, according to the geography of the poem, and figuratively true as well, as the descent into the self, *intra nos* is the prerequisite for the kind of transcendent knowledge that all men desire. It is a journey that cannot be undertaken without a guide and here too, Virgil spans the gap that separates Dante from the pre-Christian or pre-conversion time represented by Ulysses.

I have said that the contrast between Virgil and Ulysses in the poem is not one of language, but rather of the *uses* to which an almost identical rhetoric is put. In literary terms, Ulysses is the man whose greatness determines epic history, while Aeneas is the man whose greatness is determined by the providential destiny thrust upon him. Both history and the individual follow a circular course in the *Odyssey,* while the pathos of Virgilian epic seems to lie in the discrepancy between the linear destiny of Rome and the cyclical turn of the seasons, to which individual men remain forever subject. Christian time shattered both circles, however, and insisted on the perfect congruence, in the geometric sense, between history and the soul. I should like to turn now to Dante's transformation of that inner circularity, the life of man as seen by the ancients. In dramatic terms, we have seen how the figure of Ulysses is undercut by the *pietas* of Aeneas. We must now examine briefly how *Aeneas* is in turn superseded by the new alter-*Aeneas* in Dante's poem.

Earlier in this paper I described Virgilian pathos with a reference to the simile of falling leaves, borrowed from Homer (*Il.* 6. 146), with which Virgil described the beginning of Aeneas' journey across the River Styx. It happens that Dante imitates that simile as the pilgrim is about to cross the River Acheron, thereby inviting the sophisticated reader to make an important structural comparison of Dante's poem with Virgil's (*Inf.* 3. 112–17):

> Come d'autunno si levan le foglie,
>   l'una appresso dell'altra fin'che il ramo
>   Vede alla terra tutte le sue spoglie,
> Similemente il mal seme d'Adamo
>   gittansi di quel lito ad una ad una,
>   per cenni come augel per suo richiamo.

> [As leaves fall in autumn, one after the other, until the branch sees all its spoils upon the ground, so the evil seed of Adam hurl themselves from that bank, one by one, as a bird to its lure.]

The purpose of the simile in both Homer and Virgil was to render some idea of the vast numbers of men who have fallen before the inexorable law of nature. Generations come and go, multitudinous as leaves which succeed one another. This purpose seems to be directly undercut by Dante's adverbial modifiers "l'una appresso dell' altra" (*Inf.* 3. 113) and "ad una ad una" (*Inf.* 3. 116) in both tercets. If the point of the original simile is in the vast numbers of men who die, then the point is blunted when the poet invites us to follow the fall of each individual leaf from bough to the ground. Dante's simile seems to insist on the fact that this fall is a collective phenomenon which is at the same time very much an individual destiny, leading to a grammatically decisive conclusion: 'fin'che 'l ramo Vede alla terra tutte le sue spoglie" (*Inf.* 3. 113–14 [until the branch sees all its spoils on the ground]). The verb personifies the bough in a daring way and substitutes its perspective for that of the detached epic poet. The word *spoglie* 'spoils' more-over suggests a wanton loss that is far from the inevitability of an autumnal fall. If this branch can look at its own spoils, presumably with sadness, then the implication is that this need not have happened: in short, that God's tree was meant to be evergreen.

The reflexive verbs in Dante's Virgilian imitation, "si levano," "gittansi," seem particularly appropriate, for the point of Dante's verses is that if this fall from God's tree is a destiny, then it is one deliberately chosen. Just as tragedy is out of place in a Christian context, so is Virgil's elegiac tone—these leaves chose to separate themselves from the tree of life. This would seem to be the difference between Virgil's introduction to the world of the dead and Dante's introduction to the world of the damned. Two different deaths are represented by these two similes: Dante would have referred to the Virgilian death as the first death, a death of the body. His own simile, however, refers to "la seconda morte"—a death of the soul (*Inf.* 1. 117). The death of the *Inferno* is a decision and not a fate. It is also irreversible. For these leaves, there is not even the biological comfort of a collective spring to come.

We should note in passing that this distinction between the two kinds of death is useful for explaining the difference between the Homeric death of Ulysses, largely irrelevant to Dante, and the death by shipwreck which he in fact portrays. The first is an organic fact of the body, but the second is a shipwreck of the soul, which can happen at any time and which, while there is life and grace, can be survived. This probably explains why Virgil asks Ulysses about his death in a curiously tortuous sentence:

> . . . ma l' un di voi dica
> Dove per lui perduto a morior gissi.'   (*Inf.* 26. 83–84)

[One of you tell / where, lost, death was arrived at by him.]

The strange passive construction was also used by Virgil in the first canto, when he said that the Emperor of Heaven did not will that "per me si vegna," that heaven be arrived at *by* me (*Inf.* 1. 126), the passive construction in both cases indicating Divine predestination, "com' Altrui piacque" (*Inf.* 26. 141) ['as pleased another']), in Ulysses' words. Furthermore, *perduto* 'lost' would be a redundancy if this were simply a question of physical death. As it is, it seems likely that Virgil's question, 'how, when you were lost, did you arrive at death,' refers to Ulysses' damnation, of which drowning is merely the figure, as it was for the fathers of the church ever since St. Ambrose.

To return to Dante's transformation of the Virgilian simile, it would seem to be emblematic of the shift in time, from the cyclical time of organic nature to the linear time of the soul. The perspective is shifted as well, from the elegiac to the theocentric, from history viewed with the momentary and poignant detachment of a poetic sensibility to history viewed from the transcendent aspect of eternity. The basis of the comparison is changed as well: the point of Virgil's simile is to compare the almost infinite number of souls to falling leaves: "Quam multa." Here, however, the comparison is in the manner of the fall—"Come." By a distortion that would probably be considered a poetic violence in the hands of a lesser poet, a horizontal motion, the crossing of a river, is compared to the downward motion of falling leaves in order to indicate that this crossing is in fact a "fall" in the spiritual sense of the word.

The last part of the simile once more stresses personal choice, in a daring and original way. Turning back to the Virgilian original, the phenomenon of the migration of birds serves to elaborate the theme of the cyclical turn of the seasons: "as birds swarm landward from the deep gulf, when the chill of the year routs them overseas and drives them to sunny lands." Dante accepts the comparison of the flight of birds as an emblem for the flight of the soul—indeed, some of the most exquisite figures of the poem derive from this comparison—but their flight is no longer an instinctive response that changes with the seasons, "Like a bird," writes Dante, "to its lure" (*Inf.* 3. 117). The terms borrowed from medieval falconry seem particularly apt for describing a motion that is at once instinctive and a conditioned response to the falconer's deception, a natural inclination toward a totally alien goal. In terms of this figure, all of the souls in Hell arrived there as did Ulysses, at the end of a "folle volo," a mad flight.

At the very beginning of Virgil's tutelage, the sharp distinctions between the poetry of the *Aeneid* and that of the *Divine Comedy* are perceptible in the most minute details. At the end of Virgil's guidance, the transformation is dramatic and definitive. At the end of the sixth book of the *Aeneid*, the famous *tu Marcellus eris* (*Aen.* 6. 883) passage is perhaps the high point of Virgilian pathos, where human grief for precocious death can derive almost no consolation from the eternity of Rome. Octavia is said to have fainted with grief for her son when the lines were first recited in the presence of Augustus. Virgil's providential history might redeem, or at least pacify the world, but the poet is powerless before death and can do nothing more than offer purple funereal lilies in mourning: "Manibus date lilia plenis" (*Aen.* 6. 883). It happens that this is the only line quoted from the original in Dante's *Divine Comedy*, but it appears, not at the ending of the voyage underworld, as one might expect, but at the ending of the *Purgatorio*, where the angels sing precisely those words to greet Beatrice's return from a precocious death with the white lilies of the Resurrection. It is only after hearing those words that the pilgrim realizes he is for the first time without his guide. The poet pays his model the supreme compliment at the moment when his poem no longer needs him.

At the beginning of this paper, I suggested a distinction between the circular and the linear forms of human time and of narrative structure and said that Dante's poem could be characterized by neither figure because it partook of both. The problematic, tentative view of the pilgrim is a novelistic, almost Dostoevskian striving toward a kind of finality which can be described as a linear goal: the death of the pilgrim and of his story. At the same time, this ending is a new beginning, for it marks the birth of the poet, who has been with us from the start. There is a circularity to the adventure as well: the voice of the poet which ends as it began. This tautology is the tautology of language itself, where the poet's intentionality pre-exists its temporal unfolding in syntax until it arrives at meaning, its point of departure. The point where circle and line, poet and pilgrim meet, is the poem's ending, specifically a vision of the incarnation. The central mystery of Christianity is at the same time the resolution of the epic and novelistic duality. The self that was, the figure of the pilgrim, and the self that is, the voice of the poet, converge in a moment which superimposes the eternity of the Redemption on the hero and now reality of the pilgrim. The detachment of the classic poet, so necessary for finding an historical coherence in the pattern, a logos of intelligibility, joins the flesh and blood experience of the pilgrim, a novelistic linear trajectory. At the final moment, the poet tells us, the circle is squared, in a poetic incarnation which is the unity of the poem and of the belief to which it bears witness.

NOTES

[1] John Freccero, "Dante's Prologue Scene," *Dante Studies* 84 (1966).
[2] Robert Hollander, *Allegory in Dante's* Commedia (Princeton, N.J.: Princeton University Press, 1969), pp. 76ff.
[3] David Thompson, "Dante's Ulysses and the Allegorical Journey," *Dante Studies* 85 (1967).
[4] E. R. Curtius, *European Literature and the Latin Middle Ages* (Princeton, N.J.: Princeton University Press, Bollingen Series, 1953), pp. 128–30.

Martha Nussbaum

ODYSSEUS IN
SOPHOCLES' *PHILOCTETES*

Odysseus invokes an oddly-matched pair of divinities on behalf of his project: "May Hermes god of guile, the escort, guide us, and Victory—Athena, guardian of the city, my constant protector" (133–4).[1] His scheme of getting control of Philoctetes and the bow is to be supported by the god of deceit and by the god who promotes the common welfare of all citizens, here identified with Victory, daughter of Zeus. Guileful Hermes seems a suitable backer for Odysseus' devious stratagem, and Athena is well known to be that hero's patroness and protector. But the significance of her being invoked in her capacity as guardian of citizens, and of her conflation in that capacity with Nike, is more obscure. In no pre-Sophoclean treatment of the exploits of Odysseus, as far as we know, does he invoke this particular Athena. We would not expect him to, since she presumably earned her title by deeds which postdate those recorded here. If this is not to be seen simply as an audience-pleasing anachronism, we must look further for an explanation. What connection is there, in Odysseus' view, between the use of guile and the protection of citizens, and how are both related to his project?

The Odysseus of Euripides' lost *Philoctetes* is an egocentric seeker after glory, always courting new risks in order to maintain and enhance his reputation. In deciding whether to adopt a certain course of action, he considers what its outcome will be for his own fame, and it is because of his constant concern with self-advancement that he is careless of the rights and interests of others.[2] In contrast to this character with his coherent, though deficient, standard of behavior, the Sophoclean figure strikes us as faceless, and has been called by one recent critic a man with "no standards of any kind."[3] It seems to me, however, that he does hold a coherent view of some interest, and that it is one of the play's main purposes to examine this view and the difficulties it presents.

In beginning to elicit the nature of Odysseus' moral view, we might consider an acute observation made by a recent critic, S. Benardete: "In Sophocles' *Philoc-*

From *Philosophy and Literature* 1, No. 1 (Fall 1976): 29–39.

tetes we can observe how an entire play can find its action reflected in the opposition of *chrē* and *dei.*"[4] These two impersonal Greek words for "must" are opposed in, broadly, the following way: *chrē* is "subjective," *dei,* "objective."[5] *Chrē* expresses the involvement of the subject in the process (he must take it upon himself to do X), whereas *dei* expresses the objective requirement of a situation or state of affairs, which compels the agent without regard to his own subjective assent to the project. We might expand these remarks a bit further: the agent who uses *chrē* thereby emphasizes the importance of some action, and of that action's being his own action, whereas the agent who describes his position with a *dei* seems to be emphasizing instead the importance of some state of affairs, to the achievement of which an action of some agent or other is regarded as a means.[6] As Benardete very briefly sketches, an examination of the play shows that Odysseus characteristically uses *dei*, Philoctetes *chrē*, and that the usage of Neoptolemus shifts at a crucial point in the action. What is the significance of this verbal point?

I would like to argue that Sophocles portrays Odysseus as a man who accords ultimate value to states of affairs, and, specifically, to the state of affairs which seems to represent the greatest possible good of all citizens. He gives his approval to any action which he believes will best promote the general welfare, and resists the argument that there are certain actions which should not be done by an agent because of his character and principles, decrying this view as a form of squeamishness. Sophocles is concerned to show us both the initial attractiveness of the Odyssean argument and its ultimate defectiveness, asking what the holder of such a view can be like as a person, how his view affects his relations with others, and what value he can give to promise-keeping, friendship, integrity, and justice—how it comes to be that the worshipper of Athena Polias, in the Odyssean sense, commits himself also to the service of Hermes, god of guile.

Through no fault of his own, by a god-sent chance (1326; cf. 1316–17), Philoctetes trespassed in the sacred precinct of Athena on the island Chryse, and as punishment he was bitten by a poisonous serpent guarding the shrine (265–7, 1327–8). His foot became ulcerous, causing him both continual distress and sudden acute attacks of pain. His very presence caused discomfort for all around him because of the evil smell of the wound (890–1; 473–4, 520, 900–1), and the blasphemous cries he uttered during his attacks prevented the army from completing essential sacrifices and libations to the gods (8–11), on which, no doubt, their prospects of military success could be thought largely to depend. To keep him with the army would be to jeopardize the fortunes of all and to cause all grave distress. To cast him out somewhere in the midst of a civilized group of island-dwellers (as in the dramas of Aeschylus and Euripides) would be to cause the same difficulties for their daily life and projects. Lack of human company increased his distress: there was nobody to help him find food, nobody to hear his complaint, nobody to apply such minimal remedies as he possessed (cf. 169ff., 183–5, 188–90, 228, 269, and esp. 279–82, 691–700). But to have given him any human companion at all would have resulted in there being two people unable to pray to the gods, one in awful pain, the other in inescapable discomfort. Though it strikes us and the Chorus as horrible that, despite his innocence of wrongdoing, he was treated so callously by those who owed much and were to owe more to his services, there is little doubt that such callousness on the part of the leaders was right from a utilitarian viewpoint. If his cries prevent the carrying-out of religious ceremonies which are essential to civilized men, it is better that he be sent to live with animals, with only the "dappled and tawny beasts" (184–5), who have no rites and no gods, and an inanimate object, the bow of Heracles, for companions. His condition will be a bit worse, but he would not in any case be cured, and no one else will suffer for the decision.

Philoctetes, however, as we might expect, is filled with resentment. The generals are realistic enough to count on his not holding their view of things. Without having seen him or heard reports of him since the abandonment, Odysseus knows he will be suspicious, filled with hatred (70ff.), unwilling now to be persuaded (103) to act for the common good, even though it means healing and glory, when before the common good had occasioned his terrible suffering. Persuasion is ruled out; and the very object which victory requires, the bow, makes capture by force impossible (103–5). Hence a stratagem must be tried, making use of the services of a young, untried soldier of sterling credentials who can win the confidence of this vindictive man.

Odysseus is an instrument of the common good, seeking not personal glory, but the best possible outcome for all. "He was given a command as one from many" (1143), in order to achieve a "common benefit" (1145). The interests of the whole army are more vivid to him than his own self-interest. Neoptolemus, he says, may defame him in any way he finds useful: "None of that will give me pain. But if you don't do this, you will cause suffering for all the Argives" (66–7). The words *ho sumpas stratos* ("the whole army," "the army as a whole") recur more than once in his arguments (1257, 1294, and cf. 1226), until at a crucial point in the action he personifies the Achaian people as a single being who will accomplish the purpose for which he works:

o: There is someone—there *is*—who will prevent you from doing this.
n: What? Who is it who will prevent me?
o: The entire Achaian populace, and I among them.... Don't you fear the
   Achaian army, in doing this?   (1241–3, 1250)

Less a person, in his own eyes, than a part of a composite political "person" whose desires are regarded as integrated into a single system, Odysseus prides himself on his adaptability to the demands of the situation: "Whenever such-and-such a man is required (*dei*), I am a man of that kind (1049)." The objective *dei* determines not only his actions, but even his character. As a perfectly flexible tool of the general welfare, there is nothing he will not do, not because he is entirely lacking in standards, but because he holds that the resulting general good is the only important standard. The only natural want he mentions (1052) is the political desire for victory—encompassing, apparently, the overall outcome as well as more immediate victories (such as that over Philoctetes) which contribute to the whole. He desires a certain result, in the accomplishment of which any sort of action, any shift in principles or character, is permissible.[7]

When he starts to instruct Neoptolemus, he begins with a bold, peculiar use of *dei:* "Child of Achilles, you must (*dei*) be *gennaios* concerning the purpose for which you came here" (50–1). The situation objectively demands, in his view, that Neoptolemus behave in a certain way. To Odysseus this is one with the demand that he "be" a certain sort of person. The word *gennaios,* etymologically and synchronically, seems to be recognized as closely connected with one's nature and heritage, even as emphasizing consistency and fidelity to nature (cf. Arist. *Historia Animalium* 488[b]19: "The *gennaion* is that which does not diverge from its own nature").[8] Being *gennaios* is being true to one's genetic heritage—hence, more importantly, being true to what is one's own essential nature (*phusis*).[9] But Odysseus, about to ask Neoptolemus to depart from his nature for the sake of the success of their project, sees nothing odd in telling him that he has got to be *gennaios* in its service, and in expressing the demand with a *dei.* Either he does not feel the connection of *gennaios* with the internal and with conformity to character, or he is offering a persuasive definition, attempting to show that the real *gennaios* is one who conforms to situational, not internal, requirements.

His injunction to Neoptolemus is that he must (*dei*) deceive Philoctetes' soul with speeches (54–5) and that he must (*dei*) work out a stratagem whereby he can steal the unconquerable weapons (77–8). But he recognizes that Neoptolemus will not be so ready as he is to bend to the demands of the situation:

> I know well, son, that you are not disposed by nature (*phusei . . . mē pephukota*) to say such things, or to devise evil tricks. But, since victory is a pleasant possession to acquire, bring yourself to do it.   (79–82)

Neoptolemus is asked to overcome his natural reluctance in order to advance the cause of victory—to give himself over (84) to the flexible Odysseus.

But his reply argues for the importance of acting consistently with one's dispositions and maintaining some harmony between *pathē* and actions:

> When I am pained at the account of an action, son of Laertes, I hate also to perform it. For it is my nature (*ephun*) to do nothing by base craft—not mine, nor, they say, my father's (*houkphusas eme*).   (86–9)

Neoptolemus says nothing about the desirability of the states of affairs resulting from various actions. His emphasis is all on the nature of the act itself, and on its harmony or disharmony with his own character, as shown in the pleasure or pain which its description elicits. Through an awareness of his feelings he knows what it is his nature to do, and the goodness of the result is of secondary importance to the fitness of the act: "I prefer, sir, to miss the goal while acting nobly (*kalōs*), rather than to gain a victory by baseness (*kakōs*)" (94–5).

Neoptolemus objects not to the project in general, but to the use of deceit, which is not in his nature. "Don't you think lying shameful?" he asks his mentor (108). The bold answer is, "No—if lies bring success (*to sothēnai*)." Odysseus does not admit that an action can be judged shameful or noble in itself—for he might have said, "Shameful, yes, but in a good cause." His position is not simply that a good end justifies the use of questionable means, but that actions are to be assessed only with reference to those states of affairs to which they contribute. If the result is overall success, what is required to produce the result cannot be morally condemned. And the complaint that it will not be possible to look the man in the eye and tell a lie is brushed aside as a form of squeamishness: "When you do something for a gain, you had better not shrink back (111)." Hermes the guileful is not to be spurned; if he can contribute to the common good—to Victory, Athena of the city—he is worthy of honor.

Such is the basic position of Odysseus. It is not immediately repugnant or implausible. Surely the denial that falsehood should ever be used in the public interest would seem excessively rigid, and there is much that is admirable in Odysseus' concern for his fellow soldiers, and in his willingness to serve the needs of the state. But, as even this cursory examination shows, his valuation of states of affairs over actions and his connected lack of concern with character result in his appearing an oddly faceless, mechanical *persona*. We shall now examine some of the other consequences of his basic position which become apparent as the drama proceeds.

First, there are problems connected with Odysseus' position on lying. For if his view is really as we have sketched it, he will have no use for stating it straightforwardly and asking for approval—unless this just happens also to be the course most advantageous for getting to his desired result. All argument becomes *ad hominem;* it is hard to see how we can even regard his conversation with Neoptolemus as a genuine moral debate. So, ironically, if Odysseus' view is what he says it is, there is no reason for us to believe his account of his view. There need be no reliable connection between his beliefs and speeches, and, given the fact that we encounter him (with the possible exception of his prayer at 133–4) only in discourse with others, what seemed at first a recognizable and consistent position begins to look hopelessly inaccessible. To the remark of Neoptolemus which so clearly exposes the conflict between valuing actions and valuing their results (94–5), Odysseus replies not with a defense of consequentialism, but with a defense of speeches (96–9). Only by resisting, *pro tempore*, these implications of the Odyssean position can we even continue to discuss his position at all.

Furthermore, we see that the man who prides himself on having no natural blocks to any sort of useful action must rely on the presence of fixed dispositions in others for the success of his stratagems. His demand to Neoptolemus is, "Give me yourself," but if that self were not a character of a certain sort, the credibility of the project would collapse, for it relies on Neoptolemus' being only a temporary servant of Odysseus, trusted as upright, with a known disposition not to lie. And

Philoctetes is likewise expected for the plan's success not to be an Odyssean: he must believe he is being told the truth. The nature of the scheme presupposes a general reliance on promises and the truthfulness of speeches. Thus, even if Odysseus believes lying for a good end is not shameful, he must allow most men to continue to think it shameful.

His view commits him, then, to secrecy and to guile: Hermes is not only a possible helper of his Athena, but is required for the success of the venture.[10]

The psychological result of this commitment to deceit is that even where candor and persuasion might be most efficacious for his purposes, he prefers guileful speeches. Thus he asks Neoptolemus to use a lie even when it seems possible that argument might have succeeded. And when guile has reached an impasse and Philoctetes bluntly refuses to accept the requirements of the situation as binding (994), Odysseus, still unable to recognize the importance of subjective assent to the project, even in the midst of a discussion of persuasion, makes the cryptic remark, *peisteon tade,* which hovers between "you must obey" and "you must be persuaded."[11] Philoctetes hears it the first way: he is, then, he says, a slave and not a free man (995)—since "you must obey" seems enforceable only by physical compulsion. But the requirements of the situation really are, as we shall see, that Philoctetes be persuaded, and not compelled. Odysseus, whose grasp of this distinction throughout the play is imperfect owing to his unwillingness to give due recognition to the desires of others, here expresses his frustration with the recalcitrance of the agent who will not look to the best result. In a bizarre confusion of the objective and the subjective, he says the man just *has* to be persuaded, whether he wants to be or not, since that is what the situation requires: he has got to (*dei*) take Troy (998), so he has got to be persuaded against his will. To such incoherence Odysseus has been led by his failure to give any independent value to actions or character.

All of Odysseus' relations with others, as we might expect, are colored by this devaluing of personal natures and of persuasion. Himself a man without a fixed nature, he treats other men as less than human. Philoctetes is to be "trapped" by a stratagem (14). Neoptolemus appropriately infers from his words that the bow and arrows "must be hunted down" (116). Philoctetes grasps the implications of Odysseus' treatment of him when he says he has been "approached by stealth" and "ensnared" (1007), and that his hands are "snared together" (1005). When the prophet Helenos was captured by Odyssean guile (608), he was taken in chains before the Achaian host, "a fine catch" (609).

Men, for him, are animals to be stalked and trapped; but it is even more strange to find him unable to make crucial distinctions between men and inanimate objects. A notorious difficulty of the play as a whole is Odysseus' lack of clarity as to whether the bow alone is required to take Troy or whether Philoctetes himself must use it, and, further, whether he must come to Troy willingly. It seems clear that the real force of the oracle is that Philoctetes must use the bow, and use it willingly (611–13, 839–41, 1332–5, 1423ff.).[12] Odysseus characteristically neglects the problem, emphasizing the importance of the bow above that of the man. If Neoptolemus is to deceive Philoctetes' soul, it is in order that he become the thief of his unconquered weapons (77–8). "This bow alone will take Troy," he tells his subordinate, "not you without it or it without you" (113, 115)—whereas the full statement of the requirement, emerging from the speech of Heracles, is: "You are not strong enough to take Troy without *him*, nor is *he* without you, but as two lions pasturing together, each guards the other" (1434–6). Although at line 102 Neoptolemus speaks of "bringing" the man, Odysseus' reply mentions only "trapping" him.[13] At a crucial point in the action, Neoptolemus, using dactylic hexameters, the metre of prophetic insight,[14] rejects the Odyssean implication that the bow is the important "catch":

> I see that we hold this catch, the bow, in vain, if we sail without him. For his is the crown: it is he whom the god has directed us to bring.   (839–41)

Odysseus is led in the same way to disregard the importance of Philoctetes' assent to the project. Deceit seems perfectly acceptable, as force apparently does later (983, 985, 1297). But the importance of his assent has been urged by Helenos (612) and by Neoptolemus recounting the prophecy (1332). Odysseus' general view, in these two related ways, leads him to make self-defeating mistakes in calculating what the situation requires.

Odysseus dehumanizes friendly associates as well as victims. The word *philos* ("friend") is used in the drama a total of thirty-one times, but never by Odysseus; whereas the demeaning *hupourgein, hupēretein,* and *hupēretes* ("serve," "servant") are used a total of six times, among which three are uses by Odysseus of others, one of himself (in relation to Zeus), and one by Philoctetes of him (15, 53 *bis*, 990, 1024). He regards Neoptolemus as a figure with a certain special power to effect the desired outcome (he first addresses him as the son of the most *powerful* of the Greeks—3), who must, in the service of the plan, become a submissive helper. The injunction which begins "You must (*dei*) be *gennaion*" turns out to mean "You must (*dei*) serve those you are here to serve" (53). The cooperation which is to make the project a "common effort" (25) will consist in Odysseus' giving instructions and Neoptolemus' heeding them (24–5). There can, it seems, be no genuine cooperation under the screen of Odyssean secrecy,[15] no friendship when *phusis* is ignored and *gennaios* is used to mean "reliably obedient in the service of the common good."[16]

In his indifference to friendship, Odysseus makes another crucial miscalculation: he neglects entirely, until it is thrust upon him, the connection between Philoctetes and Heracles—the fact that he won the bow by doing a service for an esteemed friend (cf. 670). Heracles is never mentioned until Philoctetes speaks of him at 262. Previously, the weapons have been called simply "his [i.e., Philoctetes'] bow" (68), "the unconquered weapon" (78), "arrows that are inescapable and bring death" (105), "this bow" (113), and "that" (115).

Odysseus' principles make it seem unlikely that he should be concerned with justice, or recognize any claims based on justice as placing limitations on his activities. The psychological consequences of his view, as sketched above, render the improbability greater, since if the individuality of others is neglected the question of giving each what is due him will not arise. And indeed, in a play concerned throughout with justice, Odysseus is conspicuous for his lack of concern: of seventeen occurrences of *dikaios* ("just") and related words, only three are in the mouth of Odysseus, and in these three the attitude expressed is ambiguous, if not contemptuous. In urging Neoptolemus to abandon his *phusis* for the sake of victory, Odysseus exhorts him: "Bear up; we'll look just some other time" (*dikaioi d'authis ekphanoumetha,* 81). The claims of justice are to be waived in favor of the sweetness of victory. Justice is something to be concerned about on some other occasion—i.e., not when considerations of justice might prove a block to the achievement of victory. And what is promised for the future is not even just behavior, but simply the reputation of justice, or justice manifest to others.[17] Perhaps Odysseus is suggesting here, as the Chorus will later, that when the outcome is generally good, men tend not to find fault with the agents. Lying is not shameful if it is done in the cause of success, and unjust deeds—while not necessarily ceasing to be unjust—will cease to be called so if they lead to a comfortable result. Consequently, justice is not a decisive or even important consideration in settling on a course of action: if one takes care to win, the praise of men will follow. Thus Odysseus, boasting later of his responsiveness to the needs of the situation, goes on to reveal again his indifference to justice: "Whenever such-and-such a man is required, I am a man of that kind, and when there is a competition of good and just men, you would not find anyone more pious than I" (1049–50). Odysseus is what the case requires—and when there is a competition among men concerning justice and goodness, he is not just or good, so much as pious. Piety, he claims, is what wins the contests waged ostensibly for justice in public life; and piety, as the play reveals, is quite different from justice.[18]

The Odyssean view of justice emerges with particular clarity in the defense of Odysseus by the Chorus at 1140 ff. Philoctetes has inveighed against Odysseus' duplicity and the irreparable harm it has done him. The Chorus assumes an acerbic, slightly condescending tone:

> It is the business of a real man (*anēr*), you know, to say that what turns out for the best (*to eu*) is just (*dikaion*)—and, having said so, not to give vent to spiteful bitterness of speech. He [sc. Odysseus] was given a command as one from many, and at their mandate achieved a common benefit for his friends.

They add to Odysseus' observation that men generally call just actions which turn out for the best the further point that this is what a real *anēr* ought to do. They praise Odysseus' position on justice as the really manly one, and join their praise with an explanation of why *to eu* should be admitted to be on his side: he was a representative of the whole army, and achieved a general benefit. But the Chorus correctly distinguishes between the job of getting Philoctetes to accept a general

principle and getting him to temper the expression of his feelings about his particular situation. A real man, they argue, will neither speak of injustice when the
outcome is for the best nor engage in unprofitable and unpleasant moaning about
the cost of the "general benefit" to his own interests.

These, then, are some of the consequences, both theoretical and psychological, of Odysseus' views. The social system administered by an Odyssean is characterized by great emphasis on secrecy and plotting, together with a demand for
blind obedience from the non-rulers. Moral training would seem for this sort of
person to consist primarily in the instruction to be orderly and to serve in the way
called for. The picture is forcefully summarized in the speech which Neoptolemus
delivers to Philoctetes as part of Odysseus' plan. As it concludes with its insincere
attack on Odysseus, it manages, ironically, to show us an Odyssean view of the
army and its leaders:

> And yet I do not blame him so much as I do the commanders. For an army,
> like a city, is entirely dependent on its leaders. And when men get out of
> order, it is through the speeches of their teachers that they become bad.
>
> (385–8)

Leaders are entirely responsible for the behavior of those under them. If there
is disorder, one can conclude that the leaders have not exercised sufficient control over moral teaching. This observation, in addition to its Odyssean claim that
subservience is virtue in the ruled and disorder invariably a bad thing, seems to
err, in the play's terms, by its neglect of both chance and *phusis*. If men get out
of hand, it is a question of teaching; a shrewd ruler can manage things so that
there is no disorder. But Philoctetes' plight, caused by "god-sent chance," is a
vivid counterexample to this view. He was disorderly and caused disorder
through nothing connected with speeches, and though the shrewd rulers have
attempted to get rid of this chance-caused confusion, it continues to plague them
as they try to execute their plans for the good. Furthermore the case of Neoptolemus has already raised doubts about the possibility of reducing all persons to
pawns by teaching. The importance of one's heritage and family ties, which the
leaders need to maintain and exploit in the cause of order, would have to be
drastically suppressed before resistance from the excellent and strong would no
longer be a threat. And even if such a project were feasible, there would be no
assurance that speeches could entirely reduce *phusis* to order. When Neoptolemus gets out of hand, it is in rebellion against the speeches of his teacher that
he becomes good.

It should be evident by now that Odysseus' position, as I have characterized
it, is a form of utilitarianism—a consequentialism aimed at promoting the general
welfare. A recent criticism of utilitarianism by Bernard Williams[19] has argued persuasively that consequentialism, because it insists that actions are to be assessed
only with reference to the resulting state of affairs, cannot give sufficient weight to
the agent's peculiar relation to *his own* actions, to questions of conformity between

character and action, and hence to considerations of personal integrity. If I am right, it is this same sort of criticism that Sophocles is voicing in his portrait of Odyssean morality. The rest of the play bears this out.

NOTES

[1] All translations from Sophocles' *Philoctetes* are my own.

[2] Cf. Dio Chrysostom, 59.

[3] B. Knox, *The Heroic Temper* (Berkeley: University of California Press, 1964), p. 124.

[4] S. Benardete, "*Chrē* and *Dei* in Plato and Others," *Glotta* 43 (1965): 297.

[5] Cf. also G. Redard, *Recherches sur* Chrē, Chrēsthai (Paris 1953), esp. 40, 53.

[6] *Dei* is, of course, used of actions as well as their results: not only "This must (*dei*) come about," but also "This must (*dei*) be done." But the necessity to act expressed with *dei* is a necessity to actualize some state of affairs, to fulfill some situational requirement; there is always an absence of emphasis on the personal engagement of the agent, on that action's being *his* action.

[7] It is perhaps not surprising that we find this characterless agent of circumstances referred to three times with the periphrasis *Odusseōs bia* (lit. "the force of Odysseus," or "the force, Odysseus": 314, 321, 592), although no other character in the play is so called. He is, indeed, a "force" in the society more than he is an agent with a character and with projects to which he is personally attached.

[8] Cf. also Aristotle, *Rhetoric* 1370^{b}22; in both passages the *gennaion* is contrasted with the *eugenes:* the latter is born of an excellent line, the former merely what does not depart from its nature, whatever that nature is.

[9] This conflation of heritage and essence has long been noted for *phusis* and related words, and plays an important role in Pre-Socratic cosmologies. Cf. esp. Charles Kahn, *Anaximander and the Origins of Greek Cosmology* (New York: Columbia University Press, 1960), pp. 200–3.

[10] *Dolos*, "guile," and *dolios*, "guileful," occur ten times in the play, much more frequently than in any other Sophoclean play; this is also the case with *logos*, "speech," which occurs forty-one times.

[11] For the first, cf. Soph. *Oed.* 1516, Eur. *Hippolytus* 1182, Plato *Apology* 19a; for the second, cf. Pl. *Republic* 365e.

[12] This is the version of the myth given in the *Little Iliad;* that Sophocles intended us to understand the requirement this way is agreed by most modern critics; exceptions are T. von Wilamowitz-Moellendorf, *Die dramatische Technik des Sophokles* (Berlin, 1917), p. 304 and, following him, D. B. Robinson, "Topics in Sophocles' *Philoctetes*," *Classical Quarterly* NS 19 (1969): 34–56. They argue that Sophocles could not have wanted the audience to think that Philoctetes *must* eventually come to Troy, since this would have robbed the plot of much of its suspense. Besides going against the evidence of the text, this argument is based on an absurdly superficial notion of what constitutes the dramatic tension of a Sophoclean tragedy. There may well have been spectators who saw in this drama no more than what we see in a suspense novel, but we may be allowed to doubt whether it was for these that Sophocles constructed his drama.

[13] Cf. A. E. Hinds, "The Prophecy of Helenus in Sophocles' *Philoctetes*," *Classical Quarterly* NS 17 (1967): 169–82, esp. 171.

[14] This has been noted by Knox (p. 131) and a number of other critics.

[15] For the case that simple utilitarianism defeats the possibility of cooperation, cf. D. H. Hodgson, *Consequences of Utilitarianism* (Oxford: Clarendon Press, 1967), and G. J. Warnock, *The Object of Morality* (London: Methuen, 1971), pp. 31–4.

[16] Cf. also 1068, where *gennaios* must, again, mean something like "reliable servant." *Phusis* and related words are used by Odysseus in only two passages, already discussed: the injunction to Neoptolemus to depart from his nature (79ff.), and the peculiar remark about his own nature (1052).

[17] R. C. Jebb (*Sophocles: Philoctetes* [Amsterdam, repr. 1966] ad loc.) insists that we must translate (supplying *ontes*) "Our honesty shall be shown forth another day." He cites two examples (Homer *Il.* 13.258, Soph. *Oed.* 1063) where the *true* nature or situation of a person comes to light. But even in these cases the emphasis of the verb *ekphainomai* is clearly on what it is that comes to light, what is manifested to the observer. Odysseus' lack of concern for natures leads in any case to a tendency for "It will become clear that we really were just" to be abandoned in favor of the claim, more important for him, "It will look to everyone as though we were just." The second reading is more consistent with

his strategy in this scene—cf. 85, 119, where what Neoptolemus will be *called* is the crucial factor. And it seems that the translation suggested here is at least as plausible as Jebb's. Even a weaker version, "We shall come to light as just," is still acceptable as emphasizing the judgment of the many.

[18] In the same spirit, later, Odysseus asks how Neoptolemus can call his actions just, when they involve disobedience to the plan of his superior (1241). Here he seems to go so far as to offer a redefinition of justice in line with his view.

[19] Bernard Williams, "A Critique of Utilitarianism," in Smart and Williams, *Utilitarianism: For and Against* (Cambridge University Press, 1973), pp. 77–150.

Richard Ellmann
JOYCE AND HOMER

As a young man Joyce notified Henrik Ibsen by letter, and W. B. Yeats by word of mouth, that higher and holier enlightenment lay beyond their reach and would have to await their successors. His admiration for these writers, while great, was not unbounded: in a poem about *Ghosts* later he would twit Ibsen for his obsession with spreading guilt, and at the end of *A Portrait of the Artist* he reproved Yeats for a nostalgic aestheticism. Imposing as they were, they were already receding into the past, precursors and not saviours. Joyce saw himself as advancing beyond them into the future of literature.

Yet he stepped backward as well as forward. Why he should have adopted ancient Greek originals for both Stephen Dedalus and Bloom is more than a literary question. Like other writers, he wished to invoke the collective past as well as his personal moment. "Ancient salt is best packing," as Yeats remarked long afterwards. In part it was for Joyce a way of aggrandizing his characters and his country, of connecting by continental drift the Ireland which in a notebook he rudely assailed as "an afterthought of Europe" with Greece. This anastomosis of antiquity, especially Greek antiquity, with a later age in another country, has been common enough from Virgil's *Aeneid* to Meredith's *Harry Richmond,* though rarely pursued by such intricate means.

Joyce could find encouragement in his epical aims from W. B. Yeats. In "The Autumn of the Body," included in *Ideas of Good and Evil* (1903), which Joyce had with him in Trieste, Yeats disagreed with Mallarmé that the present age would make its one medium the lyric and argued instead for a new *Odyssey.* "I think that we will learn again," Yeats wrote, "how to describe at great length an old man wandering among enchanted islands, his return home at last, his slowly gathering vengeance, a flitting shape of a goddess, and a flight of arrows, and yet to make all these so different things . . . become . . . the signature or symbol of a mood of the divine imagination."[1] Yeats was envisaging something on the order of his own *The*

From *Critical Inquiry* 3, No. 3 (Spring 1977): 567–82.

214

Wanderings of Oisin, in which Oisin too wanders among enchanted islands and eventually returns to Ireland. Into this fable Yeats had woven much of his own history. But while Yeats supposed that a modern *Odyssey* would depict armed combats, Joyce had for some time been toying with a different idea, that such adventures might be internalized. He was prodded to this by a conviction that his own nature was cast in the heroic mold, although physically he was as cowardly as morally he was intrepid. Flights of arrows were not likely to issue from his bow. Yet another heroism, too everydayish to be recognized as such, might be secretly at work in a seemingly unheroic age.

I

The epic possibilities of his subject had been with him from the start. In Trieste he read in Vico that Homer, and Dante after him, were figures of *ricorso,* that stage in a historical cycle when the whole cycle was known and leaped beyond. Vico, in his "Discovery of the True Homer," argued that Homer was not so much an individual as the entire Greek people, with the *Iliad* and *Odyssey* representing two stages of national development. Joyce aspired to give his own work a stature and significance for the modern period comparable to Homer's in the classical period, as to Dante's in the medieval one. *A Portrait of the Artist* belonged to the old stage and *Ulysses* to the new one.

In his reading Joyce began to find unexpected confirmation of his procedure. Remarkable coincidences seemed to confirm that the Homeric analogy could provide a key to the world. At the beginning of the *Odyssey* Ulysses is on Calypso's island, Ogygia. This was the name that Plutarch gave to Ireland and was the title of a well-known early history of the country by Roderic O'Flaherty, *Ogygia, seu, Rerum Hiberniarum Chronologia* (1685). Such intermeshing made clear to Joyce that he had a right to his epic parallel. He set about multiplying these correspondences.

I know that some readers, including Ezra Pound, have discounted parallels with the *Odyssey* as mere scaffolding. Joyce ventured to disagree. It is of course true that he is not on his knees before Homer. As Samuel Butler said of Homer, in an essay Joyce had read, "He was after all only a literary man, and those who occupy themselves with letters must approach him as a very honoured member of their own fraternity, but still as one who must have felt, thought, and acted much as themselves. He struck oil, while we for the most part succeed in boring only; still we are his literary brethren, and if we would read his lines intelligently we must also read between them." But if Joyce did not abase himself, he deferred. When he began to serialize *Ulysses* in *The Little Review,* he insisted that Homeric titles be prefixed to the episodes. Later he expunged these, but they remained in his mind if not on the paper. Both before and after publication day he circulated to his favorite critics one or the other of the two schemes he had prepared, in which the

Homeric titles continued to identify the episodes. In writing to his aunt Josephine Murray, whom he was anxious that the book should please, he urged her to read first a prose version of the *Odyssey* before tackling his own book.[2] When she was slow to comply, he repeated after publication the same instruction he had given earlier (1:193). Stuart Gilbert's book, and Frank Budgen's, both written under Joyce's eye a decade after *Ulysses* had appeared, kept also to the Homeric pattern. In later life Joyce sometimes reversed this process, and responding to Vladimir Nabokov's respectful comments about his knowledge of Homer, he disclaimed any special acquaintance with the *Odyssey* or with Greek. To those who read the book as an ordinary work of fiction, he wished to make clear its elaborate structure; to those who addressed themselves to the structure, he pointed to the novelistic element. This is no more than to say that in the human body DNA is based upon the double helix and could not exist without it.

The broad outlines of Joyce's narrative are of course strongly Homeric: the three parts, with Telemachus' adventures at first separate from those of Ulysses, their eventual meeting, their homeward journey and return. Equally Homeric is the account of a heroic traveller picking his way among archetypal perils. That the *Odyssey* was an allegory of the wanderings of the soul had occurred to Joyce as to many before him, and he had long since designated the second part of a book of his poems as "the journey of the soul" (2:20). He had also construed Stephen's progress in *A Portrait* as a voyage from Scyllan promiscuity in chapter 2 to Charybdian simon-purity in chapter 3, and to reconciliation in chapter 4. Although in *Ulysses* he diverged sharply from Homer in the order of events, Joyce clearly adapted the Homeric settings and what he chose to consider the prevailing themes. He found the *Odyssey* beautifully all-embracing in its vision of human concerns. His own task must be to work out the implications of each incident like a Homer who had long outlived his time and had learned from all subsequent ages. Joyce once asked his friend Jacques Mercanton if God had not created the world in much the same way as writers compose their works; but he then bethought himself and murmured, "Perhaps, in fact, he does give less thought to it than we do." Neither God nor Homer could compete with Joyce in self-consciousness.

Although Joyce was modest about his knowledge of ancient Greek, he had more than a smattering of it and did not neglect the classical infusion of his material which could be secured through language. On a principle, shared with Goethe, of letting the adversary propel, however crookedly, the book's themes, he has Mulligan quote tags from Herodotus and Homer and, after mentioning *epi oinopa ponton,* the winedark sea, has him invent two post-Homeric epithets, the snotgreen and scrotumtightening sea. The very first words of the book, "Stately, plump Buck Mulligan," instead of the more normal English order, "Buck Mulligan, stately and plump," seem to Homerize English, as do more consciously Greek epithets such as "bullockbefriendingbard." The description of the Citizen in the Cyclops episode as "a broadshouldered deepchested stronglimbed frankeyed redhaired freelyfreckled shaggybearded widemouthed largenosed longheaded deepvoiced barekneed brawnyhanded hairylegged ruddyfaced sinewyarmed hero," salutes the epithet even while mocking it. The Aeolus episode offers two sentences which sound like an exercise in Homer's formulaic composition: "Grossbooted draymen rolled barrels dullthudding out of Prince's stores and bumped them up on the brewery float," followed by "On the brewery float bumped dullthudding barrels rolled by grossbooted draymen out of Prince's stores." Joyce seems determined to burst the confines of English by allying it with the stylized language in which Homer clothes his mythical materials, or by a linguistic innovation as radical as Dante's decision, in another *ricorso,* to use the vernacular. (*Finnegans Wake* best realized the latter aspiration.) He began now his habit of taking out the space between compound adjectives, a small hellenization to which he subjected *A Portrait* in its last stages and a new edition of *Chamber Music* as well. While Homer's use of traditional phrases and archaic forms could not be precisely duplicated, Joyce achieved something of the same effect by having his characters quote well-known phrases from past authors.

In cementing his bond with Homer, Joyce soon realized that he must become familiar with Homeric scholarship. Commentators could draw his eye to particulars which he might otherwise overlook. The three to whom he attended most closely were Butler, Bacon, and Bérard—an unlikely trio, but no less handy for that reason. Critics who have mentioned the importance to Joyce of one or other of these commentators have not taken into account how opposed to each other they were. Joyce had to decide which of them to follow, and faced with this decision, he tended as was his wont to follow them all, up to a point.

He said later, in a letter (1:401), that he had encountered Bérard only when he was three-quarters through *Ulysses;* his library in Trieste also suggests that Joyce used Butler and Bacon first. Of Butler he read both *The Authoress of the Odyssey* and *The Humour of Homer,* as well as *Erewhon* and *Erewhon Revisited,* in which there are Homeric overtones. Butler had a radical conception of the poem and its geography and authorship. For him Homer was not an Athenian but a Sicilian, that is, a Greek living in a settlement in Sicily, and moreover, not a man but a woman. The voyages which Butler sketched for Ulysses all took place in or near Trapani. That Homer was a woman and no sailor was proved for Butler by amateurish details; so Ms. Homer describes Ulysses' placing a rudder on his raft "to steer by," as if a rudder might have some other function. Bérard, however, thought Ulysses an expert seaman.

Victor Bérard, later the dean of French classicists, could in fact hardly have been more at odds with Butler. His huge work in two volumes, *Les Phéniciens et l'Odyssée,* which he published in Paris in 1902 and 1903, took issue as well with all established theories. For Bérard Homer was by no means the Greek people (he specifically opposed Vico on this point); instead he was a cosmopolitan man, a Greek working with foreign materials. As a landlubber, like other Greeks, Homer knew nothing of the western Mediterranean, where most of the action of his poem occurred; he therefore relied upon the sailing manuals of the Mediterranean's best sailors, who were the Phoenicians, a Semitic people. In Bérard's view, Homer was a Hellene, Ulysses a Phoenician rover. Joyce could conveniently assume that all Semites were alike, Phoenicians and Hebrews being for his purposes (if not for history's) interchangeable, and so he could claim Bérard's authority for that climactic encounter in *Ulysses* when "jewgreek meets greekjew."

Bérard attributed to Homer the same painstaking accuracy of description that Joyce sought to attain, and in fact made him a Joyce of the classical age. Bérard's Homer invented nothing, though he sometimes combined a mainland scene with one on an island. (Bérard does not allow Homer to be fanciful, that is, inaccurate, by more than a sea mile or two.) Like Joyce, he worked with fixities and definites. Bérard's main contribution, and what he considered the key of his work, was the doublet, which he claimed was the basis of Homer's epic. For the Greek names given by Homer to various places made no sense in Greek, but in Hebrew and Phoenician made perfect sense. As an example, Circe's island is called by Homer Nesos Kirkes and also Aiaia. Aiaia means nothing in Greek but in Hebrew means the island of the She-Hawk. From this Homer devised the toponym Nesos Kirkes which means the island of the She-Hawk in Greek. To allow for a more complex provenance, Bérard suggested that Homer may have worked with an Egyptian epic based upon a Phoenician sailing manual. In other words, the whole Middle East played its part.

If Joyce had had to evaluate these scholars as scholars, he might well have been sceptical of both. Butler's theory flew in the face of traditional associations of places throughout the Mediterranean with scenes in the *Odyssey*. Bérard's theory worked with such associations as far as possible but, to make them tally with Homer, urged modifications of Homer's text—interpolations or omissions or transpositions—and claimed that many important passages, such as Menelaus' battle with Proteus, were spurious. But Joyce liked the idea of a Semitic original for the Greek poem, and he welcomed Bérard's insistence that Homer was a realist and not a fabulist. The poem offers a stable world of scenes described at secondhand, often inaccurately, but on the best authority.

What Butler saw in it was, however, helpful too. He gave the poem a homely familiarity by locating its scenes, just as confidently as Bérard, on Sicily and small islands nearby. No sailing manual was needed: the places were all instantly recognizable still. This view required even more special pleading than Bérard's, as when Butler insists that the whole voyage from Phaeacia to Ithaca was only a mile or two. While Joyce did not have to believe that the *Odyssey* was written by a woman, he had already come to the conclusion that every artist is a womanly man or manly woman. Butler's identification of the woman author with Nausicaa encouraged Joyce to allow both Nausicaa and Penelope to have their say in his own book, and he tested Butler's contention that the principal female figures were aspects of one person rather than separate beings. Finally, Butler insisted, as Bérard denied, that the *Odyssey* was just like other fictional works in being covertly autobiographical: the events in it arose out of the circumstances of the authoress's life, the people in it were people she knew, and some of them could be identified even at a distance of almost three millennia in time. Joyce concurred, in so far as the origins of his own book were concerned.

A third item in Joyce's Odyssean kit was Francis Bacon's *The Wisdom of the Ancients,* which Vico also found useful; Joyce had two copies of it. Bacon differed with both Bérard and Butler by disdaining to see any naturalism or autobiography in the *Odyssey.* For him the book was a method of imparting intellectual lessons through fables. That is, Bérard and Butler treated the fabulous as factual; Bacon, with Vico after him, treated the factual as fabulous. Instead of hunting for the location of Scylla and Charybdis, Bacon held that Homer meant to illustrate by this emblem the rocks of distinctions and the whirlpool of universals. Joyce accepts this Baconian symbolism, modifying its details as needed. I think he was also impressed by the legend, which Bacon retails with scepticism, that Penelope was unfaithful to Ulysses not with one suitor alone but with all of them, the offspring of this large-scale mating being Pan or universal nature. This legend, and others like it, encouraged Joyce to make his Penelope, Molly Bloom, unfaithful too, to compile a list of her lovers as long as Don Giovanni's but more putative than real, and to allow her in her reverie to run through an epic history of fallen man, like Michael's to Adam in *Paradise Lost.*

Following Bérard, then, Joyce patiently established geographical details and made his poem like Homer's a melting pot of the races. Following Butler, he saw in the poem an extrapolation of Homer's autobiography, for which he could more or less substitute his own. Following Bacon, he found both voyage and voyager to be symbolic. Thanks to these scholiasts and others, the reading of the *Odyssey* offered admission to a drama of violent disagreement.

II

Another form of commentary on the *Odyssey,* besides scholarly exegesis, was its sequels. The final voyage of Ulysses, which Tiresias had prophesied and Homer had chosen not to provide, became a subject for later writers. Joyce accepted Dante's view that Ulysses sailed beyond Gibraltar on a last voyage, but instead of shipwrecking him on the Mount of Purgatory he brought him safely to Ireland's shores. Aside from Dante, three post-Homeric treatments of this theme won his attention.

The first, a ludicrous one, but fully accepted in the epic cycle of Greece, was the *Telegony* written by Eugammon of Cyrene about two centuries after Homer. Eugammon dispatched Ulysses on a shorter voyage than Dante's, to the land of Thesprotia, where the hero marries the queen Callidike. That Joyce had Eugammon in mind is proven by the scheme of his own book which he sent to Carlo Linati in September 1920. He indicates there that Molly Bloom serves in the fourth chapter as both Callidike and Calypso, as if to combine Eugammonic and Homeric treatments. From Joyce's point of view, on Butler's principle of the union of female characters, Molly Bloom might be seen under these aspects as well as under those of Penelope or Nausicaa. The later history that Eugammon presents, if Proclus' summary of the lost epic can be trusted, had a kind of perfunctory unity. Callidike bears Ulysses a son and dies. When the son is grown, Ulysses, having heard that some young man is ravaging Ithaca, returns to his own country. He does not know that the marauder is really Telegonus, his son by Circe, who is in search of his father. Failing to recognize each other, the two do battle and Ulysses is killed. Telegonus, having discovered his mistake, takes his father's body and, accompanied by Penelope and Telemachus, brings it to Circe's island for burial. Circe confers immortality on Telemachus and Telegonus; then Telemachus marries her while Telegonus marries Penelope. Eugammon was ready to tie up loose ends at any cost. Joyce had a study of the lost *Telegony* in his library; what interested him particularly was the reiteration in the sequel of the theme of a son's searching for his father: Telegonus is as pessimistic a version of filial piety as Telemachus is optimistic. He was mindful also of the incestuous joining of Penelope and Telegonus and probably found there a hint for Molly's quasi-incestuous fantasy about Bloom's quasi-son Stephen. The presence in the *Telegony* of three sons of Ulysses encouraged Joyce to give Bloom two.

To some extent Joyce wished his book to be a sequel to the *Odyssey*, to some extent a reenactment of it. The best model for this dual purpose was Virgil's *Aeneid*, which followed the *Telegony* by seven hundred years. Joyce had in his library copies of the *Aeneid* both in the original and in translation. Though Virgil wrote from the point of view of Ulysses' adversaries, the Trojans, he followed Homer none the less, as typologically as the New Testament follows the Old. Virgil, like Joyce after him, changes the order of the episodes but retains many of them in somewhat altered form. Calypso becomes Dido, and Aeneas descends to the shades not to see his mother, as Ulysses did, but like Bloom in Nighttown to see his father. Other incidents could also be displaced. If Aeneas meets in Hades an angry Dido, Bloom might meet in Circe's palace, which is hellish too, all the women about whom he feels guilty. But the principal Virgilian connection was the incident of the Trojan horse, which Homer did not present. Joyce's handling of this, as will appear, was exceedingly multiform.[3]

In more recent times, Joyce found support in an unexpected quarter, Fénelon's *Les Aventures de Télémaque* (1699). This attempt to present the model rearing of a model young man does not sound like Joyce's sort of thing, and W. B. Stanford, in his fine book on *The Ulysses Theme* (1963), gives it scant notice. But Joyce had Fénelon's book in his library, and found in it an imitation by Telemachus of Ulysses' adventures which could not fail to be useful. Télémaque too goes to Calypso and he too must escape her toils. He too is shipwrecked. For Joyce this parallelism could suggest the nub of his own treatment, that Ulysses and Telemachus, instead of voyaging independently, might put in to the same ports. (Meredith's Harry Richmond also blends Ulysses and Telemachus.) Fénelon's book was in eighteen episodes, another point which Joyce eventually followed. In the eighteenth the young man and his father at last meet, an encounter heralded throughout the book. But Fénelon handles it in a remarkably muffled way: his Telemachus does not learn until after Ulysses has departed that it was to his father he was speaking. It is one of those resonant unfulfilments like Wordsworth's discovery that he has crossed the Alps without knowing it. Joyce had here an unusual precedent for the equally resonant and yet extremely muted ingathering of Bloom and Stephen.

On the basis of all or most of this reading, Joyce embarked on his own work. In using the *Odyssey* as his model, he knew he was risking everything. Nothing easier than to founder on that rock. To name it *Ulysses* was like calling one's book the Bible.

There were certain restraints upon him. He had to keep his new work separate from both *A Portrait,* which he finished in 1914, and *Exiles,* which he began in 1913 a few months before he commenced the actual writing of *Ulysses.* Since one of these works dealt with a dramatic departure, the other with an equally dramatic return to Dublin, his new hero might best be kept inside the city from beginning to end. Not only must Homer's sea become dry land, but physical exploits must be made less sensational. The only bloodletting at the end of Joyce's book is menstrual. Joyce might have simply intellectualized Homer, as Bacon did, but he did not intend to give up the physicality of the *Odyssey* altogether. Certain incidents which did not show Ulysses at his most winning or magnanimous, how- ever, Joyce was glad to omit. For example, the first stop of Ulysses, in the land of the Ciconians, ends in the slaughter of the men and the sharing of the women, diversions interrupted by the arrival of Ciconian reinforcements. This savage treat- ment was perhaps inserted by Homer to offer a foretaste of Ulysses' vengeance and to surround the tale of his adventures with a ferocity which most of the intervening incidents do not permit him to exert but only to suffer. Joyce left out the Ciconians altogether.

Some adventures could be abridged: one visit to Circe was enough (Homer has two). But other incidents were expanded, the Lotus-eaters for example, where in an atmosphere of *dolce far niente* Bloom like the rest whiles away his time, at moments bathing in inconclusive sensation as Ulysses does not, yet converging with Ulysses in his close scrutiny of the individuals he meets and the institutions to which they belong. When he decided to make the climax of his book the visit to Circe's brothel, rather than the return to Penelope's Ithaca, Joyce did not surrender this contrast altogether: his Nausicaa, though her own innocence is somewhat qualified, is islanded between two foul-mouthed episodes.

I imagine Joyce as reading and rereading Homer with a special delight because of his ulterior motivation. He testified to his pleasure in the episode where Ulysses, grizzled and scarred, or as Joyce said to a friend, "perhaps baldheaded," yet still eligible, is a suppliant before the virginal seventeen-year-old Nausicaa. That the shipwrecked man should be naked made Joyce think of emphasizing what he called "the parts that mattered" by Gerty's coyness about them. Homer's hero, after having covered these parts with a leafy branch, addresses the princess in fulsome style, "I kneel to thee,—Queen, are you goddess or mortal?" This is blarney but it works. Nausicaa responds to these attentions by indicating how very mortal she is, so mortal indeed that she is quite prepared to marry him if asked. Joyce adapts Homer so that Gerty's mortal-immortal being is evoked by a similar confusion between the original Gerty seated on the strand and the Virgin Mary ensconced in the Star of the Sea church nearby. Coy miss and sacred myth interact. Votive offerings are made to the two shrines simultaneously. These elements were present in Homer, though admittedly latent. Joyce not only brings them to the surface but couches them in a style which, at once adulatory and lubricious, seems also to be asking with Ulysses, "Are you goddess or mortal?"

The rationale of making Ulysses Irish was more difficult. That the Irish were like the Greeks no one will deny; what Western people is not? The earliest invaders of Ireland, the Firbolgs, were legended to have come from Greece. A scribal note in the *Book of Armagh* (folio 22, column a) makes a claim that Saint Patrick himself abstained from making in his *Confessio,* that he was the great grandson of Ulysses. Joyce sports with this imaginary ancestry in his book. What was more extraordinary was to make Ulysses not simply an Irishman but an Irish Jew. I will not trace here Joyce's developing interest in the Jews, but besides having Jewish friends in Dublin, he became in Trieste the English teacher of a large number of Jewish pupils. Among them was Ettore Schmitz (Italo Svevo), a fellow-writer of genius, from a family which like Bloom's had migrated from Hungary; like Bloom, too, Svevo had married a Gentile who was part Jewish. Svevo was as witty as Oliver Gogarty, but without malice; much of his humour was turned upon himself, and his books explored amorous contretemps in a way that Joyce admired and learned from. The personality of Svevo gave Joyce the impulsion he needed to form a new character, a blend of Svevo, himself, and other prototypes.

More largely, the Wandering Jew was in Joyce's mind, as it was in his library in Eugene Sue's version. (He had also read Heijermans's *Ahasver* and Mark Twain's less reverent treatment of the same subject in *The New Pilgrim's Progress.* Other wanderers such as Wagner's *The Flying Dutchman* played their part.) So was the idea of the oldest people wandering in exile century after century and still maintaining, in spite of oppression, an identity. Although Joyce did not read Bérard's conception of a Semitic *Odyssey* until he was well advanced on his book, in Dublin (before he left in 1904) he had come upon another writer who could offer him support. This was the eighteenth-century comparative mythologist, General Charles Vallancey, a follower of Jacob Bryant. In a lecture he gave in Trieste in 1907, Joyce cited Vallancey's theory that the Irish were of Phoenician origin. It appeared that Vallancey and Bérard, each unknown to the other, had made both Greeks and Irish Semitic. It was as difficult not to be Jewish as not to be Greek.

But no Dubliner of Joyce's generation had to rely upon scholars for the comparison of the Irish to the Jews. In October 1901, at a meeting of the Law Students' Debating Society, John F. Taylor made the famous speech in which he brilliantly compared the Hebrews in Egypt to the Irish under foreign domination. Joyce probably heard the speech: it was said at University College that his own oratorical manner was like Taylor's. But in any case he had access to *The Language of the Outlaw,* a four-page leaflet published privately but in large numbers (5,000 or 10,000 copies) in 1904 or 1905. The pamphlet explained that the only record of Taylor's remarks was contained in a letter to the Manchester *Guardian* signed "X," which it then reprinted:

Sir,—May I venture to send you a few words as to a speech made by Mr. J. F. Taylor last November at the University College Debating Society? Mr. Taylor's gifts as an orator were of a very remarkable order—and a most learned judge on the Irish Bench has remarked that he had never heard at the Bar a more remarkable speech than that given by Mr. Taylor at a certain trial. I myself only once heard him speak—at this meeting—and the memory of it is very distinct with me.

The discussion was on the question whether the Irish people might be allowed to know or take an active interest in their own language. Lord Justice Fitzgibbon had made a dialectical discourse of a kind with which we are all familiar on platforms; only, as might be expected of his ability, he surpassed the ordinary advocate in the skilful irrelevance of his argument and in the covering vehemence (no less skilful) of his manner of delivery.

After his conventional fireworks Mr. Taylor rose. He had been very ill, and had come straight from his bed, and without food.

He began with some difficulty, but his power increased as he went on to repudiate the test of commercial success as being the final end of a nation's life, or of long misfortune as being any reason for abandoning faith and loyalty to one's own people.

He compared, in one passage, the position of the Irish language under the English rule to the position of the Hebrew language under Egyptian rule. He set out the arguments which a fashionable professor with an attachment to the Egyptian Court might have addressed to Moses: —

"Your prejudices are very antiquated and sentimental," he would have said. "Do just look at the matter in a reasonable light, like a man of the world. Here your people have been now for hundreds of years in the brickfields. The fact is patent that they have never been able to rise out of this miserable position.

They have no education; the mass of them are poor, demoralised, and despised. They have no history outside their brickfields, and within them they are the foolish prey of agitators who set them clamouring for straw. Instead of adopting the enlightened and philosophic religion of Egypt, they still cling through all these generations to a superstitious and obscurantist faith, mischievous and altogether behind the times.

Their language is rude and provincial. It is incapable of expressing philosophic thought.

It is, of course, useless for commercial purposes. As for literature, the fragments that remain are well known to be either superstitious or indecent—in any case quite unfit for ordinary people.

You must recognise that the interest your race attaches to it is derived from mere ignorance and obstinacy; it would be quite unworthy of a man of culture, and certainly impossible in a man of the world or moving in society. Consider, on the other hand, the Empire to which you now, happily for you, belong—its centuries of civilisation, its ancient history, its buildings, its arts, its literature. Observe its splendid Imperial organisation, its world-wide fame, its ever-increasing dominions, its satisfactory foreign relations with the Great Powers, the lustre of its achievements, which put it for ever in the rank of one of the greatest Empires which the world can know to the end of time. Why, then, do you not frankly throw in your lot with this magnificent and successful organisation? A handful of obscure peasants as you are, you would at once share in its renown and its prosperity.

Of course, you could depend on being generously treated by rulers of such standing. Something would doubtless be done for those poor labourers of the brickfields. More favourable terms could be made for them—who knows? A supply of straw at a reasonable price; security of tenure of their mud huts; lower rents even.

The deserving could enter the Egyptian service, or make a start in commerce, or learn industry from this great and progressive country. Only get rid of those brickfield agitators. Give up your outlandish, and useless language. Reconsider your superstitious sort of religion. Put an end to all this nonsense, quite out of place in good society—to local dialects, out-of-date provincial patriotisms, and illiterate sentimentalities which Providence itself condemns by casting them out into mud huts and brickfields and acre holdings."

"And," broke out the speaker, "if Moses had listened to those arguments, what would have been the end? Would he ever have come down from the Mount with the light of God shining on his face and carrying in his hands the Tables of the Law written in the language of the outlaw?"

Joyce welcomed the analogy even if he spurned the argument for Irish against English. The language movement did not appeal to him at all, and in fact was the point where he felt at odds with the separatist movement. But it was a great speech, and Joyce designed a great answer to it. He put the description of Taylor's speech in the mouth of Professor MacHugh and ventured to improve upon its style while at the same time casting doubt upon its content. MacHugh follows the *Guardian* letter in first introducing Mr. Justice Fitzgibbon's speech:

— It was the speech, mark you, the professor said, of a finished orator, full of courteous haughtiness and pouring in chastened diction, I will not say the vials of his wrath but pouring the proud man's contumely upon the new movement. It was then a new movement. We were weak, therefore worthless.

Then begins some of the elaborately observed stage business which gradually asserts itself as a countermovement to oratory:

He closed his long thin lips an instant but, eager to be on, raised an outspanned hand to his spectacles and, with trembling thumb and ringfinger touching lightly the black rims, steadied them to a new focus.

IMPROMPTU

In ferial tone he addressed J. J. O'Molloy:

— Taylor had come there, you must know, from a sick bed. That he had prepared his speech I do not believe for there was not even one shorthand-writer in the hall. His dark lean face had a growth of shaggy beard round it. He wore a loose neckcloth and altogether he looked (though he was not) a dying man.

His gaze turned at once but slowly from J. J. O'Molloy's towards Stephen's face and then bent at once to the ground, seeking. His unglazed linen collar appeared behind his bent head, soiled by his withering hair. Still seeking, he said:

— When Fitzgibbon's speech had ended John F. Taylor rose to reply. Briefly, as well as I can bring them to mind, his words were these.

He raised his head firmly. His eyes bethought themselves once more. Witless shellfish swam in the gross lenses to and fro, seeking outlet.

He began:

— *Mr Chairman, ladies and gentlemen: Great was my admiration in listening to the remarks addressed to the youth of Ireland a moment since by my learned friend. It seemed to me that I had been transported into a country far away from this country, into an age remote from this age, that I stood in ancient Egypt and that I was listening to the speech of some highpriest of that land addressed to the youthful Moses.*

His listeners held their cigarettes poised to hear, their smoke ascending in frail stalks that flowered with his speech. *And let our crooked smokes.* Noble words coming. Look out. Could you try your hand at it yourself?

— *And it seemed to me that I heard the voice of that Egyptian highpriest raised in a tone of like haughtiness and like pride. I heard his words and their meaning was revealed to me.*

FROM THE FATHERS

It was revealed to me that those things are good which yet are corrupted which neither if they were supremely good nor unless they were good could be corrupted. Ah, curse you! That's saint Augustine.

— *Why will you jews not accept our culture, our religion and our language? You are a tribe of nomad herdsmen; we are a mighty people. You have no cities nor no wealth: our cities are hives of humanity and our galleys, trireme and quadrireme, laden with all manner merchandise furrow the waters of the known globe. You have but emerged from primitive conditions: we have a literature, a priesthood, an agelong history and a polity.*

Nile.

Child, man, effigy.

By the Nilebank the babemaries kneel, cradle of bulrushes: a man supple in combat: stonehorned, stonebearded, heart of stone.

— *You pray to a local and obscure idol: our temples, majestic and mysterious, are the abodes of Isis and Osiris, of Horus and Ammon Ra. Yours serfdom, awe and humbleness: ours thunder and the seas. Israel is weak and few are her children: Egypt is an host and terrible are her arms. Vagrants and daylabourers are you called: the world trembles at our name.*

A dumb belch of hunger cleft his speech. He lifted his voice above it boldly:

— *But, ladies and gentlemen, had the youthful Moses listened to and accepted that view of life, had he bowed his head and bowed his will and bowed his spirit before that arrogant admonition he would never have brought the chosen people out of their house of bondage nor followed the pillar of the cloud by day. He would never have spoken with the Eternal amid lightnings on Sinai's mountaintop nor ever have come down with the light of inspiration shining in his countenance and bearing in his arms the tables of the law, graven in the language of the outlaw.*

He ceased and looked at them, enjoying the silence.[4]

Against this euphony Joyce and Stephen assert a reality principle. MacHugh belches. His glasses are full of witless shellfish seeking outlet. Stephen thinks, "Noble words coming," and when they have come, tersely comments, "Dead noise." His one voiced reaction is to invite the company for a drink. On the way to it he tells his own "Parable of the Plums" as foil to Taylor's parallel, as the blade of truth amid the airbags of oratory. There is no Moses on Pisgah, there is no promised land, only two old women spitting out plumstones on Dublin from the top of Nelson's pillar.

Joyce did not accept Taylor's argument for the Irish language, but he welcomed with all its shortcomings the analogy of the races. It would seem that Hebraism and Hellenism, far from being opposites as Arnold and Auerbach have contended, had been brought into touch by the theories of Bérard, and Celticism with them by the theories of Vallancey and Taylor. The imagery of Moses and the promised land was in fact a cliché of revolutionary poems and songs of the period, as Louis Hyman informs me. Joyce's compatriot, Oscar Wilde, had urged "a new hellenism," and in his early critical writing Joyce spoke with only the faintest irony of Ireland's becoming "the hellas of the north." It is part of Mulligan's obtuseness that he can at once urge Stephen to join with him in hellenizing the island and not perceive the secret affinity of Greece and Palestine. To be anti-Semitic, as Mulligan is, is to challenge the foundations of Joyce's book.

Joyce was aware that the conjunction of Greek, Irish, and Jewish had a humorous aspect. He depicts Bloom as eager to incorporate Aristotle, whom Stephen so much admires, into the Hebraic tradition on the grounds that Aristotle had received instruction from a rabbi, whose name has somehow slipped Bloom's mind. But if there was a humorous aspect to this and other matters, it was comedy of a special sort, comedy with teeth and claws. Vico had pointed out that Homer was not a delicate writer, delicacy being too small a virtue for so large a mind. Joyce was not eager to be delicate either. To hellenize the island meant to combat its dark insularity. As Hegel noted, a belligerent situation is the one most suited to epic. Joyce dismissed the idea of devoting half his book, as Homer had done, to vengeance, and even countered Homer by bringing Bloom to complaisance rather than to indignation over his wife's adultery. But he hit upon the plan of combining the assault upon the suitors with the adventures of Ulysses. A war, even if undeclared and bloodless, is waged from the start.

NOTES

[1] Yeats brilliantly converted Jacob Boehme's word "signature," which in Boehme's *De Signatura Rerum* means God's unmistakable imprint on all things, to artistic uses. Joyce followed him by having Stephen declare as artist at the beginning of the Proteus episode, "Signatures of all things I am here to read . . ."

[2] *Letters*, ed. Stuart Gilbert and Richard Ellmann, 3 vols. (New York, 1957–66), 1:174. All subsequent citations are to this edition.

[3] To begin with, he dotted his book with references to horses, from the first page where Mulligan's face is "equine in its length," and continuing with Boylan (who is Bloom's antitype as Mulligan is Stephen's) as son of a man who not only unpatriotically sold horses to the British during the Boer war, but—treachery within treachery—sold them twice over. Molly is "a gamey mare and no mistake." Then there is the horse race that day: Boylan bets on Sceptre, but it is the lowly Throwaway who wins, as Bloom had unwittingly prophesied earlier. (In his true witness he betters Dante's Ulysses, who burns in hell because of bearing false witness about a horse.) Joyce's larger view of the matter is expressed by Joe Hynes when he says of Bloom in the Cyclops episode, "He's a bloody dark horse himself." That is, he is an innocuous seeming man whose independence of spirit mines the city, whether the city knows it or not. This view of him is held up to examination by ridicule in the brothel scene, when Bloom, like Aristotle in the medieval legend Joyce quotes, is "bitted, bridled, and mounted" by Bello Cohen. He is measured and found to be fourteen hands high. The society ladies promise to dig their spurs into him up to the rowel. His womanly manliness makes him describe the tangle he is in as "a pure mare's nest."

Joyce does not leave Stephen out of this imagery. It is Stephen who pulls together the Trojan horse designed by Ulysses with the wooden cow designed by his avatar Daedalus, when he speaks of Helen as "the wooden mare of Troy in whom a score of heroes slept . . ." Not all these hoofbeats of the Trojan horse can be heard—Joyce did not mind so long as the book thudded with them. And in a way the book itself, as well as its two principals, was a Trojan horse, parading as a monument, but armed for battle.

[4] *Ulysses* (New York, 1961), pp. 141–43.

Jean Pépin
THE PLATONIC
AND CHRISTIAN ULYSSES

I. Philosophos Odysseus[1]

Several philosophical schools in antiquity made use of the figure of Ulysses. Take the case of the Cynics, to begin with, who put him forward as an *exemplum*. The idea is already suggested in the fifth century B.C. by the founder of the Cynic movement, Antisthenes. Ulysses is for him a sage who knows life, the gods and men—and women!—and who knows how to adapt his speech in relation to different interlocutors.[2] The same kind of evaluation of Ulysses is found two centuries later in Bion.[3] It becomes a literary cliché in the apocryphal letters of the Cynics, which date from the imperial period and which see in Ulysses, notably in his clothes (that is, his rags), the incarnation of the kind of life advocated by Cynicism.[4] It was to be expected that the Stoics, who admitted to being under Cynic influence in their ethics, would in turn choose Ulysses as a model of morality. In fact, no trace of this is found in the documents relating to the founders of Stoicism, but it is a well-established idea in the Stoics of the imperial period: Seneca, then Epictetus, and in two texts influenced by Stoicism that probably date from the first or second century A.D., the *De Vita et Poesi Homeri* of Pseudo-Plutarch and the *Quaestiones Homericae* of Heraclitus. In these texts we find a Ulysses extolled because of his endurance, his indifference to pain, his contempt for pleasure.[5]

Parallel to this Cynic and Stoic tendency, there developed another philosophical use of Ulysses, of which I would like to give a representative sample. The reader must forgive the length of this passage in view of the fact that I will use it in the following pages as a point of comparison. It concerns the episode of the Sirens, which Plutarch prides himself in using to show that there is no conflict between Homer and Plato (*Republic* X, 517B):

From *Neoplatonism and Christian Thought,* edited by Dominic J. O'Meara (Norfolk, VA: International Society for Neoplatonic Studies, 1982), pp. 3–18.

Now Homer's Sirens, it is true, frighten us, inconsistently with the Platonic myth; but the poet too conveyed a truth symbolically, namely that the power of their music is not inhuman or destructive; as souls depart from this world to the next, so it seems, and drift uncertainly after death, it creates in them a passionate love for the heavenly and divine, and forgetfulness of mortality; it possesses them and enchants them with its spell, so that in joyfulness they follow the Sirens and join them in their circuits. Here on earth a kind of faint echo of that music reaches us, and appealing to our souls through the medium of words, reminds them of what they experienced in an earlier existence. The ears of most souls, however, are plastered over and blocked up, not with wax, but with carnal obstructions and affections. But any soul that through innate gifts is aware of this echo, and remembers that other world, suffers what falls in no way short of the very maddest passions of love, longing and yearning to break the tie with the body, but unable to do so. (Trans. Sandbach)[6]

Although Plutarch puts this passage in the mouth of the Platonic speaker in his dialogue, the exegesis thus presented is not specifically Platonic, but is Pythagorean, as can be seen from some comparisons.[7] There were, therefore, at a time which is hard to determine, Pythagoreans for whom the song of the Homeric Sirens represented the planetary music that enthralls souls after death and agitates them already in this life, on the condition that their ears are not sealed by carnal passions as wax blocked the ears of Ulysses' companions.[8] This exegesis must also have been a very significant part of a larger whole that is only partially known, that is, the allegorical interpretation of the figure of Ulysses in the Pythagorean tradition.[9] It is likely that this Pythagorean Ulysses influenced the image that the later followers of Plato would have of the Homeric hero, an image some aspects of which will be traced in the following pages.

In looking back over what has been noted about the way in which the Cynics, Stoics, and Pythagoreans saw the figure of Ulysses, and anticipating what will be seen about its meaning in Neoplatonism, we see a clear difference that, from different angles, separates these four philosophical movements into two groups of two. First, while the Cynics and the Stoics also take into account Ulysses' actions in the *Iliad*,[10] the Neoplatonists and, as far as we can tell, the Pythagoreans concern themselves exclusively with the figure of the *Odyssey*, that is, with his maritime adventures.[11] Further, as we have quickly seen in the case of the former group and as we will see in more detail concerning the latter group, Pythagoreans and Neoplatonists agree to confer on Ulysses a metaphysical dimension—to discover in his legend the history of the soul—whereas the other group confines itself to extolling him as a moral ideal. Hence the former are forced to make use of an allegorical exegesis which goes far beyond the immediate meaning of the poem,[12] contrary to the Cynics and Stoics who could be satisfied with an almost literal reading.[13]

II. The Neoplatonic Exegesis

1. Three Stages in a Long Tradition

Ulysses freeing himself from Circe and Calypso, despite their charms, so as to escape to his fatherland, Ithaca, which he loves is Homer's reminder to us to return to our fatherland on high, tearing ourselves away from the beauties of the sensible world. Such is Plotinus' interpretation in his famous treatise *On Beauty:*

> This would be truer advice, "Let us fly to our dear country." What then is our way of escape, and how are we to find it? We shall put out to sea, as Ulysses did, from the witch Circe or Calypso—as the poet [Homer] says (I think with a hidden meaning) (αἰνιττόμενος)—and was not content to stay though he had delights of the eyes and lived among much beauty of sense. Our country from which we came is there, our Father is there. (Trans. Armstrong)[14]

Proclus, in turn, sees in Ithaca "that mystical port of the soul (μυστικὸς ὅρμος τῆς ψυχῆς) to which the poet brings back Ulysses after the long wanderings of his life, and to which we rather must return, that is, if we wish to be saved."[15] As to the wandering in which the soul is commonly caught and the ascent which will deliver it, these Proclus discerns in the order of knowledge; throughout this epistemological odyssey, the soul will transcend successively sensations, images, opinions, sciences, discursive reason itself, to reach a "life according to the intellect, which alone possesses stability."[16] Here the progressive return of Ulysses is used as an illustration and guarantee of the hierarchy of knowledge defined in Books VI and VII of the *Republic*. Elsewhere, the same Proclus finds in the sea in which Ulysses struggles the symbol of the world of coming-to-be, whose temptations are embodied by the Sirens. Hence Plato's advice (*Phaedrus* 259A) to avoid the Sirens:

> As to souls, who live in the world of coming-to-be, they should "sail past them," imitating Homer's Ulysses—if it is true that the sea also is the image of coming-to-be (θάλασσα γενέσεως εἰκών)—so as not to allow themselves to be bewitched (θέλγωνται) by coming-to-be.[17]

Eustathius of Thessalonica, a Byzantine scholar of the twelfth century, has preserved many Neoplatonic allegories concerning the Homeric poems. One of these, on Ulysses and Calypso, coincides substantially with Plotinus' exegesis, but weighs it down with plays on etymology and by establishing detailed correspondences; Calypso, meaning she who "envelops" (συγκαλύπτουσαν), stands for our body, envelope of the soul; she held back Ulysses as the flesh fetters man; if her island is said to be "encircled by currents of water" and "planted with trees," it is because the body on the one hand is traversed, as Plato says, by a liquid flux, and, on the other hand, consists of a matter similar to wood and dense as a forest; but, Ulysses returns to his beloved fatherland, which, according to the Platonists,[18] denotes the intelligible world, the true fatherland of souls.

2. Two Important Texts

(a) HERMIAS, In Phaedrum 259A

Eustathius is a witness to the fact that, nine centuries after Plotinus, there were still readers interested in his interpretation of Ulysses. Of this long history, for which we have just picked out three witnesses who expressly name the Homeric hero, one can find many other traces which are more vague and more limited. At any rate, I have not yet discussed the texts which are most instructive. I must present them now.

One of these texts is found in the commentary on Plato's *Phaedrus* which has been transmitted under the name of Hermias (second half of the fifth century A.D.), but which is inspired by Syrianus, the teacher of Proclus. The passage of Plato commented on is the beginning of the myth of the crickets (*Phaedrus* 259A–B), which, paraphrased, follows: At noon the crickets are singing in the trees above Socrates and Phaedrus. Socrates imagines that the crickets are watching them, and that if they saw the two men give in to sleep, as if enchanted by their magic (κηλουμένους), they would mock them; if, on the contrary, Socrates says, they see us "sailing past them as if they were Sirens, resisting their spells, then perhaps they would give us the gift they have from the gods to give to men,"[19] that is, as what follows shows (259C), the privilege of singing until death and then becoming the couriers of the Muses.

This is how Hermias comments on this text:

> Just as those, [Plato] says, who are attracted and bewitched (κατακηλούμενοι) by the Sirens forget their own fatherland, so also we, if we give in to the magic of these sights and these crickets and are plunged into sleep, forget our fatherland and our ascent to the intelligible (τῆς εἰς τὸ νοητὸν ἀναγωγῆς). But if we awaken in ourselves discernment and vigilance, if we refuse the attraction of the sweetness of life, we sail past (παραπλέομεν) like Ulysses, we avoid life here below (τὸν ἐντῦθα βίον), we become worthy of our own fatherland and of our ascent toward the intelligible. "The gift that they have from the gods";—if, then, it were to happen, [Plato] says, that we would be able to sail past the Sirens (παραπλεῦσαι), the Sirens who are in the sensible world (ἐν τῷ αἰσθητῷ κόσμῳ), which is to say the demons who hold back souls in the proximity of coming-to-be (περὶ τὴν γένεσιν), then at that moment the crickets, that is, the divine souls and the gods, seeing us revolting against coming-to-be (γενέσεως) and living like gods, would give us the greatest gift for men, which is to treat us as companions. For as the gods are vigilant in their own activity, so we also should awaken ourselves as far as possible, and it is then that we awaken ourselves, if we reactivate the reason (λόγον) which is in us. The most speculative of the exegetes of the *Iliad* and the *Odyssey* [have said that it is]

also the ascent (ἄνοδον) [of the soul which Homer has portrayed]; they understand the *Iliad* thus: it is because the soul fights [so as to leave] matter that [the poet] represented battles, wars and suchlike; as to the *Odyssey*, it is [Ulysses] sailing past the Sirens (παραπλέοντα), escaping Circe, the Cyclops, Calypso, and all the obstacles in the way of the ascent (ἀναγωγήν) of the soul, leaving them for his fatherland, that is, for the intelligible (νοητόν).[20]

It is clearly the comparison—incidental, fleeting, and, it seems, purely literary—made by Plato ὥσπερ Σειρῆνας that led Hermias to have recourse to Ulysses and to his interpretation in Neoplatonism. The weakness of this starting point makes the commentator, especially at the beginning, attribute to Plato much more than he actually says, not indeed without some arbitrariness, since the Sirens and the crickets, united first in that their magic produces in their respective victims forgetfulness of the fatherland, are immediately afterwards set in opposition as maleficent demons and helping divinities. The Homeric exegesis itself appears to conform, as more complete and systematic, to the elements which we found in Plotinus, Proclus, and Eustathius: the difficult return of Ulysses to his fatherland represents the ascent of the soul to the intelligible; the soul is blocked by obstacles corresponding to those which Ulysses had to overcome; among these obstacles, the Sirens represent the lure of life here below, the sensible world, or better, the demons which imprison the soul in coming-to-be. The end of the commentary adds an important piece of information: the Neoplatonists (it is certainly these, or some of these, that are indicated by "the most speculative of the exegetes") apply this framework not only, as one might expect, to the *Odyssey*, but also to the battles of the *Iliad*.

If the allegory developed by Hermias goes far beyond the tiny reference in Plato to the Sirens and imputes to him some adventurous assumptions, nevertheless the passage of the *Phaedrus* has influence on the interpretation of the figure of Ulysses by introducing elements which do not normally appear there; this is the case of the ideas of sleep (to which is related the idea, which is absent from Homer's account of the Sirens, of a forgetting of the homeland), of the awakening of the soul (conceived as a reactivation of the λόγος), of vigilance, of the divine aid assured for souls which imitate the gods and rebel against genesis.

But the principal interest of this page of Hermias is that it establishes a connection between the exegesis of Ulysses and that of *Phaedrus* 259A. Hermias is not the only witness to this connection, which has been pointed out already here in relation to two texts in Proclus,[21] and which might probably be found in many other places. There is one indicator that the source of this connection is earlier in date. For after Hermias, but already before him, many pagan and Christian authors, of whom we will see some examples, wishing (outside all visible reference to the passage of the *Phaedrus*) to make clear that Ulysses avoided the rock of the Sirens and "sailed past," use the verb παραπλέειν.[22] But if one is to believe the concordances,[23] this verb is absent from the passages of the *Odyssey* dealing with the Sirens, and if it appears in the poem, and then only once,[24] it is in another episode.

It therefore cannot have been suggested to these authors by a reading of Homer. For those, such as Hermias and Proclus after him, who refer explicitly to the *Phaedrus*, it is clear that it is from there that they derive παραπλέοντάς σφας ὥσπερ Σειρῆνας. But one must suppose that all their predecessors, who have recourse to the same verb when commenting on the Homeric passage from which it is absent, witness in turn to a certain dependence, immediate or at a distance, in relation to the Platonic dialogue. The initiative, illustrated by Hermias and Proclus, of having recourse to *Phaedrus* 259A in order to interpret the Homeric episode of the Sirens should thus be viewed as anterior to the earliest use of παραπλέειν in this context. We will see presently how far back this hypothesis will allow us to go. One should note also that Hermias and Proclus agree in discerning in the Sirens the evil demons who hold back souls caught in coming-to-be, whereas there is nothing pejorative in the brief mention of them in Plato. If it is true, as I have said above, that the Pythagoreans and Neoplatonists agreed in reading into the navigation of Ulysses the history of the soul, the latter did not keep the imagery that seemed essential to the former and which had the Sirens appearing as soul-guiding and helping musicians.

(b) PORPHYRY, *De Antro* 34–35

The other Neoplatonic text which should be studied carefully was written about two centuries earlier than Hermias. It is part of Porphyry's little treatise *De Antro Nympharum:*

> For it is my opinion that Numenius and his school were correct in thinking that for Homer in the *Odyssey*, Odysseus bears a symbol of one who passes through the stages of genesis (γενέσεως) and, in doing so, returns (ἀποκαθισταμένου) to those beyond every wave (κλύδωνος) who have no knowledge of the sea,
>
> > "Until you come to those who are unacquainted with the sea,
> > men who do not eat food mixed with salt."
>
> The deep, the sea, and the sea-swell are, according to Plato as well, material substance. (πόντος δὲ καὶ θάλασσα καὶ κλύδων καὶ παρὰ Πλάτωνι ἡ ὑλικὴ σύστασις). (Trans. Westerink)[25]

The same exegesis continues a few lines further on:

> But rather, the man [Ulysses] who had dared these things was pursued by the wrath of the gods of the sea and of matter. (ἁλίων καὶ ὑλικων θεῶν) ... But he will be past all toil when, entirely removed from the sea, he finds himself among souls so ignorant of everything that has to do with the sea, that is to say, with matter (θαλασσίων καὶ ἐνύλων ἔργων), that his oar is thought to be a winnowing-fan, because of the utter ignorance of nautical instruments and activities.[26]

This interpretation of the figure of Ulysses is substantially similar to that found before Porphyry and especially after him. The distinctive character of Porphyry's exegesis is to find in the sea the symbol, not only of the world of coming-to-be, but more widely of matter, doubtless because of the fluid and disorganized nature they share in common. This symbolism is referred back to Plato. Various Platonic texts, all quite distant, might be invoked in relation to this.[27] The nearest text is without doubt the famous myth in the *Politicus* 272D–273E, where the universe, at certain moments of its existence and in consequence of its corporeal constitution, is compared to a boat buffeted by the storm and very near to sinking "in the bottomless ocean of unlikeness."[28] In fact, the Neoplatonists saw in this ocean the image of matter,[29] and it is therefore this that Porphyry must have in mind. At any rate, Plato is not the source of the idea of personifying the hostile forces of the sea-matter by the gods of that element (Poseidon) bent on destroying Ulysses; however, he (that is, the soul of which he is the image) will triumph in overcoming one by one the degrees of coming-to-be and will be restored to his pristine state.[30] Finally, another aspect peculiar to Porphyry is the skillful reading of the return of the soul to its first condition, not only in the return to Ithaca, but also in the prophecy of Teiresias, whose shade is called forth by Ulysses, that the hero will not receive from Poseidon complete rest until he goes to the people who know nothing of the sea (*Od.* xi. 121–129), in other words, the souls who have not had experience of coming-to-be.

But the important thing in Porphyry is clearly the attribution of this exegesis to Numenius. One may doubt if the reference to Numenius in chapter 34 of the *De Antro* extends, as the editors of the fragment believe, to include the reference to Plato. But one is reassured in this regard by another fragment of Numenius that is independent of this one and in which matter, held from on high by the Demiurge, is assimilated (certainly in relation to *Politicus* 272Dff.) in some detail to the sea which the pilot masters from his ship.[31] Thus we are brought back for this exegesis of Ulysses to a period prior to Plotinus—to the first half of the second century A.D.

There might be, perhaps,[32] another indicator of the pre-Plotinian character of this interpretation in a contemporary of Numenius, the Platonic rhetor Maximus of Tyre. The episode of the *Odyssey* concerned is no longer that of the Sirens, as in the majority of the texts we have seen, but the passage in the poem (v. 333–353) where the goddess Leucothea takes pity on Ulysses against whom the elements rage, and gives him a veil which, stretched under his chest, will serve as a life belt. Maximus finds in this scene the image of the philosophy which saves the human soul plunged into the tempest of the sensible world and ready to succumb:

> Thrown into the tumult here below and abandoning itself to the irresistible waves which carry it, the soul swims in an adverse sea, until philosophy itself takes it under its protection by slipping under it[33] its arguments, just as Leucothea did for Ulysses with her veil.[34]

This interpretation of Ulysses as the symbol of the soul which is not resigned to its fall is very similar, despite the differences, to Neoplatonic exegesis, and could thus be its earliest formulation.

III. Christian Exegesis

1. Main Features

Parallel to the Platonic tradition, appearing almost at the same time as it and also lasting for several centuries, there evolves a Christian reading of the figure of Ulysses, of his navigation and especially of his victory over the Sirens. One will not be surprised to find that Christian exegesis made use here of pagan materials, just as did the Christian art of the time.[35] It even goes beyond the pagan sources in that it systematically confers an allegorical meaning on all of the details of the Homeric episode, whereas the Platonists left some details in the shadow. Here are the principal elements of this new exegesis.

The sea in which Ulysses struggles represents the world in the Johannine sense of that word, the hostile *saeculum* whose pleasures are represented by the Sirens. The rock to which the latter lure the sailors symbolizes the body on which is broken the discernment of spiritual intelligence. Ithaca is the celestial fatherland (paradise) to which we must return, escaping from here and living the true life; the means of return is the Church, a traditional image of which is a ship.

Up to this point, with the exception, obviously, of the last idea, the exegesis of Christian authors is not specifically Christian. But it becomes so with the meaning it gives to the figure of Ulysses. Certainly, as before, he embodies the human condition, but also much more: tied to his mast which symbolizes the Cross, he represents the crucified, and, with less emphasis, the Christian saved by the wood, and even all of humanity. His companions are to be understood as the more distant adherents to whom, however, the shadow of the Cross reaches, such as the good thief. Finally, even the wax stopping up their ears is given meaning; that is, it represents Scripture.

2. The Main Texts

This detailed description corresponds to the final complete stage of Christian exegesis, as it is found in the fifth century A.D., and where a place is found for almost all the elements of the Homeric story relative to the Sirens. But this fairly late stage was naturally preceded by attempts that were less complete.[36]

One of the earliest attempts was that of Clement of Alexandria (late second to early third centuries A.D.). For him the Sirens represent the misdeeds of habit and the lures of pleasure, and Ulysses who fools them by tying himself to his mast is the image of the Christian who triumphs over perdition by clinging to the wood of the Cross.

> Let us flee (Φύγωμεν), then, habit (συνήθειαν); let us flee it as we would a dangerous promontory, the menace of Charybdis, or of the Sirens of legend. Habit strangles man, turns him away from the truth and from life, is a trap, an abyss, a ditch, it is a keen evil.

"Far from this smoke, far from these waves take
Your ship."

Let us flee (**Φεύγωμεν**), then, my sailor companions, let us flee these waves, they vomit forth fire; there, there is an accursed island on which are piled bones and corpses; in that place a bold courtesan (that is, pleasure) sings, delighting in vulgar music:

"Come here, famous Ulysses, supreme glory of the Achaians!
Halt your ship to hear a more divine voice."

She praises you, sailor, speaking your great fame, and she seeks, this prostitute, to capture him who is the glory of the Greeks. Leave her to feed on her corpses; a heavenly wind (**πνεῦμα οὐράνιον**) comes to your aid. Sail past pleasure (**πάριθι τὴν ἡδονήν**), it is a deceiver:

"Neither let a lewd woman make you lose your mind;
Her flattering chatter is only interested in your barn."

Sail past (**παράπλει**) this song, it produces death. Just want it (**ἐὰν ἐθέλῃς**) and you will conquer perdition. Chained to the Wood, you will be delivered from all corruption; you will have for pilot the Word (**λόγος**) of God; you will reach the port of the heavens, thanks to the Holy Spirit (**τοῖς λιμέσι καθορμίσει τῶν οὐρανῶν τὸ πνεῦμα τὸ ἅγιον**). Then you will contemplate my God; you will be initiated into these sacred mysteries; you will enjoy these realities hidden in the heavens and which I keep, "which no ear hath heard and which have not risen to the heart" of anyone.[37]

The first point that strikes one in this text is the attack on habit, **συνήθεια**, which seems unduly vehement. In fact, Clement indicates by this word the weight of pagan traditions which chain the Greeks to their religious practices, notably to the cult of divine images, and which prevent them from adhering to the Christian truth, which is something new: "One pushes one to the abyss, that is habit; the other raises one to heaven, that is truth."[38] It should be noted too that the denunciation of habit, nurse of vice, belonged to the literary genre of protreptics,[39] among which figures, even in its title, Clement's work. These two circumstances make less surprising the offensive he mounts against **συνήθεια**, to the point of making it the main subject of the allegory of the Sirens (and also of Charybdis). As to the other danger which the Sirens represent, it is pleasure; especially, it seems sexual pleasure, since the Sirens are given the traits of a tempting prostitute who solicits by means of song and flattery. Ulysses is exhorted to flee this song of death in terms that seal his transposition into Christianity: the wood to which he chains himself prefigures that of the Cross; the divine Word is at his rudder; the Holy Spirit which is at first a puff of wind, **πνεῦμα οὐράνιον**, fills his sails and pushes him to the port of salvation.

We can see that Clement picks out here the positive aspects of the figure of Ulysses. It is quite different some pages earlier where the same author, opposing to the believers in love with eternal salvation the others who mock it, places the latter under the patronage of the Greek hero:

> But the others, stuck to the world like seaweed stuck to the rocks in the sea, make little of immortality, and, in the manner of the old man of Ithaca (καθάπερ ὁ Ἰθακήσιος γέρων), take as object of their desire, not the truth nor the heavenly fatherland, nor further the true light, but ... smoke.[40]

The portrait of Ulysses on which this text is based is the product of bringing together some verses taken from the first books of the *Odyssey:* i. 57–59 (held back by Calypso, Ulysses, who wants only to see again the smoke of Ithaca, calls for death); v. 135–136 and vii. 256–257 (Calypso in vain makes an offer to Ulysses to keep him from death and old age, ἀθάνατον καὶ ἀγήραον); and v. 203–209 (Ulysses wants to return to his terrestrial homeland, ἐς πατρίδα γαῖαν, instead of becoming immortal). Ulysses' refusal to escape old age explains in part the curious circumlocution which Clement uses in referring to him as "the old man of Ithaca," but this formula must also have the purpose of emphasizing, as expressed in one of its major heroes, the oldness of paganism whose inertia blocks the arrival of the newness of Christianity. In other words, Ulysses is enrolled here in the camp of perverse "habit," whereas, on the contrary, in the text cited earlier, he escapes from its grasp under the cover of his flight far from the Sirens. We can see that Clement is a master of allegorical practice, of which one of the axioms is that the same mythical figure can produce many different, even opposed, interpretations. Besides, we might note that Clement's stern evaluation of Ulysses' sacrifice of immortality in order to return to Ithaca and to see its smoke again takes the opposite tack to the praises conferred on him in the Stoic tradition, which sees in this same behavior the proof of the hero's moderation and of his love for his fatherland.[41]

As for the Sirens, another interpretation can also be found in Clement, who sees them as the image of pagan Greek culture in its relation to Christian catechesis: the converts registered to receive baptism fear lest the melodious pagan knowledge, like the Sirens, block their way to the faith, and they prefer, like Ulysses' sailors, to stop their ears with corks of ignorance. But their instructor will not imitate them in their summary refusal; he will know how to select from pagan culture elements of use to catechesis, on condition that he does not dally with it and does not compromise his return to the Christian philosophy which is his fatherland. It is understood that he will profit by the song of the Sirens without losing himself in it; he will take Ulysses as his model. These preliminaries prepare us for reading Clement's own text:

> But it appears that most of those who register themselves, just like Ulysses' companions, hold to the word like peasants. They pass by, not the Sirens, but

their harmony and their music; it is from ignorant prejudice that they stop their ears, knowing well that if they listen only once to the teaching of the Greeks, they will never be able to return. But he who selects from it, on behalf of the catechumens, what is useful, especially if they themselves are Greeks ("the earth belongs to the Lord and all which fills it"), he does not have to abstain, as do irrational animals, from the love of knowledge. He should rather collect from it as much help as possible for his flock. This is on condition, however, that he does not become attached to it, only for the use that can be made of it, so as to be able, once the borrowing is done and becomes his property, to return in himself to the true philosophy, in possession of that solid conviction of the soul which is security guaranteed by all means.[42]

There is a noteworthy appreciation of the song of the Sirens in this praise of Ulysses who listened to it without succumbing to it and in this reproval of those who did not wish to (in reality, who could not) hear anything. Other Christian authors would again see in the song the image of the seduction of pagan culture and philosophy, but most often only to reject these entirely,[43] or to reduce them to the vanity of fine speech.[44] Clement was less original when the call of the Sirens evoked for him the call of the pleasures of the senses. One might note again, at any rate, that in the case of the Sirens, as before in the case of Ulysses, he does not neglect to subject the same mythical figure to different allegorical interpretations.

We will spend less time with the Fathers of the Church who, in various ways, took up and extended the great exegesis in *Protrepticus* XII. They do not in any case require as much attention on this point. A few years after Clement, Hippolytus of Rome, in his account of Basilides the Gnostic, reminds us of the episode of the Sirens, after he had named quickly the mythical monsters of the sea around Sicily— the Cyclops, Charybdis, and Scylla. The sea-crossing full of obstacles is now that of the Christians in the midst of the doctrines of the heretics. Let the Christians use as a model the cunning Ulysses, who fills the ears of his companions with wax, whereas he himself, tied to the mast, "sails past the Sirens without obstacle" (παραπλεῦσα ἀκινδύνως τὰς Σειρῆνας) while clearly hearing their song. The weaker will not listen to the heresies, which are quite able to drag them where they wish; but the man of faith will hear them without being disturbed as long as he is chained to the wood of Christ.[45] This last phrase (ἑαυτὸν τῷ ξύλῳ Χριστοῦ προσδήσαντα), which assimilates the mast of Ulysses to the Cross of Christ, is taken almost word-for-word from Clement (τῷ ξύλῳ προσδεδεμένος) despite the fact that the two authors give the Sirens a quite different meaning. One will note also that Hippolytus gives value to a detail in the story in the *Odyssey* (the wax in the ears of the sailors) that his predecessor, at least in the *Protrepticus,* did not single out.

The debt to Clement is admitted from the start, near the end of the third century, by Bishop Methodius of Olympus, who indeed calls Ulysses ὁ Ἰθακήσιος γέρων,[46] and explains the latter's behavior by the fact that he wished neither to deny himself the uncontrolled pleasure of hearing the song of the Sirens, nor to expose himself to the death which followed this song. But Methodius uses the Homeric episode mainly as a foil: to the mortal song of the Sirens he opposes the divine and saving voices of the choir of the Prophets and of their interpreters, the Apostles; to hear this song which produces, not death, but a better life, there is no need to block the ears of our companions or to tie ourselves.[47] Besides this completely negative approach, and indeed because of it, we may note that this author, quite different in this from his two predecessors, avoids assimilating Ulysses' mast to the wood of the Cross.

A century later Saint Ambrose takes up the tradition, making himself its first important representative in Latin Christianity. For him the sea is the deceiving world, the *saeculum* (*Quod autem mare abruptius quam saeculum tam infidum?*); the Sirens are the pleasures of the senses which ensnare the mind and sap its strength; the rocks on which they live are the body that softens spiritual keenness; far from blocking our ears, let us open them to the voice of Christ; let us bind ourselves, not like Ulysses hurrying back to his fatherland (*Ulixem illum...festinantem ad patriam*), with corporeal bindings to the mast, but spiritually with the knots of the soul to the wood of the Cross.[48] This entire allegory is in its substance found already in the Greek Fathers, with the exception, perhaps, of the assimilation of the rock of the Sirens to the human body. Ambrose also introduces some innovations in some minor details: among the circumstances delaying Ulysses' return he cites, besides the Sirens, the sweet fruits of the Lotus-Eaters and the gardens of Alcinous (*Od.* vii. 112–132; ix. 82–104). As is natural for a Latin author, he mixes into his memory of Homer allusions to Aeneas' navigation according to Virgil (*Aeneid* I. 536 and II. 23). Finally he notes that the prophet also named the Sirens,[49] one of the several mythological allusions he believes are to be found in Scripture.

The Christian exegesis of the victory of Ulysses over the Sirens in a sense reaches perfection in the fifth century in a homily by Bishop Maximus of Turin.[50] Several expressions taken word-for-word from Ambrose show his debt to Ambrose. But he contributes much to this exegesis: the item-to-item correspondence between the episode of the *Odyssey* and its Christian application is now pushed to the limit. In his detailed parallels, Maximus capitalizes on nearly all the contributions of his predecessors and his weakness for rhetorical amplification helps him orchestrate these with ingenuity. The prolixity of these passages makes quotation difficult. In any case, we already know their substance, since my account of the "main features" of patristic exegesis as sketched above is drawn almost exclusively from him. It remains that this last stage in the exegesis represents the completion of some parallels that were only suggested before. Thus Maximus finalizes the correspondence between Ithaca and the *patria paradysi, de qua primus homo exierat*. More important, Ulysses chained to his mast becomes for Maximus the image, no longer only, as before, of the incorruptible Christian, but of Christ Himself on the Cross: to *de Ulixe illo refert fabula quod eum arboris religatio de periculo liberarit* the response is given *Christus dominus religatus in cruce est*.

3. The Relation to Platonism

This Christian tradition, which lasts from the third to the fifth century, is approximately contemporaneous with the exegesis of Ulysses that we traced from Numenius to Proclus. The differences between these two parallel developments are evident. The most fundamental difference consists naturally in the fact that the Christian truth which is supposed to be found in the myth, or which is at least illustrated by it, is without equivalent in the exegesis of the Platonists. This is clear. But there are also other differences, even if we limit ourselves to the episode of the Sirens.

Christian exegesis, from the beginning, seems to be more complete in that it integrates, and even views as essential, aspects of the legend not picked out by the Platonists. This is the case in relation to Ulysses tied to the mast, the ears of his companions stopped up by wax (we have seen, however, that this last aspect is given meaning when, by amalgamating the Sirens of Homer and of Plato, Plutarch gives an eschatological interpretation of the Sirens with reference to the harmony of the spheres; but this is, it seems, a Pythagorean and not strictly a Platonic exegesis).

On the other hand, several meanings which Platonic exegesis was fond of introducing are not echoed by the Christians. This is the case for the notion of genesis whose identification with the hostile sea of the *Odyssey* is a constant theme in Platonic exegesis from Numenius to Proclus. Another case is that of the practice, which continues from Hermias to Eustathius, of discerning in the fatherland Ithaca the intelligible world. One should note, however, that these ideas do not fail to evoke fairly close substitutes in Christian exegesis. The deceiving world (*saeculum*) of Ambrose, more merciless than the sea, is not without affinities to the world of coming-to-be from which the Neoplatonists wish to rescue the soul. As for the intelligible world, we know that some later Christians had begun to assimilate it to the Kingdom of God of Scripture, only to blame themselves for this later on.[51] This suggests that the distance can be shortened between the Platonic notion and the "heavens" of Clement of Alexandria, or the "Paradise" of Maximus of Turin.

In saying this we cannot fail to recognize in Clement and his successors the presence of elements found in the Platonic tradition. We can begin with some aspects of vocabulary. We saw above the important clues that are yielded by the use in Hermias and Proclus of the verb παραπλέειν in order to express Ulysses' giving a wide berth to the Sirens. Unless I am mistaken, this word is the sign that the Sirens of the *Odyssey* were interpreted in the light of the Sirens of the *Phaedrus*. But here we find, about two centuries before these pagan authors, the same word παραπλέειν used several times in the same fashion, as we have seen, by Clement[52] and by Hippolytus—a fact that suggests that the contamination I have pointed out (between the *Odyssey* and the *Phaedrus*) originated at the beginning of the third century at the latest. It does not appear that we can push the date back further than this, or at least not further back than Lucian of Samosata, twenty or thirty years earlier.[53]

Another word to note is the present imperative φεύγωμεν used twice by Clement as a sort of retraction, since he used, some lines earlier, also twice, the aorist φύγωμεν. But we found the same word in Plotinus where it is part of a short quotation from the Iliad, having as its background a memory of the famous "flight" of Plato's Theaetetus 176A: χρὴ ἐνθένδε ἐκεῖσε φεύγειν.[54] It is therefore possible to assume the same literary and doctrinal context for Clement's φεύγωμεν, who would again, therefore, have anticipated the Neoplatonists. One can probably find further signs of a vocabulary shared in common. Thus, the same verb παρέρχεσθαι is used both by Clement and by Hermias to indicate that we must avoid worldly pleasures.[55]

Other similarities go beyond the level of words and have to do with doctrine. The grandiose symbolism that Christian authors progressively confer on the figure of Ulysses is grafted on an exegetical foundation which is substantially the same as that of the Platonists. For both, the hero embodies man in love with salvation and fighting against the hostile forces that are part of the sensible world. In this perspective salvation is conceived of as a return to the fatherland. As Numenius strikingly expresses it in a clever use of the very verses of the Odyssey, the fatherland's essential characteristic is to be irreducible to the actual world. Furthermore, if this fatherland is so "dear" to us, it is because it was the point of departure before being the point of arrival; πατρὶς ... ὅθεν παρήλθομεν in Plotinus (I 6,8,21) harmonizes in this respect with Maximus of Turin's patria paradysi, de qua primus homo exierat. Reestablishment in a place or previous state is what is well expressed by Numenius (or Porphyry) by the use of a word that reminds us of that eschatological reestablishment which is Origen's "apocatastasis." Finally, since the world here below has as its mythical image the ocean, the place of salvation will naturally be represented by a port: when Proclus discovers in Ithaca the μυστικὸς ὅρμος τῆς ψυχῆς, he takes up the allegory in Clement which has Ulysses arrive at τοῖς λιμέσι ... τῶν οὐρανῶν.[56]

The pilot whom Clement credits with steering towards salvation is none other than the divine Logos; the reactivation of the immanent logos is for Hermias the condition of our awakening, by means of which we approach the vigilance that constitutes the gods. Another fundamental idea common to the two traditions is that the necessary condition for salvation is the desire to be saved; on this point Clement's ἐὰν ἐθέλῃς μόνον is an exact anticipation of Proclus' ἐὰν ἄρα σώζεσθαι θελῶμεν.[57] I will end with a comparison that requires attention, even though it relates only to Origen and not to any of the Christian authors quoted above. The Platonists I have examined above introduce a kind of "demonization of the cosmos:"[58] for Hermias the domain of coming-to-be has its demons who imprison captive souls in it. These demons are what the Sirens are. Porphyry previously made note in a similar way of the gods of the sea, that is, of matter, who vengefully pursued Ulysses. We know, on the other hand, that in the cosmogonies

of the ancient Near East, including Jewish cosmogony, the apparition of the organized
world was conceived as a victory of God over a primordial hostile ocean populated
with sea monsters.[59] Early Christianity preserves a trace of this archaic image when
it gives the devil the features of a monstrous fish. This is the case notably in Origen
and in Ambrose in whom we find expressions such as *cetus, diabolus scilicet.*[60] Why
then would not the Sirens, who are also sea monsters, have featured in the *pompa
diaboli?* This connection has not left as many traces as one would expect. However,
H. Rahner found one[61] in an exegetical fragment of Origen on the Lamentations of
Jeremiah, in which one finds the Sirens of the pagan myth identified with corrupting
demons, πονηρὰ πνεύματα.[62] How can one avoid comparing this interpretation
to that of Porphyry and especially that of Hermias?

These many literary and doctrinal resemblances suggest that these two traditions of exegesis of the figure of Ulysses are not two completely independent
totalities. There is nothing to suggest that the Platonists were acquainted with
Christian interpretation. It is reasonable, then, to suppose that the latter, especially
at the beginning, borrowed from the Platonists elements to which I have drawn
attention. This must be the case in particular in relation to Clement of Alexandria:
all of the aspects he shares in common with Hermias, Proclus, and so on, show that
the Platonic exegesis predates Neoplatonism and that he was familiar with its main
lines. Added to what we have seen earlier about Numenius, Maximus of Tyre, and
Lucian, this indicates that the Platonic Ulysses was composed in the second century
A.D. The Middle Platonist Numenius, in particular, is very likely to have been one of
Clement's sources. Clement knew his work well and is even used as the nearest
terminus ante quem for the dating of Numenius. Concerning what might be specific
to the Middle Platonic Ulysses, we have only the few texts and fragments studied
above to go on. Might not Clement provide some supplementary information? In
particular, at that place in *Protrepticus* IX where the "old man of Ithaca" is blamed
for not having had any desire for the truth, for the celestial fatherland, or for the
true light, does Clement have in mind, as has been thought,[63] interpreters for
whom Ulysses embodied man striving for these three things? This attractive idea
loses its probability when we see that Clement is attacking the Stoic glorification of
Ulysses, and not the meaning of Ulysses for Platonists.

4. The Gnostic Ulysses

Without doubt Christian exegesis of Ulysses begins at a period earlier than
Clement. We know that the Gnostics were very interested in Homeric myths and
their interest in the navigation of the *Odyssey* has left some traces in Hippolytus.
Thus, Simon the Mage seems to have referred to the "moly" plant, a magic herb
which Hermes gave as a gift to Ulysses in order to counter the evil deeds of
Circe.[64] Again, for the Naasenes, Penelope's suitors whose souls are called forth by
Hermes stand, in fact, for men whom the action of the Logos brings back from
sleep and makes remember (ἐξυπνισμένων καὶ ἀνεμνησμένων) the dignity

which they have lost.[65] This Gnostic exegesis is all the more interesting in that the same episode of the *Odyssey* will be given a similar meaning in Neoplatonism, a meaning preserved in Proclus: when Homer speaks of sleep and of awakening, we must understand by this the descent of the souls into coming-to-be and their ascent from it by means of the recollection of true realities.[66] But sleep and forgetting, awakening through the action of the Logos, the fall of souls into coming-to-be and their ascent out of it—these are also the themes thanks to which Hermias interprets the episode of the Sirens in the light of the *Phaedrus*. To come back to the Naasenes, one might remember also that J. Carcopino attributed to them the construction and decoration of a famous grave in the Viale Manzoni, on whose walls are represented, according to him, the return of Ulysses to Ithaca, with Penelope, her loom, and her suitors.[67]

There is indeed a Nag Hammadi treatise (II 6), *The Exegesis on the Soul*, which gives a firsthand example of a Valentinian author of the end of the second century[68] referring to Ulysses' symbolic meaning:

> For no one is worthy of salvation who still loves the place of erring (πλάνη). Therefore it is written in the poet: "Ulysses sat on the island weeping and grieving and turning his face from the words of Calypso and from her tricks, longing to see his fatherland and smoke (καπνός) coming forth from it. And had he not [received] help from heaven, [he would] not [have been able to] return to his fatherland." (Trans. Robinson, modified)[69]

There is no doubt but that these lines contain themes which have been met throughout this article. The Gnostic author anticipates Plotinus who also made the break with the same symbolic Calypso the condition of Ulysses' return to his fatherland on high. Furthermore, the definition of the condition of salvation by means of the union of will (the hate of wandering) and of celestial aid has its equivalent in Clement and in Hermias. As to the traits chosen in the composition of the Gnostic image of Ulysses, notably the homesick desire for the smoke of Ithaca, we have found several of these also in Clement. It is even possible that the immortality that is denied by Ulysses is understood here in the "words of Calypso." All that would be lacking in this sympathetic account is Clement's attack on "the old man of Ithaca." It is true that we have not yet met the striking image of Ulysses sitting on the shore in tears. But this image is not unknown to the philosophers, to Epictetus, for example, who even provides a severe evaluation of it, along the lines used by Clement.[70] In any case, from the fact that the Valentinian treatise's general theme is the fall and the ascent of the soul,[71] there can be no doubt that the allegory of Ulysses in it is controlled by the same inspiration as that which governs the allegory in the contemporaneous Middle Platonists. This glance at Gnostic literature harmonizes with our earlier inquiry into the Ulysses allegory. It is probably the most noteworthy example of a Greek myth for which the Christians were able, at the beginning, to make use of Platonic exegesis, and yet to reach finally a result in which the myth seems made expressly to receive a Christian meaning.

NOTES

[1] Ὁ Φιλόσοφος Ὀδυσσέυς, "the philosopher Ulysses," is an expression used by the twelfth century Byzantine exegete Eustathius, *Comm. ad Hom. Odysseam* I 51, vol. I (Leipzig, 1825), p. 17, 10; X 241, p. 379, I, etc.

[2] See the two antithetical declamations *Ajax* and *Ulysses*, ed. F. Decleva Caizzi, *Antisthenis Fragmenta* (Testi e docum. per lo studio dell' Antichità 13) (Milano-Varese, 1966), pp. 24–28, with fragments 51, 52A, and 54, pp. 43–45 and the corresponding notes, pp. 105–108. See also R. Höistad, *Cynic Hero and Cynic King: Studies in the Cynic Conception of Man* (Diss. Uppsala, 1948), pp. 94–102.

[3] Cf. *testim.* 2B and 12, and fragment 15 in J. F. Kindstrand, *Bion of Borysthenes: A Collection of the Fragments with Intro. and Comment.* (Acta Univ. Upsal., Studia Graeca 11) (Uppsala, 1976), pp. 106, 108, and 116, with the corresponding commentary, pp. 134, 155, and 204.

[4] Thus *Diogenis Epist.* VII 2 and XXXIV 2–3, ed. Hercher, pp. 237 and 248; cf. W. Capelle, *De Cynicorum Epistulis* (Diss. Göttingen, 1896), pp. 23–24; H. W. Attridge, "The Philosophical Critique of Religion under the Early Empire," in *Aufstieg und Niedergang der römischen Welt* II 16, I (Berlin–New York, 1978), pp. 64–65 dates the pseudepigraphic Cynic letters to the first century A.D. One will note that later Ulysses ceased to be an *exemplum* for the Cynics, as can be seen in *Cratetis Epist.* XIX, pp. 211–212; cf. W. Capelle, op. cit. pp. 52–53. The same change is found in "Un recueil de diatribes cyniques, Pap. Genev. inv. 271," edited by V. Martin, *Museum Helveticum* 16 (1959), col. XIV 42–57, pp. 104–105, trans. pp. 82–83. On the Cynic Ulysses, see also W. B. Stanford, *The Ulysses Theme: A Study in the Adaptability of a Traditional Hero* (Oxford, 1954), pp. 96–100; F. Buffière, *Les Mythes d'Homère et la pensée grecque* (Thèse Paris, 1956), pp. 367–374.

[5] Cf. W. B. Stanford, op. cit., pp. 121–127; F. Buffière, *op. cit.*, pp. 374–380.

[6] Plutarch *Quaest. Conviv.* IX 14, 6, 745DF. A probable reminiscence, as noted by F. Buffière, op. cit., p. 480 (cf. pp. 476–481), of Plato *Phaedrus* 249B–250A, on the quasi-amorous emotion of the soul which remembers the former sights.

[7] Thus Theo of Smyrna, *Expos.* ed. Hiller, p. 147, 3–6, credits the Pythagoreans with having meant by the Sirens the harmony of the spheres. Furthermore, two famous Pythagorean *akousmata* (in Iamblichus *De Vita Pythag.* 18, 82, = 58 C 4 Diels-Kranz, I, p. 464, 6–7) seem to testify, the one to a belief in a planetary sojourn of the souls after death (the Sun and Moon as the Islands of the Blessed), the other to the symbolic equation Sirens = cosmic harmony (the harmony in which the Sirens ⟨sing⟩). See finally the attribution to Pythagoras of a theory of the Milky Way as the resting place of the souls that have left their bodies (Porphyry *De Antro Nymph.* 28, ed. Westerink et al. p. 28, 1–2; Proclus *In Plat. Rempubl. Comment.* ed. Kroll II, p. 129, 24–26; Macrobius *Comment. in Somn. Scip.* I 12, 3; all three authors depend on Numenius: cf. *Testim.* 42, 44, 47 Leemans and pp. 151–152 of his collection), on which see P. Boyancé, *Études sur le Songe de Scipion* (Biblioth. des Univ. du Midi 20) (Bordeaux-Paris, 1936), pp. 136–137. There are, however, some reservations about this; see most recently I. P. Culianu, " 'Démonisation du cosmos' et dualisme gnostique," *Revue de l'Hist. des Religions* 196 (1979), pp. 4–10.

[8] On this exegesis see A. Delatte, *Études sur la littérature pythagoricienne* (Biblioth. de l'École des Hautes Études, Sciences histor. et philol. 217) (Paris, 1915), pp. 133–134, 259–264, 276; F. Cumont, *Recherches sur le symbolisme funéraire des Romains* (Biblioth. archéol. et histor. des Antiquités de Syrie et du Liban 35) (Paris, 1942), pp. 23 and 328–331; E. Kaiser, "Odyssee-Szenen als Topoi," *Museum Helvet.* 21 (1964), pp. 114–115. P. Boyancé, "Études philoniennes," *Revue des Études Grecques* 76 (1963), pp. 76–77, draws attention to a similar exegesis of the same origin (it is in fact simply a literary rapprochement, and not an allegory), in Philo *Quaest. in Gen.* III 3. The Pythagoreans also developed a more banal interpretation in which the murderous songs of the Sirens represent sensual pleasures; cf. Porphyry *Vita Pythag.* 39 and Clement of Alexandria *Strom.* I 10, 48, 6.

[9] Cf. A. Delatte, op. cit., pp. 128ff., 129: "Il semble que tous les mythes et toutes les légendes de l'*Odyssée* en particulier furent traités par l'interprétation symbolique." We must admit that we lack sufficiently well-established facts about this Pythagorean Ulysses, despite the efforts of M. Detienne, "Ulysse sur le stuc central de la Basilique de la Porta Maggiore," *Latomus* 17 (1958), pp. 270–286, and especially *Homère, Hésiode et Pythagore: Poésie et philosophie dans le pythagorisme ancien* (Collection Latomus 57) (Bruxelles, 1962), pp. 52–60.

[10] See the discussion between Socrates and Hippias in Plato *Hippias Min.* where we meet again with Antisthenes' preoccupations. The discussion in fact has to do with a quotation from *Iliad* IX 308–314 (365AB).

[11] Notably in the episodes of Calypso (*Od.* v 55–269; vii 241–267), Circe (x 210–574; xii 8–143), the Sirens (xii 39–54 and 158–200), Charybdis and Scylla (xii 73–126 and 222–262).

[12] Proclus *In Plat. Rempubl.* ed. Kroll, I, p. 131, 7–8 thus mentions those who "transpose to other deeper meanings (ἐπ᾽ ἄλλας ὑπονοίας) what is called the wandering" of Ulysses.

[13] This difference impressed I. Heinemann, "Die wissenschaftliche Allegoristik der Griechen," *Mnemosyne* IVa ser., 2 (1949), pp. 15–16 who opposes Numenius to Heraclitus *Quaest. Homer.* 70 (note that this last text contains several instances of the word "allegory", but it relates to a moral allegory on the surface of the text).

[14] *Enn.* I 6 [1] 8, 16–21, ed. Henry-Schwyzer², p. 102; the first words Φεύγωμεν … φίλην ἐς πατρίδα come from *Iliad* II 140 = IX 27 where they are spoken by Agamemnon, but φίλην ἐς πατρίδα is also found, in relation to Ulysses, in *Od.*, v 37. There is a possible allusion to the return of Ulysses to his fatherland after much wandering in *Enn.* V 9 [5] 1, 20–21.

[15] *In Plat. Parmen.* V, ed. Cousin², col. 1025, 33–37; the mention of Ulysses is induced by the word πλάνη in *Parm.* 136E2.

[16] Ibid., col. 1025, 1–33.

[17] *In Plat. Crat.* 158, ed. Pasquali, p. 88, 20–23; the passage commented on is *Crat.* 403D–E, which has to do with the Sirens of Hades (Proclus distinguishes them from those of *genesis*). There are comparable texts, including the reference to the *Phaedrus*, in Proclus *In Rempubl.* II, p. 68, 3–16 and especially p. 238, 23–26: "… τῶν γενεσιουργῶν … Σειρήνων, ἃς δὴ καὶ αὐτὸς (Plato) ἀλλαχοῦ συμβουλεύει κατὰ τὸν Ὁμηρικὸν ἐκεῖνον Ὀδυσσέα παραπλεεῖν." See Festugière's notes ad loc., vol. III, p. 195. Proclus' word θέλγειν, "to bewitch," is already applied to the Sirens at *Od.* xii 40 and 44. On the sea as image of coming-to-be, see Proclus *In Plat. Tim.* ed. Diehl, I, p. 113, 30–31, τὴν εἰς τὸν πόντον τῆς γενέσεως … τῆς ψυχῆς φοράν; Julian *Orat.* VIII *In Matrem Deor.* 9, 169D; the soul flees γένεσιν καὶ τὸν ἐν αὐτῇ κλύδωνα; F. Cumont, op. cit., p. 66 n. 1 and p. 326.

[18] *Comment. ad Hom. Odysseam* I 51, 1389, Leipzig ed. (Weigel, 1825) I, p. 17, 9–16; see for more details F. Buffière, op. cit., pp. 461–464. The most remarkable aspect of this passage is its skill in combining Homeric and Platonic themes: the body as "envelope" (ἔλυτρον) comes from *Republ.* IX 588E; but the assimilation of the enveloped soul to a pearl (μάργαρον) connects with the comparison with the oyster in *Phaedrus* 250C; the island surrounded by currents (νήσῳ ἐν ἀμφιρύτῃ) of *Od.* i 50 evokes for the commentator *Timaeus* 43A on the body which receives and excretes a liquid flux (ἐπίρρυτον σῶμα καὶ ἀπόρρυτον), etc.

[19] 259A–B; παραπλέοντάς σφας ὥσπερ Σειρῆνας ἀκηλήτους, ὃ γέρας παρὰ θεῶν ἔχουσιν ἀνθρώποις διδόναι ταχ᾽ ἂν δοῖεν.

[20] Hermias *In Plat. Phaedrum Schol.* 259A, ed. Couvreur, p. 214, 4–24; the words between square brackets give mostly the restitutions or clarifications in Couvreur's apparatus. For the idea that the true fatherland of the souls is the intelligible world, see already ad 230CD, p. 32, 26.

[21] *In Crat.* p. 88, 20–23 and *In Rempubl.* II, p. 238, 23–26.

[22] This is the case for Proclus, *In Rempubl.* II, p. 68, 11 παραπλεύσεται; the verb here is intransitive, as it often is; it can also have an object in the accusative as we have seen in Hermias and in Proclus following *Phaedrus* 259A: παραπλέοντάς σφας.

[23] Thus H. Dunbar, *A Complete Concordance to the* Odyssey *of Homer* (Oxford, 1880; Hildesheim², 1962, ed. B. Marzullo), p. 293B; A. Gehring, *Index Homericus* (Leipzig, 1891–1895; Hildesheim–New York², 1970 ed. U. Fleischer), col. 656.

[24] In xii 69, where the ship Argo alone sailed past (παρέπλω) the Wandering Rocks. Yet here the verb is used in its Ionian form παραπλώω.

[25] Porphyry *De Antro Nymph.* 34, ed. Westerink, p. 32, 13–21. The two verses quoted are *Od.* xi 122–123. The reference to Numenius is *Testim.* 45 Leemans, pp. 103, 25–104, 2 = Fragment 33 des Places, p. 84. The word ἀποκαθισταμένου, which denotes a reestablishment in a former state, has been studied by W. Theiler, *Forschungen zum Neuplatonismus* (Quellen und Studien zur Geschichte der Philos. X) (Berlin, 1966), p. 27 and n. 48, and *Untersuchungen zur antiken Literatur* (Berlin, 1970), p. 536: he attempts to show that the well-known *apocatastasis* doctrine in Origen derives to some degree from Numenius, via Ammonius Saccas.

[26] Ibid., 35, pp. 32, 29–30 and 34, 4–7. Ulysses' "audacity" is to have blinded the Cyclops, hence Poseidon's hate (*Od.* i 68–75), which is to say: one does not free oneself of the life of the senses by blinding it in one blow. P. 34, 5 ἐν ψυχαῖς ἀπείροις, "with people who do not know …", is Westerink's correction of the MS reading ἔμψυχος ἀπείρων and of the reading ἄπειρος given by Hercher followed by Nauck; it has the advantage of harmonizing better with *Od.* xi 122–129 and with ch. 34 of

the *De Antro*, where it is the people among whom Ulysses must arrive, and not obviously Ulysses himself, who know so little of the sea as to make the mistake in question.

[27] Thus, in the geographical myth toward the end of the *Phaedo*, we find a devaluation of the sea, a place of corruption, imperfection, decay (110A and E); in *Republ.* X 611B–612A the soul, joined to the body, is disfigured like the submerged statue of Glaucus, and will only show her true nature by leaving the sea (ἐκ τοῦ πόντου) in which she is; in *Laws* IV 704D–705A the proximity of the sea (θάλαττα) ruins morals; etc.

[28] 273D: εἰς τὸν τῆς ἀνομοιότητος ἄπειρον ὄντα πόντον (τόπον codd.); the whole context is ostensibly nautical: the Demiurge is described at length as a pilot who moves between the tiller and his observation post. One can understand then why πόντον would have been substituted for the supposedly authentic τόπον, whereas the reverse change would be harder to explain. The Neoplatonists in any case generally read πόντον. For the comparison, see J. B. Skemp, *Plato's Statesman* (London², 1961), pp. 95–97. For the relation with *De Antro* 34, see F. Cumont, op. cit., p. 500.

[29] Thus Proclus *In Tim.* I, p. 179, 25–26: ... ὕλη, ἣν ἀνομοιότητος πόντον ἐν τῷ Πολιτικῷ προσείρηκε [sc. Plato], and pp. 174, 10–11; 175, 18–20 (178, 15–16), etc.

[30] We must note here a very similar image in a text which, by all accounts, is important to Porphyry. It is the alleged oracle of Apollo which he quotes in his *Life of Plotinus*. If Ulysses is not named in this text, his figure can be read between the lines, for in this text victory over corporeal subjection is assimilated to a swift swim to the coast; the nausea and dizziness produced by carnal food are compared to sea sickness. Plotinus' striving for salvation is presented as an escape from the bitter waves, in the midst of the billows (ἐν μεσάτοισι κλύδωνος) (*Vita Plot.* XXII 25–27 and 31–33).

[31] Numenius Fr. 27 L., pp. 141, 16–142, 2 = Fr. 18, 2–10 des Pl., pp. 58–59, = Eusebius *Prae. Evang.* XI 18, 24, in particular *in fine*: "The Demiurge resides over her (i.e., matter) as if above a ship on that sea which is matter" (thus I think one should translate, in the light of the reference to Plato in the preceding fragment and keeping the received text: αὐτὸς μὲν ὑπὲρ ταύτης ἵδρυται, οἷον ὑπὲρ νεὼς ἐπὶ θαλάττης, τῆς ὕλης). This is an actual quotation from Book VI of Numenius' treatise *On the Good*.

[32] As thinks J. F. Kindstrand, *Homer in der Zweiten Sophistik: Studien zu der Homerlektüre und dem Homerbild bei Dion von Prusa, Maximos von Tyros und Ailios Aristeides* (Acta Univ. Upsal., Studia Graeca 7) (Uppsala, 1973), pp. 179–180.

[33] ὑποβαλοῦσα, a reading proposed with reason by J. F. Kindstrand, op. cit., p. 179 n. 81 instead of Hobein's ὑπολαβοῦσα.

[34] Maximus of Tyre *Philos.* XI 10 h (= XVII 10 Dübner), ed. Hobein, p. 142, 8–12.

[35] J. Huskinson, "Some Pagan Mythological Figures and Their Significance in Early Christian Art," *Papers of the British School at Rome* 42 (1974), pp. 80–81 has shown, à propos of the scene of Ulysses and the Sirens in early Christian art, that in most cases it is a re-use of pagan images by Christians in decorating their churches. For the same scene in early Christian art and its interpretation in the light of pagan and Christian literary documents, see T. Klauser, "Studien zur Entstehungsgeschichte der christlichen Kunst," VI, in *Jahrbuch für Antike und Christentum* 6 (1963), pp. 71–100.

[36] The principal work on the Christian allegories of this episode in H. Rahner, *Symbole der Kirche: Die Ekklesiologie der Väter* (Salzburg, 1964), pp. 247–267; see also, by the same author, "Antenna crucis, I: Odysseus am Mastbaum," *Zeitschrift für katholische Theologie* 65 (1941), pp. 123–152. See also, especially for the Latin Fathers, P. Courcelle, "Quelques Symboles funéraires du néo-platonisme Latin. Le vol de Dédale.—Ulysse et les Sirènes," *Revue des études anciennes* 46 (1944), pp. 73–91 (he gives also many details about pagan Neoplatonic exegesis); and again, by the same author, "L'interprétation evhémériste des Sirènes—courtisanes jusqu'au XIIᵉ siècle," in *Mélanges L. Wallach* (Monographien zur Geschichte des Mittelalters 11) (Stuttgart, 1975), pp. 33–48.

[37] Clement of Alexandria *Protrept.* XII 118, 1–4, ed. Stählin, p. 83, 8–30. I have profited by Mondésert's translation in the "Sources chrétiennes" series, 2. The prose quote at the end of the text comes from I Cor. 2:9. The last of the three poetical quotes is pure ornament and comes from Hesiod *Works* 373–374. The first two, on the other hand, are taken from *Od.* xii 219–220 and 184–185 (at 185 θειοτέρην, a "more divine" voice, is substituted for the νωιτέρην of the text, "our" voice). There is furthermore an allusion to verses 45–46 (the island crowded with human bones) and 178 (Ulysses tied to his mast). This is good confirmation that Clement is really developing an exegesis of the Homeric episode.

[38] *Protrept.* X 109, 1, p. 77, 29–30; same opposition at X 89, 2 and 99, 3, as well as at XII 118, 1. On the word as applied to the cult of idols, see IV 46, 1; X 99, 1; 101, 1 and 3. These texts are referred to by H. Rahner, op. cit., pp. 254–255.

[39] L. Alfonsi, "La *Consuetudo* nei *Protrettici,*" *Vigiliae Christ.* 18 (1964), pp. 32–36 gives several examples of this; let us make note of Cicero *Hortensius* Fr. 63 Ruch p. 134 (*consuetudo vitiosa*), Seneca *De Ira* II 20, 2: plurimum potest consuetudo, quae si gravis est alit vitium.

[40] *Protrept.* IX 86, 2, p. 64, 27–37. This text has been very well analyzed by M. L. Amerio, "Su due similitudini del *Protrettico* di Clemente Alessandrino (*Prot.* 9, 86, 2)," *Invigilata Lucernis* (Bari), I (1979), pp. 7–37.

[41] I have drawn in this analysis from M. L. Amerio, *art. cit.,* especially pp. 12, 21–24 and 28–32 where a complete study may be found.

[42] *Strom.* VI 11, 89, 1–3, ed. Stählin, p. 476, 14–26; the quotation in brackets is from Psalm 23, 1 = I Cor. 10:26; it expresses at the same time the fact that Christian recruitment does not have ethnic limitations and that all knowledge is at the service of the faith. See the commentary on this text in A. Méhat, *Étude sur les* Stromates *de Clément d'Alexandrie* (Patristica sorbonensia 7) (Paris, 1966), pp. 67, 132–133, 287, 327.

[43] Thus Paulinus of Nola (fourth to fifth century) *Epist.* XVI (*ad Jovium philosophum*) 7, ed. Hartel, pp. 121, 6–122, 2, cited by P. Courcelle, *art. cit.,* p. 89.

[44] Like [Justin] *Cohort. ad Gentiles* (date uncertain) 36, ed. Otto, pp. 116–118: Plato and Aristotle seduce only by their δοκιμότης φράσεως and their εὐγλωττία; let us stop our ears with wax so as to escape the sweet death produced by these Sirens. One will note that Clement himself had recourse to the Sirens in order to denounce the magic of Sophists and the leading of the soul based on the charm of language; let us not repeat the trial of Ulysses, "it is quite enough for one man to have had to sail past the Sirens (Σειρῆνας δὲ παραπλεύσας)" (*Strom.* I 10, 48, 6, p. 32, 8–10). On these texts see H. Rahner, op. cit., pp. 255–256.

[45] Hippolytus *Elenchus* VII 13, 1–3, ed. Wendland, pp. 190, 21–191, 11.

[46] Cf. V. Buchheit, "Homer bei Methodios von Olympos," *Rheinisches Museum* 99 (1956), pp. 19–23.

[47] Methodius *De Autexusio* I 1–5, ed. Bonwetsch, pp. 145, 3–147, 1.

[48] Ambrose *Expos. in Lucam* IV 2–3, ed. Schenkl, pp. 139, 12–141, 3; the connection with the text of Luke seems very loose.

[49] Isaiah 13:21; there are thus "Sirens" in the Septuagint and in the Latin translation of the Old Testament read by Ambrose, but Jerome dared to use the word only once in the Vulgate, as Is. 13:22; cf. P. Antin, "Les Sirènes et Ulysse dans l'oeuvre de saint Jérôme, *"Revue des Études Lat.* 39 (1961), pp. 232–234; E. Kaiser, art. cit., p. 126.

[50] *Sermo* XXXVII 1–3, lines 1–43, ed. Mutzenbecher, pp. 145–146 = *Homilia* 49, Migne *Patrologia Latina* 57, 339B–340B.

[51] This is the case in Augustine; see my work *"Ex Platonicorum persona": Études sur les lectures philosophiques de saint Augustin* (Amsterdam, 1977), p. xiii.

[52] Besides *Protrept.* XII 118, 3, see *Strom.* I 10, 48, 6, quoted supra note 44.

[53] *Nigrinus* 19: one must, imitating Ulysses, sail past (παραπλεῖν) the seductions of Roman life, but without binding one's hands or stopping one's ears with wax, so as to hold them, in full knowledge and liberty, in contempt. Every opinion on this point is of course full of uncertainty, given the lack of any collection of references which is near being exhaustive. I base myself on the rich repertory in E. Kaiser, art. cit., where one finds seven instances of παραπλεῖν applied to the Sirens (pp. 128, 130, 131, 132, 134, 135, 136). If we eliminate the instances where this verb means "sail beside," and not "avoid," there remain only four texts of which two only are early enough to be of interest to our inquiry, one in Philostratus (*Heroicus* 11), who must be a little later than Clement, and that in Lucian, who must be a little earlier.

[54] For the connection of the theme of flight with that of the return to the fatherland, see H. Merki, ʹΟΜΟΙΩΣΙΣ ΘΕΩ *Von der platonischen Angleichung an Gott zur Gottähnlichkeit bei Gregor von Nyssa* (Paradosis VII) (Freiburg/Schweiz, 1952), p. 127. Hermias, loc. cit., p. 214, 22 does not have φεύγωμεν, but has ἐκφεύγοντα τὴν Κίρκην, etc.

[55] Clement, loc cit., p. 83, 21: πάριθι τὴν ἡδονήν; Hermias, p. 214, 9–10; παρερχόμεθα τὸν ἐνταῦθα βίον.

[56] See on this theme the classic article by C. Bonner, "Desired Haven," *Harvard Theological Review* 34 (1941), pp. 49–67.

[57] *In Parmen.* V, col. 1025, 36–37.

[58] See the title of the article by I. P. Culianu cited supra n. 7.

[59] Cf. P. Reymond, *L'eau, sa vie et sa signification dans l'Ancien Testament* (Supplements to *Vetus Testamentum* VI) (Leiden, 1958), pp. 123–124 and 182–198.

[60] Thus Origen *Hom. in Gen.* I 10; *Hom. in Levit.* VIII 3; *In Epist. ad Rom.* 5, 10; Ambrose *De Fide* V 2, 31; *Expos. in Lucam* IV 40. I take these references from H. Rahner, op. cit., pp. 291–292.

[61] Op. cit., p. 253, where indeed no reference is made to Hermias.

[62] Origen Fr. 95–96 *In Thren.* 4, 3, ed. Klostermann p. 270, 2–12: τὰς κατὰ Σύμμαχον Σειρῆνας ἀκούσει τὰ πονηρὰ πνεύματα … Κατὰ γὰρ τὸν ἔξω μῦθον αὗται διὰ τῆς ἡδονῆς τοὺς προστυχόντας ἀπώλλυον.

[63] P. Boyancé, "Écho des exégèses de la mythologie grecque chez Philon," in *Philon d'Alexandrie: Actes du colloque de Lyon 1966* (Paris, 1967), p. 170.

[64] Hippolytus *Elenchus* VI 15, 4–16, 2, ed. Wendland, pp. 141, 22–142, 5; this concerns *Od.* x 286–306.

[65] Ibid., V 7, 30–32, pp. 85, 23–87, 3, on which see H. Leisegang, *La Gnose*, French trans. (Biblioth. histor.) (Paris, 1951), pp. 89–90; the Homeric passage is *Od.* xxiv 1–5; ἀνεμνησμένων, a word-play with μνηστῆρες, "suitors."

[66] Proclus *In Rempubl.* II, p. 351, 7–17, a reference given by the editor Wendland, p. 86.

[67] J. Carcopino, *De Pythagore aux Apôtres: Études sur la conversion du monde romain* (Paris, 1956), especially pp. 177, 188, 211–213.

[68] As thinks W. Foester, intro. to *The Exegesis on the Soul*, in R. McL. Wilson (ed.), *Gnosis* vol. II (Oxford, 1974), p. 103.

[69] *The Exegesis on the Soul*, ed. M. Krause and P. Labib, *Gnostische und Hermetische Schriften aus Codex II und Codex VI* (Glückstadt, 1971), pp. 85–86 = p. 136, 26–35 of the Codex. What is given as a quotation from Homer is based on a compilation of several passages from *Od.* i 55–59 (Ulysses weeps and wants to see again the smoke of Ithaca), iv 555–558 (on Calypso's island, Ulysses weeps at not being able to return to his fatherland), v 82–83 and 151–158 (each day Ulysses weeps sitting on the cape), v 219–220 (Ulysses wants to return), xiii 299–301 (Athena never stopped helping Ulysses), etc.

[70] Epictetus *Discourses* III 24, 18–21, notably: "if Ulysses cried and lamented, he was not a noble man."

[71] See the excellent article by M. Scopello, "Les citations d'Homère dans le traité de *L'exégèse de l'âme*," in M. Krause (ed.), *Gnosis and Gnosticism* (Nag Hammadi Studies VIII) (Leiden, 1977), p. 3: the treatise is "une exposition du mythe gnostique de l'âme déchue dans le monde"; the purpose of the biblical and Homeric quotations is to "justifier le thème gnostique de la remontée de l'âme au Plérôme."

R. B. Rutherford

THE PHILOSOPHY OF
THE *ODYSSEY*

rursus quid virtus et quid sapientia possit
utile proposuit nobis exemplar Ulixen,
qui domitor Troiae multorum providus urbis
et mores hominum inspexit, latumque per aequor,
dum sibi, dum sociis reditum parat, aspera multa
pertulit, adversis rerum immersabilis undis.
Sirenum voces et Circae pocula nosti;
quae si cum sociis stultus cupidusque bibisset,
sub domina meretrice fuisset turpis et excors,
vixisset canis immundus vel amica luto sus.
nos numerus sumus et fruges consumere nati,
sponsi Penelopae, nebulones, Alcinoique
in cute curanda plus aequo operata iuventus,
cui pulchrum fuit in medios dormire dies et
ad strepitum citharae cessatum ducere curam.

(Horace, Epistles i 2.18–31)

So let us now turn from the vigour and combat of the *Iliad* to the *Odyssey* with its *ethos*. For that poem too is not altogether devoid of wisdom (ἀφιλοσόφητος).

([Heraclitus], Homeric Allegories 60)

The ancient critics are well known—some might say notorious—for their readiness to read literature, and particularly Homer, through moral spectacles.[1] Their interpretations of Homeric epic are philosophical, not only in the more limited sense that they identified specific doctrines in the speeches of Homer's characters, making the poet or his heroes spokesmen for the views of Plato or Epicurus,[2] but

From *Journal of Hellenic Studies* 106 (1986): 145–62.

also in a wider sense: the critics demand from Homer not merely entertainment but enlightenment on moral and religious questions, on good and evil, on this life and the after-life. When they fail to find what they seek, they follow Plato and find him wanting.[3]

In modern criticism of Homer this approach has not been altogether abandoned, but it has perhaps become less prominent. In the case of the *Odyssey*, the moralistic reading of Odysseus' character, well exemplified in the lines of Horace's poem quoted above, would probably be met with considerable scepticism today. Horace's reading of the *Odyssey*, it may fairly be said, is too limited and one-sided to do justice to the complex character of the hero, in whom we find not only wisdom, prudence and endurance, but also curiosity, vanity and above all a delight in crafty tricks and lies. Odyssean criticism seems not yet to have reconciled the poem's dominantly moral tone and the moral status of its hero. It is a commonplace that the *Odyssey* as a whole is, much more than the *Iliad*, a moral tale, in which, for example, the unjust man meets with the censure and punishment of the gods, whereas the suppliant, the stranger and the guest-friend are under their protection.[4] But how far are these and other ethical principles adequately represented and championed by the hero of the poem? To put the question another way, is Odysseus too rich and complex a character for the poem to accommodate?

What is here being suggested is that, although moral interpretation of the *Odyssey* is familiar and even orthodox in modern critical writings, the insight of the ancients, that such morality must be embodied in or illustrated by the hero himself, has been lost. This parting of the ways is disturbing not only because critics such as Horace or Plutarch or the Stoic allegorists merit a hearing, nor even because of the influence which the concept of Odysseus as a moral example, a symbol of man's voyage through life and quest for wisdom, has had upon later times;[5] it is also hard to deny that the moral reading of Odysseus' character and adventures gains considerable support from the poem itself. It is neither frivolous nor fanciful to observe that Odysseus, in abandoning Calypso for Penelope, exchanging eternal pampered passivity for a real and active mortal existence, shows exceptional self-denial and devotion.[6] Allegory, one of the chief weapons of the ancient critic, also has its origins in poetry, not least that of Homer himself;[7] and it may be seen, just below the surface, in episodes such as the escape from the Lotus-Eaters and the Sirens, or in the transformation of Odysseus' men by Circe. The trials and labours of Odysseus, like those of Heracles, were seen by the ancients as both a moral training and a testing-ground for virtue;[8] though we may not wish to endorse the specific allegories which they detected, it remains true, I think, that they saw something fundamental to the poem, and as important for its design and structure as for its ethos. Furthermore, the poet often makes Odysseus himself voice moral warnings and describe the condition of man: many of the themes of the poem are summed up, for example, in the powerful speech in which he cautions the decent suitor Amphinomus (xviii 125ff.). The hero is also the exemplar of the good king, who is a father to his people (ii 230ff., cf. 47; iv 690ff., v 7ff., xix 365ff.).[9] When he comes home, as one famous passage implies, the land will be restored to health and fertility, the crops will flourish once more; with the homecoming of the rightful king, prosperity will come again to Ithaca (see xix 107ff.). In short, we can hardly claim that the character and experiences of Odysseus are not a central concern of the poet; and, as is proper and perhaps inevitable in serious poetry, they have a moral dimension.

It can still be asked, however, how important and coherent is the moral picture of Odysseus which is presented in the poem. My purpose in this paper is to chart the development of Odysseus, and to suggest some of the ways in which the changes in his behaviour and responses serve to illustrate and develop important themes of the poem. For the conception of a character developing is not anachronistic or inappropriate in the study of ancient literature, despite what some critics have maintained.[10] This is not to say that we should read the Homeric poems as psychological novels, but that Odysseus, like Achilles, reacts to and is changed or affected by circumstances and experience.[11] Odysseus too, though not a tragic hero, learns and develops through suffering: he undergoes 'an enlargement of experience and comprehension'.[12] In the course of this paper, I shall attempt to trace the main stages in this process of enlargement; I shall try also to show that the ethical framework, the 'philosophy', of the *Odyssey,* is less clear-cut and more realistic than is sometimes implied; and that Odysseus, though a complicated and not always virtuous character, is none the less a coherent one, and a proper vehicle for that philosophy.

Inasmuch as Homeric morality is upheld, however capriciously, by the gods, they naturally feature from time to time in this paper; but I do not propose to linger on the thorny questions of Homeric theology, or to treat in full such questions as the similarity or differences between Iliadic and Odyssean religion,[13] the programmatic remarks of Zeus in Book i of the *Odyssey,*[14] or the relationship of the divine pantheon in either poem to contemporary belief or cult.[15] It is hardly possible, however, to avoid offering a few preliminary comments, which I hope will be relatively uncontroversial.

In general, I take for granted the presentation of the Iliadic gods in a number of recent works, perhaps most conspicuously in the last two chapters of Jasper Griffin's eloquent study *Homer on Life and Death* (Oxford 1980). The gods of the *Iliad* are beings of terrible power and majesty, yet also often frivolous, selfish, vindictive, and above all able to abandon or ignore their human protégés, to turn their eyes away from mortal suffering.[16] In the *Odyssey,* the picture is obviously rather different; the problem is to decide precisely how different. We may observe that the gods appear less frequently, and that fewer of them are actually involved in the action. There are divine councils only at the openings of Books i and v; Athene and Poseidon, though for different reasons deeply concerned with the destiny of Odysseus, seem prepared to forget about him for several years; and of all the gods in the *Odyssey,* only Athene has anything of the fullness of characterisation which we find in the divinities of the *Iliad.* The gods are, then, less well known to us; and their purposes are obscure to the characters of the poem.[17] They move in disguise among men (esp. xvii 482–7). Although they are said, and sometimes seen, to uphold justice, there are disturbing exceptions (in particular, the punishment of the Phaeacians by Poseidon, endorsed or at least condoned by Zeus himself, hardly corresponds to any human canons of justice);[18] and although in her plea to Zeus on Odysseus' behalf Athene praises the hero's piety (i 60–2, cf. 65–6), her own affection for him is based on their similarity of character (xiii 330–1).[19] In other words, the successful return and revenge of Odysseus is a special privilege, not a general law. Men should be pious, but piety does not automatically win rewards. Similarly, the gods may warn men, and (as we shall see) such warnings can never safely be ignored, but obedience may be impossible (as in the case of the starving companions of Odysseus in Book xii), and virtue and generosity, such as the Phaeacians show to Odysseus, cannot always save the unfortunate mortal from the anger of the offended god. The actions of Poseidon and Helios in the *Odyssey* recall the ruthlessness of the gods of the *Iliad* when they act in defence of their honour.[20] The divine background of the *Odyssey* shows little change: the gods, like human kings and overseers,[21] may show favour to certain selected mortals, and may at times even feel under some ill-defined obligation to step in and exercise their authority in support of the just cause, but that is not their normal or perennial preoccupation.

It is time now to return to Odysseus and his function within the moral structure of the poem. We have seen that ancient writers, including Horace, often saw him as a philosopher, a moral authority, even a *sapiens*. As has already been indicated, this picture needs refining: the difficulty is to reconcile it with his deviousness, his greed and appetite, his ingenious spinning of lies, his almost comical pleasure in his own cleverness. On the one hand we have Odysseus the πολύτλας, the man of sorrows, who suffers yet finds the inner strength and wisdom to endure despite all his trials; on the other, the πολυμήχανος, the crafty schemer.[22] In imitation and interpretation of the *Odyssey* we generally find that one side or the other is adapted or emphasised: already in classical times, later authors prefer to choose between the philosopher and the crook.[23] In Sophocles, for example, we find the Odysseus of the *Ajax* to be a sombre and compassionate statesman, whereas in the same author's *Philoctetes* it is the other side of the Homeric portrait which is stressed, and Odysseus emerges as an arch-sophist, a time-serving and scheming politician.[24]

Homer himself, however, combines both these aspects, the liar and braggart and the moral avenger, within the same poem. It seems plausible that the earlier tradition had stressed the more disreputable, unheroic aspects of the character. In the *Iliad*, his capacity for deception is treated with veiled allusion by Achilles (ix 308–314) and open insult by Agamemnon (iv 339). His very appearance is unconventional and deceptive (iii 209–224, cf. *Od.* viii 159–64). He deceives Dolon without a qualm (*Il.* x 383); his successes in the funeral games are not quite innocently won (xxiii 725ff.); his retreat from the battlefield in the eighth book of the *Iliad*, ignoring Diomedes' appeal and Nestor's plight, was the occasion of considerable debate among the scholiasts (viii 97 with ΣBT).[25] In the *Iliad*, he is a fine speaker and a quick thinker (as shown especially by his presence of mind in Book ii, when he saves Agamemnon from disgrace); but we are obviously meant to see him as a lesser hero and a less noble figure than Achilles. It is striking that what moralising Odysseus does offer in the earlier poem, in Book xix, is, and seems meant to appear, trite and insensitive (*Il.* xix 160ff., 216ff., esp. 225).[26] In the *Odyssey*, we hear of his relationship with the arch-thief and oathbreaker Autolycus (xix 393–412), and in the first book we are also told of his use of poisoned arrows (i 257–64), though for dramatic as well as moral reasons the poet does not admit their use in the actual slaughter.[27] We may also observe that his womanising overseas with glamorous goddesses has been discreetly kept to a minimum, though not entirely bowdlerised. (There is some evidence that in other tales Odysseus' fidelity to Penelope was less uncompromising, his sexual morals more lax.[28]) All in all, the poet has not chosen a hero who can readily become the vehicle or the spokesman of ethical teachings.

Traditional analysis might see the wily trickster and the moral hero as originally two different treatments or traditions lying behind the tale of Odysseus, unhappily stitched together to create a patchwork.[29] More plausibly, refined analysis might deduce from the evidence so far given that the poet of the *Odyssey* imposed a moralising picture on recalcitrant material, in an effort to transform folk-tale or fable into a narrative with greater ethical and religious significance.[30] Naïve unitarianism might reply by simply appealing to human nature: people are complicated, characters in fiction as in real life possess many qualities and these may often be inconsistent; the character of Odysseus and the poem itself are the richer for this variety, which reflects the hero's chameleon-like versatility. Such a defence, superficially attractive, will seem less so if we believe that most classical literature characteristically imposes pattern and integrates contradictions within an artistic and formally structured whole. It is not usual for ancient authors to present their readers with loose ends, random juxtapositions or unrelated elements. Their preference is to include contrasting and conflicting scenes or viewpoints within a carefully organised, unified structure.[31]

In the rest of this paper I shall attempt to offer a more refined version of the unitarian position, based on the assumption that Odysseus' character does change or develop, and that this development is not simply of psychological interest, but serves to reinforce, to convey more vividly and more thoughtfully, the moral lessons of the *Odyssey*.

When we first meet Odysseus in the *Odyssey*, on the island of Calypso in Book v, his wanderings are of course well advanced. He has been stripped by ill fortune and divine persecution of ships, comrades, treasure, all that was once his. Part of the point of structuring the poem in this way is in order to introduce us to the hero at the very nadir of his fortunes, just as in geographical terms he is at the outer limits of the known world. But it will be more convenient to go through Odysseus' adventures chronologically, and this means moving directly to the opening of the hero's narrative to the Phaeacians, in Book ix.

There is a certain difficulty here, given that these stories are told by Odysseus himself at a later date.[32] There are indeed some touches of bravado and the occasional reference to his own foresight or achievements, for instance at x 156ff., the episode in which he kills a mighty stag. It seems deliberate, and amusing, that he dwells so long on the episode, even repeating, in a matter of ten lines, the formula which emphasises the beast's enormous size (x 171 = 180 μάλα γὰρ μέγα θηρίον ἦεν); similarly, he takes the trouble to mention how long his followers spent gazing at the dead animal in wonder. But in spite of these boastful passages in the first-person narrative,[33] it remains the case that Odysseus does tell us a fair amount, sometimes ruefully and grimly, about his own errors as well as his companions' misdeeds.

From Troy, Odysseus sailed to the land of the Cicones. Here again, his narrative betrays a breezy heroic bravado: 'there I sacked their city and killed the people' (ix. 40; cf. e.g. *Il.* ix 326–9, 594–5). But a sterner note is heard when the men go on looting, despite Odysseus' warnings (ix 44 τοὶ δὲ νήπιοι οὐκ ἐπίθοντο). This disobedience sets the keynote of Odysseus' difficult relations with his followers. As a result, the neighbouring allies spring a counter-attack, and six men from each ship are lost before the rest can make their escape.

The second mishap is Odysseus' doing: indeed, the whole débâcle of the Cyclops episode is due, as he himself admits, to his insatiable curiosity, and to his eagerness to win friends and acquire gifts. Particularly noteworthy are his retrospective comments at ix 224ff., in which he recalls the moment when he and his men had entered the Cyclops' cave. 'There my companions begged me to let them take away some of the cheeses and depart, driving kids and lambs out of their pens and aboard our swift ship, and setting out once more over the salt sea. But I did not heed them[34]—better, far better, if I had! I was still eager to see the owner of the place and find out if he would give me a guest-gift. But it was no kind host that my companions were to meet there . . .'. The rest of the story needs no summary here. Odysseus succeeded in getting some of his companions out of this predicament, but only after having got them into it. Furthermore, he cannot resist the temptation to mock the Cyclops from the apparent safety of his ship, taunting him in the fashion of an Iliadic warrior.[35] This is almost disastrous when Polyphemus hurls boulders at them; still worse, Odysseus has to exult in his own personal successs, revealing his own identity and so making it possible for the Cyclops to harm him through his prayer to Poseidon. Here again, the companions desperately try to restrain Odysseus, but he pays no attention (ix 492ff.).

In the episode of the bag of winds (x 1–79), the situation is more complicated, for it seems that both Odysseus and his men are at fault: Odysseus for his characteristic lack of trust, never telling his men more than is absolutely necessary, always taking delight in his superior knowledge. Understandably, they do not trust *him,* and proceed to loot their captain's luggage (× 44f.). As a result, when actually within sight of Ithaca, they are driven off course by the battling winds. Odysseus is filled with unequalled misery at this fresh setback: he considers hurling himself into the sea (50–2), but instead, as he puts it, 'I endured (53 ἔτλην) and remained; veiling my head, I lay in the ship'. This moment of self-control and restraint of his emotions (we are not told that Odysseus weeps, though the companions certainly do, 49) points the way forward to Odysseus' later endurance and patience in adversity. But it has yet to become the dominant, controlling force in his character. In these early adventures he is still something of a dashing buccaneer; he has yet to become the brooding, deep-thinking planner and almost Stoic moralist whom we see in the making during the Phaeacian books and in action in the second half of the epic.[36]

These episodes help to explain the general tension between Odysseus and his companions, particularly Eurylochus, in subsequent adventures, notably the Circe episode. They admire, fear and even care about him, but they also distrust him. This emerges from × 198–202, 244–73, and especially the splendid scene at 428ff., when Odysseus returns from his encounter with Circe, to tell his waiting friends that all is well. At this point Eurylochus makes a panicky speech which culminates in an accusation of Odysseus: he says (in essence) 'where are you off to, you fools? She'll turn you all into pigs or wolves or lions; it'll be just like the Cyclops affair all over again, when our friends died because of *his* rash folly (× 437 τούτου γὰρ καὶ κεῖνοι ἀτασθαλίῃσιν ὄλοντο)'.[37] Although Odysseus draws his sword in fury and has to be restrained by his more timid friends (× 443, 'No, descendant of Zeus, let's leave him here, if you bid us do so . . .'), we may well feel that there is some truth in what the rebellious Eurylochus says.

The next episode involving a warning that is not heeded occurs in Book xii, with the warnings of Circe when Odysseus finally leaves her island. She tells him privately of the dangers of the Sirens, but, knowing that he will not be able to resist listening to their song, she gives him instructions how to do so in safety.[38] These he follows to the letter: the story illustrates once again his curiosity, his fascination with new experiences, but it also indicates his greater prudence in comparison with earlier episodes in which he took unnecessary risks or forced his companions to do so. But Circe also warns him of the danger from Scylla and Charybdis: here he cannot avoid losing some men, and must be content if the ship itself is saved. At this point the heroic spirit of Odysseus the sacker of cities reasserts itself, and he asks if there is no way to make a stand against Scylla. The enchantress replies:

> Self-willed man (σχέτλιε), is your mind still set on war-like deeds, on struggle and toil? Will you not bow to the deathless gods themselves? Scylla is not of mortal kind; she is an immortal monster.   (xii 116–8)

Odysseus needs to learn that the old heroic code of facing your foe in head-on defiance, kill or be killed, cannot always work.[39]

In what follows, Odysseus shows that these lessons are only partially learnt. He retails the warnings to his companions, but with typical caution tells them only part: 'Of Scylla I did not speak, that inexorable horror, for fear the crew in panic might cease from rowing and huddle themselves below in the hold' (xii 223–5). But he himself forgets Circe's warning—the familiar story-pattern once again makes its appearance—dons his armour and tries to threaten Scylla, to no avail (xii 226ff.). Six of his comrades are lost, in one of the most spine-chilling scenes of the *Odyssey*, and one which speaks clearly in the language and images of men's nightmares.

> ... I saw only their feet and hands as they were lifted up; they were calling out to me in their heart's anguish, crying out my name for the last time ... Scylla swung my writhing companions up to the rocks, and there at the entrance to her cave, she began to devour them as they shrieked and held out their hands to me in the extremes of agony. Of all the things I saw with my eyes, of all the trials I underwent in my quests of the paths of the sea, that was the most pitiful.   (xii 248–59)[40]

The next trial that Odysseus and his crew have to undergo is the episode of the Oxen of the Sun. Both Tiresias and Circe had been particularly insistent in warning Odysseus about this (xi 104ff., xii 127–41). If Odysseus lands on Thrinacia, he must not harm these animals, or his homecoming will be late and hard, and before that he must lose all his comrades (xi 114 = xii 141). In Tiresias' speech of warning one line in particular stands out for its thematic importance, extending beyond this episode to the poem as a whole: 'If you are prepared to restrain your desire, and that of your comrades', (xi 105 αἴ κ' ἐθέλῃς σόν θυμὸν ἐρυκακέειν καὶ ἑταίρων ...). Self-restraint and self-denial remain important themes throughout the rest of Odysseus' career, not just during the wanderings.[41]

Odysseus himself would have preferred to steer past the islands altogether, but again it is Eurylochus who protests, rebelling against their leader's strictures (xii 271–302), and Odysseus is forced to yield, though not without insisting that his companions swear an oath not to touch the beasts. Needless to say, in the end, with the winds unfavourable and starvation looming, the companions, urged on by Eurylochus, forget their oath and embark upon the fateful meal (xii 339ff.). On this occasion they are clearly the offenders, but Odysseus' own position is ambiguous, since he had left them alone when he went away to pray and fell asleep, as he had before in the episode of the bag of winds. He tells the Phaeacians that the gods sent this disastrous sleep on him (xii 338, cf. 370ff., esp. 372 ἄτην).[42] A convenient excuse, as in Agamemnon's famous 'apology' (*Il.* xix 86 ff.),[43] or a malicious deity at work, or a more complex theological paradox, by which the gods, like Jehovah in the Old Testament, lead their human victims into sin?[44] At all events, the companions perish while Odysseus is saved, but he too is punished, still dogged by the curse of Poseidon, now reinforced by the anger of Helios. As Tiresias warned him:

εἰ δέ κε σίνηαι, τότε τοι τεκμαίρομ' ὄλεθρον
νηΐ τε καὶ ἑτάροισ'. αὐτὸς δ' εἴ πέρ κεν ἀλύξῃς,
ὀψὲ κακῶς νεῖαι, ὀλέσας ἄπο πάντας ἑταίρους,
νηὸς ἐπ' ἀλλοτρίης· δήεις δ' ἐν πήματα οἴκῳ ...

If you harm them, I foretell destruction for your ship and your companions; and if you yourself escape, you will come home late and hard, after losing all your companions, a passenger on another's ship; and you will find troubles in your house ...   (xi 112–5)

This story pattern is an important part of Homer's legacy to tragedy: the omens ignored, the warning inadequate, defied or recalled too late.[45] We may remember the case of Creon in the *Antigone,* of Pentheus and Hippolytus, of the doomed Polynices in the *Oedipus Coloneus.* Like many characters in Greek tragedy, like Orestes and Oedipus, for example, the companions of Odysseus seem trapped by a problem that has no solution.[46] Precautions and warnings are not always enough. The travel books of the *Odyssey* do not offer us a simple, black and white fable in which Odysseus is always right and the companions always wrong or wicked. Eurylochus is not a hubristic figure or a *theomachos.* A more realistic and thoughtful pattern seems to emerge: Odysseus survives not because he is pious or guiltless or devoid of vices, nor even because he does not make mistakes, but because he is able to learn from them, to adapt, to use what help he can get from others and stay on top. He learns, slowly and painfully, to curb both his heroic impulses (the instinctive desire to taunt an enemy, to fight on even when it is hopeless), and his more dangerous, more idiosyncratic quality, his curiosity. Moreover, we see him growing into a more sombre figure, isolated from his own kind after the deaths of his remaining friends, turned in upon himself and absorbed in his own loneliness and grief, suspicious even of those who offer help and support.

Here we turn back to Book v, in which our first glimpse of Odysseus is as he sits weeping on the shore of Ogygia (151–8), and in which, after many years of captivity, he is finally told by Calypso that he can go. His suspicious response is striking: in surly fashion, he replies: 'you have something else in mind, goddess, you have no thought of sending me home, you who now bid me traverse the vast gulf of the sea on a raft ...' (v. 173–4). Nor is this a unique case: he reacts similarly to the overtures of the sea-nymph Ino, who offers him help when his raft has been shattered (v 333ff., esp. his speech at 356–59). This is a negative and unprofitable suspicion; it appears again when he wakes up on the shores of Ithaca and immediately supposes, against all probability, that the Phaeacians have betrayed him (xiii 203–14). Their actual fate, as presented in the preceding scene, makes still clearer the unfairness of this suspicion and creates a poignant irony (esp. line 213–4). It reappears once more when he will not believe Athene's assurance that he is at last home, even after she has revealed her identity (xiii 312ff., esp. 324–8). Suspicion is one aspect of the gloomy pessimism which possesses Odysseus in the early books, especially v–viii. Tossed by fate and abandoned, perhaps even hated (x

73–5) by the gods,[47] he is now preoccupied with his own miseries, and loses no opportunity to comment on them to others. Thus in Book v, when Calypso warns him that there are further troubles in store for him when he reaches his home, he replies in words which prefigure, and perhaps provide the model for, Aeneas' speech of *praemeditatio* in response to the parallel warning of the Sibyl in the sixth book of Virgil's *Aeneid* (103–5):[48]

> Even so, my desire and longing day by day is still to reach my own home and to see the day of my return. And if this or that deity should shatter my craft on the wine-dark sea, I will bear it (τλήσομαι), and keep a heart within me that can endure sorrow. For now indeed I have suffered and toiled long on the waves and in war; let new tribulations now join the old.   (*Od.* v 219–24)

This gloomy yet stoical fatalism appears further in the Phaeacian books, for instance in Odysseus' appeal to Nausicaa: '... and now some deity has cast me here, I suppose so that I can suffer some further misfortune. For I don't suppose it is at an end; no, the gods have further things in store for me ...' (vi 172–4). Nausicaa's reply produces the standard fatalistic thinking of early Greek literature, though we may here also suspect that the poet, as so often in the *Phaeacis*,[49] is having a little fun with his creations. Her words are: 'Stranger, since you do not seem to me a bad or foolish man, remember that Zeus himself, the Olympian, dispenses blessings to mankind, to good men and also to bad, to each as he chooses. This fate he has, we may be sure, given to you, and it is for you to endure it' (vi 187–90; τετλάμεν again).[50] These remarks are doubtless very true and salutary; they come close, in fact, to Odysseus' own words to Calypso in the fifth book; but there is a gentle humour in Odysseus' hard-won insights being echoed thus by Nausicaa's sententious naïveté.

In the Phaeacian books we find further pessimistic remarks and unhappy speeches by Odysseus even after he has been hospitably received (vi 325, vii 208ff.); and in general in Book viii he remains apart, brooding and weeping, reluctant or unable as yet to reveal himself and partake in their frivolous and peaceful existence (further, see viii 154–5, 182–3, 231–2, 478, ix 12ff.). It is a commonplace, which I would endorse, that Phaeacia is a 'transitional' episode, a half-way stage between the magical, other-worldly fairyland of Odysseus' earlier adventures and the familiar Greek geography and society of Ithaca.[51] The Phaeacian books also prepare for and include events which foreshadow Odysseus' later experiences in Ithaca.[52] Most important, Phaeacia provides a suitable environment for Odysseus to recover from his adventures beyond the known world. He is able to mix with human beings again, to experience their compassion, their hospitality and finally their wonder and admiration. He regains some of his old self-confidence in the course of Book viii; he also realises with delight that his old ally Athene has returned to aid him (viii 199–200). In short, he begins to emerge from his shell of self-pity and self-centred despair; for the *Odyssey* no less than the *Iliad* is concerned with the role of man in society, with the preservation or the destruction of the bonds, social, emotional and moral, between a man and his fellows.[53]

No episode of the Phaeacian books is as moving and suggestive in charting the progress of Odysseus as the concluding scene of Book viii, the account of the third song by Demodocus and its aftermath.[54] Full of food and drink and pleased with himself, Odysseus asked Demodocus to change his song, turning to the fall of Troy. Tell us, he says, of the Wooden Horse, 'which Odysseus had brought into the citadel as a ruse' (viii 494). Demodocus obliges with a detailed account of the sack of Troy highlighting Odysseus and his struggles. We expect the disguised hero to be pleased and flattered. But instead he weeps, and his tears are described in one of Homer's most moving similes, in which he is compared with a woman who weeps over the body of her husband, who fell protecting his city and their children, while she is left alive to be dragged off into slavery (viii 521–31). Not precisely Andromache (for the woman in the simile reaches her husband's body before he draws his last breath), the wife in the simile stands for all the widowed women of Troy, all those who suffered in the sack, and suffered at Odysseus' hands. Now the victor and the victim are united in suffering and grief: ll. 530–1 beautifully bring this out by the verbal echo:

τῆς δ' ἐλεεινοτάτῳ ἄχεϊ φθινύθουσι παρειαί·
ὡς 'Οδυσεὺς ἐλεεινὸν ὑπ' ὀφρύσι δάκρυον ἔιβεν.

Here we see Homer contrasting different ideas of what poetry does and what it is for. What Odysseus expects is, in effect, a panegyric of his own strategic and military successes. There seems no reason to doubt that in the aristocratic society of early Greece and Ionia, such poems would be common, as in many other oral traditions, and familiar to Homer (cf. Hes. *Th.* 80–93).[55] But what Odysseus actually gets is something deeper and more characteristically Homeric: not a partisan version, but one that sees both sides, Trojan and Greek. For when we look back at the summary of Demodocus' song, we find that it dwells on the delusion and the cruel destiny of the Trojans (511 αἶσα γὰρ ἦν ἀπολέσθαι, κ.τ.λ.; cf. Virg. *Aen.* ii 54), and how near they came to destroying the horse. The situation and the chain of events would be familiar to Odysseus, who had himself been inside the horse (iv 271–88), and we might expect him to remember this crisis with satisfaction and relief. It needs the eloquence and the compassion of a Homeric poet to open the springs of pity in Odysseus and to make him see that the victory he won all those years ago has become a matter for history and poetry; that the profits which he gained have slipped through his fingers; and above all that his own sufferings and his own separation from wife, child and home are not *more* important than the sufferings of the Trojans, but mirror-images of them (as is brought out by the marital theme in the simile).[56]

It has often been remarked that Odysseus weeps *twice* at Demodocus' songs, the first time being earlier in the day when he sang of the quarrel between Odysseus and Achilles. We may expect a recognition then, but Alcinous' tact leads him to stop the singing and divert the stranger in other ways. The second weeping-scene caps the first, not only because it is more emotional and prolonged,[57] but also because of the subject of the song and the object of Odysseus' grief and pity. In the earlier scene, he wept for himself and his comrades; in the scene we have just considered, he realises, like Achilles, the common ground between friend and foe. This is the lesson of shared and common suffering, common not just to friends and allies, but to all mankind.[58]

In the later books of the *Odyssey*, this principle animates some of Odysseus' sternest and most serious speeches of warning to the suitors. Their offence has a broader moral significance because it ignores the humility and fragility of man. The suitors believe that they can live like gods, eternally feasting, unpunished (νήποινοι, a recurrent word: see i 377, 380, etc.).[59] Experience has taught Odysseus that such arrogant optimism is a delusion. As he says to Amphinomus, the one suitor who regularly has misgivings about what they are doing:

> I have something to say to you, and do you listen, and store it in your heart. Of all things that breathe and move upon the earth, earth mothers nothing more frail than man. For as long as the gods grant him prosperity, as long as his limbs are swift, he thinks that he will suffer no misfortune in times to come. But when instead the Blessed Ones send him sorrow, that too he has to bear, under compulsion, with enduring heart. The father of gods and men makes one day unlike another day, and men on the earth must change their thoughts in accordance with this. I too once seemed marked out as a fortunate man; I did many reckless things (139 ἀτάσθαλ') to sate my desire for power and mastery, putting great faith in my father and brothers. And so I would have no man be lawless (ἀθεμίστιος); rather, let each accept unquestioningly what-ever gifts the gods grant him.   (xviii. 130–42)[60]

There is falsehood here, and the story bears affinities to Odysseus' large-scale lies;[61] but like them it contains elements of truth about his travels and his past; and it also involves moral truths and warnings which draw on the basic ethical framework of the *Odyssey*: rashness, boldness, overconfidence coming to grief; and, by contrast, the advocacy of generosity, mercy, gentleness (see above all Penelope's speech at xix 325ff.).[62]

If Phaeacia prepares Odysseus for the role that he must play in Ithaca and the second part of the poem, it is the scene with Athene in Book xiii, on the beach in Ithaca itself, which provides the pivot and completes the change in Odysseus' condition.[63] With Book xiii we move from predominantly sea-going adventures to land, and from more magical and supernatural countries to a familiar part of Greece. The reunion with Athene marks the new upward turn in Odysseus' fortunes. From now on, instead of being the victim of the gods and the child of ill fortune,[63a] he will be in control; instead of receiving warnings, he will give them; instead of being a passive figure who merely endures, he will become the active strategist and avenger; instead of indulging in self-pity and brooding on the past, instead of carrying grief or vanity or boastfulness to extremes, he learns the crucial lesson of self-restraint and self-control.

This is shown first when in Book xvi he beholds his son after their long separation (xvi 1ff.). The point is skilfully made through the use of a simile describing a father welcoming his son, the simile being applied not, as would be natural, to Odysseus, but to Eumaeus.[64] Eumaeus plays the role of a surrogate father to Telemachus (who calls him ἄττα, e.g. xvi 31), and the spontaneous joy and openness of the swineherd's greeting to his young master (23 ἦλθες, Τηλέμαχε, γλυκερὸν φάος) provide a perfect foil to the silent presence of the disguised Odysseus in the background. The poet keeps Odysseus silent, and refrains from describing his emotions for some time; he does not break this silence until xvi 90, when he is his usual collected self, and it is only later, after the recognition between father and son has taken place, that Homer gives some hint, however delicately, of the hero's feelings. Now we again see a father kissing and shedding tears; but what was only a simile before is now reality.

ὣς ἄρα φωνήσας υἱὸν κύσε, κὰδ δὲ παρειῶν
δάκρυον ἧκε χαμᾶζε· πάρος δ' ἔχε νωλεμὲς αἰεί

With these words he kissed his son, and shed a tear that fell down his cheeks and to the ground; until that moment he had held the tear back always.[65]

(xvi 190–1)

The self-discipline of Odysseus receives its severest trial in the encounter with Penelope in Book xix.[66] Here too he must mask his emotions and hold back his tears, even when he is forced to watch Penelope weep at the very words he himself utters; and here again, the poetic device of contrasting similes vividly communicates the lesson which Odysseus has now learned:

ἴσκε ψεύδεα πολλὰ λέγων ἐτύμοισιν ὁμοῖα
τῆς δ' ἄρ' ἀκουούσης ῥέε δάκρυα, τήκετο δὲ χρώς.
ὡς δὲ χιὼν κατατήκετ' ἐν ἀκροπόλοισιν ὄρεσσιν,
ἥν τ' εὖρος κατέτηξεν, ἐπὴν ζέφυρος καταχεύῃ,
τηκομένης δ' ἄρα τῆς ποταμοὶ πλήθουσι ῥέοντες·
ὡς τῆς τήκετο καλὰ παρήϊα δάκρυ χεούσης,
κλαιούσης ἑὸν ἄνδρα παρήμενον.[67] αὐτὰρ Ὀδυσσεὺς
θυμῷ μὲν γοόωσαν ἑὴν ἐλέαιρε γυναῖκα,
ὀφθαλμοὶ δ' ὡς εἰ κέρα ἕστασαν ἠὲ σίδηρος
ἀτρέμας ἐν βλεφάροισι· δόλῳ δ' ὅ γε δάκρυα κεῦθεν.

He moulded all these falsehoods of his to resemble truth, and as the queen listened, her tears flowed and her cheeks grew wet. It was as when the snow melts on lofty mountains; the west wind brought it, the east wind melts it, and at its melting the rivers swell up to overflowing. So did her lovely cheeks grow wet as she shed tears and wept for the husband who sat so near her. As for Odysseus, his heart went out to his weeping wife, but beneath his eyelids his eyes kept firm as horn or iron; he still dissembled, and showed no tears.

(xix 203–212, tr. W. Shewring)

Clearly, the similes are antithetical; melting snow versus hard iron or horn; over-flowing emotion versus containment and control.

The meeting between Odysseus and Athene in Book xiii is also important in other ways for the thematic design of the poem. Two aspects in particular require comment: delayed recognition and testing (πειράζειν and cognates are key words in the second half of the *Odyssey*).[68] Athene deceives Odysseus, disguising herself and concealing from him the fact that he is now back in Ithaca; thus she has the pleasure and satisfaction of making the revelation herself. There is a sophisticated and humorous psychological point here: Homer understands the superiority we feel when we are in a position to reassure or bring good news to others, how we are often willing to delay giving the news, hoping thus to enhance their suspense and our pleasure. This is the superiority that Odysseus himself enjoys throughout the second half of the poem. In almost all the recognition scenes it is he who chooses the moment of revelation (the exceptions are Argos, who does not really count, being a dog, and Eurycleia, where Odysseus has indeed slipped up, but remains in command of the situation and avoids further exposure). Athene, then, is showing him the way, but also demonstrating that she can play his game and deceive him. The scene is rich in witty ironies and double-bluffs.[69] Athene deceives Odysseus successfully (he does not recognise who she is) and she makes her revelation (he is in Ithaca); but even in his moment of delight he does not give himself away. Instead of a spontaneous outburst of joy we find him responding with exquisite self-possession: 'Ah yes, Ithaca ... yes, I've heard of that place, even far off in my home in Crete ...' (xiii 256): these words form the prelude to one of his outra-geous but splendidly circumstantial lies. In the end, Athene has to admit defeat and reveal her own identity (xiii 287–309, 330ff.; note esp. 332–5, in which she praises his self-control).

Thus the poet prepares for the themes which will dominate subsequent books. Odysseus will move disguised among his household, *testing*, seeking out loyalty and treachery, good and evil.[70] Only when the test is passed will he reveal the truth. The scene in Book xiii is an ironic, touching but charming anticipation of the scenes of suspense, tension and drama which are to follow. As often, the gods of Homeric poetry are like mortals, their actions are analogous, but there are also crucial differences. Athene is like Odysseus, and that is why she loves him; but it is also why she tests his calibre and seeks to deceive and only later to undeceive him. Teasing and deception are characteristic of the gods, even when dealing with their favourites.[71] It is also often true that what is serious and even tragic for mortals is light-hearted and even unimportant for the gods, a point well illustrated by the *amour* of Ares and Aphrodite (viii 266–366).[72] So too here, Athene's deception and testing of Odysseus' mettle is amusing, for her and for us; but nothing depends on it for her. As a goddess, she can, if she wishes, play such games, with no fear of human retaliation, whereas in the later books the tests and deceptions which Odysseus practises are very different. Despite all the ingenuity and brazenness that he employs, we know that his life depends on his keeping his identity secret until the right moment.

The analogy between Athene's actions and those of Odysseus is also themat-ically important in another respect. It has been well observed that Odysseus him-self, with his superior knowledge and power, is to some degree in the position of a Homeric god, avenging insults and defending his honour.[73] This analogy has also a moral dimension. Odysseus' seemingly lowly status, which in fact conceals terrible power and anger, is close to the stories, common in many cultures and found, for example, in the Old Testament, which tell of gods visiting men in disguise in order to test the hospitality they receive, and to find out whether their hosts are just and pious (cf. esp. xvii 482–7; Paul, *Hebrews* xiii 1 'be not forgetful to entertain strangers, for thereby some have entertained angels unawares').[74] And if Odysseus is like a god in his testing of men's behaviour, he is also like one in the punishment that he exacts, which, like many actions of the gods, is both just and terrible. We may compare the ruthlessness with which Poseidon punishes the Phaeacians (xiii 125–87), or the punishment that Apollo and Artemis exacted (also with the bow) from the family of Niobe (*Il.* xxiv 605ff.; Soph. *Niobe* fr. 441 Radt). This analogy has further implications for a number of scenes in the later books of the *Odyssey.*

First, as regards Penelope. When she awakens after the slaughter and hears the news that Eurycleia brings her, she cannot at first believe that it is truly Odys-seus who accomplished it (her scepticism mirrors the earlier suspiciousness of her husband;[75] both Odysseus and Penelope need to learn that there is a time for trust and acceptance to supersede disbelief). Instead, Penelope supposes that it must be a god, who has come down from Olympus to punish the suitors for their villainy (xxiii 63ff.). The scene which follows shows Penelope, in the midst of her confusion and doubt, formulating a plan to test the identity of the stranger (see esp. xxiii 108–110, 113–4). Once before, in Book xix, she had attempted to do so (see esp. 215 νῦν μὲν δή σευ ξεῖνε γ' ὄϊω πειρήσεσθαι), but there Odysseus had side-stepped.[76] Now we see the tables turned, the bitter bit, in the famous counter-test of the bed (see esp. xxiii 181 ὡς ἄρ' ἔφη πόσιος πειρωμένη). Here Odysseus' celebrated caution and control vanish, and he bursts out with indignation. This scene not only trumps Odysseus' previous testing and Penelope's own failure in Book xix; Penelope here also goes one better than Athene in Book xiii, for even Athene, though she deceived Odysseus and he failed to recognise her, could not make him give himself away; *impasse.* Penelope is the only person who could outwit Odysseus in such a test, and this shows, like so many other details and parallelisms between them, how well matched husband and wife truly are.[77] Fur-ther, it is not just the test itself, Odysseus' knowledge of their secret, which makes Penelope believe in him, but his moment of angry passion, of uncontrolled emotion. As commentators have pointed out, a god could have known the truth, but no mortal in the Homeric poems can trick or deceive a god; and the automatic, unthinking surge of anger at the thought of *his* bed, his wonderful creation, being violated, is wholly human.[78] As often in Homer, the emotions of human relation-ships are more intense and more precious than those shared between god and man; in this sense too, the reunion between Odysseus and Penelope 'trumps', and has greater force or seriousness than, the encounter of Odysseus and Athene.

In the course of the poem, as I have tried to show, Odysseus acquires greater severity and self-control, and wins a deeper understanding of human feelings and motives, perhaps even of the wider condition of man.[79] In this sense, and in his role as avenger and instrument of divine justice, he is a hero with special moral authority. This is not the whole story, however. The 'philosophic' Odysseus never totally displaces the older, wilier Odysseus; rather, the moral side coincides with and controls his instinctive sense of curiosity (as in the testing scenes), his greed (as in the scene in which the suitors offer Penelope gifts, and Odysseus inwardly rejoices (xviii 281–3)), and his vanity (as in the scenes in which he teases praise of himself from others). The moral task of testing and dealing out justice offer a suitable channel for Odysseus' native character and talents, as they were described by Athene (xiii 291–9, 306–310, and esp. 330–338). The older, craftier side of his personality is not dead (though it may seem so for a time in Phaeacia), but it is *controlled* in a way that it was not always before (most conspicuously not in the Cyclops episode). He still, for instance, enjoys making up the most detailed and persuasive lies about his background, using a different one for each new auditor (cf. xii 452–3).[80] But these lies now serve a necessary purpose, are suited to the addressee, and convey through their fictions a serious and consistent moral lesson.[81]

If these observations are correct, they may point the way to a better understanding of one of the most controversial scenes in the poem, the encounter of Odysseus with Laertes in Book xxiv, in which the hero conceals his own identity, describes a meeting with Odysseus long before, and generally leads his father to the grim conclusion that his son is lost to him forever.[82] It is important, not least in considering the question of the episode's authenticity, to observe that the scene continues the vocabulary of testing and recognition which we have seen to be recurrent throughout the second half of the poem (see xxiv 216, 238, 345–6). Here we come to the core of the problem with this scene. It has long been seen that there is no reason for Odysseus not to reveal himself at once and spare his father so much agony. Where is our 'moral' hero, or even moderately affectionate son, now? The curious form which the scene does in fact take has been explained as the work of a bungling and insensitive hack,[83] and as the conditioned reflex of an oral poet still working within the limits of a set theme, the 'testing' theme, which is no longer relevant to the actual situation.[84] Perhaps there is room for a further suggestion.

We may note first that Odysseus does hesitate when he sees his father's sorry condition. Having previously proposed to test him (216), he now ponders for some time whether to do so, or to reveal himself at once (235–40). In other words, he has some qualms, as he never had before. Why, then, does he proceed? Perhaps the conditioned reflex is not Homer's, but Odysseus': he has lived so long with danger and the need for concealment that it has become almost second nature. Or again, he may still be smarting at having been outwitted by Penelope; he hopes to execute one more triumphant deception along the usual pattern, with himself the bringer of unforeseen good news and unhoped-for pleasure to his father.[85] At all events, the poet presents Odysseus here in a more dubious light, though he is not incomprehensible or despicable. What was previously a necessity and a dangerous game of self-preservation becomes a more mischievous, almost malicious joke on Odysseus' part. The 'moral' aspect of the testing theme slips away with the victory won and safety restored; now, the hero has one more moment of self-indulgence, of 'playing God', following the example of Athene in Book xiii. There too, we should remember, the deception was unnecessary.[86]

But the scene in Book xxiv backfires when the trick hurts Laertes, and hence Odysseus himself, much more than the latter had expected. Laertes cannot cope and hit back with skilful rhetoric and counter-play; he cannot control or contain his emotion as Odysseus did in Book xiii (where in any case the news was good). Instead he collapses in despair, whereupon Odysseus, filled with grief and dismay, pours out the truth with unprecedented suddenness and openness (xxiv 318ff.). The episode shows Odysseus, and us, that self-protection through deception is not an end in itself: there is a time also for openness and trust. Here again, the analogy between god and man also highlights the contrasts: Odysseus cannot play games with his fellow-men and his family forever, but needs to learn to show himself to his father as he has, in each case after delay, to his son and his wife. Here again, as in those scenes and when he heard the song of Demodocus, others' grief and pain bring home his own emotion, his own *humanity*, more acutely. Since he lacks the detachment of a god, Odysseus' own distress (318–9) answers that of Laertes (as we have seen, the hero's moments of open, unsuppressed emotion form a significant sequence in the poem). Odysseus and Laertes share their feelings at last, as Odysseus and Penelope did in the preceding book and as Achilles (mutatis mutandis) finds common ground and speaks only with Priam in *Il.* xxiv.[87] In short, the *Odyssey* no less than the *Iliad* offers a subtle and many-sided presentation of human behaviour and relationships; and the moral insight of the poet guides and stimulates the moral judgement of the reader in his assessment of the hero of the poem no less than the villains.

NOTES

[1] See further e.g. Pl. *Rep.* x 620, Antisth, *frr.* 51–62 Caizzi, Sen. *Const. Sap.* 2.1, Dio Chr. *Or.* lv, lvii, Plut. *De Audiendis Poetis*, M. Aur. xi 6, Max. Tyr. *Or.* xxvi Hobein, [Plut.] *De Vita et Poesi Homeri* 133–40, etc., [Heracl.] *Alleg. Hom.* 70 and passim. For the Stoics, see esp. P. de Lacy, *American Journal of Philology* lvi (1948) 241–71. For a very full and thorough history of such criticism see F. Buffière, *Les Mythes d'Homère et la pensée grecque* (Paris 1956), esp. 365–91; also W. B. Stanford, *The Ulysses Theme*[2] (London 1963), esp. ch. ix; H. Rahner, *Greek Myths and Christian Mystery* (Eng. tr., London 1963), esp. ch. viii.
[2] Cf. esp. Sen. *Ep.* 88.5–8, with A. Stuckelberger's commentary; early instances cited by him include Anaxag. AI D.-K., Pl. *Prt.* 316d.
[3] Pl. *Rep.* x 607b 'there is an ancient quarrel between poetry and philosophy'; and for Homer as the poet *par excellence* see 595b, 607d1, and passim. Further, see Plut. *aud. poet.* 15c, 16a–d, 17de, etc. (with E. Valgiglio's notes on 16a–b); [Heracl.] *Alleg. Hom.* 1 πάντα γὰρ ἠσέβησεν, εἰ μηδὲν ἠλληγόρησεν; [Longin.] 9.7 *init.*
[4] On the gods see esp. nn. 13–18 below. On the institution of ξενία, see M. I. Finley, *The World of*

Odysseus[2] (London 1980) 95–103; see e.g. *Od.* iv 169f., ix 125ff., 267–80, 477–9, xiv 56–9, 402–6. Guests and suppliants associated: e.g. viii 546 ἀντὶ κασιγνήτου ξεῖνος θ' ἱκέτης τε τέτυκται. On supplication in the *Odyssey*, see J. Gould, *Journal of Hellenic Studies* xciii (1973) 74ff., esp. 80, 90–4. The pattern of hospitality and generosity granted (as by Nestor, Menelaus, the Phaeacians and Eumaeus), denied (as by the Cyclopes, the Laestrygonians and the suitors), or offered on certain terms or after delay (Calypso, Circe) is as vital to the poem's structure as to its ethics.

[5] Cf. Rahner (n. 1) passim; E. R. Dodds, *Pagan and Christian in an Age of Anxiety* (Cambridge 1965) 100–1.

[6] Cf. W. S. Anderson, in *Essays on the Odyssey*, ed. C. H. Taylor, Jr. (Indiana 1963) 73–86 on this episode; also J. Griffin, *Homer on Life and Death* (Oxford 1980) [hereafter Griffin] 59–60; B. Fenik, *Studies in the Odyssey*, Hermes Einzelschr. xxx (Wiesbaden 1974) 62.

The temptation to forget home and abandon oneself to a softer, less demanding existence is another recurrent challenge for Odysseus and his companions (the Lotus-eaters, life with Circe; the temptation of knowledge offered by the Sirens; Calypso, Nausicaa). On the Sirens see further Rahner (n. 1) 354 f.; E. Vermeule, *Aspects of Death in Early Greek Art and Poetry* (Berkeley and L.A. 1979) 201ff. Vermeule 131 suggestively speaks of 'Lethe, . . . the key theme of the *Odyssey*'; cf. N. Austin, *Archery at the Dark of the Moon* (Berkeley and L.A. 1975) 138–9. Calypso, as her name implies, seeks to *conceal* Odysseus, to rob him of fame and memory (cf. i 235–43); she beguiles him (i 55–6), trying to make him *forget* Ithaca (56 ἐπιλήσεται; cf. ix 97, 102, x 236, 472). In the *Odyssey*, importance also attaches to remembering or failing to recall the past; see, from various angles, iii to 103ff., iv 118 (contrast the drug-scene, 219ff.), xiv 170, xix 118; also ii 233–4, xvi 424–447.

[7] E.g. Eris, Hypnos, Phobos, Thanatos, Kudoimos, Ate and the Litai. For stout denial of allegory's presence in Homeric poetry, see D. Page, *History and the Homeric Iliad* (Berkeley and L.A. 1959) 303; contra, see M. L. West's commentary on Hesiod's *Theogony* (Oxford 1966) 33–4; H. W. Clarke, *Homer's Readers* (London and Toronto 1981) 64ff.

[8] E.g. Sen. *Const. Sap.* 2.1, *Tranq.* 16.4, Epict. i 6.32–6, iii 22.57 with Billerbeck's note; Dio Chr. *Or.* vii. 28–35; Max. Tyr. *Or.* xv 6, xxxviii 7; G. Galinsky, *The Heracles Theme* (Oxford 1972) chs. v and ix; Buffière (n. 1) 377.

[9] The social dimension of the *Odyssey* means that we should not be concerned solely with Odysseus, but also with his people: see e.g. xiv 92ff., xvci 360ff., xx 105ff., 209–25, xxi 68ff. Further, H. D. F. Kitto, *Poiesis* (Berkeley and L.A. 1966) ch. iii, esp. 133–40. The suitors want not only Penelope, but the throne: cf. A. Thornton, *People and Themes in Homer's Odyssey* (Otago 1970) ch. vi; H. Clarke, *The Art of the Odyssey* (New Jersey 1967) 20–3; Finley (n. 4) 88–91, etc. For the passage from Book xix, see esp. West on Hes. *Op.* 225ff.; also Aesch. *Supp.* 625ff., *Eum.* 916ff.; I. du Quesnay, *Papers of the Liverpool Latin Seminar* i (Liverpool 1976), 61–6. E. A. Havelock, *The Greek Concept of Justice* (Cambridge, Mass. and London 1978) chs. viii–x also discusses these topics.

[10] On this issue see most recently the thoughtful paper by C. Gill, *Classical Quarterly* xxxiii (1983) 469–87. Tacitus' account of Tiberius (esp. *Ann.* vi 51) is usually prominent in such discussions, but vi 48 (Arruntius' comment) shows that a more developmental model of character was available to Tacitus; conversely, modern accounts of personality also stress the emergence of potential and the development of already existing tendencies (which is what I essentially argue for Odysseus: cf. n. 41). The debates of the sophists (Pl. *Meno* 70a, with Thompson's n.; *Clitopho* 407b; Eur. *El.* 367ff., *I.A.* 558–62; Antiph. B. 62, etc.) reveal a keen interest in the relative importance of φύσις ἄσκησις, and διδαχή: cf. W. K. C. Guthrie, *Hist. of Greek Philosophy* iii (Cambridge 1969), esp. 250ff.; K. J. Dover, *Greek Popular Morality* (Oxford 1974) 85–95.

We may distinguish between the development of a *young* man's character (scholars have long recognised the *Telemachy* as the ancestor of the *Bildungsroman;* cf. the case of Neoptolemus in Sophocles' *Philoctetes*), and the rarer but not unknown phenomenon of character changing once the personality is adult and mature. In early literature, besides the case of Achilles, see esp. Croesus in Hdt. i 207, iii 36 (another case of 'learning through suffering': i 207.1); Croesus advances in understanding sufficiently to assume himself the role of 'wise adviser' which Solon had played to him, i 30–33. (For a different view, see H. P. Stahl, *Yale Classical Studies* xxiv [1974] 19–36.) Note also Adrastus in Eur. *Supp.* (n. 62); Soph. *O.C.* 7–8 (significant even if disproved by events, cf. 854–5, 954). And in Euripides the corruption of individuals through hardship of ill-treatment is a recurring theme (esp. *Med., Hec., El., Or.*). In comic vein, compare Ar. *Vesp.* 1457f., Men. *Dysc.* 708–47 with Handley's n; Ter. *Ad.* 855–81.

[11] For the debate on Achilles see e.g. Griffin 50 n. 1; P. C. Wilson, *Transactions and Proceedings of the American Philological Association* lxix (1938) 557–74; F. Hirsch, *Der Charakter Achills und die Einheit der Ilias* (diss. Innsbruck 1965).

[12] C. W. Macleod, *Homer: Iliad xxiv* (Cambridge 1982) 23, speaking of Achilles.

[13] See e.g. E. R. Dodds, *The Greeks and the Irrational* (Berkeley and L.A. 1951) 10–11, 29–35; Griffith 164–5.

[14] See esp. Dodds (n. 13) 31–3.

[15] Wilamowitz, *Der Glaube der Hellenen*[3] i (Basel and Stuttgart 1959) 311–34; G. Murray, *Rise of the Greek Epic*[4] (Oxford 1934) 145, 265; G. M. Calhoun, in *A Companion to Homer*, edd. A. B. Wace and F. W. Stubbings (London 1962) 442–50; W. Burkert, *Griechische Religion der archaische und klassische Epoche* (Stuttgart 1977) 191–6 (= Eng. tr., 1985, 119–25).

[16] I allude particularly to *Iliad* xiii 1–9, cf. Griffin 131. Contrast *Il.* xvi 388 and context, or Hes. *Op.* 248–55, passages which imply that the gods maintain a constant surveillance over the doings of mankind. In the *Odyssey*, note esp. the contrast at vii 78–81 (the departure of Athene to Athens and her place of honour), juxtaposed with αὐτὰρ ʼΟδυσσεὺς ... (81), as the all-too-human hero prepares to enter a new and unfamiliar society. Contrast also v 478ff. with vi 41ff. (C. W. Macleod, marginalia). For Virgilian developments of this vital contrast, see e.g. *Aen.* v. 859–61 (the falling, dying Palinurus contrasted with the effortless flight of the god); x 464–73 (developing the passage of *Iliad* xiii); xii 875–884.

[17] Note esp. the tactics of disguise and deception that Athene adopts in relation to Telemachus and Odysseus (contrast her openness with Diomedes in *Iliad* v). See also vii 199–203: the gods' practice with the fairy-tale Phaeacians, who are akin to them (v 35, vii 56ff., xix 279) offers a contrast to their behaviour with ordinary men. Further, H. J. Rose, *Harvard Theological Review* xlix (1956) 63–72.

[18] Note esp. that the Phaeacians are seafarers, protégés of Poseidon (and their king is his descendant, see vii 56–63).

[19] So too in the *Iliad* Aphrodite favours Paris, whose view of life and whose amorous gifts are like her own: cause and effect are inseparable (cf. *Il.* iii 39, 64–6, 391–4).

The 'piety' of Odysseus is embodied in his sacrifices; compare the praise of Hector in *Il.* xxiv 34, 69–70 (cf.xxii 170, etc.; Griffin 185 f.; *h.Dem*.311–2 and Richardson's n.). It thus remains ambiguous, and deliberately so, how far the gods favour mortals for their virtue and how much they are swayes by personal motives and consideration of their own τιμή. In the last book of the *Iliad* the poet seems to bring this question—whom and for what reasons will the gods support?—sharply into focus: cf. Macleod (n. 12) on xxiv 33–76 and add xviii 356–68. Cf. nn. 43–4.

[20] Cf. esp. *Il.* vii 442–63 (Poseidon protests at the building of the Achaean wall). Here κλέος, human and divine, is the issue (451, 458): Poseidon is jealous of the Greek achievement. Cf. *Od.* xiii 128 f. οὐκετ' ἐγώ ... τιμήεις ἔσομαι, ὅτε με βροτοὶ οὔ τι τίουσι, 141 οὔ τι σ' ἀτιμάζουσι θεοί (140 = *Il.* vii 455).

[21] For the parallel between gods and kings cf. Griffin 186.

[22] The epithets of Odysseus are studied by Austin (n. 6) 40–53; W. Whallon, *Formula, Character and Context* (Washington 1969) 6–9, 87–91.

[23] See esp. Stanford's absorbing study (n. 1), not entirely superseding a series of earlier articles by the same author.

[24] On Odysseus in Sophocles see Stanford (n. 1) 104–11.

[25] N. J. Richardson, *CQ* xxx (1980) 273. On Odysseus in the *Iliad* see Stanford (n. 1) 12–21, 25–9; Griffin 15–16; J. D. Folzenlogen, *Classical Bulletin* xli (1965) 33–5.

[26] Contrast the deeper humanity and sensitivityof Achilles' words to Priam in Book xxiv, where again persuasion to eat is in question. So also in *Iliad* ix, Odysseus' highly rhetorical and calculated speech employs the arguments which would convince *himself*: gifts, glory and gain, with added touches of flattery.

[27] See S. West's commentary ad loc.; G. Murray (n. 15) 129–30.

[28] R. Lattimore in *Classical Studies Presented to B. E. Perry* (Illinois 1969) 101 n. 41. I owe my knowledge of this essay to the late T. C. W. Stinton.

[29] See further the surveys by A. Lesky, *Homeros* (repr. from *RE* Suppl. xi [1968]) coll. 108–23; A. Heubeck, *Die homerische Frage* (Darmstadt 1974) 87–130; H. W. Clarke (n. 7) esp. ch. iv. For speculation on the pre-Homeric Odysseus see Stanford (n. 1) ch. ii; P. Philippson, *Museum Helveticum* iv (1947) 8–22.

[30] Cf. W. Schadewaldt, *Harvard Studies in Classical Philology* lxiii (1958) 15–32, *Studi in onore di L. Castiglioni* (Florence 1960) 861–76, both reprinted in his *Hellas und Hesperien* i (Zurich-Stuttgart 1960). For comment, see Fenik (n. 6) 208ff.; Clarke (n. 7) 182–6.

[31] These generalisations are doubtless questionable, and I would admit e.g. Euripides as a notable and influential exception; but a full defence of the assertion in the text would require at least an article of its own; I hope to return to the topic elsewhere. For ancient concepts of unity and diversity see esp.

Brink on Hor. *Ars* 1ff. (*Horace on Poetry* ii, 77–85); for unity of character, esp. Arist. *Poet.* xv. 1454a 22–36, Hors. *Ars* 125–7. For an interesting modern discussion, see A. Dihle, *Studien zur Griechischen Biographie* (Göttingen 1956) 69–81.

[32] Further, see *Od.* xi 364ff. (Alcinous' complimentary remarks nevertheless associate Odysseus—and poetry—with lies: cf. Hes. *Th.* 27, Solon *fr.* 29 West, etc.); Juv. 15.16, with Courtney's notes; Lucian *VH* i 3. See also W. Suerbaum, 'Die Ich-Erzählungen des Odysseus', *Poetica* ii (1968) 150–77.

[33] For further possible touches of bravado and boastfulness in the first-person narrative see ix 19–20, 160, 213–5 (this foresight seems somewhat implausible, cf. D. Page, *The Homeric* Odyssey [Cambridge 1955] 8), 442–5, 550–1, x 447 (?), xi 512, 524, xii 208–212 (contrast the humility of Aeneas in Virgil's imitation of the last passage, *Aen.* i 198–208). I would also include in this category xi 565 f. (contra Page, op. cit. 26–7).

[34] 228 ἀλλ’ ἐγὼ οὐ πιθόμην echoes 44 οὐκ ἐπίθοντο (of the companions); cf. also 500.

[35] See e.g. B. Fenik, *Typical Battle Scenes in the* Iliad, *Hermes* Einzelschr. xxi (Wiesbaden 1968) 222.

The episode is also disquieting because of Odysseus' possible blasphemy in 525, which already worried ancient critics: see Antisth. *fr.* 54 Caizzi, Arist. *fr.* 174 Rose, Buffière (n. 1) 370–1. Readers may differ as to whether this does constitute blasphemy, but if it does, the ancient excuses are certainly not sufficient to palliate it.

[36] For this interpretation see further K. Reinhardt, *Traditions und Geist* (Göttingen 1960) 47–124, esp. 65ff.; also Fenik, *Studies* (n. 6) 161.

[37] For ἀτασθαλίαι cf. *Il.* iv 409, xxii 104 (only); *Od.* i 7, 34, xxii 437, xxiii 67, etc. (normally used of the suitors). Note that Odysseus does later attribute ἀτάσθαλα to himself (below, p. 156 on xviii 139)—again an indication of his greater insight and his increased capacity for self-criticism.

[38] There is a pointed discrepancy between Odysseus' account to his men (xii 160 οἶον ἔμ’ ἠνώγει ὅπ’ ἀκουέμεν) and Circe's actual words (49 αἴ κ’ ἐθέλησθα)! Circe suspects that Odysseus himself will not be able to resist listening.

[39] Cf. J. Griffin, *Homer* (Past Masters series, Oxford 1980) 57.

[40] On these lines see further H. Fränkel, *Early Greek Poetry and Philosophy*, Eng. tr. (Oxford 1975) 49; C. Moulton, *Similes in the Homeric Poems* (Göttingen 1977) 104, 119. Note the reversal in xxii 383ff., where Odysseus is the fisherman viewing his dying catch. So too xxii 388 (τῶν μέν τ’ ἠέλιος φαέθων ἐξείλετο θυμόν) recalls the wrath and vengeance of Helios in Book xii; now Odysseus fills a comparable role (cf. nn. 73–4 below).

[41] Telemachus too has to learn to conceal his emotions (as he fails to do in book ii) and to contain his wrath: see esp. xvi 274–7, xvii 484–91, xxi 128–9. This is one of many ways in which the development and adventures of Telemachus parallel those of his father: cf. n. 10, and *Proceedings of the Cambridge Philological Society* n.s. xxxi (1985) 138–9. Notice also, of Odysseus himself, xi 84–9, xvii 238, 284, xviii 90–4, xx 9–30. In xix 479ff. (esp. 481 ἐρύσσατο), Odysseus restrains Eurycleia, as also in book xxii, when the nurse is about to utter a cry of exultation over the dead suitors (cf. n. 79).

Odysseus' self-restraint is not altogether a new thing: see Menelaus' narrative, iv 269–89, esp. 270–1 (271 ἔτλη), 284 κατέρυκε καὶ ἔσχεθεν ἱεμένω περ, and compare the description of him as ταλασίφρων in 241, 270. Both Menelaus' and Helen's tales prefigure later events of the poem (thus S. West on iv 244, comparing xix 386ff.); either we must see Odysseus' endurance here as a thematic reflection of a major motif of the poem, or we may suppose that self-restraint of this kind, in a martial context, is exceptional but less demanding, more conventional, than Odysseus' later ordeals (for heroic 'endurance' see Macleod (n. 12) 22 n. 2; and for the qualities required of a hero in an ambush, *Il.* xiii 275–86).

[42] On ἄτη see Dodds (n. 13) 5f.; Barrett on Eur. *Hipp.* 241.

[43] Contra Dodds (n. 13) 1–6, 13–16. This passage, like Priam's words to Helen in *Il.* iii 164–5, has perhaps been too readily treated as central in discussions of Homeric theology and psychology. Dodds himself observes (*ibid.* 11) that we must distinguish between the poet's statements and the words of his characters (cf. Arist. *frr.* 146, 163 Rose); in the passages in question, Agamemnon seeks a portentous formulation which will appease his opponent without putting himself in a bad light; and Priam's generosity to the guilt-ridden Helen exemplifies his typical kindness to her (cf. xxiv 770). This principle also affects the view we take of the gods' concern for justice in the *Iliad:* the Greeks, believing themselves in the right, sometimes declare that the gods must think likewise (esp. as regards the breaking of the truce): cf. iv 157ff., 235ff., vii 350ff; xiii 623–32. But the scenes on Olympus which the poet allows us to witness do not generally bear this out. See also Hutchinson on Aesch. *Sept.* 4–9.

[44] See esp. *Exodus* vii–ix, x 1 (cf. Hdt. vii 12ff., ix 109.2, etc.); A. Dihle, *The Theory of Will in Classical*

Antiquity (Berkeley and L.A. 1981) 75f., 198n. 31. In the *Odyssey*, note especially the way in which Athene leads the suitors on into further crime: xvii 360–4, xviii 155–6, 346–8 = xx 284–6 (contra H. Lloyd-Jones, *The Justice of Zeus* [Berkeley and L.A. 1971] 29, 31f., 44).

[45] Cf. *Journal of Hellenic Studies* cii (1982) 149, esp. n. 21, adding Aesch. *Septem* 778, *Ag.* 709, and esp. Fenik, *Studies* (n. 6) 158ff.

[46] Fenik (n. 6) 208–232.

[47] Cf. J. E. B. Mayor's comm. (London 1873) on *Od.* ix and part of x, on x 72, citing e.g. xiv 366, xix 275, 363f.

[48] On Aeneas' *praemeditatio* here (glossed by Sen. *Ep.* 77. 33ff.), cf. Norden on 103–5; further, Nisbet-Hubbard on Hor. *Odes* ii 10.14; P. Rabbow, *Seelenführung* (Munich 1954) 160ff., 182ff., 344ff.

[49] Note esp. the skilful use of repetition at viii 166 (Odysseus' retort ἀτασθάλῳ ἀνδρὶ ἔοικας snubs Euryalus and caps his sneer at 164 οὐδ᾽ ἀθλητῆρι ἔοικας). See also Alcinous' embarrassed speech at viii 236–55 (esp. 248–9; in 251–3 he has to revise his claims for his people, using the same phrasing as in 101–3!). As Plutarch observed, the tale of Ares and Aphrodite is appropriate to the pleasure-loving Phaeacians (*Aud. Poet.* 18F, 19F–20A). See further Lattimore (n. 28).

[50] On these *topoi*, see further Richardson on *h.Dem.* 147f.

[51] C. Segal, *Arion* i 4 (1962) 17–63, *Parola del Passato* cxvi (1967) 321–42; Fenik (n. 6) 54–5; P. Vidal-Naquet, in *Myth, Religion and Society*, ed. R. Gordon (Cambridge 1981) 90–4, 248 n. 58.

[52] Cf. *Proceedings of the Cambridge Philological Society* n.s. xxxi (1985) 140–43. I should also have mentioned there that from this perspective the notorious 'recapitulation' of Odysseus' adventures to Penelope (xxiii 306–43) corresponds to the full narrative to the Phaeacians in the first half of the poem.

[53] Cf. the suggestive comments of Buffière (n. 1) 384; also Colin Macleod's review of Griffin, *Homer on Life and Death*, in *London Review of Books* 6–14 Aug. 1981, p. 21: 'If the *Iliad* is "the poem of death" . . . the *Odyssey* might be called the poem of social existence, or, to use the more eloquent Latin word, of *humanitas.*'

[54] See esp. C. W. Macleod, *Collected Essays* (Oxford 1983) ch. i.

[55] See R. Finnegan, *Oral Poetry* (Cambridge 1977) 188–92, 226–7. In later Greece, we may compare the 'court poetry' of Simonides, Bacchylides and Pindar, though the Homeric influence enriches their encomia with an awareness of the temporary and fragile quality of their addressees' achievements.

[56] There is a somewhat similar progression in the third book of the *Aeneid*. In l. 273 the Trojan refugees pass Ithaca, and curse the 'terram altricem *saevi . . . Ulixi*' (cf. ii 762, etc.). Later in the book, the pathetic Achaemenides (an honest version of Sinon) supplicates them, presenting himself as 'comes *infelicis* Ulixi' (613). After hearing his tale and escaping from the perils which Ulysses had endured before him, Aeneas himself finds it possible to use the same epithet when speaking of Ulysses (691).

[57] So Fenik (n. 6). 102–4.

[58] Cf. *Journal of Hellenic Studies* cii (1982) 158–60; add esp. J. Hornblower, *Hieronymus of Cardia* (Oxford 1981) 104–6.

[59] Compare and contrast the world of the gods: in the song of Demodocus, although Aphrodite is caught *in flagrante*, she may depart with impunity (cf. n. 72), though there is some talk of compensation and surety (esp. viii 348). But this is a very different thing from the 'payment' Odysseus will exact. Note that the suitors do try to offer compensation at xxii 55–67, but Odysseus rejects their pleas in words that seem to echo those of the impassioned Achilles (xxii 61–4, compared with *Il.* ix 379–87, xxii 349–54; on the general question whether the *Odyssey*-poet knew the *Iliad*, see n. 87).

That the suitors are aspiring to the condition of gods is further suggested by the close analogy between *Od.* xviii 401ff. (cf. xvii 219–20, 446), and *Il.* i 575–6 (Hephaestus). Everlasting and contented feasting is godlike: cf. Pind. *Py.* 10.30ff.

[60] The significance of this speech is also observed by Macleod (n. 54) 14, and treated from a more sociological standpoint in a thoughtful essay by J. M. Redfield, in *Approaches to Homer*, edd. C. A. Rubino and C. W. Shelmerdine (Austin, Texas 1983), esp. 239–44. For its legacy in tragedy see esp. Aesch. *Pers.* 588ff., *Ag.* 1327–30, Eur. *Hcld.* 608ff.; contrast the lighter, more hedonistic attitude deduced from the same premises by the buffoonish Heracles in Eur. *Alc.* 780–96 (see further Bond on Eur. *Her.* 503–5). See also n. 62.

[61] For instance, the father and brothers of xviii 140 can be related to the fuller version in xiv 199–210 (cf. xix 178–81); the 'me quoque' structure (138 καὶ γὰρ ἐγώ) and the reference to past prosperity are analogous to xvii 419–24 and xix 75–80, and so on. For other aspects of this and parallel speeches, see Fenik (n. 6) 185.

[62] See further Odysseus' speeches at xvii 414ff., xix 71ff., Eurycleia's at xix 370ff., Philoetius' at xx 194ff.,

205ff., all of which reinforce these themes.

In tragedy, a further parallel is provided by Euripides' *Supplices*, in which we should note the fresh authority with which Adrastus, enlightened by experience, breaks his long silence at 734 (in a speech which echoes that of Theseus earlier, 549ff.): see Collard ad loc. and on 634–777 in general. Acknowledgement of past folly and error leads the ὀψιμαθής to a clearer view of human rashness and of morality in general. Now Adrastus is to *teach* the young Athenians (842–3). Note also Soph. *O.C.* 607ff.: Theseus is wise and compassionate (562ff.), but idealistic; the insight that Oedipus has gained through age and suffering means that he can see further than the young king.

[63] On the scene, see the admirable discussion in Fenik (n. 6) 30–7; also H. Erbse, *Beiträge zum Verstandnis der* Odyssee (Berlin 1972) 143–65. Athene's practical motives are explained in xiii 189–93, which have been unjustly attacked by analytic criticism. Moreover, like Odysseus himself, she enjoys deception and partial or gradual revelation: cf. esp. xviii 160–2 (crassly handled by Page [n. 33] 124f.); here, as in ibid. 191, the motives described are Athene's, not Penelope's (cf. C. Emlyn-Jones, *Greece and Rome* xxxi [1984] 9–12). On divine deception cf. n. 71. In Book xiii, notice the subtle ironies of 219–20, 230 (Athene really *is* a goddess; contrast the successful flattery of vi 149–52); 234 (εὐδείελος is elsewhere used only of Ithaca); and especially the mischievous delaying tactics of Athene in 237ff. The phrases she uses there to describe Ithaca, before actually naming it, echo more explicit descriptions of their homeland by Telemachus and Odysseus himself (iv 605ff., ix 25ff.)—yet another self-conscious and creative use of formulaic language.

[63a] For Odysseus' name and interpretations thereof, see i 55, 60–2, v 340, 423, in contrast with the explicit etymologising at xix 407–9. In the first four cases Odysseus is the victim and sufferer, and the etymological play presents him as persecuted by the gods. In xix 407 ὀδυσσάμενος may be middle or passive; if middle, and active in sense, this again brings out the reversal of fortunes in the second half of the poem. Odysseus, who was dogged by ill fortune, now becomes the persecutor and punisher. See further L. P. Rank, *Etymologiseerung en verwante Verschijnselen bij Homerus* (diss. Utrecht 1951) 52–60, who seems also to prefer the active sense here, as preparation for the slaughter. See also W. B. Stanford, *Harvard Studies in Classical Philology* xlvii (1952) 209–13. G. E. Dimock, 'The Name of Odysseus', *The Hudson Review* ix (1956) 52–70, reprinted in various collections, is also suggestive, though some of his interpretations are wild. In general on significant names of this kind in Homer and elsewhere, see Rank, op. cit.; R. Pfeiffer, *History of Classical Scholarship* i (Oxford 1968) 4–5; Fraenkel on Aesch. *Ag.* 687, Collard on Eur. *Supp.* 497, M. Griffith, *Classical Philology* lxxxii (1978) 83–6; and the brilliant discussion of Oedipus' name by B. Knox, *Oedipus at Thebes* (New Haven and London 1957) 127f. (esp. *O.T.* 397).

[64] Further, Moulton (n. 40) 132–3. Cf. xvi 25 and 60, in which Eumaeus calls the boy τέκος and τέκνον. The swineherd greets Telemachus *as though* he has been parted from him for ten years; Odysseus really *has* been separated from him for twice that time. The simile speaks of an *only* son, μοῦνον; compare the actual circumstances of Odysseus' house (xvi 118–20).

[65] A further simile at xvi 213–9 marks the moment of acceptance and recognition by Telemachus and 'caps' the simile used by Eumaeus. By drawing a parallel with the *loss* of children, the poet stresses what might have been (Telemachus has just escaped the suitors' ambush). But the comparison with birds of prey reminds us of what is in store, revenge and punishment (for warriors compared with birds see e.g. *Il.* xiii 531, xvi 428, *Od.* xxiv 538; Moulton [n. 40] 35). Thus the similes are complementary; but whereas the first seemed to mark a conclusion, with the long-lost son happily home, the second looks ahead to new and destructive action. The sinister implications of the comparison are intensified in Aeschylus' imitations (e.g. 49–59, *Cho.* 246–9).

[66] For a fine treatment of this scene, see C. Emlyn-Jones, *Greece and Rome* xxxi (1984) 1–14 (besides its positive merits, his article decisively refutes the mistaken view, held in various forms by different critics, that Penelope recognises Odysseus, whether subconsciously or otherwise, before the dénouement of Book xxiii). Judicious observations also in Fenik (n. 6) 39–46. Buffière (n. 1) 310 points out the contrast between Odysseus' self-discipline and the suitors' brash and emotional responses to Penelope's appearances.

[67] On the phrasing here see Macleod (n. 12) 41. On the stylistic devices of this passage see also J. D. Denniston, *Greek Prose Style* (Oxford 1952) 80. Note that the key word τήκετο was also used of Odysseus' weeping at the end of Book viii (522).

[68] On recognition in Homer and tragedy see esp. Arist. *Poet.* xiv and xvi; also Satyrus, *Vita Eur.*, fr. 39, vii Arrighetti. For modern studies see F. Solmsen, *Kleine Schriften* iii (Hildesheim 1982) 32–63; N. J. Richardson, *Papers of the Liverpool Latin Seminar* iv (Liverpool 1983) 219–35.

For the testing-theme, see esp. *Od.* xi 442ff., 454–6, xiii 336, xiv 459, xv 304, xvi 304–5, xvii 363, xix 45, 215, xxiii 108–10, 114 πειράζειν, 181, 188, 202, 206. Anticipations of the theme do appear in the first half, e.g. at ix 74; but there Odysseus' expedition is imprudent, and no effective test takes place. See further Thornton (n. 9) ch. iv; Havelock (n. 9) 163–76.

[69] Cf. n. 63. Note also how Odysseus' speech at 311ff., after Athene has revealed herself, picks up and counters some of her phrasing: thus 312 ἀντιάσαντι echoes 292 καὶ εἰ θεὸς ἀντιάσειε; and each begins by praising the other and proceeds to criticise, Athene fondly and humorously, Odysseus with genuine chagrin. Such responsion between speeches is a frequent and highly-wrought Homeric technique: cf. Macleod (n. 12) 9–10, 52–3, and in the *Odyssey* compare especially xxiii 166–80 (n. 77 below).

[70] Cf. esp. xiv 459, xv 304, xvi 304f., xix 215.

[71] See Fenik (n. 6) 38. On a grander and far from light-hearted scale in the *Iliad*, compare the deception or delusion of Hector, who is led on by Zeus to his disastrous end (cf. Griffin 41, 169). For deception of man by the gods see esp. *Il.* ii 1–83 (Agamemnon's dream sent by Zeus), iv 68–104 (Pandarus deceived by Athene with divine approval), xxii 214–99, esp. 247, 276 (Athene and Hector). Deception is again contemplated in *Il.* xxiv 24, but is ruled out by Zeus (71–2); in the end Achilles is told outright what is to happen and why (xxiv 133–40), and Hermes deals kindly, if not altogether openly, with Priam.

[72] Cf. n. 59; and esp. the *laughter* of the gods in the tale: see viii 326, 343. Yet at the end of the story Aphrodite remains φιλομμειδής (362); she is unashamed and unrepentant (cf. Griffin 200–1). The laughter of the gods is employed to similar effect in the *Iliad* (esp. i 595–6, 599; also in the theomachy, e.g. xxi 389, 408, 423, 434, 491, 508).

[73] See esp. E. Kearns, *Classical Quarterly* xxxii (1982) 2–8.

[74] Further, cf. *Genesis* 18.1ff., 19.2; Richardson on *h. Dem.* 93, 96; Hollis on Ov. *Met.* viii 611–724; Kearns, *art. cit.* esp. 6.

[75] Elsewhere in the poem the same pattern of encouragement and good news being met with disbelief is used with Telemachus (esp. iii 218–21) and Eumaeus (xiv 121–32, an important passage; 166–7, 361–8). The encounter with Eumaeus and his refusal to accept Odysseus' assurances foreshadow the more emotional ὁμιλία with Penelope cf. Fenik (n. 6) 155, 157, and compare esp. xiv 151 and 391 with xxiii 72.

[76] For seminal observations on the deceptive move here, see Arist. *Poet.* 24 1460a 18ff., with Richardson (n. 68), esp. 221–3; Hor. *Ars* 150 'atque ita mentitur, sic veris falsa remiscet', with Brink's note.

[77] Further, compare above all the paired similes at v 394–9 and xxiii 231–40 (cf. Moulton [n. 40] 128f.): these similes are complementary in their application and parallel in structure (note esp. the triple repetition of ἀσπάσιος in both). Also parallel and equal in length are the probing speeches by Odysseus and Penelope before the latter's test (xxiii 166–72, 174–80): δαιμονίη is answered by δαιμόνιε; both address the old nurse; both feign a concession while hoping for submission or revelation; both give instructions about a bed (171, 179). For further cases of affinity compare xxiii 168 with xiii 333–8 (Macleod, marg.); xix 325ff. with 107ff. (κλέος in 108 echoed in 333); xx 87–8 with 93–4 (telepathy?). The praise grudgingly given to Penelope by Antinous (ii 116–22) emphasises her exceptional intelligence; and her character throughout the poem reveals her self-control and restraint. She is regularly ἐχέφρων (e.g. xxiv 294), as is Odysseus (xiii 332).

[78] Cf. Stanford (n. 1) 57–9 and the note in his commentary on xxiii 182.

[79] In xxii 409 Odysseus restrains the overjoyed Eurycleia (411–2 ἐν θυμῷ, γρηῦ, χαῖρε ... οὐχ ὁσίη κταμένοισιν ἐπ' ἀνδράσιν εὐχετάασθαι). Contrast the typical behaviour of the Iliadic hero (cf. n. 35; A. W. H. Adkins, *Classical Quarterly* xix (1969) 20ff. on εὔχομαι et sim.). This again shows the authority and wisdom of Odysseus. It is not simply a matter of different rules for war-time and peace; the behavior of Clytemnestra in Aeschylus (*Ag.* 1394 ἐπεύχομαι) or of Electra in Euripides (*El.* 900ff.) makes plain the degree of callousness and pride which was conceivable, even if horrifying, in success. Note also xxiv 545, where Odysseus *rejoices* at Athene's command to make peace (χαῖρε δὲ θυμῷ, a phrase ridiculed by Page [n. 33] 114). Odysseus welcomes peace in Ithaca; to battle without cause, against his own people, would be folly indeed.

[80] On Odysseus' lies see further C. R. Tranham, *Phoenix* vi (1952) 31–43; P. Walcot, *Ancient Society* viii (1977) 1–19; Fenik (n. 6) 167–71.

[81] Cf. nn. 58, 60–2 above. Does *Od.* xiv 156f. mischievously allude to the famous opening of Achilles' main speech in *Iliad* ix, lines in which he implicitly criticises Odysseus (308ff.)?

[82] I am of course aware that the status of the so-called 'Continuation' of the *Odyssey* (xxiii 296–xxiv 548) is still very much *sub judice*, and it seems to me that there are good arguments on both sides. Those

who are convinced of the spuriousness of the scene under discussion may be reassured to know that I intend to base no important conclusions on that scene alone. Arguments for excision, good and bad, are assembled by Page (n. 33) ch. v, esp. 111–2; contrast W. B. Stanford, *Hermathena* c (1965) 1–21; Erbse (n. 63) esp. 166–250; D. Wender, *The Last Scenes of the* Odyssey, *Mnemosyne* Suppl. lii (1978); Fenik (n. 6) 47–53. C. Moulton, *Greek, Roman, and Byzantine Studies* xv (1974) 153–69 is perhaps the most balanced short account.

[83] Page, loc. cit. (n. 82).

[84] Fenik, loc. cit. (n. 82); also, with some additional points, Richardson (n. 68) 227–9.

[85] It may be objected that to attribute complex motives of this kind to the hero without the support of comment from the author is to come dangerously close to the documentary fallacy. But Homer does sometimes leave the reader to draw his own conclusions or deductions (Griffin 51, 61–6), and if we reject authorial incompetence as an explanation, then the oddity of Odysseus' behaviour compels us to explore these possibilities.

[86] Fenik (n. 6) 48–9 also sees this scene as the closest analogy to the encounter with Laertes.

[87] Perhaps not only an analogy but a direct imitation, as Mr E. L. Bowie suggests to me. Achilles weeps with and for a substitute father, his true father being far away, helpless and grief-stricken (*Il.* xxiv 538–42, imitated (?) at *Od.* xi 494–503). But Odysseus regains his real father, and is able to do for him and his family what Achilles longs to do (*Od.* xi 496, 501–3).

The comparison of Achilles' fate with Odysseus' is prominent at the beginning of *Od.* xxiv, as it was in the first Nekuia: cf. Wender (n. 82) 38–44. In particular, Agamemnon's words at xxiv 192 cap his words of greeting to Achilles earlier in the scene (36), and strikingly modify a standard formula. Seven times in the *Iliad* and 15 times in the *Odyssey,* Odysseus is addressed with the line διογενὲς Λαερτιάδη, πολυμήχαν' 'Οδυσσεῦ. Here alone the phrase is modified, and the line begins ὄλβιε Λαέρταο πάι . . . , for only now could Odysseus be so described. Only Achilles and Odysseus are addressed as ὄλβιε in the whole poem, and it seems plausible to see the poet as measuring Odysseus against the great figures of the *Iliad,* and above all its hero. Already these characters are natural opposites: cf. further Pl. *Hipp. Min.* 365e; Hor. *Odes* iv 6.3–24. The *Odyssey* is often thought to be an attempt to rival the *Iliad* in scale (the Cyclic poems, to judge by the number of books recorded, were notably shorter); and, as [Longinus] 9.12 observed, it forms a fitting sequel, filling in the story since the tale of the *Iliad* with remarkable economy. For further argument, see nn. 59, 81; A. Heubeck, *Der* Odyssee-*Dichter und die* Ilias (Erlangen 1954) 39 (analogies between *Od.* ii and *Il.* ii); Macleod (n. 12) 1–4.

Sheila Murnaghan

ODYSSEUS AND
THE SUITORS

The episode, spanning Books 21 and 22 of the *Odyssey*, in which Odysseus makes himself publicly known as he strings the bow, shoots through the axes, and turns on the suitors is at once the central recognition scene of the poem and the most anomalous. It lacks the essential characteristics of the scenes analyzed in the previous chapter, for it contains no element of reciprocity or mutuality. While its central action is the removal of disguise, it is devoid of recognition. Odysseus neither seeks the suitors' recognition nor receives it, and he offers the suitors no acknowledgment in return. Although Odysseus' self-revelation in this episode has many of the features of a divine epiphany, it lacks the ringing announcement of his name that occurs in most of the other recognition scenes of the *Odyssey*. He does not enter into negotiations with the suitors but begins to attack them at once; it is only after he has killed Antinous that he tells the suitors who he is, and even then he does so indirectly in a speech of relentless hostility. "ὦ κύνες, οὔ μ' ἔτ' ἐφάσκεθ' ὑπότροπον οἴκαδ' ἱκέσθαι / δήμου ἄπο Τρώων, ὅτι μοι κατακείρετε οἶκον," "You dogs, you didn't believe I would still come back/home again from Troy, and so you lay waste my household. . . ." (*Od.* 22.35–36). He makes no attempt to distinguish among them but addresses them collectively as *"kunes,"* "dogs," less than humans.

Nor do the suitors acknowledge the claim to be Odysseus that is implicit in his speech and actions. Eurymachus, even in a speech designed to placate Odysseus and to deny that any of them but Antinous has really ignored Odysseus' rights, betrays his insincerity by refusing to concede absolutely that this is Odysseus. "εἰ μὲν δὴ 'Οδυσεὺς 'Ιθακήσιος εἰλήλουθας, / ταῦτα μὲν αἴσιμα εἶπως, ὅσα ῥέζεσκον 'Αχαιοί," "If you really are Odysseus of Ithaca, having returned, / then what you have said is fair about what the Achaeans have done to you. . . ." (*Od.* 22.45–46).[1] When this speech is unsuccessful, and the hostility between them has

---

From *Disguise and Recognition in the* Odyssey (Princeton: Princeton University Press, 1987), pp. 56–68, 74–77, 82–90.

become open and violent, Eurymachus, calling the rest of the suitors to arms, refers to Odysseus as "οὗτος ἀνήρ," "this man," attributing to him the anonymity appropriate to an enemy. As the public announcement of his return, Odysseus' self-revelation in the hall does lead to his general recognition, but the recognition comes not from the suitors but from the faithful maidservants, with whom he celebrates a reunion after the battle is over (Od. 22.497–501).

Odysseus reveals himself to the suitors not to cure their ignorance but to punish it, so that, instead of bringing them to life, their encounter with him leads to their death. The suitors learn his identity too late and only acknowledge it when they are dead. It is only in retrospect, when Amphimedon in the underworld gives his account of Odysseus' return, that the suitors can recognize Odysseus. In Amphimedon's version Odysseus is identified by name as soon as he arrives on Ithaca, and his return is attributed to the activity of a god at his side. "καὶ τότε δή ῥ' Ὀδυσῆα κακός ποθεν ἤγαγε δαίμων / ἀγροῦ ἐπ' ἐσχατιήν," "Just then an evil divinity brought Odysseus back from somewhere / to the edge of his estate...." (Od. 24.149–150). Again, when his definitive act of self-revelation, his stringing the bow, is related, he is given his name, although none of the suitors was willing to concede it at the time. "αὐτὰρ ὁ δέξατο χειρὶ πολύτλας δῖος Ὀδυσσεύς, / ῥηϊδίως δ' ἐτάνυσσε βιόν, διὰ δ' ἧκε σιδήρου," "Then much-enduring Odysseus took the bow in his hand / and easily strung it and shot an arrow through the iron" (Od. 24.176–177).[2] Odysseus' association with the gods is acknowledged when Amphimedon says that Zeus inspired him to hide the armor (Od. 24.164), and the recognition of that association is actually included in the narrative of the battle "γνωτὸν δ' ἦν ὅ ῥά τίς σφι θεῶν ἐπιτάρροθος ἦεν," "It could be seen that one of the gods was his helper" (Od. 24.182)—although this wasn't seen by any of the suitors at the time. Finally, the suitors' inferiority to Odysseus is linked to their inability to recognize him as the same formula, "οὐδέ τις ἡμείων δύνατο," "not one of us was able," introduces both a report of the suitors' key physical inadequacy, their inability to string Odysseus' bow, and, just before, a statement that they were unable to recognize him (Od. 24.159, 170).[3]

This very different version of a recognition scene defines the very different relationship Odysseus has with the suitors than with the loyal members of his household, a relationship that is competitive and one-sided rather than cooperative and mutually supportive. Through his refusal to recognize the suitors and his ability to make their recognition of him coincide with their death, Odysseus shows himself to be irremediably hostile and unquestionably superior to them. His ability to make this decisive and final show of superiority depends on the disguise through which he blinds them to his presence until the bow is in his hands. Thus Odysseus' superiority is closely related to the exceptional assurance of divine favor and the exceptional similarity to a god expressed by his assumption of a disguise. And, like those qualities, it is tied to his homecoming.

Odysseus' ability to disguise himself from the suitors indicates a godlike superiority over a group of men who represent his competitors, a superiority that a hero normally doesn't have. The series of recognition scenes analyzed in the previous chapter shows that, within the extended family that constitutes his household, the hero can depend on acknowledgment of his claims to a heroic preeminence that is as secure and permanent as his identity. This acknowledgment represents a form of recognition, in which the broader and narrower senses of that English term are inextricable, that is intrinsic to familial and certain quasi-familial relations. The way the loyalty over time of Odysseus' supporters within his immediate household is rooted in permanent relations of kinship assures him an acknowledgment as continuous as that which the gods can command. But the breadth of a hero's aspirations is such that he wants the recognition of a much wider audience than his immediate household; his ambition is to be known throughout his society and eventually to be remembered by people he has never met, living in places where he has never been and in times he has not survived into. Thus he hopes, by playing a leading role in the joint enterprises of his society, either by fighting especially hard and well or by taking on some institutional role that automatically guarantees recognition, to earn from his fellow men a degree of honor like that accorded to the gods—an honor that is continuous and lasting[4] and sets him apart from the community, the undifferentiated group of people from whom this honor comes, as a whole.[5]

But this unfailing recognition is much more difficult to achieve in a wider society populated by non-kin than it is within the family. The hero must try to earn recognition from others who have no automatic obligation to recognize him and are not "naturally" subordinated to him by virtue of their youth, age, gender, or social status. He seeks the recognition of his contemporaries and social equals, who may possess similar heroic capabilities. Thus, a hero is always seeking acknowledgment from others who are also his competitors, who are always prepared to challenge his claims and to demand recognition for themselves, and thus who resist classification into an undifferentiated category of people among whom the hero stands out. Furthermore, because mortals' powers are not unfailing, as gods' are, they must be continuously displayed if they are to be continuously recognized. Thus the evaluations that prevail within a society are always subject to challenge and revision. This instability is tempered by the existence of institutionalized arrangements regularizing acknowledgment, such as the political institution of kingship, but even they do not guarantee stability, as Agamemnon's problems in the *Iliad* make clear. In the wartime setting that the *Iliad* depicts, this insecurity is especially acute for all heroes because they are called on to prove themselves constantly, and the chances of failure are very high. And because the expedition against Troy is a pan-Hellenic enterprise, it provides individual heroes, each of whom may be preeminent wherever he comes from, with the opportunity to win wider recognition from a larger and more far-flung group of people but also with a corresponding need to face greater danger and sharper competition.[6]

The *Odyssey*'s story of its hero's *nostos* is an account of his return to a place, his own home, where he should no longer need to compete with a group of peers to win recognition. Although the conditions of this setting limit the sphere in which he is recognized, they also eliminate the need to acknowledge and compete with the society of peers with whom he has constantly to come to terms during an enterprise undertaken jointly with other heroes away from home, such as the expedition against Troy. The great but also circumscribed advantages of operating within this sphere are well illustrated in the final episode of the *Odyssey,* where they are seen pursued to their limits. Odysseus is able to defend his house up to the boundary created by the edge of his holdings with a band of warriors composed of family members and dependents—his father, his son, and his family retainers—whose ability to help him is sufficient but falls short of threatening his own position of preeminence.[7] He does not, therefore, have to reach any accommodation with the unrelated contemporaries and social equals who shared both the burden and the glory during the expedition to Troy. All figures of that kind now appear as the enemy; the entire adult male population of Ithaca, with whom Odysseus must compete for any recognition outside his own household, is represented as a body of people with whom Odysseus is overtly and understandably in conflict.

Odysseus' near destruction of the last remaining Ithacans from the vantage of his own house illustrates, as does Achilles' near destruction of the Achaeans through his withdrawal from the Achaean cause, the way the hero's desire for preeminence makes him potentially hostile to the whole of the community of his peers that lies beyond his own family and household. If he can arrive at a position in which he no longer needs the cooperation of outsiders, then the hero can afford to become their enemy. This is something Achilles seems to achieve through the favor that Thetis obtains for him from Zeus, but the achievement proves illusory since Achilles cannot detach himself wholly from the Achaean cause. Odysseus attains a much truer state of self-sufficiency as he recovers his home, and would gladly dispense with the rest of Ithacan society if Athena did not finally intervene to preserve the larger community and to indicate the limits of his undisputed power. Odysseus achieves something similar to Achilles' impossible wish that he could forget the rest of the Achaeans and take the citadel of Troy, aided only by Patroclus, the one member of the Achaean army with whom he has a noncompetitive, quasi-familial relationship (*Il.* 16.97–100). Odysseus is actually able to win a war with the help only of those with whom he has the kind of relationship that Achilles has with Patroclus.[8]

As Odysseus achieves the genuine distance from the world of combat that Achilles only simulates, he becomes progressively less dependent on, and progressively more hostile towards, the various groups of men who, in successive settings, represent a society of his peers: the other Achaean warriors, his own companions on the homeward journey, the suitors, and finally the suitors' kinsmen. In its presentation of Odysseus' separation and distinction from his peers, the poem is able to find justification for their increasing treatment as his enemies. This justification is closely allied both to Odysseus' acquisition of continuous divine aid in the figure of

Athena, who is regularly at his side, and to his own assimilation to the role of a god.

It is with the suitors that Odysseus succeeds best in doing what every hero would like to do: he asserts an unqualified superiority over his rivals as he removes them forever. Furthermore, he does so in a setting in which this action represents the restoration of order and the execution of justice. The suitors define themselves as transgressors by choosing to compete with Odysseus in the one realm in which he ought not to have to compete with his peers, the household, in which he is entitled to a position of uncontested eminence created through a network of relationships with subordinates and dependents. This fundamental fact of human social organization is endorsed and charged with moral significance in the Homeric epics by the way a hero's claims are upheld systematically by the gods in this setting, as they are not in the less stable and highly competitive environment of the wartime camp. It is in relation to the rights and obligations of the individual household that the Homeric gods act according to principles that are sufficiently consistent to be identified with justice. They support heroes who are avenging offenses against the integrity of their households and impose certain obligations, associated with the institution of hospitality, on the household in its relations with the outside world.[9]

Odysseus acquires the undivided sponsorship of one of the gods only for that part of his story that is concerned with his repossession of his house. Although, as Nestor recalls (*Od.* 3.218–222), Athena has always shown favor to Odysseus, at Troy as well as elsewhere, in the *Iliad* she helps other heroes, such as Diomedes, as well, and in the *Odyssey* she is Odysseus' constant patron only during the time he is specifically engaged in regaining his house.[10] She actively helps him only from the moment he is destined to make his solitary journey from Calypso's island and shows open support for him only from the time he actually reaches the shores of Ithaca. As long as he is in the wider world beyond Ithaca, he is still in the realm where other heroes, with other gods helping them, have conflicting claims, which make Athena's partnership neither possible nor appropriate.

During the time of his wanderings, Odysseus is subject to the wrath that Athena turns against all of the returning Achaeans (*Od.* 5.105–109).[11] In Homer, divine wrath, whatever its often inscrutable cause, expresses itself at the point of mortal limitation; it is evoked against mortals as they experience the limits of their knowledge, cleverness, strength, or luck. Athena's generalized anger against the Achaeans corresponds to their time at sea, the time when they are outside the limited realm in which human society mitigates the violence and precariousness of human existence. Then Athena's help is unavailable to Odysseus, and Zeus sides with Polyphemus and Helios against him, despite Odysseus' claims to justice.[12]

Athena's aid to Odysseus becomes open only as his return progresses. First she works only behind the scenes, persuading Zeus to send Hermes to secure Odysseus' release from Calypso; in Phaeacia she herself acts to help him but, out of deference to Poseidon, appears only in disguise (*Od.* 6.328–331). It is only when he reaches Ithaca and is no longer subject to Poseidon's wrath that Athena appears to him openly and offers him unlimited support (*Od.* 13.341–343). And at the end of the poem, when Odysseus begins to move outside his household again, stepping beyond the boundaries of his farm to attack a segment of the Ithacan population that has not invaded his house, Athena no longer is automatically on his side; rather, she forces him to reach an accommodation with his rivals. He is now in a situation like that of the Achaean camp, in which he must acknowledge the claims of others who are his peers, and so her final epiphany is not, like earlier ones, a sign of unqualified support for his assertion of himself. It is, rather, like her appearance to Achilles at the beginning of the *Iliad*. Achilles interprets the appearance as a sign of partnership, asking her if she has come to witness Agamemnon's misdeeds. But Athena's appearance is actually inspired by Hera's equal love for Achilles and Agamemnon and is intended to stop Achilles from destroying his rival (*Il.* 1.193–218).

The values of the poem, then, are such that the suitors, by virtue of the setting they have chosen for themselves, condemn themselves to the role of the poem's villains and eventually to being the victims of a divine plot. The poem at once develops this characterization, portraying the suitors as murderous and uncivilized, and allows it to be seen that this characterization is a function of setting. Odysseus' role as just avenger is successfully established but not left entirely unquestioned.

In particular, Odysseus' treatment of the suitors as an undifferentiated group is shown to be questionable. He asserts an undiscriminating superiority to all of them and makes no attempt to recognize their individual merits or degrees of culpability. But, on the basis of the evidence presented by the *Odyssey*, it is, in fact, impossible to arrive at any stable collective characterization or moral assessment of the suitors. After Odysseus has decisively revealed both his identity and his intentions towards the suitors by killing Antinous, Eurymachus tries to save the others by claiming that only Antinous was to blame for the suitors' transgressions (*Od.* 22.45–59). Coming from Eurymachus, the speech is hypocritical, and the claim is false, but the underlying contention that not all the suitors are equally culpable has a merit that Odysseus chooses to ignore. Certainly the ringleaders, notably Eurymachus and Antinous, are more blameworthy than the others. Furthermore, the portrayal of the relationship between individual suitors and the suitors as a group, a relationship that is often expressed in the alternation between speeches attributed to the suitors as a whole and speeches attributed to individuals, tends to shift. For example, when Antinous throws a footstool at the disguised Odysseus in Book 17, the rest of the suitors collectively reproach him, reminding him of the possibility that the stranger could be a god (*Od.* 17.483–487). But when this episode is replayed in Book 18, and Eurymachus throws a footstool at the beggar, the suitors respond collectively by wishing the stranger had never come to ruin their feast (*Od.* 18.400–404), and only Amphinomus speaks up in favor of the stranger's rights (*Od.* 18.414–421).

Odysseus, however, absolves himself of any obligation to discriminate among the suitors. In the explanation he gives for his refusal to pardon the seer Leodes, he insists that if Leodes associated with the suitors he must have shared their unforgivable desire that he, Odysseus, never return to recover his house, and thus Leodes cannot escape their fate (*Od.* 22.322–325). That Odysseus' undiscriminating hostility to the suitors is a function of their situation in the house is most clear in the similarly unsettling episode in which Odysseus urges Amphinomus to leave, but Athena binds him there to be killed eventually by Telemachus (*Od.* 18.119–157). Athena looks out for Odysseus' interests in this episode by keeping even this sympathetic and upright rival in the one place where Odysseus' hostility has the unwavering support of the gods.[13]

The unqualified superiority that Odysseus asserts against the suitors is dramatized by his success in concealing his identity from them and taking them by surprise. The gap between the truth of their situation and their understanding of it defines a distance between them and him comparable to that between mortals and the gods whose epiphanies his self-revelation mimics. The failure of mortals to recognize a disguised god, which is a prominent feature of accounts of divine disguise in the Homeric epics and the Homeric Hymns, is echoed in the suitors' failure to recognize Odysseus. The significance of failed recognition in those parallel stories, especially as it relates to setting, can illuminate the role of similar failures in the *Odyssey*'s depiction of the suitors' just subordination to Odysseus. ⟨...⟩

No one on Ithaca can be expected to recognize Odysseus as long as he maintains his disguise, and no one does (with the exception of his dog, whose instincts even a disguise cannot baffle). But the nonrecognition of the suitors takes on an entirely different quality from that of Odysseus' loyal supporters; it can be related to broader failures of recognition of which they are also guilty. Odysseus' supporters are sometimes dull to the possibility, which always exists, that the gods could work a miracle, the fact of which Athena, as Mentor, reminds Telemachus that, "ῥεῖα θεός γ᾽ ἐθέλων καὶ τηλόθεν ἄνδρα σαώσαι," "A god, if he wished, could easily bring back a man, even from far away" (*Od.* 3.231), and this causes them to lose hope when they ought not to. When they express their despair in the presence of the disguised Odysseus, the resulting irony makes it clear that they are suffering beyond what is necessary. But Penelope's suitors not only are blind to the possibility of miracles but also fail to recognize the ordinary principles of human behavior that the gods routinely uphold.[14] The suitors ignore the alignment of the gods with the proper functioning of the household, an alignment that constitutes a pattern of divine behavior that ought to be recognizable even to mortals too shortsighted to identify a god when they see one. Thus, while the suitors cannot be expected to perceive Odysseus' presence, their failure to do so is bound up in their cases with their failure to recognize him in ways they can be expected to.

The suitors can be expected in a certain way to recognize Odysseus even when he is absent: they ought to recognize his right to his household even when he is not there to assert it or when it resides in a legitimate representative who is too weak to assert it. (Which of these possibilities actually describes the situation on Ithaca remains, in the absence of information about Odysseus' fate, unclear.) Thus the suitors can be expected to acknowledge Telemachus' right to the house even if he cannot yet defend it. Odysseus' entitlement to his household entitles him, in that one sphere, to the kind of recognition of his power, even when it is not manifested, that the gods can always claim.

The suitors can also be expected, in another way, to recognize Odysseus in the form in which he is present to them, the form of a homeless beggar. Whether or not they know who he is, they ought to receive him with hospitality and thereby to confer on him a measure of recognition. In the Homeric world, hospitality is a social institution that provides outsiders, who are by nature without status, with that place in society that constitutes an identity. As James Redfield puts it, "the household is obligated through household ceremonies to convert the stranger from a nonentity to a person with a status."[15]

On Ithaca, Odysseus' friends and enemies differ—not in their ability to see through his disguise, but in their willingness to accord him the kind of recognition entailed by hospitality. His supporters offer him an hospitable reception that (as we will see in the next chapter) both substitutes for and results in the recognition of his identity. In contrast, the suitors and their allies repeatedly reject him. And in doing so they are not simply failing to see his particular heroism as expressed by Athena's steady protection; they are failing to recognize the generalized association with divine protection that he enjoys as a stranger and suppliant. The suitors disregard an alliance between strangers and Zeus that anyone could be expected to recognize because it is expressed in a general principle—the principle that "πρὸς γὰρ Διος εἰσιν ἅπαντες / ξεῖνοί τε πτωχοί τε," "all strangers and beggars are under the protection of Zeus" (Od. 6.207–208)—rather than in a momentary and veiled encounter with a god. Concern for strangers is not an isolated event but a regular attribute of Zeus, who is referred to as "Ζεύς Ξείνιος," "Zeus, Protector of Strangers," or "Ζεύς Ἱκετήσιος," "Zeus, Protector of Suppliants." In addition, the suitors are blind to the universal precariousness of human fortune, the possibility that anyone might someday be a homeless wanderer, that makes Zeus' protection of strangers so necessary and so highly valued. The suitors miss the hints embedded in the stranger's fictional autobiography and lack the sense of potential similarity between Odysseus and the stranger that is, for Penelope (Od. 19.358–360) and for Eumaeus and Philoetius (Od. 21.204–207), a significant step towards recognition.

Odysseus' entrance into his household in a beggar's disguise broadens the significance of his return so that his personal triumph over his enemies becomes also an exemplary vindication of the laws of hospitality. Odysseus' achievement of recognition for his exceptional heroism simultaneously enforces the principle of social life that demands recognition even for those without status. As each interprets the meaning of the suitors' death, both Odysseus and Penelope point out that the suitors have inverted this principle: instead of honoring even poor beggars, they have honored no one, "οὔ τινα γὰρ τίεσκον ἐπιχθονίων ἀνθρώπων, / οὐ κακὸν οὐδὲ μὲν ἐσθλόν, ὅτις σφέας εἰσαφίκοιτο," "they honored no one of all earthly men / whether base or noble, who came to them" (Od. 22.414–415; 23.65–66). In other words, the suitors entirely misunderstood the nature of τιμή, "recognition": they honor only "οὖτις," "no one"—a contradiction in terms because to honor someone is to make him someone other than "οὖτις." Like the Cyclops, whose encounter with Odysseus this line recalls, the suitors help to create the disguise that enables Odysseus to defeat them. By making him "οὖτις," by keeping him unrecognized, they make themselves vulnerable to his surprise attack. Further, unlike the Cyclops, they are situated in the realm of human civilization so that they are expected to know better. Here Odysseus' claim to be acting in consort with Zeus and the other gods is not a hollow boast, as it is when he makes it to Polyphemus. ⟨. . .⟩

When the suitors are finally confronted with the actual figure of the disguised Odysseus, they give repeated demonstrations of their inability to recognize him and of the reckless disregard for his rights—both as Odysseus and as the stranger—that lies behind their failure. Odysseus tests them with veiled, hypothetical, or incomplete disclosures of his identity like the hints of his presence with which he animates Penelope. These disclosures may consist of the display of a godlike attribute or of victory in a contest or of a recognition that does not happen but is talked about, prophesied, or threatened. They correspond structurally and conceptually to the partial epiphanies with which disguised gods test mortals, such as Demeter's sudden transformation on the threshold of Celeus' house or Dionysus' evasion of his fetters. In these episodes the god's disguise slips a bit—indeed no mortal could recognize a god who wished to conceal his identity entirely—and mortals are tested by their reaction to or interpretation of this event.[16]

Odysseus' prolonged interaction with the suitors while he is in disguise becomes a protracted verbal battle over the interpretation of such episodes. The issue of their meaning becomes the focus of a growing hostility between them and the stranger that is the surface expression of the latent enmity between them and Odysseus. Their original refusal to recognize Odysseus' claims to his house, which has occurred in the past and in his absence, is recapitulated in their active inability to recognize his identity in the present and in his presence; their inability to recognize his identity is similarly recapitulated in their refusal to respond to him with hospitality.

While the issue of whether the suitors will suffer for these offenses is, in one sense, a matter of suspense and depends on the outcome of the trial of the bow, that contest is repeatedly anticipated—not for the poem's characters but for its audience—and repeatedly won by Odysseus in these preliminary verbal skirmishes. The suitors and Odysseus encounter each other in an arena of mutual deception in which the contest, as in the dialogue of Eurymachus and Telemachus at the end of Book 1 discussed above, is between forms of duplicity. Both Odysseus and the suitors often speak falsely, and both think that they understand and control the relationship between what they are saying and the actual truth. But only Odysseus knows the central, unrevealed fact on which their contest implicitly centers: his own return. For the audience of the poem the issue between Odysseus and the suitors becomes the question of who is in control of the meaning of his own words, of who controls the ironies that pervade their dialogue. And the issue of who controls the meaning of the dialogue comes to stand for the larger issue of who controls the territory in which the dialogue takes place, of who controls the house of Odysseus. In this poem, based on the premise that he who should control it will do so (for that is the meaning of the gods' support for Odysseus), the possession of the truth becomes equated with the right to possess the house. The narrative weight given to Odysseus' encounters with the suitors when he is still in disguise causes the question that is settled through action when he reveals himself, the question of who is stronger, to be recast and prejudged in another form, the question of who the stranger is. Odysseus' identity becomes the reference point for all the poem's evaluations, and the advantage to Odysseus of this shift is one more expression of the advantage that he gains from his disguise.

Odysseus' victory in his fight with the beggar Irus in Book 18 is one of the most overt of his partial epiphanies, and it generates a revealing debate about its meaning.[17] Odysseus conceals its significance, modifying the spectacular feat of which he might be capable to prevent the suitors from recognizing him (*Od.* 18.94). But the suitors still condemn themselves through their misinterpretation of Odysseus' victory. They thank Odysseus for ridding them of Irus, whom they will now ship off to the mainland, and they say that they hope Zeus and the other gods will grant Odysseus whatever he desires most. Odysseus, we are told, "χαῖρεν δὲ κληηδόνι," "was pleased at the omen" (*Od.* 18.117). The suitors, having seen only a display of power sufficient to defeat Irus, interpret it as only that and respond with a cheerful generosity that would never extend to someone they considered competition for themselves. But the redefinition of their speech as an omen, in which poet and hero conspire in the construction of line 117 (and have already conspired in the presentation of Odysseus in disguise), takes its meaning out of their hands and turns it against them. The susceptibility of their words to this treatment is itself a sign of the inevitable defeat those words now invoke; the suitors' inadvertent irony causes them, in effect, to work towards their own defeat.

As a verbal battle develops between Odysseus and his supporters, and the suitors and their supporters, over the significance of this and other such events, the unacknowledged conflict over who is speaking the truth becomes a purposeful and explicit conflict over who is capable of perceiving the truth, a conflict in which the suitors actively betray their ignorance. Shortly after the battle with Irus, Odysseus gives a more subtle hint of his power by offering to tend the lamps in the hall.[18] This partial epiphany is instantly rejected in an abusive speech by the suitors' accomplice, Melantho. She treats Odysseus' offer as a form of madness, which she attributes either to drunkenness or to overconfidence after his victory over Irus, and she goes on to warn him against meeting a better man than Irus. Thus, she equates what we know to be an accurate response to his victory with madness (*Od.* 18.327–336).

Shortly afterwards Eurymachus refers to Odysseus with what he thinks is a parody of a speech acknowledging a divine epiphany.

> οὐκ ἀθεεὶ ὅδ' ἀνὴρ Ὀδυσήϊον ἐς δόμον ἵκει·
> ἔμπης μοι δοκέει δαΐδων σέλας ἔμμεναι αὐτοῦ
> κὰκ κεφαλῆς, ἐπεὶ οὔ οἱ ἔνι τρίχες οὐδ' ἠβαιαί.

Not without divine providence has this man come to the house of Odysseus.
It certainly seems to me that he can provide torchlight
from his head, since there aren't any hairs on it, not even a few.

(Od. 18.353–355)

Not only is Eurymachus unwittingly speaking the truth about Odysseus' association
with the gods, but his speech precisely indicates that his mistake is due to Odysseus'
disguise. The feature of Odysseus' appearance that he makes fun of by pretending
to claim that it makes him godlike—Odysseus' baldness—is actually part of his
disguise; in that sense it does make him godlike.

Odysseus responds, in essence, by suggesting a recognition scene. In response
to Eurymachus' taunting offer of work on his estate, Odysseus proposes a contest
between the two of them and claims that he would win it (Od. 18.365–380). He
then turns against Eurymachus the kind of accusation he himself has already had
from Melantho. He impugns Eurymachus' mental faculties, claiming that his opponent is incapable of accurate judgment, and then goes on to warn Eurymachus of
a more formidable enemy—in this case, Odysseus.

ἀλλὰ μάλ᾽ ὑβρίζεις καί τοι νόος ἐστὶν ἀπηνής·
καί πού τις δοκέεις μέγας ἔμμεναι ἠδὲ κραταιός,
οὕνεκα πὰρ παύροισι καὶ οὐκ ἀγαθοῖσιν ὁμιλεῖς.
εἰ δ᾽ Ὀδυσεὺς ἔλθοι καὶ ἵκοιτ᾽ ἐς πατρίδα γαῖαν,
αἶψά κέ τοι τὰ θύρετρα, καὶ εὐρέα περ μάλ᾽ ἐόντα,
φεύγοντι στείνοιτο διὲκ προθύροιο θύραζε.

But now you insult me and your spirit is harsh,
and doubtless you think of yourself as someone tall and powerful
because you associate with few men and ones who aren't brave.
But if Odysseus should return and reach his fatherland,
suddenly the gates of the house, although they are very broad,
would hem you in as you fled out through the door.   (Od. 18.381–386)

The last three lines of this speech vividly express the idea that this whole series of
episodes illustrates, the idea that the recognition of Odysseus that will eventually be
forced upon the suitors will involve a sudden and dramatic reversal of their perceptions.

Eurymachus responds in the same words used by Melantho: he suggests that
Odysseus must be drunk, deranged, or overly elated by his victory (Od. 18.389–
393). While Odysseus' speech may represent a veiled self-revelation, to Eurymachus it is simply an act of insolence by someone he refuses to accept as a guest.
When he converts words into action by throwing the pitcher, his blindness to
Odysseus' presence takes the form of an inhospitable act, and the debate over who
is sane is expanded to serve as a test of hospitality, as well. The suitors respond by
rejecting the guest who has proved an irritant rather than the boorishness of
Eurymachus: they wish the guest had never come and complain that the quarrel he
has provoked is ruining the feast (Od. 18.401–404). This complaint is countered by

two speeches in favor of Odysseus that, taken together, reinforce the links between receptivity to the stranger's outlook, sanity, and hospitality. Telemachus, knowing the stranger's identity, identifies his own view with sanity, and accuses the suitors of being mad or drunk themselves; he also, in effect, corrects their identification of the stranger, suggesting that it is a god, not a beggar, who has stirred them up (*Od.* 18.406–409). His speech is seconded by Amphinomus who, dissociating himself from the rest of the suitors, proposes that Telemachus has spoken justly and should be allowed to treat the stranger as his guest (*Od.* 18.414–421).

The conflict between Odysseus and the suitors, which is, at base, a conflict over whether they have to acknowledge his authority when he is not there to enforce it, has become a conflict over whose perceptions are reliable. In this conflict each accuses the other of distorted vision, but it is Odysseus and his supporters who possess the truth. This conflict continues right up until the moment of Odysseus' disclosure. Theoclymenus' fantastic vision is yet another intimation of Odysseus' presence and elicits another accusation of insanity from Eurymachus (*Od.* 20.360–362). Here, too, the contrast in perceptions is identified with a contrast in attitudes toward hospitality. Eurymachus associates Theoclymenus' madness with his foreignness (*Od.* 20.360), and when Theoclymenus goes off to be received properly by Peiraeus, the suitors taunt Telemachus about his two guests and suggest they should be sold into slavery (*Od.* 20.376–384).

On the day of the trial, each move Odysseus makes as he comes closer to actually revealing his identity is wildly misinterpreted by the suitors. When Odysseus asks to take the bow, Antinous, like Melantho and Eurymachus in Book 18, assumes he must be deranged (*Od.* 21.288–292). He accuses him of being drunk and goes on to cite the highly inappropriate parallel of the centaur Eurytium—an exemplum that applies far better to the suitors than to Odysseus[19]—and to make an inaccurate prediction about what will happen if Odysseus should succeed in stringing the bow (*Od.* 21.305–310). When Odysseus takes the bow and examines it in a proprietary fashion, the suitors contemptuously decide that he must be either a craftsman or a thief. This failure of recognition is followed by another unintentionally ominous statement (*Od.* 21.397–403). Odysseus' success in stringing the bow and shooting through the axes should tell the suitors who he is, especially since that success is confirmed by *sēmata*, "signs," from Zeus. Yet it does not, although Odysseus himself points out that his feat his discredited their perceptions: "ἔτι μοι μένος ἔμπεδον ἐστιν, / οὐκ ὡς με μνηστῆρες ἀτιμάζοντες ὄνονται," "My strength is still steady, / not as the suitors scornfully claimed, doing me no honor" (*Od.* 21.426–427). When he directs his next arrow at Antinous, his victim is taken completely by surprise, not understanding that the situation has changed, that this is no longer a normal feast. Nor do the rest of the suitors realize even then. They believe, as they have often before, that Odysseus could not have acted as he did intentionally, misinterpreting entirely the situation and its consequences for them.

'Ίσκεν ἕκαστος ἀνήρ, ἐπεὶ ἦ φάσαν οὐκ ἐθέλοντα
ἄνδρα κατακτεῖναι· τὸ δὲ νήπιοι οὐκ ἐνόησαν,
ὡς δή σφιν καὶ πᾶσιν ὀλέθρου πείρατ' ἐφῆπτο.

Each one was speculating, for they really thought he had not intended
to kill the man. The fools did not realize
that upon every one of them the bonds of death had been fastened.

(*Od.* 22.31–33)

The suitors, particularly when viewed as group and not as represented chiefly by Eurymachus, often seem to be the victims of a divine plot that they can hardly be expected to discern; thus they seem to represent the perpetual disadvantage of all mortals in a world controlled by gods capable of deceiving them. But in the *Odyssey* that divine plot is paralleled by a human plot that is not a secret conspiracy but a public network of benefits and obligations binding people together in a more-or-less orderly society; the *Odyssey*'s world is such that those who observe that human plot do not have to uncover the divine one. A final example of an episode in which the suitors' blindness is contrasted to Odysseus' knowledge will illustrate how these two plots can parallel each other.

During the battle between Odysseus and the suitors, Athena makes an appearance disguised as Mentor. Odysseus recognizes her but does not show that he does, addressing her as if she were Mentor.

"Μέντορ, ἄμυνον ἀρήν, μνῆσαι δ' ἑτάροιο φίλοιο,
ὅς σ' ἀγαθὰ ῥέζεσκον· ὁμηλικίη δέ μοί ἐσσι."
ὣς φάτ', ὀϊόμενος λαοσσόον ἔμμεν' Ἀθήνην.

"Mentor, come to my aid, remember me, your beloved companion,
I who have done you many favors. For you grew up with me."
Thus he spoke, but he thought it was Athena, rouser of armies.

(*Od.* 22.208–210)

One of the suitors, Agelaus, failing to recognize the goddess, also addresses her as if she were Mentor: he warns Mentor against joining with Odysseus, saying that when Odysseus is defeated, as he surely will be, the suitors will kill Mentor and deprive his wife and children of their house (*Od.* 22.213–223). The issue of recognition is, in a sense, irrelevant to the significance of this exchange: the critical difference between Odysseus and the suitors is made clear in terms of human morality, in the difference between the respect with which Odysseus addresses Mentor and the boorish disregard with which Agelaus tries to bully him. The overt content of Odysseus' speech is an adequate substitute for the recognition it conceals; it replaces direct acknowledgment of Athena's divinity with a gesture towards the kind of recognition that occurs between men, an attempt to revive a long-standing and reciprocally beneficial relationship.

The substitution that Odysseus makes here deliberately and slyly can also be made unwittingly. By following the scenarios written for them by society, especially scenarios for the reception of strangers (one of the most ritualized activities in the Homeric world and one of the most clearly patterned sequences in Homeric narrative), characters can act in ways that compensate for their failure to see through a disguise and that even eventually lead to the removal of that disguise.

NOTES

[1] The use here of εἰ with the indicative is of the type that Pierre Chantraine categorizes as serving "pour poser une hypothèse comme realisée" (*Grammaire homérique* [Paris: Librairie C. Klincksieck, 1958, 1963], II, 416, p. 283) and thus expresses well that Eurymachus regards Odysseus' identification as a hypothesis, not a fact. Cf. the closely parallel statements made by Penelope and Laertes before they are willing to recognize Odysseus at *Od.* 23.107–109 and 24.328–329.

[2] It is significant that Amphimedon here acknowledges Odysseus' heroic character through his use of the epithet "πολύτλας," "much-enduring." Usually when the suitors refer to Odysseus, they do not use those epithets that characterize him as intelligent or enduring. See Norman Austin, *Archery at the Dark of the Moon* (Berkeley: University of California Press, 1975), 51.

[3] Amphimedon's account occurs in a context in which recognition in a variety of forms is a dominant motif: when the suitors' shades arrive, Achilles is hearing an account of the funeral with which the Achaeans honored him after his death; the encounter begins when Agamemnon recognizes Amphime-don (*Od.* 24.102) and they revive their old relationship of guest-friendship; after Amphimedon's narrative, Agamemnon offers a speech of praise for Odysseus and, especially, Penelope, in which he prophesies that Penelope will win undying *kleos* for her fidelity.

[4] This notion of honor that is not only permanent but also uninterrupted is expressed in the adjective *aphthiton*, "unfailing," which is regularly applied to *kleos*. As Gregory Nagy has shown, the basic association of this adjective is with a continuous or unfailing stream of liquid. *Comparative Studies in Greek and Indic Meter* (Cambridge, Mass.: Harvard University Press, 1974), 244.

[5] In the *Iliad* Hector twice formulates a fantasy of being immortal or the child of a god as a desire to be honored just as Athena and Apollo are honored (*Il.* 8.540; 13.827). While this aspiration may be fulfilled outside epic in the institution of the hero cult, within epic, as Gregory Nagy points out (*The Best of the Achaeans* [Baltimore: The Johns Hopkins University Press, 1977], esp. 148–150), it is impossible and heroes are obliged to act within the constraints of mortality, searching for honor that simulates that of the gods. Thus Sarpedon includes in the list of honors that heroes fight for that "πάντες δὲ θεοὺς ὡς εἰσορόωσι," "all men look on us as if we were gods" (*Il.* 12.312); the members of Agamemnon's embassy promise Achilles that if he returns to them the Achaeans will honor him like a god (*Il.* 9.302, 603); and heroes are frequently said to be honored by their communities as if they were gods if they hold an office that routinely confers honor, either the political office of king (*Il.* 9.155, 297; 10.33; 11.58; 13.218; cf. Hesiod *Theogony* 91) or the religious office of priest (*Il.* 5.78; 16.605). While these expressions may contain latent references to cult worship, as Nagy has recently argued ("On the Death of Sarpedon," in *Approaches to Homer*, edited by Carl A. Rubino and Cynthia W. Shelmerdine [Austin: The University of Texas Press, 1983], 197–203), their recurrent formulation as a comparison maintains the distinction between men and gods that the worship of heroes blurs. The focus of the epics remains on the glory men win as men and through human institutions (note the emphasis in these expressions on the *dēmos*, the people, as the source of honor).

[6] A good example of a hero who is greatly honored at home but eclipsed by others when he comes to Troy is Thoas, who is not a particularly prominent hero in the *Iliad* but is said to be "the best of the Aetolians" (*Il.* 15.282) and to be honored like a god by the *dēmos* (*Il.* 13.218).

[7] Not only can Odysseus rely only on family members, but he can rely only on family members whose relationship to him is notably unequal, for he has no brothers. In other words, he lacks the kind of relative with whom he would have a relationship most similar to the one between fellow warriors who are not related by blood. This may seem to be a disadvantage, because it means that he cannot put together even a rudimentary army to confront the suitors. But it can also be seen as an advantage: it requires Odysseus to adopt the kind of clandestine strategy at which he excels and for which he can

get all the glory. The underlying advantage of brotherlessness is indicated obliquely during the encounter between Odysseus and Telemachus in Book 16: Odysseus asks Telemachus if it is because his brothers are inadequate to help him that he is oppressed by the suitors (*Od.* 16.95–98), and Telemachus explains that he has no brothers by citing his genealogy, thus pointing to the source of his and Odysseus' power (*Od.* 16.118–120).

[8] Not only does the *Odyssey* focus on Odysseus' actions in the context in which he can be solely triumphant, but in it Odysseus describes the taking of Troy in terms that surpass even Achilles' wish, claiming to have destroyed the city in partnership only with Athena (*Od.* 13.388). See Pietro Pucci, "The Proem of the *Odyssey*," *Arethusa* 15 (1982): 44–45. On the other hand, when he conceals his identity from the Cyclops, Odysseus must suppress that claim and so gives all the credit for the taking of Troy to Agamemnon (*Od.* 9.264–266).

[9] On the inconsistency between the view of the gods as just that is associated with the account of Odysseus' return to Ithaca and the view of them as arbitrary and capricious that is associated with the account of Odysseus' adventures, see Bernard Fenik, *Studies in the* Odyssey, (Wiesbaden: F. Steiner, 1974), 209–227; Jenny Strauss Clay, *The Wrath of Athena* (Princeton: Princeton University Press, 1983), 213–239. Awareness of this opposition within the *Odyssey* must qualify any attempt to distinguish between the morality of the *Odyssey* and the morality of the *Iliad* along the lines suggested by Werner Jaeger ("Solons Eunomie," *Sitzungsberichte der Preussischen Akademie der Wissenschaften, Phil. hist. k.* 11 [1926]: 69–85) and Felix Jacoby ["Die geistige Physiognomie der *Odyssee*," *Die Antike* 9 [1933]: 159–194). On the way the *Odyssey* contrasts settings in which human institutions, such as agriculture and sacrifice, are operative with settings in which they are not, see Pierre Vidal-Naquet, "Valeurs religieuses et mythiques de la terre et du sacrifice dans l'*Odyssée*."

[10] Cf. Jenny Strauss Clay's explanation of Athena's resumption of support for Odysseus: "It is not so much Odysseus himself, but the pressure of events on Ithaca that compels Athena to release Odysseus and to bring him home to set things right." *The Wrath of Athena*, 234.

[11] Odysseus' exposure to Athena's wrath is discussed at length by Jenny Strauss Clay, who argues that Odysseus does not simply suffer from Athena's wrath by virtue of being one of the returning Achaeans, but that he provokes her wrath through his nearly godlike cleverness. *The Wrath of Athena*, 43–53, 209.

[12] When Odysseus is in transit between this world and his home, Zeus plays a role that could be called transitional, siding partly with Poseidon and partly with Odysseus as he negotiates a reduced punishment for the Phaeacians.

[13] In these respects the treatment of the suitors should be compared to that of Odysseus' companions. They too are presented as an undifferentiated group, and the fact that they die while Odysseus survives (which is an essential element of his return—cf. *Od.* 13.340) is attributed to their own reckless actions. This is especially true in the prologue, in which the justification of Odysseus' return without his companions is made virtually the first business of the poem. (Cf. especially the characterization of their behavior as "*atasthalia*," "reckless actions," a term that, as Jenny Strauss Clay has recently shown, is used "to place the blame for a destructive act on one party while absolving another." *The Wrath of Athena* 37.) The actual narrative of the homeward journey, like the overall portrayal of the suitors, shows, however, that Odysseus' companions cannot be so easily lumped together or blamed for their own destruction. They are not all lost under the same circumstances, and the loss of those who survive the encounters with the Ciconians, the Cyclops, and Scylla is doubly motivated, stemming both from Odysseus' refusal to forego identifying himself to the Cyclops (*Od.* 9.533–535) and from the companions' own inability to resist the temptation to eat the cattle of the sun (*Od.* 11.114–115). In accord with their situation in the story of the homeward journey rather than in the hero's house, the case against Odysseus' companions is made much more mildly than that against the suitors; it has an ambiguous quality that corresponds to their intermediate position between Odysseus' highly esteemed fellow warriors in the Achaean camp and his deadly enemies, the suitors. Odysseus' refusal to accept any of the companions as a legitimate rival is dramatized when he overreacts to Eurylochus' challenge to his leadership (*Od.* 10.428–448). Eurylochus' claim to compete with Odysseus is reinforced by the fact that he is Odysseus' close kinsman (*Od.* 10.441).

[14] For a detailed account of the suitors' transgressions against the laws of human society and of the importation of the bestial into the realm of civilization, see Suzanne Saïd, "Les Crimes des prétendants, la maison d'Ulysse et les festins de l'*Odyssée*," *Études de Littérature Ancienne,* Paris (1979): 9–49.

[15] James Redfield, *Nature and Culture in the* Iliad (Chicago: The University of Chicago Press, 1975), 197–198. To be another person's guest is to be someone. When being someone's guest is institution-

alized in the relationship of guest-friendship, that simple recognition can become a permanent and impressive mark of identity. "Mentes," for example, identifies himself to Telemachus in part by saying that he and Odysseus claim one another as guest-friends (*Od.* 1.187–188). Like other aspects of identity, guest-friendship is not only permanent but also inheritable. Telemachus, as he both discovers and discloses his heritage as son of Odysseus, inherits his father's relations of guest-friendship with Nestor and Menelaus. As a way of institutionalizing mutual recognition between people who are usually absent from one another, guest-friendship is an important example of a social institution that systematically assures for mortals the continuous recognition that the gods enjoy. Very good hosts, such as the Phaeacians, are said to honor their guest as if he were a god (*Od.* 5.36; 19.280; 23.339).

[16] Cf. the remarks on Odysseus' repeated rejection by the suitors of Albert Lord, who writes, "These incidents are multiforms of a single theme . . . whose meaning, deeply imbedded in the myth underlying the story, is that the resurrected god in disguise is rejected by the unworthy, who cannot recognize him." *The Singer of Tales* (Cambridge: Mass.: Harvard University Press, 1960), 175.

[17] As Albert Lord puts it, this episode is "a frustrated, a vestigial recognition scene brought about by accomplishing a feat of strength possible only to the returned hero" that is closely parallel to the trial of the bow. *The Singer of Tales,* 175. Before fighting Irus, Odysseus is transformed physically by Athena, and as in other recognition scenes, there is the suggestion of rejuvenation. The battle is, several times, treated as a contest of young against old (*Od.* 18.21, 31, 52–53); thus, this contest is, like the final one (cf. *Od.* 21.282–284), a test of whether Odysseus' strength is what it was in his youth. Odysseus puts aside his rags in much the same gesture as accompanies his ultimate self-disclosure during the contest of the bow (*Od.* 18.67, cf.22.1). The response is that which usually follows an act of self-revelation or a divine epiphany: amazement (*Od.* 18.71). When the contest is over, Odysseus takes up his wallet once again, effectively reassuming his entire disguise (*Od.* 18.108–109). For further parallels between this episode and the contest of the bow, see Daniel Levine, "*Odyssey* 18: Iros as Paradigm for the Suitors," *Classical Journal* 77 (1982): 200–204.

[18] Odysseus' offer suggests the sudden bright light which is one of the most common features of a divine epiphany. See N. J. Richardson, *The Homeric Hymn to Demeter* (Oxford: Clarendon Press, 1974), 189. For radiance as a sign of the hero, see Michael Nagler, *Spontaneity and Tradition* (Berkeley: University of California Press, 1974), 117–118; Cedric H. Whitman, *Homer and the Heroic Tradition* (Cambridge, Mass.: Harvard University Press, 1958), 128–153. Cf. also *Od.* 4.71–75, where Telemachus thinks Menelaus' palace must be like Zeus' because everything is gleaming, and *Od.* 19.34, where Athena reveals herself to Odysseus and Telemachus by providing a light for them as they remove the armor from the hall.

[19] See the discussion of this passage by W. Büchner, "Die Penelopeszenen in der *Odyssee,*" *Hermes* 75 (1940), 161.

CHRONOLOGY

c. 700 B.C.E.	Setting down of the *Iliad* and the *Odyssey*
c. 490 B.C.E.	Pindar, *Nemean Ode* 7
c. 440 B.C.E.	Sophocles, *Ajax*
425 B.C.E.	Euripides, *Hecuba*
409 B.C.E.	Sophocles, *Philoctetes*
c. 408 B.C.E.	Euripides, *Cyclops*
c. 1307–21	Dante, *Inferno*
c. 1602	Shakespeare writes *Troilus and Cressida* (published 1609)
1833	Tennyson writes "Ulysses" (published in *Poems,* 1842)
1922	James Joyce, *Ulysses*
1938	Nikos Kazantzakis, *Odyseia* (English translation 1958)

CONTRIBUTORS

HAROLD BLOOM is Sterling Professor of the Humanities at Yale University and Henry W. and Albert A. Berg Professor of English at the New York University Graduate School. He is a 1985 MacArthur Foundation Award recipient, served as the Charles Eliot Norton Professor of Poetry at Harvard University (1987–88), and is the author of nineteen books, the most recent being *The Book of J* (1990). Currently he is editing the Chelsea House series Modern Critical Views and The Critical Cosmos, and other Chelsea House series in literary criticism.

GEORGE DE F. LORD is a former Professor of English at Yale University. Among his many books are *Homeric Renaissance: The* Odyssey *of George Chapman* (1956), *Heroic Mockery: Variations on Epic Themes from Homer to Joyce* (1977), *Trials of the Self: Heroic Ideals in the Epic Tradition* (1983), and *Classical Presences in Seventeenth-Century English Poetry* (1987).

G. E. DIMOCK, JR. is Professor Emeritus of Classical Languages and Literatures at Smith College. He is the author of *The Unity of the* Odyssey (1989), has translated Euripides' *Iphigeneia at Aulis* (1978; with W. S. Merwin), and has written articles on Homer, Aeschylus, Euripides, and Vergil.

HUGH KENNER, one of the most distinguished critics of our time, is Andrew W. Mellon Professor of the Humanities at Johns Hopkins University. Among his many works are *Flaubert, Joyce and Beckett: The Stoic Comedians* (1962), *The Pound Era* (1971), *A Colder Eye: The Modern Irish Writers* (1983), *The Mechanic Muse* (1987), and *A Sinking Island: The Modern English Writers* (1988). He has also written books on G. K. Chesterton, James Joyce, and T. S. Eliot.

GEORGE SCOUFFAS, Professor of English at the University of Illinois, has also written on J. F. Powers.

W. R. ELTON, Professor of English at the City University of New York Graduate School, is the author of King Lear *and the Gods* (1966) and *Shakespeare's World: Renaissance Intellectual Contexts* (1979; with Giselle Schlesinger).

R. F. STORCH is a Associate Professor Emeritus of English at Tufts University. He has written articles on Coleridge and Romantic poetry.

MICHAEL BEAUSANG teaches at the Sorbonne and has written articles on Samuel Beckett, Andrey Sinyavsky, and *Finnegans Wake.*

JOHN FRECCERO is Rosina Pierotti Professor of French and Italian at Stanford University. He is the author of *Dante: The Poetics of Conversion* (1986) and editor of *Dante: A Collection of Critical Essays* (1965).

MARTHA NUSSBAUM is Professor of Philosophy and Classics at Brown University. She has compiled an edition with commentary of Aristotle's *De Motu Animalium* (1978) and has written *The Fragility of Goodness: Luck and Ethics in Greek Tragedy and Philosophy* (1986), and has edited G. E. L. Owen's *Logic, Science, and Dialectic: Collected Papers in Greek Philosophy* (1986).

RICHARD ELLMANN was, until his death in 1987, Goldsmiths' Professor of English Literature at Oxford University and Fellow of New College, Oxford. His principal publications are *The Identity of Yeats* (1954), *James Joyce* (1959), *Ulysses on the Liffey* (1972), *The Consciousness of Joyce* (1977), *Oscar Wilde* (1987), and *A Long the Riverrun: Selected Essays* (1988).

JEAN PÉPIN is the author of *Mythe et allégorie: Les Origines grecques et les contestations judeo-chrétiennes* (1958), *Dante et la tradition de l'allégorie* (1970), and *Idées grecques sur l'homme et sur Dieu* (1971).

R. B. RUTHERFORD is Lecturer in Classical Languages and Literature at Christ Church, Oxford. He has written *The* Meditations *of Marcus Aurelius: A Study* (1989).

SHEILA MURNAGHAN, Professor of Classics at the University of Pennsylvania, is the author of *Disguise and Recognition in the* Odyssey (1987) and of articles on Homer and Sophocles.

BIBLIOGRAPHY

Adamson, Jane. *Troilus and Cressida.* Boston: Twayne, 1987.

Adkins, Arthur W. H. "Basic Greek Values in Euripides' *Hecuba* and *Hercules Furens.*" *Classical Quarterly* 16 (1966): 193–219.

Almeida, Hermione de. *Byron and Joyce through Homer.* London: Macmillan, 1981.

Andersen, Øyvind. "Odysseus and the Wooden Horse." *Symbolae Osloenses* 52 (1977): 5–18.

Anderson, Linda. "Problem Comedies." In *A Kind of Wild Justice: Revenge in Shakespeare's Comedies.* Newark: University of Delaware Press, 1987, pp. 127–44.

Austin, Norman. *Archery at the Dark of the Moon: Poetic Problems in Homer's* Odyssey. Berkeley: University of California Press, 1975.

———. "Name Magic in the *Odyssey.*" *California Studies in Classical Antiquity* 5 (1972): 1–19.

Banks, G. V. "Giraudoux's Ulysse in Word and Deed." In *Literature and Society: Studies in Nineteenth and Twentieth Century French Literature Presented to R. J. North,* edited by C. A. Burns. Birmingham: University of Birmingham, 1980, pp. 153–65.

Baum, Paull F. "A Note on 'Ulysses.'" In *Tennyson: Sixty Years After.* Chapel Hill: University of North Carolina Press, 1948, pp. 299–303.

Belmont, David E. "Twentieth-Century Odysseus." *Classical Journal* 62 (1966): 49–56.

Beye, Charles Rowan. *The* Iliad, *the* Odyssey, *and the Epic Tradition.* Garden City, NY: Doubleday/Anchor, 1966.

Bien, Peter. *Kazantzakis: Politics of the Spirit.* Princeton: Princeton University Press, 1989.

Blundell, Mary Whitlock. *Helping Friends and Harming Enemies: A Study in Sophocles and Greek Ethics.* Cambridge: Cambridge University Press, 1989.

———. "The Moral Character of Odysseus in *Philoctetes.*" *Greek, Roman, and Byzantine Studies* 28 (1987): 307–29.

Bowra, C. M. *Sophoclean Tragedy.* Oxford: Clarendon Press, 1944.

Bradley, Edward M. "The Hybris of Odysseus." *Soundings* 51 (1968): 33–44.

Brooks, Harold. *"Troilus and Cressida:* Its Dramatic Unity and Genre." In *"Fanned and Winnowed Opinions": Shakespearean Essays Presented to Harold Jenkins,* edited by John W. Mahon and Thomas A. Pendleton. London: Methuen, 1987, pp. 6–25.

Brown, Calvin S. "Odysseus and Polyphemus: The Name and the Curse." *Comparative Literature* 18 (1966): 193–202.

Campbell, Oscar James. *Comicall Satyre and Shakespeare's* Troilus and Cressida. San Marino, CA: Huntington Library, 1938.

Chiasson, E. J. "Tennyson's 'Ulysses'—A Re-interpretation." *University of Toronto Quarterly* 23 (1953–54): 402–9.

Clarke, Howard W. *The Art of the* Odyssey. Englewood Cliffs, NJ: Prentice-Hall, 1967.

Considine, P. "Moses and Odysseus." *Proceedings of the African Classical Associations* 10 (1967): 23–28.

Culler, A. Dwight. "From Ulysses to Sir Bedivere." In *The Poetry of Tennyson.* New Haven: Yale University Press, 1977, pp. 84–105.

Dasenbrock, Reed Way. *"Ulysses* and Joyce's Discovery of Vico's 'True Homer.'" *Éire-Ireland* 20 (1985): 96–108.

293

Dimock, George E. *The Unity of the* Odyssey. Amherst: University of Massachusetts Press, 1989.

Duncan, Edgar Hill. "Tennyson: A Modern Appraisal." *Tennessee Studies in Literature* 4 (1959): 13–30.

Eagleton, Terence. *"Troilus and Cressida."* In *Shakespeare and Society.* New York: Schocken Books, 1967, pp. 13–38.

Ellmann, Richard. *Ulysses on the Liffey.* New York: Oxford University Press, 1972.

Everett, Barbara. "The Inaction of *Troilus and Cressida.*" *Essays in Criticism* 32 (1982): 119–39.

Farron, S. G. "The *Odyssey* as an Anti-Aristocratic Statement." *Studies in Antiquity* 1 (1979–80): 59–101.

Findlay, L. M. "Sensation and Memory in Tennyson's 'Ulysses.'" *Victorian Poetry* 19 (1981): 139–49.

Finley, John H. *Homer's* Odyssey. Cambridge, MA: Harvard University Press, 1978.

Finley, M. I. *The World of Odysseus.* New York: Viking Press, 1954.

Flaumenhaft, Mera J. "The Undercover Hero: Odysseus from Dark to Daylight." *Interpretation* 10 (1982): 9–41.

Galperin, William H. "The Defeat of the Suitors: Homer and Joyce Once More." *James Joyce Quarterly* 20 (1982–83): 455–59.

Gilbert, Stuart. *James Joyce's* Ulysses: *A Study.* New York: Knopf, 1930.

Goldberg, S. L. *The Classical Temper: A Study of James Joyce's* Ulysses. London: Chatto & Windus, 1961.

Goslee, David. *Tennyson's Characters: "Strange Faces, Other Minds."* Iowa City: University of Iowa Press, 1989.

Gray, Wallace. *Homer to Joyce.* New York: Macmillan, 1985.

Griffin, Jasper. *Homer on Life and Death.* Oxford: Clarendon Press, 1980.

Grudin, Robert. "Ulyssean Irony in *Troilus and Cressida.*" *Anglia* 93 (1975): 55–69.

Havelock, Eric A. "Parmenides and Odysseus." *Harvard Studies in Classical Philology* 63 (1958): 133–43.

Heatherington, M. E. "Chaos, Order, and Cunning in the *Odyssey.*" *Studies in Philology* 73 (1976): 225–38.

Hogan, James C. "The Temptation of Odysseus." *Transactions and Proceedings of the American Philological Association* 106 (1976): 187–210.

Hogan, Patrick Cohn. "Lapsarian Odysseus: Joyce, Milton, and the Structure of *Ulysses.*" *James Joyce Quarterly* 24 (1986–87): 55–72.

Holtsmark, Erling B. "Spiritual Rebirth of the Hero: Odyssey 5." *Classical Journal* 61 (1965–66): 206–10.

Kain, Richard M. *Fabulous Voyager: James Joyce's* Ulysses. Chicago: University of Chicago Press, 1947.

Kaula, David. "Will and Reason in *Troilus and Cressida.*" *Shakespeare Quarterly* 12 (1961): 271–83.

Kearns, Emily. "The Return of Odysseus: A Homeric Theoxeny." *Critical Quarterly* 32 (1982): 2–8.

Kimbrough, Robert. *Shakespeare's* Troilus and Cressida *and Its Setting.* Cambridge, MA: Harvard University Press, 1964.

Kirkwood, G. M. *A Study of Sophoclean Drama.* Ithaca: Cornell University Press, 1958.

Kitto, H. D. F. "The *Odyssey.*" In *Poiesis: Structure and Thought.* Berkeley: University of California Press, 1966, pp. 116–52.

Kleinstuck, Johannes. "Ulysses' Speech on Degree as Related to the Play of *Troilus and Cressida.*" *Neophilologus* 43 (1959): 58–63.

Knight, W. F. Jackson. *Many-Minded Homer: An Introduction.* Edited by John D. Christie. London: George Allen & Unwin, 1968.

Knights, L. C. "The Theme of Appearance and Reality in *Troilus and Cressida.*" In *Some Shakespearean Themes.* London: Chatto & Windus, 1959, pp. 65–83.

Knox, Bernard M. W. *The Heroic Temper: Studies in Sophoclean Tragedy.* Berkeley: University of California Press, 1964.

Konstan, David. "An Anthropology of Euripides' *Cyclops.*" *Ramus* 10 (1981): 87–103.

Kozicki, Henry. *Tennyson and Clio: History in the Major Poems.* Baltimore: Johns Hopkins University Press, 1979.

Leggett, B. J. "Dante, Byron, and Tennyson's Ulysses." *Tennessee Studies in Literature* 15 (1970): 143–59.

Leventhal, A. J. "The Jew Errant." *Dubliner* 2 (1963): 11–24.

Levitt, Morton P. *The Cretan Glance: The World and Art of Nikos Kazantzakis.* Columbus: Ohio State University Press, 1980.

———. "A Hero for Our Time: Leopold Bloom and the Myth of Ulysses." *James Joyce Quarterly* 10 (1972–73): 132–46.

Linforth, Ivan M. "Philoctetes: The Play and the Man." *University of California Publications in Classical Philology* 15 (1956): 95–156.

Mahaffy, J. P. "The Degradation of Odysseus in Greek Literature." *Hermathena* 1 (1874): 265–75.

Merton, Stephen. "*The Tempest* and *Troilus and Cressida.*" *College English* 7 (1945–46): 143–50.

Meyer, George Wilbur. "Order Out of Chaos in Shakespeare's *Troilus and Cressida.*" *Tulane Studies in English* 4 (1954): 45–56.

Mitchell, Charles. "The Undying Will of Tennyson's Ulysses." *Victorian Poetry* 2 (1964): 87–95.

Muir, Kenneth. "*Troilus and Cressida.*" In *Shakespeare's Comic Sequence.* Liverpool: Liverpool University Press, 1979, pp. 108–24.

Newton, Rick M. "The Rebirth of Odysseus." *Greek, Roman, and Byzantine Studies* 25 (1984): 5–20.

Nisetich, Frank J. *Pindar and Homer.* Baltimore: Johns Hopkins University Press, 1989.

Nowottny, Winifred M. T. "'Opinion' and 'Value' in *Troilus and Cressida.*" *Essays in Criticism* 4 (1954): 282–96.

Osborn, R. E. "Modern Man's Search for Salvation—Nikos Kazantzakis and His *Odyssey.*" *Encounter* 35 (Spring 1974): 121–31.

Page, Denys. *The Homeric* Odyssey. Oxford: Clarendon Press, 1955.

Palumbo, Donald. "Death and Rebirth, Sexuality, and Fantasy in Homer and Joyce." *Colby Library Quarterly* 20 (1984): 90–99.

Parr, Mary. *James Joyce: The Poetry of Conscience.* Milwaukee: Inland Press, 1961.

Pettigrew, John. "Tennyson's 'Ulysses': A Reconciliation of Opposites." *Victorian Poetry* 1 (1963): 27–45.

Phillips, E. D. "The Comic Odysseus." *Greece and Rome* 6 (1959): 58–67.

————. "Odysseus in Italy." *Journal of Hellenic Studies* 73 (1953): 53–67.

Pitts, Gordon. "A Reading of Tennyson's 'Ulysses.'" *West Virginia University Philological Papers* 15 (1966): 36–42.

Poe, Joe Park. *Heroism and Divine Justice in Sophocles'* Philoctetes. Leiden: E. J. Brill, 1974.

Prevelakis, Pandelis. *Nikos Kazantzakis and His* Odyssey. Translated by Philip Sherrard. New York: Simon & Schuster, 1961.

Prier, Raymond Adolph. "Joyce's Linguistic Imitation of Homer: The 'Cyclops Episode' and the Radical Appearance of the Catalogue Style." *Neohelicon* 14 (1987): 39–66.

Quick, Jonathan R. "The Homeric *Ulysses* and A. E. W. Mason's *Miranda of the Balcony.*" *James Joyce Quarterly* 21 (1984–85): 31–43.

Raizis, M. Byron. "Kazantzakis' Ur-Odysseus, Homer, and Gerhart Hauptmann." *Journal of Modern Literature* 2 (1971–72): 199–214.

Raleigh, John Henry. "Bloom as a Modern Epic Hero." *Critical Inquiry* 3 (1976–77): 583–98.

————. *The Chronicle of Leopold and Molly Bloom:* Ulysses *as Narrative.* Berkeley: University of California Press, 1977.

Ricks, Christopher. *Tennyson.* New York: Macmillan, 1972.

Riquelme, John Paul. *Teller and Tale in Joyce's Fiction: Oscillating Perspectives.* Baltimore: Johns Hopkins University Press, 1983.

Robbins, Tony. "Tennyson's 'Ulysses': The Significance of the Homeric and Dantesque Backgrounds." *Victorian Poetry* 11 (1973): 177–93.

Ronan, Clifford J. "Daniel, Rainolde, Demosthenes, and the Degree Speech of Shakespeare's Ulysses." *Renaissance and Reformation* 21 (1985): 111–18.

Roppen, Georg. "'Ulysses' and Tennyson's Sea-Quest." *English Studies* 40 (1959): 77–90.

Rose, Gilbert P. "The Swineherd and the Beggar." *Phoenix* 34 (1980): 285–97.

Rose, Peter W. "Sophocles' *Philoctetes* and the Teachings of the Sophists." *Harvard Studies in Classical Philology* 80 (1976): 49–105.

Rosenmeyer, Thomas G. "*Ajax:* Tragedy and Time." In *The Masks of Tragedy.* Austin: University of Texas Press, 1963, pp. 155–98.

Rossiter, A. P. "*Troilus and Cressida.*" In *Angel with Horns and Other Shakespeare Lectures.* Edited by Graham Storey. New York: Theatre Arts Books, 1961, pp. 129–51.

Rubino, Carl A., and Cynthia W. Shelmerdine, ed. *Approaches to Homer.* Austin: University of Texas Press, 1983.

Schwarz, Daniel R. *Reading Joyce's* Ulysses. New York: St. Martin's Press, 1987.

Scully, Stephen. "Doubling in the Tale of Odysseus." *Classical World* 80 (1986–87): 401–17.

Segal, Charles. "*Kleos* and Its Ironies in the *Odyssey.*" *L'Antiquité Classique* 52 (1983): 22–47.

————. "Pindar's Seventh Nemean." *Transactions and Proceedings of the American Philological Association* 98 (1967): 431–80.

————. "Transition and Ritual in Odysseus' Return." *Parola del Passato* No. 116 (1967): 321–42.

Seidel, Michael, and Edward Mendelson, ed. *Homer to Brecht: The European Epic and Dramatic Traditions.* New Haven: Yale University Press, 1977.

Senn, Fritz. "Bloom among the Orators: The Why and the Wherefore and All the Codology." *Irish Renaissance Annual* 1 (1980): 168–90.

Shackford, Martha Hale. "Dramatic Characterization of Ulysses: *Troilus and Cressida.*" In *Shakespeare, Sophocles: Dramatic Themes and Modes.* New York: Bookman Associates, 1960, pp. 84–96.

Sheppard, J. T. "Great-Hearted Odysseus: A Contribution to the Study of 'Stock-Epithets' in Homer's *Odyssey.*" *Journal of Hellenic Studies* 56 (1936): 36–47.

Skulsky, Harold. "Circe and Odysseus: Metamorphosis as Enchantment." In *Metamorphosis: The Mind in Exile.* Cambridge, MA: Harvard University Press, 1981, pp. 10–23.

Stavrou, C. N. "Mr. Bloom and Nikos' Odysseus." *South Atlantic Quarterly* 62 (1963): 107–18.

Stein, Arnold. "*Troilus and Cressida:* The Disjunctive Imagination." *ELH* 36 (1969): 145–67.

Stewart, Douglas J. *The Disguised Guest: Rank, Role, and Identity in the* Odyssey. Lewisburg, PA: Bucknell University Press, 1976.

Sultan, Stanley. *The Argument of* Ulysses. Columbus: Ohio State University Press, 1964.

Tanner, Rollin H. "The 'Οδυσσῆς of Cratinus and the *Cyclops* of Euripides." *Transaction and Proceedings of the American Philological Association* 46 (1915): 173–206.;

Taylor, Charles E., Jr. "The Obstacles to Odysseus' Return: Identity and Consciousness in the *Odyssey.*" *Yale Review* 50 (1960–61): 569–80.

Tennyson, Hallam, ed. *Studies in Tennyson.* Totowa, NJ: Barnes & Noble, 1981.

Thornton, Agathe. *People and Themes in Homer's* Odyssey. London: Methuen, 1970.

Tillyard, E. M. W. "*Troilus and Cressida.*" In *Shakespeare's Problem Plays.* Toronto: University of Toronto Press, 1949, pp. 36–93.

Tracy, Robert. "Leopold Bloom Fourfold: A Hungarian-Hebraic-Hellenic-Hibernian Hero." *Massachusetts Review* 6 (1965): 523–38.

Trahman, C. H. "Odysseus' Lies (*Odyssey,* Books 13–19)." *Phoenix* 6 (1952): 31–43.

Ussher, R. G. "The *Cyclops* of Euripides." *Greece and Rome* 18 (1971): 166–79.

Vivante, Paolo. *The Homeric Imagination.* Bloomington: Indiana University Press, 1970.

Voth, Grant L. "Ulysses and 'Particular Will' in *Troilus and Cressida.*" *Shakespeare Jahrbuch* 113 (1977): 149–57.

Ward, Arthur D. "'Ulysses' and 'Tithonus': Tunnel-Vision and Idle Tears." *Victorian Poetry* 12 (1974): 311–19.

Whitman, Cedric H. *Homer and the Heroic Tradition.* Cambridge, MA: Harvard University Press, 1958.

Williams, Harry. "Viewing the Stubble: A Note on the *Odyssey.*" *Classical Journal* 68 (1972–73): 75–78.

Wilson, Colin. "The Greatness of Nikos Kazantzakis." *Minnesota Review* 8 (1968): 159–80.

Woodhouse, W. J. *The Composition of Homer's* Odyssey. Oxford: Clarendon Press, 1929.

Wright, David G. *Characters of Joyce.* Dublin: Gill & Macmillan, 1983.

ACKNOWLEDGMENTS

"The Philosophy of *Troilus and Cressida*" by G. Wilson Knight from *The Wheel of Fire*, © 1930 by Oxford University Press, © 1949 by Methuen & Co. Reprinted by permission of Methuen & Co.

"Odysseus in the *Ajax*" by W. K. C. Guthrie from *Greece and Rome* 16, No. 3 (October 1947), © 1947 by Oxford University Press. Reprinted by permission of Oxford University Press.

"The Stage Villain" by W. B. Stanford from *The Ulysses Theme: A Study in the Adaptability of a Traditional Hero* by W. B. Stanford, © 1954, 1964 by Basil Blackwell Ltd. Reprinted by permission of Basil Blackwell Ltd.

"The Song of the Sirens: Encountering the Imaginary" by Maurice Blanchot from *The Gaze of Orpheus and Other Literary Essays* by Maurice Blanchot, translated by Lydia Davis, © 1959 by Editions Gallimard, English translation © 1981 by Lydia Davis and Station Hill Press. Reprinted by permission.

"The Torrent and the Sun" by Andonis Decavalles from *Poetry* 95, No. 3 (December 1959), © 1959 by the Modern Poetry Association. Reprinted by permission of *Poetry* and the author.

The Songs of Homer by G. S. Kirk, © 1962 by Cambridge University Press. Reprinted by permission of Cambridge University Press.

"The Phaeacians and the Symbolism of Odysseus' Return" by Charles Paul Segal from *Arion* 1, No. 4 (Winter 1962), © 1962 by *Arion*. Reprinted by permission of the Trustees of Boston University and the author.

"Taking Over Homer" by Anthony Burgess from *Re Joyce* by Anthony Burgess, © 1965 by Anthony Burgess. Reprinted by permission of W. W. Norton & Co. and Faber & Faber Ltd.

"Homer and Sophocles' *Ajax*" by G. M. Kirkwood from *Classical Drama and Its Influence*, edited by M. J. Anderson, © 1965 by Methuen & Co. Reprinted by permission of Methuen & Co.

"Interpretation and Misinterpretation: The Problem of *Troilus and Cressida*" by Derick R. C. Marsh from *Shakespeare Studies* 1 (1965), © 1965 by *Shakespeare Studies*. Reprinted by permission of *Shakespeare Studies*.

"The *Cyclops*" by D. J. Conacher from *Euripidean Drama: Myth, Theme and Structure* by D. J. Conacher, © 1967 by the University of Toronto Press. Reprinted by permission of the University of Toronto Press.

"The Unknown Ulysses" by Karl F. Thompson from *Shakespeare Quarterly* 19, No. 2 (Spring 1968), © 1968 by The Shakespeare Association of America, Inc. Reprinted by permission of *Shakespeare Quarterly*.

"The Odysseys within the *Odyssey*" by Italo Calvino from *The Uses of Literature* by Italo Calvino, translated by Patrick Creagh, © 1982 by Giulio Einaudi editore S.p.A., Torino, English translation © 1986 by Harcourt Brace Jovanovich, Inc. Reprinted by permission of Harcourt Brace Jovanovich, Inc.

"Giraudoux's *La Guerre de Troie d'aura pas lieu* and Homer's *Iliad:* The Scales of Zeus as Dramatic Device" by Brian Pocknell from *Modern Drama* 24, No. 2 (June 1981), © 1981 by the University of Toronto, Graduate Study for Study of Drama. Reprinted by permission of *Modern Drama.*

"*Philoctetes:* Society, Language, Friendship" by Charles Segal from *Tragedy and Civilization: An Interpretation of Sophocles* by Charles Segal, © 1981 by the Board of Trustees, Oberlin College. Reprinted by permission.

"The Name of Odysseus" by Jenny Strauss Clay from *The Wrath of Athena: Gods and Men in the* Odyssey by Jenny Strauss Clay, © 1983 by Princeton University Press. Reprinted by permission of Princeton University Press.

The Measures of Praise: Structure and Function in Pindar's Second Pythian and Seventh Nemean Odes by Glen W. Most, © 1985 by Vandenhoeck & Ruprecht. Reprinted by permission of Vandenhoeck & Ruprecht.

"Beautiful Other Worlds: The Dramatic Monologues of 1832 and 1842" by Linda K. Hughes from *The Manyfacèd Glass: Tennyson's Dramatic Monologues* by Linda K. Hughes, © 1987 by Linda K. Hughes. Reprinted by permission of Ohio University Press/Swallow Press.

" 'Ulysses' " by Kenneth M. McKay from *Many Glancing Colours: An Essay in Reading Tennyson, 1809–1850* by Kenneth M. McKay, © 1988 by the University of Toronto Press. Reprinted by permission of the University of Toronto Press.

"Recasting an Epic Journey of the Soul" by Theoharis Constantine Theoharis from *Joyce's* Ulysses: *An Anatomy of the Soul* by Theoharis Constantine Theoharis, © 1988 by the University of North Carolina Press. Reprinted by permission.

"The *Odyssey* and the Western World" by George de F. Lord from *Sewanee Review* 62, No. 3 (July–September 1954), © 1954 by *The Sewanee Review.* Reprinted by permission.

"The Name of Odysseus" by G. E. Dimock, Jr., from *Hudson Review* 9, No. 1 (Spring 1956), © 1956 by The Hudson Review, Inc. Reprinted by permission of The Hudson Review, Inc.

"Homer and Hamlet" by Hugh Kenner from *Dublin's Joyce* by Hugh Kenner, © 1956 by Hugh Kenner. Reprinted by permission of Indiana University Press and Aitken & Stone.

"Kazantzakis: Odysseus and the 'Cage of Freedom' " by George Scouffas from *Accent* 19, No. 4 (Autumn 1959), © 1959 by *Accent.* Reprinted by permission of the author.

"Shakespeare's Ulysses and the Problem of Value" by W. R. Elton from *Shakespeare Studies* 2 (1966), © 1967 by The Center for Shakespeare Studies. Reprinted by permission of *Shakespeare Studies.*

"The Fugitive from the Ancestral Hearth" (originally titled "The Fugitive from the Ancestral Hearth: Tennyson's 'Ulysses' ") by R. F. Storch from *Texas Studies in Literature and Language* 13, No. 1 (Summer 1971), © 1971 by The University of Texas Press. Reprinted by permission of The University of Texas Press.

"Seeds for the Planting of Bloom" by Michael Beausang from *Mosaic* 6, No. 1 (Fall 1972), © 1972 by The Editors, *Mosaic,* The University of Manitoba Press. Reprinted by permission of *Mosaic.*

"Dante's Ulysses: From Epic to Novel" by John Freccero from *Concepts of the Hero in the Middle Ages and Renaissance,* edited by Norman T. Burns and Christopher J. Reagan, © 1975 by State University of New York. Reprinted by permission of the State University of New York Press.

"Odysseus in Sophocles' *Philoctetes*" (originally titled "Consequences and Character in Sophocles' *Philoctetes*") by Martha Nussbaum from *Philosophy and Literture* 1, No. 1 (Fall 1976), © 1976 by The University of Michigan–Dearborn. Reprinted by permission of The Johns Hopkins University Press and the author.

"Joyce and Homer" by Richard Ellmann from *Critical Inquiry* 3, No. 3 (Spring 1977), © 1977 by Richard Ellmann. Reprinted by permission of The University of Chicago Press.

"The Platonic and Christian Ulysses" by Jean Pépin from *Neoplatonism and Christian Thought,* edited by Dominic J. O'Meara, © 1982 by the International Society for Neoplatonic Studies. Reprinted by permission of the International Society for Neoplatonic Studies.

"The Philosophy of the *Odyssey*" by R. B. Rutherford from *Journal of Hellenic Studies* 106 (1986), © 1986 by the Society for the Promotion of Hellenic Studies. Reprinted by permission of the Society for the Promotion of Hellenic Studies.

"Odysseus and the Suitors" by Sheila Murnaghan from *Disguise and Recognition in the Odyssey* by Sheila Murnaghan, © 1987 by Princeton University Press. Reprinted by permission of Princeton University Press.

INDEX